A-Z CORBY & K

CONTENT

REFERENCE

A Road	A14	Car Park (Selected)	P
B Road	B670	Church or Chapel	†
Dual Carriageway		Cycleway (Selected)	
One-way Street	⟶	Fire Station	■
Traffic flow on A roads is indicated by a heavy line on the driver's left.	⟶	Hospital	H
Restricted Access		House Numbers A & B Roads only	298 77
Pedestrianized Road		Information Centre	i
Track		National Grid Reference	⁴90
Footpath		Police Station	▲
Residential Walkway		Post Office	★
Railway	Tunnel / Station / Level Crossing	Toilet: without facilities for the Disabled / with facilities for the Disabled	▽ / ▽
Built-up Area	DENE CL	Educational Establishment	
Local Authority Boundary	— ·· — ··	Hospital or Hospice	
Posttown Boundary		Industrial Building	
Postcode Boundary (within posttown)	— ·· — ··	Leisure or Recreational Facility	
		Place of Interest	
Map Continuation	20	Public Building	
		Shopping Centre or Market	
		Other Selected Buildings	

SCALE 1:15,840   4 inches (10.16cm) to 1 mile   6.31cm to 1 km

```
0        ¼              ½              ¾          1 Mile
0     250      500      750 Metres    1 Kilometre
```

Copyright of Geographers' A-Z Map Company Limited

Fairfield Road, Borough Green, Sevenoaks, Kent TN15 8PP
Telephone: 01732 781000 (Enquiries & Trade Sales)
01732 783422 (Retail Sales)

www.a-zmaps.co.uk

Copyright © Geographers' A-Z Map Co. Ltd.

Ordnance Survey® This product includes mapping data licensed from Ordnance Survey® with the permission of the Controller of Her Majesty's Stationery Office.

© Crown Copyright 2004. All rights reserved. Licence number 100017302

EDITION 1 2006

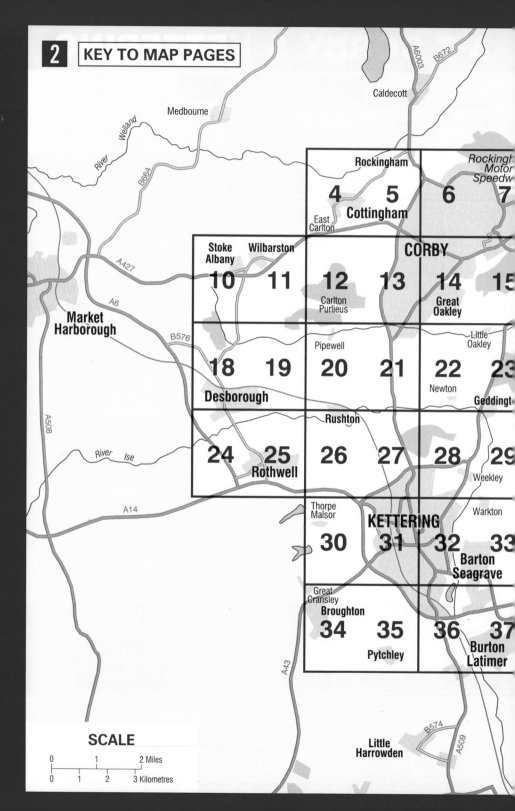

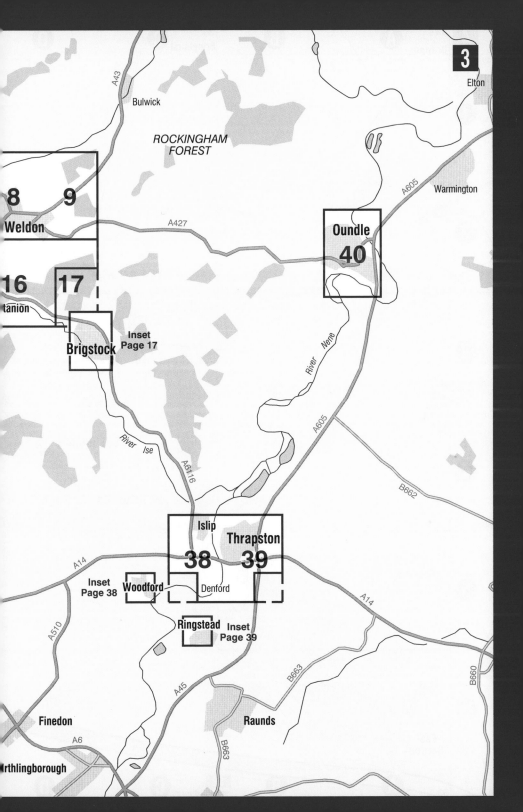

Elton

A43

Bulwick

ROCKINGHAM FOREST

A605

Warmington

8 **9**

Weldon

A427

Oundle

40

16 **17**

tanion

Brigstock

Inset
Page 17

River Nene

A605

B662

River Ise

A6116

Islip

Thrapston

A14

38 **39**

Inset
Page 38

Woodford

Denford

A14

Ringstead Inset
Page 39

A510

A45

B663

B660

Finedon

Raunds

A6

B663

rthlingborough

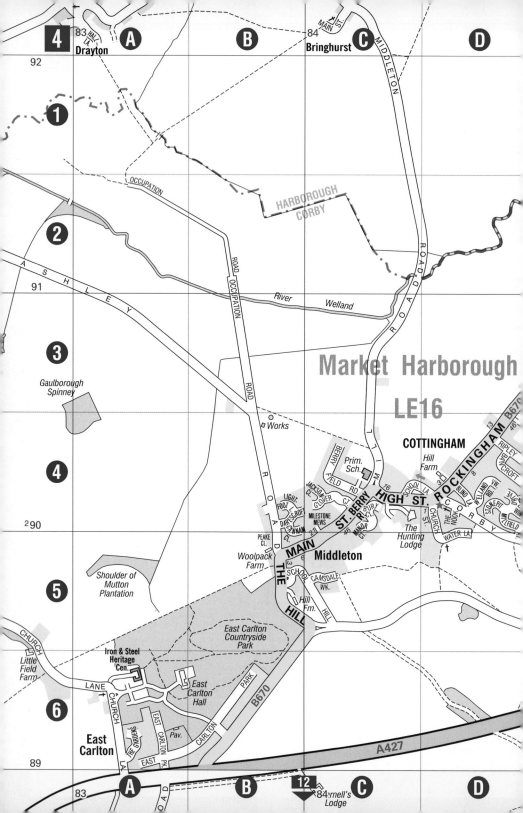

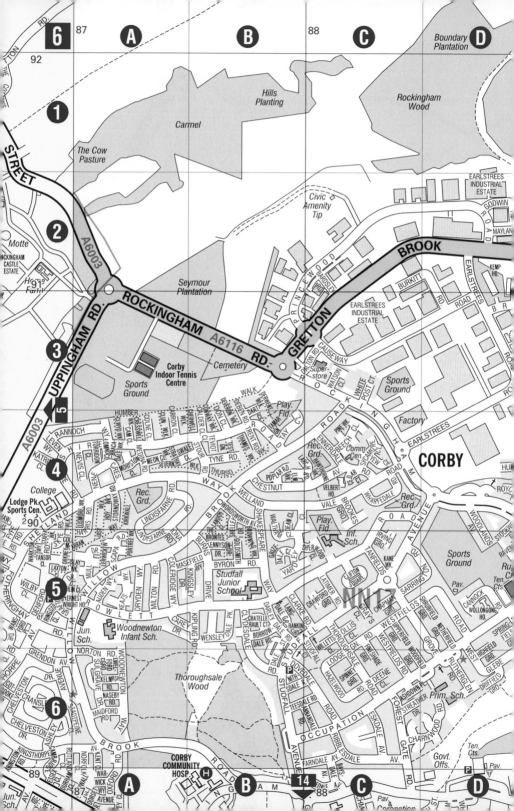

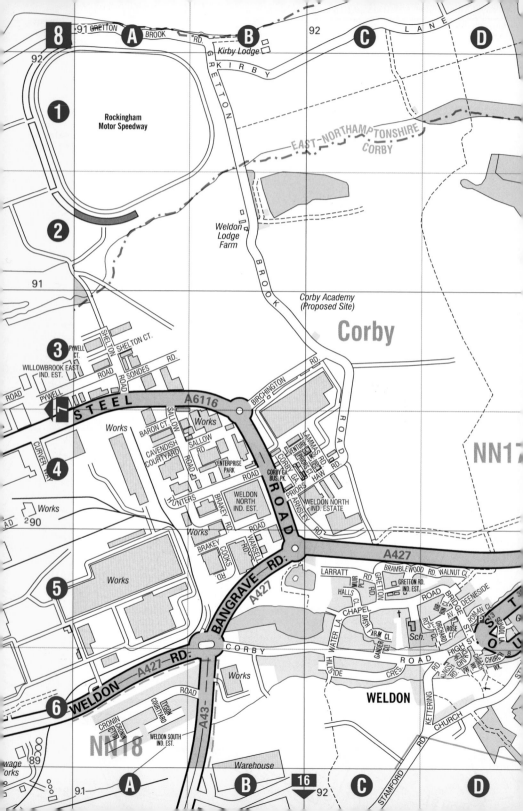

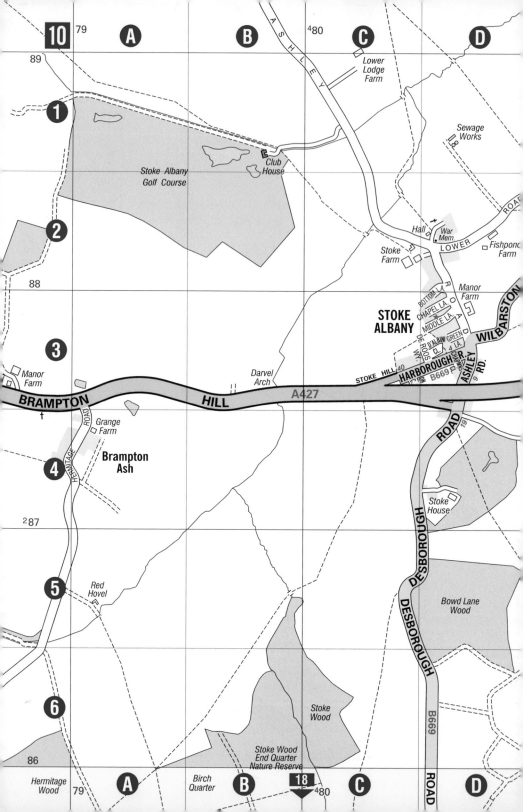

A **B** ⁴80 **C** **D**

89

❶

Lower
Lodge
Farm

Sewage
Works

Stoke Albany
Golf Course

Club
House

Hall

War
Mem.

LOWER

ROAD

Fishpond
Farm

❷

Stoke
Farm

Manor
Farm

88

**STOKE
ALBANY**

BOTTOM LA.

CHAPEL LA.

MIDDLE LA.

DE ROOS

❸

Manor
Farm

Darvel
Arch

STOKE HILL

40

D'ALBINI GREEN

D'ALBINI
WY.

4 LA.

TOOMING CL.

WILBARSTON

HARBOROUGH R.

B669

ASHLEY RD.

†

BRAMPTON   HILL   A427

ROAD

19

HERMITAGE

Grange
Farm

ROAD

❹

**Brampton
Ash**

Stoke
House

²87

DESBOROUGH

❺

Red
Hovel

Bowd Lane
Wood

❻

ROAD

DESBOROUGH

B669

86

Stoke
Wood

Hermitage
Wood   79

A   Birch
Quarter   **B**   **18**   ⁴80   **C**   ROAD   **D**

Stoke Wood
End Quarter
Nature Reserve

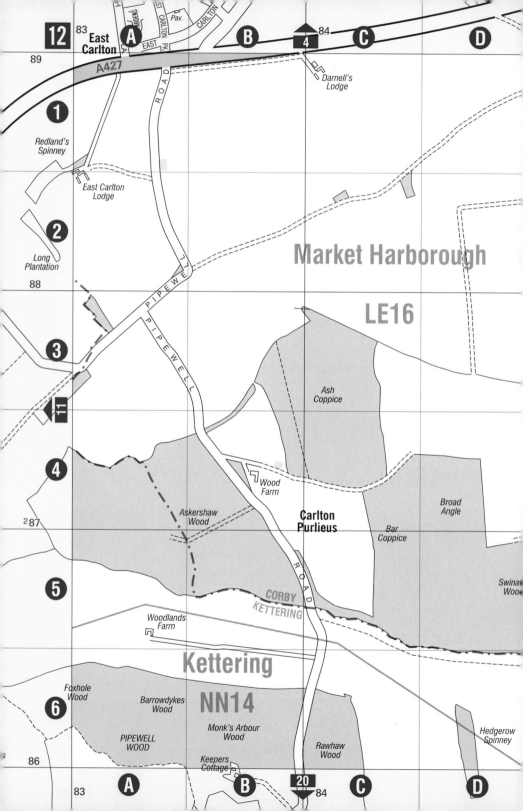

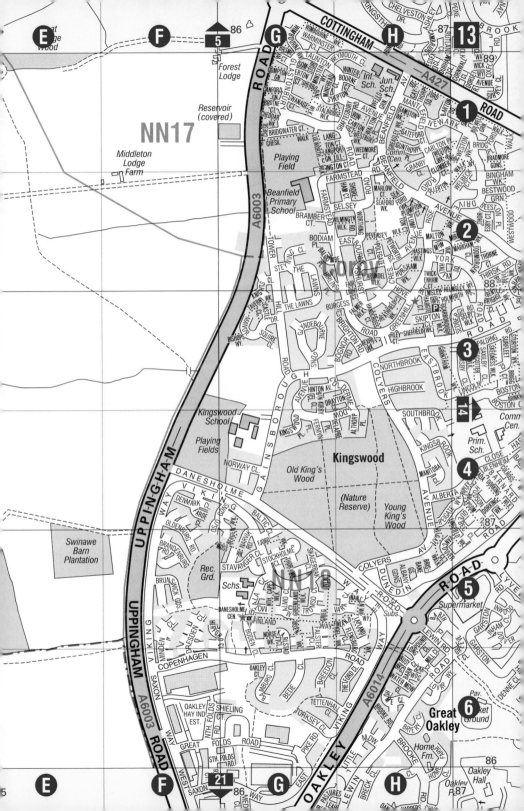

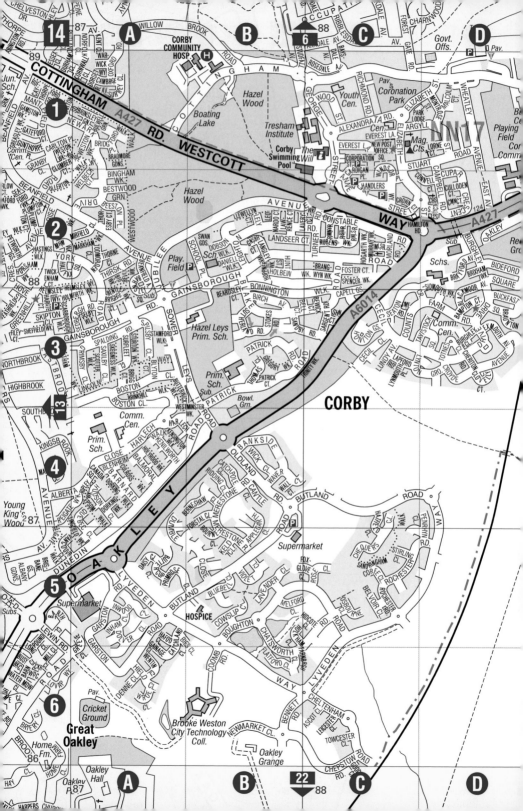

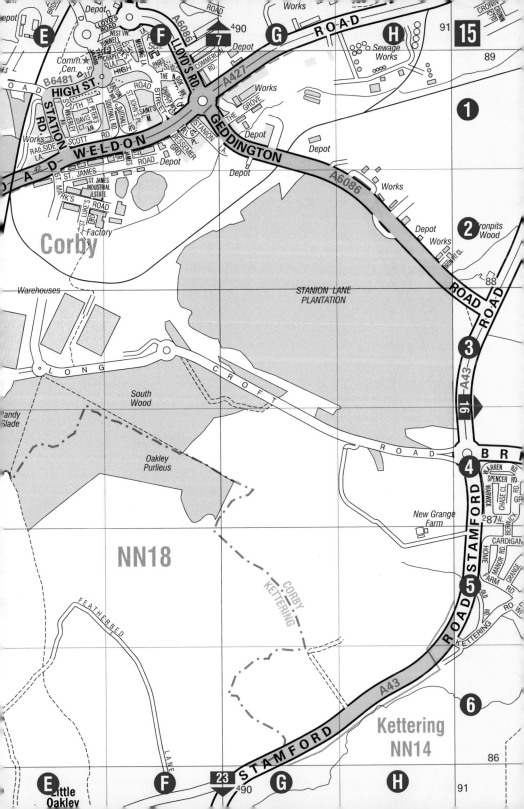

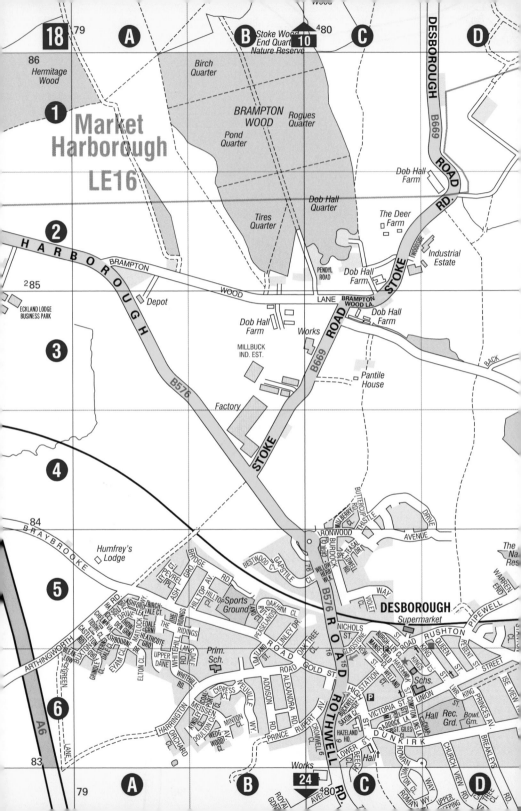

18 79

A

B Stoke Wood End Quarter Nature Reserve ▲ **10** 480

C

D DESBOROUGH B669 ROAD RD.

86
Hermitage Wood

Birch Quarter

1

Market Harborough LE16

BRAMPTON WOOD

Pond Quarter

Rogues Quarter

Dob Hall Quarter

Tires Quarter

Dob Hall Farm

The Deer Farm

Industrial Estate

2 HARBOROUGH

BRAMPTON

WOOD

LANE

PENDYL ROAD

Dob Hall Farm

STOKE

²85

Depot

ECKLAND LODGE BUSINESS PARK

BRAMPTON WOOD LA.

Dob Hall Farm

3

B576

Dob Hall Farm

Works

B669 ROAD

MILLBUCK IND. EST.

Pantile House

BACK

Factory

STOKE

4

84

BRAYBROOKE

Humfrey's Lodge

BUTTERCUP
MULBERRY CL
THISTLE

DRIVE

AVENUE

The Na Res

IRONWOOD
BURDOCK
SPE. TEASEL
ZINWEL RD.
WILLOW HERB WLK.

WARREN END

5

BESTWOOD CL

GAPSTILE

B576 ROAD

WAY VIOLET CL

DESBOROUGH
Supermarket

PIPEWELL

CL

CL

CZ
PEVREL
EZ PPL
ASH

BRIDGE
ORG
RD.

HILLTOP AV.
HILLTOP CL.

Sports Ground

OAKHAM CL

NICHOLS ST

RUSHTON

WARREN END

RD.
BIRCH-
VALE CT.
THE
RIDINGS

OAK
CLANDONS
PEASELAND
RD

LINLEY DR.

GLADSTONE
MANSFIELD RD.
BURGH LEY CL

ROAD

KING
ST.

QUEEN ST

PEGENT ST

STREET

ARTHINGWORTH
CASTLETON RD
TUDLEY CL
BUXTON CL
BLEA CL
LOWE

CHELMARSH
DEN GRN
ASHBOURNE
DR
EDALE
CGRN
MATLOCK
HEATHCOTE
GRO

WHITEHILL
LANE
VALE

UPPER
DANE

ROAD

OAKTREE CL
GOLD ST

ROAD

KINGS CL
HAVELOCK
WELLAND CL

Schs.

KING
ST.
PRINCES CL
ISE VIEW CL

EYAM CL

Prim. Sch.

Hall

Schs.

UNION ST.

Rec. Grd.

Bowl. Grn.

ORCHARD
HARRINGTON

KINGSCOUR
MEISSEN CL
DOULTON CL
MINTON CL
WEDG-
WOOD
AV. CL

CYPRESS
CL

NEVILLE WY.

ADDISON

ALEXANDRA RD.

RUPERT AV.
CROMWELL CL

Hi. STATION RD.
BUCKWELL LA.
SAXON CL
VICTORIA ST.
COMPTON
HAZELAND HO.

ROTHWELL
LOWER

WIR. RD.
COMPTON UNI. LA.
ST. GILES CL
SADDOCK LA.
DUNKIRK
ROMAN
BEECH ST.

CHAP.

WITTON CL
CHURCH VIEW RD.
ROMAN WY.

BREAKLEY

A6

83

6

79

A

B

▼ **24** 480

C

D

Works

ROYAL GDN
Hall

UPPER KEEPING

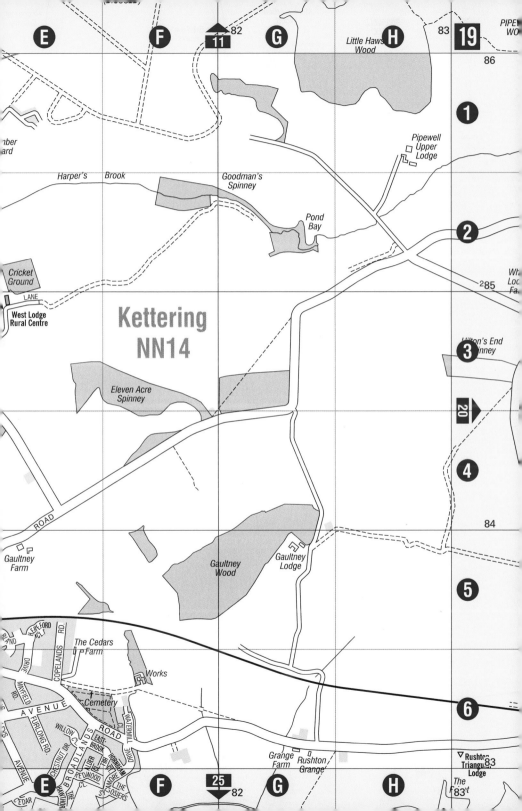

E **F** ▲82 **11** **G** Little Haws Wood **H** 83 **19** *PIPEW WO*

86

1

Pipewell Upper Lodge

Harper's Brook Goodman's Spinney

Pond Bay

2

Wh
Loc
Fa

285

Cricket Ground

LANE

West Lodge Rural Centre

Kettering
NN14

Ulton's End inney

3

20 ▶

Eleven Acre Spinney

4

84

ROAD

Gaultney Farm

Gaultney Wood Gaultney Lodge

5

H.CROFT CL. The Cedars Farm

COPELANDS

DRIVE

MAYFIELD RD.

Works

AVENUE

Cemetery

WILLOW

FURLONG RD.

6

CHESTNUT DR. THE BROADLANDS ROAD EAST BROOK HORNBEAM WATERMILL DRIVE

REDWOOD CL. ALDER THE SYCAMORE THE COSIERS

AVENUE

CEDAR

Grange Farm Rushton Grange ▽ Rushton Triangu. Lodge 83

The
83'it

E **F** 25 ▼82 **G** **H**

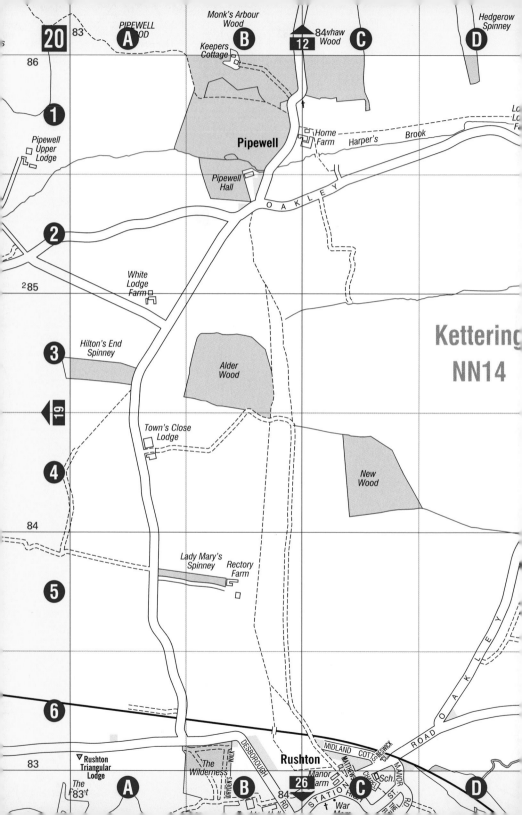

20 83

PIPEWELL
WOOD
A

Monk's Arbour
Wood
B

84 vhaw
Wood
C

Hedgerow
Spinney
D

86

1

Keepers
Cottage

12

Pipewell
Upper
Lodge

Pipewell

Home
Farm

Harper's

Brook

2

Pipewell
Hall

O A K L E Y

²85

White
Lodge
Farm

Hilton's End
Spinney

3

Alder
Wood

Kettering
NN14

19

Town's Close
Lodge

New
Wood

4

84

5

Lady Mary's
Spinney

Rectory
Farm

O A K L E Y

6

83

Rushton
Triangular
Lodge

The
F 83 t

A

The
Wilderness

DESBOROUGH

B

84

Rushton

MIDLAND

COTT

 ESWICK

Manor
Farm

26

STATION

HIGH

Sch.

War

ROAD   O A K L E Y

MANOR   ST

C

D

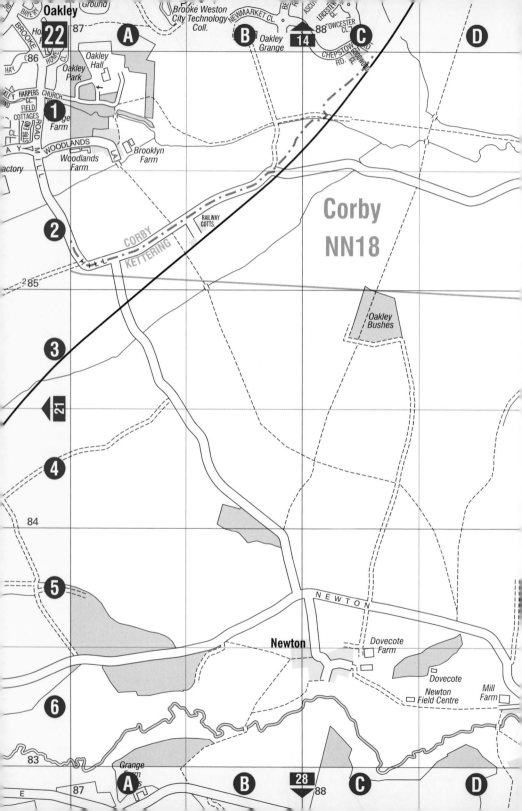

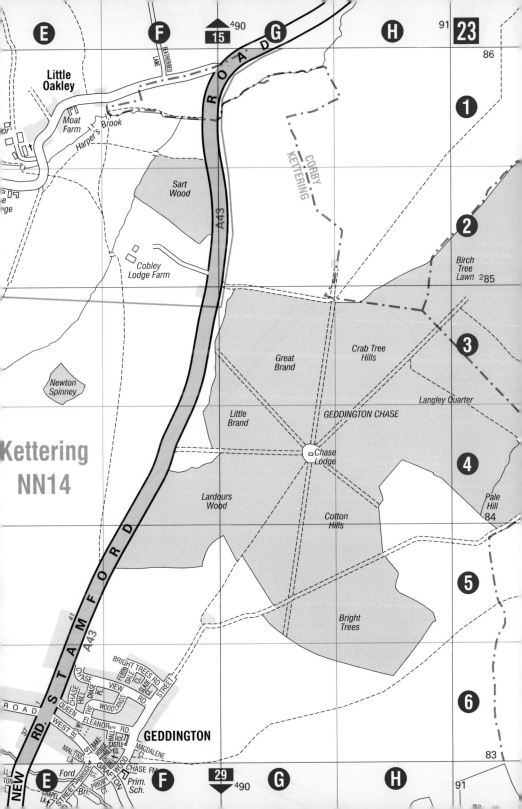

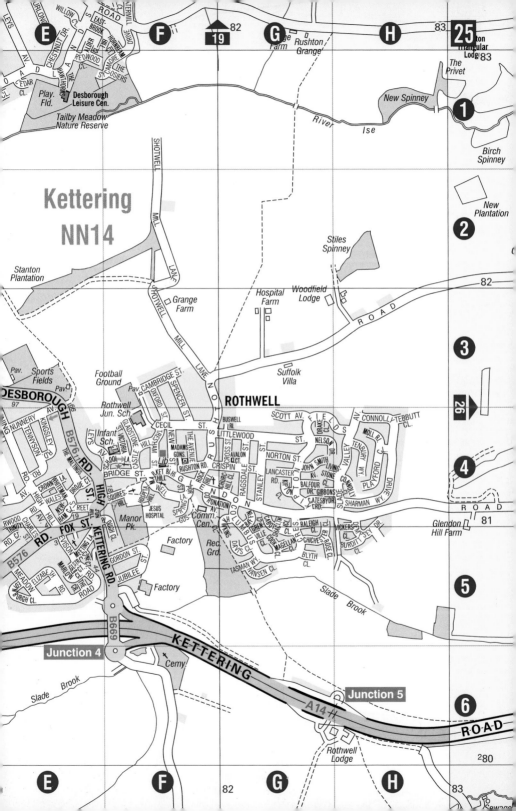

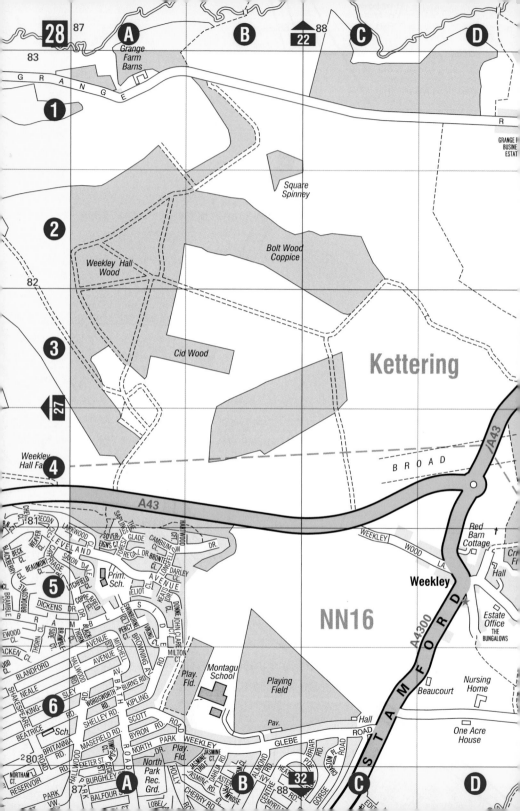

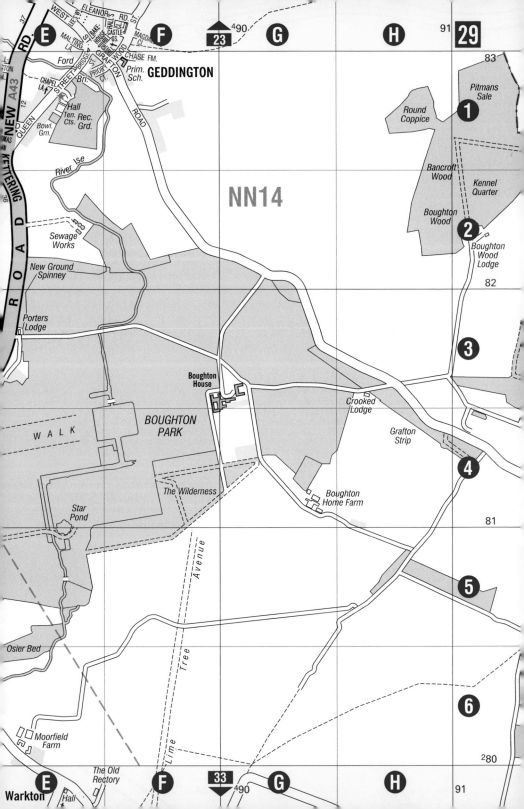

WEST LEES
MALTING LA.
ELEANOR RD. ST.
GRAFTON ST.
BAKE
HILL
HOUSE GS.
CASTLE
CHASE FM.
PRIORY CT.
MAGDA. CL.
Prim. Sch.
GEDDINGTON
490
83

Ford
CHAPEL LA.
Hall
Ten. Cts.
Rec. Grd.
Bowl. Grn.
Queen
River Ise
NEW A43
KETTERING ROAD
37
12
36

GRAFTON ROAD

NN14

Round Coppice

Pitmans Sale

1

Bancroft Wood

Kennel Quarter

Boughton Wood

2

Boughton Wood Lodge

82

Sewage Works

New Ground Spinney

Porters Lodge

3

Boughton House

BOUGHTON PARK

WALK

The Wilderness

Star Pond

Crooked Lodge

Grafton Strip

Boughton Home Farm

4

81

5

Osier Bed

Avenue

Lime Tree

6

Moorfield Farm

The Old Rectory

Warkton

Hall

490

280

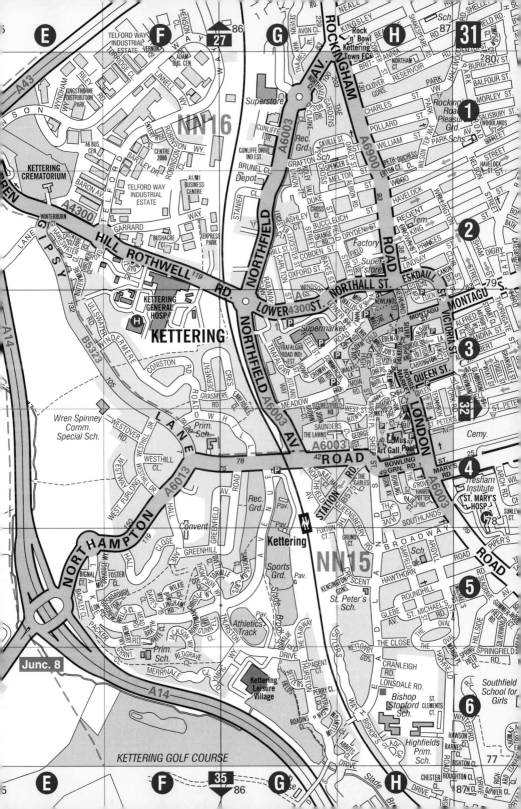

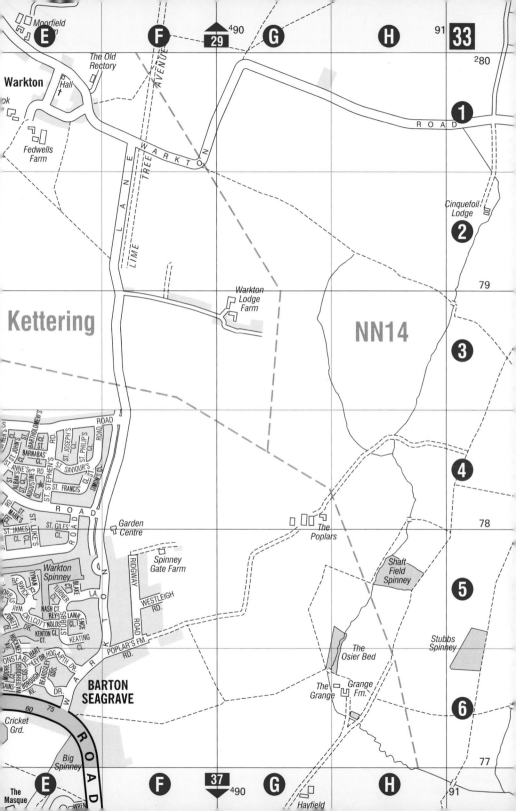

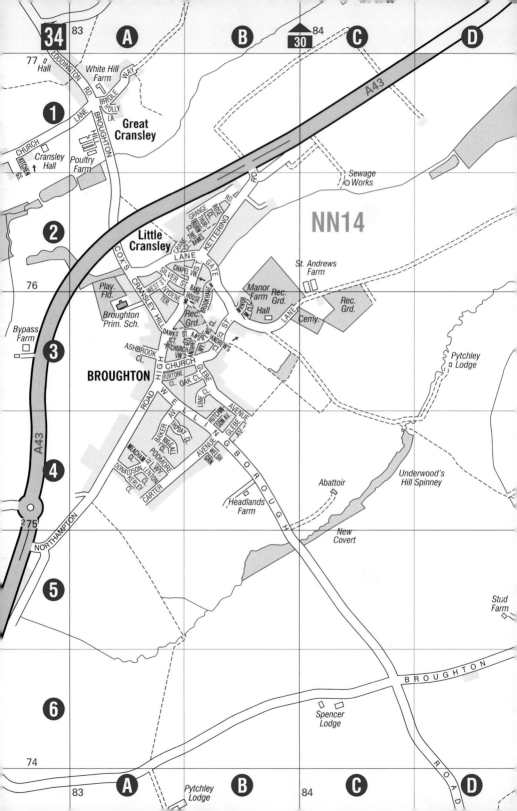

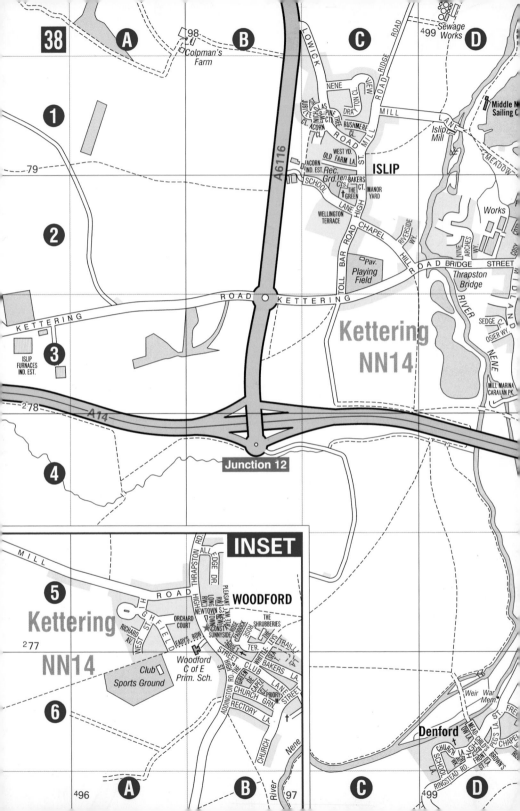

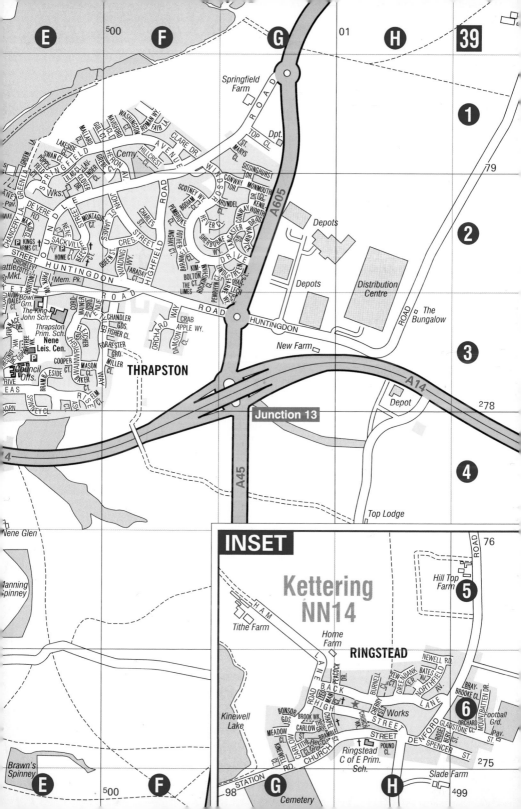

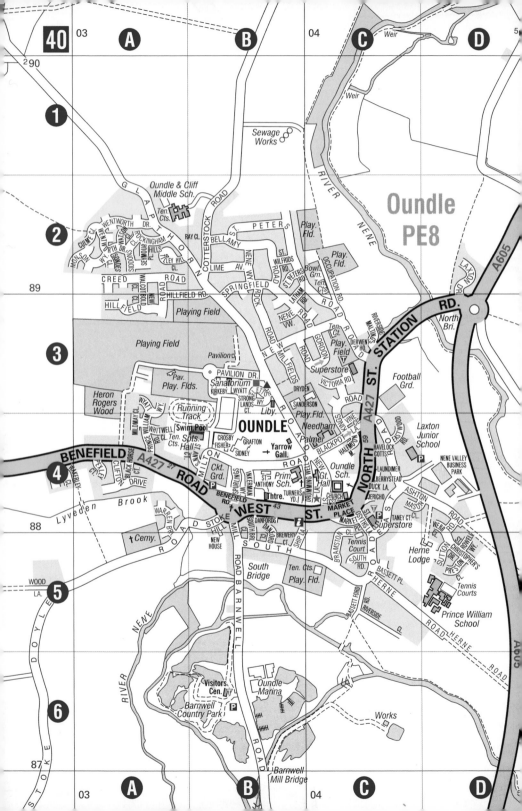

INDEX

Including Streets, Places & Areas, Hospitals & Hospices, Industrial Estates,
Selected Flats & Walkways, Stations, and Selected Places of Interest.

HOW TO USE THIS INDEX

1. Each street name is followed by its Postcode District and then by its Locality abbreviation(s) and then by its map reference;
e.g. **Abbots Cl.** NN15: Kett . . . .6H **31** is in the NN15 Postcode District and the Kettering Locality and is to be found in square 6H on page **31**.
The page number is shown in bold type.

2. A strict alphabetical order is followed in which Av., Rd., St., etc. (though abbreviated) are read in full and as part of the street name;
e.g. **Ash Ct.** appears after **Ashbrook Cl.** but before **Ashdown Cl.**

3. Streets and a selection of flats and walkways too small to be shown on the maps, appear in the index with the thoroughfare to which it is connected shown in
brackets; e.g. **Acre Ct.** NN16: Kett . . . .2B **32** (off Acre St.)

4. Addresses that are in more than one part are referred to as not continuous.

5. Places and areas are shown in the index in **BLUE TYPE** and the map reference is to the actual map square in which the town centre or area is located and not to the
place name shown on the map; e.g. **BARTON SEAGRAVE** 5E **33**

6. An example of a selected place of interest is **Manor House Mus.** 4H **31**

7. An example of a station is **Kettering Station (Rail)** 5G **31**

8. An example of a hospital is **CORBY COMMUNITY HOSPITAL** 1B **14**

GENERAL ABBREVIATIONS

Av. : Avenue
Bri. : Bridge
Bldgs. : Buildings
Bus. : Business
Cvn. : Caravan
Cen. : Centre
Cl. : Close
Cotts. : Cottages
Ct. : Court
Cres. : Crescent
Cft. : Croft
Dr. : Drive

E. : East
Est. : Estate
Fld. : Field
Flds. : Fields
Gdns. : Gardens
Ga. : Gate
Grn. : Green
Gro. : Grove
Ho. : House
Ind. : Industrial
Info. : Information
La. : Lane

Lwr. : Lower
Mnr. : Manor
Mdw. : Meadow
M. : Mews
Mus. : Museum
Nth. : North
Pde. : Parade
Pk. : Park
Pas. : Passage
Pl. : Place
Ri. : Rise
Rd. : Road

Sth. : South
Sq. : Square
St. : Street
Ter. : Terrace
Up. : Upper
Va. : Vale
Vw. : View
Wlk. : Walk
W. : West
Yd. : Yard

LOCALITY ABBREVIATIONS

Bart S : **Barton Seagrave**
Bramp : **Brampton Ash**
Brigs : **Brigstock**
Bring : **Bringhurst**
Brou : **Broughton**
Bur L : **Burton Latimer**
Corby : **Corby**
Cott : **Cottingham**
Cran : **Cransley**
Deene : **Deene**

Denf : **Denford**
Desb : **Desborough**
East C : **East Carlton**
Gedd : **Geddington**
Glen : **Glendon**
Gt O : **Great Oakley**
Ish : **Isham**
Islip : **Islip**
Kett : **Kettering**
Lit O : **Little Oakley**

Midd : **Middleton**
Newt : **Newton**
Ound : **Oundle**
Pipe : **Pipewell**
Pytc : **Pytchley**
Ring : **Ringstead**
Rock : **Rockingham**
Roth : **Rothwell**
Rush : **Rushton**
Stan : **Stanion**

Sto A : **Stoke Albany**
Tho M : **Thorpe Malsor**
Tho U : **Thorpe Underwood**
Thrap : **Thrapston**
Wark : **Warkton**
Week : **Weekley**
Weld : **Weldon**
Wilb : **Wilbarston**
Wood : **Woodford**

A

A1/M1 Bus. Cen. NN16: Kett 2F **31**
A6 Bus. Cen. NN16: Kett 1E **31**
Abbots Cl. NN15: Kett 6H **31**
Abington Rd. NN17: Corby 6H **5**
Acorn Cl. NN14: Islip 1C **38**
NN15: Bart S 2F **37**
Acorn Ind. Est. NN14: Islip 1C **38**
Acorn Pk. NN15: Bur L 3H **37**
Acre Cl. NN16: Kett 2B **32**
(off Acre St.)
Acre St. NN16: Kett 2B **32**
Adam Bus. Cen. NN16: Kett 1F **31**
Adams Dr. NN14: Roth 4D **24**
Addington Rd. NN14: Wood 6B **38**
Addison Rd. NN14: Desb 6B **18**
Admiral Ct. NN16: Kett 2A **32**
(off Club St.)
Afan Cl. NN16: Kett 6G **27**
Alanbrooke Cl. NN15: Kett 4C **32**
Albany Gdns. NN18: Corby 5H **13**
Alberta Cl. NN18: Corby 4H **13**
Albert St. NN16: Kett 3A **32**
(not continuous)
Albion Rd. NN16: Kett 2H **31**
Alder Cl. NN14: Desb 6E **19**
Alexander Ct. NN17: Corby 3E **7**
Alexandra Rd. NN14: Desb 6B **18**
NN17: Corby 1C **14**
Alexandra St. NN15: Bur L 6F **37**
NN16: Kett 3A **32**
Alfred East Art Gallery, The 4H **31**
Alfred St. NN16: Kett 3A **32**
Alice Dr. NN15: Bur L 6F **37**
Alice Gdns. NN16: Kett 2B **32**
All Saints Ter. LE16: Wilb 2E **11**
(off Carlton Rd.)
Almond Rd. NN16: Kett 1B **32**
Alness Cl. NN15: Kett 5C **32**

Altendiez Way NN15: Bur L 3E **37**
Althorpe Pl. NN16: Kett 2B **32**
Althorp Pl. NN18: Corby 4H **13**
Anderson Gro. NN15: Kett 4D **32**
Angel Yd. NN16: Kett 3H **31**
Angus Ho. NN17: Corby 1D **14**
(off Argyll St.)
Annandale Rd. NN17: Corby 6C **6**
Anne St. NN17: Corby 2C **14**
Ann Sq. NN16: Kett 2C **32**
(not continuous)
Anson Cl. NN17: Corby 6H **5**
Applegarth Cl. NN16: Kett 5B **14**
Arden Cl. NN15: Bart S 2D **36**
Argyll Ho. NN17: Corby 1C **14**
(off Argyll St.)
Argyll St. NN15: Kett 5H **31**
NN17: Corby 1C **14**
Arkwright Rd. NN17: Corby 4G **7**
Arnsley Rd. NN17: Corby 4B **8**
Arran Way NN11: Corby 5A **6**
Arthingworth Rd. NN14: Desb 6A **18**
Arthur's Way NN16: Kett 3A **32**
Arundel Cl. NN14: Thrap 2G **39**
Arundel Ct. NN15: Kett 5D **32**
Arundel Wlk. NN18: Corby 2H **13**
Ascot Cl. NN18: Gt O 6C **14**
Ashbourne Dr. NN14: Desb 5A **18**
Ashbrook Cl. NN14: Brou 3A **34**
Ashburn Cl. NN14: Thrap 3E **39**
Ashdown Cl. NN15: Bart S 2E **37**
Ashdown Pl. NN17: Corby 6C **6**
Ashes, The NN17: Weld 5E **9**
Ashford Lea NN14: Desb 5A **18**
Ash Gro. NN14: Desb 5A **18**
Ashley Av. NN17: Corby 6H **5**
Ashley Cl. NN16: Kett 2G **31**
Ashley Rd. LE16: Midd 2A **4**
LE16: Sto A 1B **10**
Ash Wlk. NN16: Kett 4B **32**
Ashton Rd. PE8: Ound 4C **40**
Ashurst Cres. NN18: Corby 2H **13**

Aspen Ho. NN15: Kett 4G **31**
(off Station Rd.)
Aster Rd. NN16: Kett 1B **32**
Athelstan Rd. NN16: Kett 2B **32**
Auden Way NN17: Corby 5A **6**
Avalon Ct. NN14: Roth 4G **25**
Avenue, The NN14: Roth 4F **25**
Avenue Ter. NN16: Kett 2C **32**
Avon Cl. NN16: Kett 6G **27**
Avondale Ct. NN14: Thrap 3E **39**
Avondale M. NN16: Kett 5B **14**
Avondale Rd. NN16: Kett 1A **32**
Aynsley Cl. NN14: Desb 6B **18**

B

Back La. NN14: Brigs 4G **17**
NN14: Desb 3D **18**
NN14: Ring 6G **39**
Backley Cl. NN15: Kett 5E **31**
Baffin Cl. NN14: Roth 4G **25**
Baird Rd. NN17: Corby 4H **7**
Bakehouse Hill NN14: Gedd 6E **23**
Bakehouse La. NN15: Bur L 4G **37**
Bakehouse M. NN14: Brou 3B **34**
Baker Av. NN14: Brou 4A **34**
Baker Ct. NN14: Thrap 3E **39**
Bakers Ct. NN14: Islip 2C **38**
Bakers La. NN14: Wood 6B **38**
Balcombe Pl. NN18: Corby 2G **13**
Balfour Dr. NN14: Roth 4G **25**
Balfour St. NN16: Kett 1A **32**
Balmoral NN18: Corby 4A **14**
Balmoral Ct. NN15: Kett 2A **36**
Baltic Cl. NN18: Corby 4G **13**
Bamburg Cl. NN18: Corby 6G **13**
Bampton Cl. NN18: Corby 3D **14**
Bancroft Rd. LE16: Cott 4D **4**
Bangrave La.
NN17: Corby, Weld 5B **8**
Banks, The NN14: Brou 2B **34**

Bankside NN18: Corby 4B **14**
Bardsley Rd. NN17: Corby 2C **6**
Barley Dr. NN15: Bur L 5G **37**
Barlow Cl. NN14: Roth 4D **24**
Barlow Ct. NN15: Bur L 6F **37**
Barlows La. LE16: Wilb 2E **11**
Barnard NN18: Corby 4A **14**
Barn's Way NN14: Brigs 6H **17**
Barn Cl. NN18: Gt O 6H **13**
Barnes Cl. NN15: Kett 6H **31**
Barnsley Sq. NN18: Corby 2A **14**
Barnwell Cl. NN14: Thrap 2F **39**
Barnwell Country Pk. 6B **40**
Barnwell Country Pk. Vis. Cen. 6B **40**
Barnwell Rd. PE8: Ound 5B **40**
Barnwell St. NN16: Kett 2B **32**
Baron Av. NN16: Kett 2E **31**
Baron Ct. NN17: Corby 4A **8**
Barron Cl. NN15: Kett 1A **36**
Barth Cl. NN18: Gt O 5H **13**
Bartley Dr. NN16: Kett 1F **31**
Barton Rd. NN15: Bur L 6B **32**
Barton Sq. NN18: Corby 1H **13**
BARTON SEAGRAVE 5E **33**
Bassett Ford Rd. PE8: Ound 5C **40**
Bassett Pl. PE8: Ound 5C **40**
Bates Av. NN14: Ring 6H **39**
Bath La. NN16: Kett 2A **32**
Bath Rd. NN16: Kett 2A **32**
Bayes St. NN16: Kett 2G **31**
Baysdale Av. NN17: Corby 1C **14**
Beanfield Av. NN18: Corby 1H **13**
Beardsley Ct. NN18: Corby 3B **14**
Beardsley Gdns. NN15: Bart S 6E **33**
Bears La. NN15: Weld 1F **17**
Beatrice Rd. NN16: Kett 6H **27**
Beatty Gdns. NN17: Corby 6H **5**
Beaufort Dr. NN15: Kett 1E **37**
Beauly Cl. NN15: Kett 5C **32**
Beaumont Cl. NN16: Kett 5H **27**
Bede Cl. NN18: Corby 6G **13**
Bedford Cl. NN15: Bart S 2D **36**

Clipstone Ct.—Furlong Rd.

Clipstone Ct. NN14: Roth 5E **25**
Clive Cl. NN15: Kett 4C **32**
Close, The NN15: Kett 5H **31**
Clovelly Ct. NN18: Corby 3D **14**
Clover Dr. NN14: Thrap 2E **39**
Clover Gdns. NN16: Kett 1H **31**
Club La. NN14: Wood 6B **38**
Club St. NN16: Kett 2H **31**
Clumber Ct. NN18: Corby 1H **13**
Clun Wlk. NN17: Corby 4A **6**
Clwyd Wlk. NN17: Corby 4A **6**
Clydesdale Rd. NN17: Corby 5B **6**
Coalport Cl. NN14: Desb 6B **18**
Cobden St. NN16: Kett 2G **31**
Cockerell Rd. NN17: Corby 5F **7**
Cocker Wood Cl. NN18: Gt O 6H **13**
Cogan Cres. NN14: Roth 5D **24**
Coldermeadow Av.
NN18: Corby 3H **13**
Coleridge Way NN17: Corby 5A **6**
Coles Cl. NN15: Bur L 5F **37**
Collingwood Av. NN17: Corby 6G **5**
Colne Cl. NN17: Corby 4A **6**
Columbus Cres. NN14: Roth 4G **25**
Colyers Av. NN18: Corby 3H **13**
Commercial Rd. NN16: Kett 3G **31**
NN17: Corby 1F **15**
Compton Grn. NN18: Corby 1G **13**
Compton Pl. NN16: Kett 3C **32**
Compton St. NN14: Desb 6C **18**
Coniston Rd. NN16: Kett 3F **31**
Connaught St. NN16: Kett 2B **32**
Connell Ct. NN17: Corby 2D **14**
Connolly Cl. NN14: Roth 4H **25**
Connolly Dr. NN14: Roth 4H **25**
Constable Cl. NN15: Bart S 6E **33**
Constable Rd. NN18: Corby 2C **14**
Constable Wlk. NN14: Wood 5B **38**
Conway Dr. NN14: Thrap 2G **39**
(not continuous)
NN15: Bur L 5E **37**
Conway Wlk. NN17: Corby 4B **6**
Cook Cl. NN14: Roth 5G **25**
Cooks Rd. NN17: Corby 5B **8**
Coomb Rd. NN18: Gt O 6B **14**
Cooper Ct. NN14: Thrap 3E **39**
Copelands Rd. NN14: Desb 6E **19**
Copenhagen Rd. NN18: Corby 6F **13**
Copperfield Cl. NN16: Kett 5A **28**
Coppertree Wlk. NN14: Thrap 3E **39**
Coppice Cl. NN15: Bur L 3G **37**
Copse Cl. NN15: Bur L 4G **37**
Cora Rd. NN16: Kett 1C **32**
CORBY 1C **14**
CORBY COMMUNITY HOSPITAL
1B **14**
Corby Ga. NN17: Corby 4B **8**
Corby Ga. Bus. Pk. NN17: Corby 4B **8**
Corby Golf Range 5E **5**
Corby Indoor Tennis Cen. 3A **6**
Corby Rd. LE16: Cott 4D **4**
NN14: Stan 4A **16**
NN17: Corby 1H **7**
NN17: Cott 6G **5**
NN17: Weld 5B **8**
Corby Swimming Pool 1B **14**
Cordwainer Gro. NN14: Thrap 3E **39**
Cornfield Way NN15: Bur L 6G **37**
Cornwall Cl. NN17: Corby 1A **14**
Cornwall Rd. NN16: Kett 2B **32**
Coronation Av. NN14: Roth 4F **25**
Corporation St. NN17: Corby 1C **14**
Cosy Nook NN14: Thrap 2D **38**
Cotswold Av. NN16: Kett 6H **27**
Cotterstock Rd. PE8: Ound 2B **40**
Cottesbrooke Rd. NN17: Corby 6H **5**
Cottesmore Av. NN15: Bart S 2E **37**
COTTINGHAM 4D **4**
Cottingham Rd. LE16: Rock 2F **5**
NN17: Corby 1A **14**
NN18: Corby 6G **5**
Cottingham Way NN14: Thrap 2D **38**
Cottingham Way Ind. Est.
NN14: Thrap 2E **39**
Cottons, The LE16: Rock 1H **5**
Counts Farm Rd. NN18: Corby 3C **14**
Courier Rd. NN17: Corby 6E **7**
Court Dr. NN16: Kett 5H **27**
Cowper St. NN16: Kett 6H **27**
Cowslip Cl. NN18: Corby 5B **14**
Cox's La. NN14: Brou 2A **34**
Crab Apple Way NN14: Thrap 3F **39**
Crane Cl. NN14: Brou 2A **34**
Cranesbill Cl. NN14: Desb 5C **18**
Cranford Av. NN15: Bur L 4H **37**
Cranford Rd. NN15: Bart S 1F **37**
NN15: Bur L 3H **37**
Cranleigh Rd. NN15: Kett 6H **31**
Cransley Gdns. NN17: Corby 6H **5**
Cransley Hill NN14: Brou 2A **34**
Crawford Gro. NN17: Corby 5C **6**
Creed Rd. PE8: Ound 2A **40**
Crescent, The NN14: Roth 5E **25**
NN15: Bur L 3G **37**
NN15: Kett 4H **31**
Cresswell Wlk. NN17: Corby 4A **6**
Crick Cl. NN17: Corby 4E **7**
Cricketers Grn. NN17: Weld 5E **9**
Crispin Pl. NN16: Kett 3H **31**
Crispin St. NN14: Roth 4F **25**
Cromarty Ct. NN17: Corby 2D **14**
Cromarty Ho. *NN17: Corby 2D **14***
(off Elizabeth St.)
Cromwell Cl. NN14: Desb 6C **18**
Cromwell Rd. NN16: Kett 3G **31**
Cronin Courtyard NN18: Corby 6A **8**
Cronin Rd. NN18: Corby 6A **8**
Crosby PE8: Ound 4B **40**
Cross Ct. NN16: Kett 2G **31**
Cross St. NN14: Roth 4G **25**
NN16: Kett 1G **31**
Crown Apartments *NN16: Kett 3H **31***
(off Dryland St.)
Crown Ct. NN17: Corby 2C **14**
Crown La. NN14: Roth 4E **25**
Crown St. NN16: Kett 2H **31**
Croxen Cl. NN15: Bur L 5G **37**
Croyde Av. NN18: Corby 3D **14**
Crucible Rd. NN17: Corby 6F **7**
Culloden Ct. NN17: Corby 2D **14**
Culloden Dr. NN15: Kett 5C **32**
Culme Cl. PE8: Ound 2A **40**
Culross Wlk. NN18: Corby 4A **14**
Cunliffe Dr. NN16: Kett 1G **31**
Cunliffe Dr. Ind. Est. NN16: Kett 1G **31**
Cupar Cres. NN17: Corby 2D **14**
Curver Way NN17: Corby 4H **7**
Cypress Cl. NN14: Desb 6B **18**
Cytringan Cl. NN15: Kett 6G **31**

D

Dahlia Rd. NN16: Kett 1B **32**
Daisybank Av. NN14: Roth 4D **24**
Daisy Cl. NN18: Corby 5A **14**
D'Albini Cl. LE16: Sto A 3D **10**
Dalby Cl. NN16: Kett 5G **27**
Dale St. NN17: Corby 6B **6**
Dalkeith Av. *NN16: Kett 3H **31***
(off British La.)
Dalkeith Pl. NN16: Kett 3H **31**
Dallacre Bus. Units LE16: Wilb 3F **11**
Dallacre Dr. LE16: Wilb 3E **11**
Dallington Cl. NN14: Gedd 1E **29**
Dalton Rd. NN17: Corby 3C **6**
Damson Cl. NN14: Thrap 3F **39**
Danesholme Cen. NN18: Corby 5G **13**
Danesholme Rd. NN18: Corby 4F **13**
Danford Cl. PE8: Ound 4B **40**
Danfords PE8: Ound 4B **40**
Daniell Wlk. NN18: Corby 2B **14**
Darescroft LE16: Midd 4B **4**
Darley Cl. NN16: Kett 5A **28**
Darley Dale Rd. NN17: Corby 5B **6**
Dart Cl. NN17: Corby 4B **6**
Darwin Ct. NN17: Corby 5G **7**
Darwin Ho. *NN17: Corby 4B **8***
(off Corby Ga.)
Darwin Rd. NN17: Corby 4G **7**
Dash Farm Cl. NN17: Weld 5C **8**
Davey Rd. NN17: Corby 5G **7**
Davis Cl. NN14: Roth 5G **25**
Davis Ct. NN17: Corby 1E **15**
Dawkins Ct. NN14: Brou 3A **34**
Deben Rd. NN17: Corby 3B **6**
De Capel Cl. NN14: Wood 6B **38**
Deeble Rd. NN15: Kett 4B **32**
Deene Cl. NN17: Corby 6C **6**
Deene End NN17: Weld 5D **8**
Deene Park 1G **9**
Deeneside NN17: Weld 5D **8**
Delamere Dr. NN15: Bart S 3E **37**
Delapre Pl. NN18: Corby 4G **13**
Dempsey Dr. NN14: Roth 5H **25**
Dene Cl. NN16: Kett 6G **27**
DENFORD 6D **38**
Denford Dr. NN15: Bart S 2D **36**
Denford Rd. NN14: Ring 6H **39**
NN14: Thrap 4D **38**
NN17: Corby 5H **5**
Denman Cl. LE16: Sto A 3C **10**
Denmark Cl. NN18: Corby 4F **13**
Denne Cl. NN18: Gt O 6A **14**
Denton Ct. NN15: Bur L 5F **37**
De Roos Way LE16: Sto A 3D **10**
Derwent Cres. NN16: Kett 3F **31**
Derwent Ho. PE8: Ound 3C **40**
Derwent Wlk. NN17: Corby 3B **6**
DESBOROUGH 6C **18**
Desborough Leisure Cen. 1E **25**
Desborough Rd. LE16: Sto A 5C **10**
NN14: Roth 3E **25**
NN14: Rush 6B **20**
Devere Rd. NN14: Thrap 2E **39**
Deveron Wlk. NN17: Corby 3B **6**
Diana Way NN15: Bur L 6F **37**
Dibbin Cl. NN17: Weld 5D **8**
Dickens Dr. NN16: Kett 5H **27**
Digby St. NN16: Kett 2A **32**
Dixon Wlk. *NN17: Corby 1E **15***
(off South Rd.)
Dobson Wlk. NN18: Corby 2B **14**
Dolver Cl. NN18: Gt O 5A **14**
Donald Greaves Ho.
*NN17: Corby 4B **6***
(off Landor Cl.)
Donaldson Av. NN14: Brou 4A **34**
Don Cl. NN17: Corby 4B **6**
Donne Cl. NN16: Kett 5A **28**
Doris Rd. NN16: Kett 1C **32**
Dorking Wlk. NN18: Corby 4A **14**
(not continuous)
Dorothy Rd. NN16: Kett 2C **32**
Dorset Rd. NN17: Corby 1A **14**
Douglas Ct. NN15: Kett 5C **32**
Doulton Cl. NN14: Desb 6B **18**
Dovecote Cl. NN15: Bart S 6D **32**
Dovedale NN14: Desb 5A **18**
Dovedale Rd. NN17: Corby 6B **6**
Drake Cl. NN14: Roth 4G **25**
NN17: Corby 5H **5**
Drayton Cl. NN14: Islip 1C **38**
NN18: Corby 3H **13**
Dresden Cl. NN18: Corby 5F **13**
Driffield Gro. NN17: Corby 6D **6**
Drill Hall Ct. NN15: Kett 4G **31**
Drive, The NN15: Kett 4H **31**
Droue Ct. NN14: Roth 4E **25**
Drumming Well La. PE8: Ound 4C **40**
Dryden PE8: Ound 3B **40**
Dryden St. NN16: Kett 2H **31**
Dryden's Wlk. NN14: Rush 1B **26**
Dryden Way NN17: Corby 5A **6**
Dryland St. NN16: Kett 3H **31**
Duchess Cl. NN16: Kett 1H **31**
Duck End NN14: Denf 6E **39**
Duck La. PE8: Ound 4C **40**
Duckworth Rd. NN17: Corby 6H **5**
Duke St. NN15: Bur L 5F **37**
NN16: Kett 2G **31**
Dumble Cl. NN18: Corby 5A **14**
Dunbar Ct. NN15: Kett 5D **32**
Duncan Rd. NN17: Corby 6H **5**
Dunedin Rd. NN18: Corby 5H **13**
Dunkirk Av. NN14: Desb 6C **18**
Durban Rd. NN16: Kett 3B **32**
Durham Cl. NN17: Corby 1H **13**
Durness Cl. NN15: Kett 5C **32**
Dusthill Rd. NN14: Brigs 5F **17**

E

Ead Rd. NN15: Bur L 6F **37**
Eady's Row NN14: Wood 5A **38**
Eagle Rd. NN14: Cran, Tho M 3B **30**
Earlstrees Ct. NN17: Corby 3D **6**
Earlstrees Ind. Est. NN17: Corby 3E **7**
Earlstrees Rd. NN17: Corby 2D **6**
East Av. NN15: Bur L 4F **37**
NN15: Kett 3B **32**
NN17: Corby 2D **14**
Eastbourne Av. NN18: Corby 2H **13**
Eastbrook NN18: Corby 3H **13**
Eastbrook Hill NN14: Desb 6E **19**
EAST CARLTON 6A **4**
East Carlton Countryside Pk. 5B **4**
East Carlton Pk. LE16: East C 6A **4**
East Cl. NN15: Kett 3B **32**
East Cres. NN17: Weld 5E **9**
East Dr. NN15: Kett 3C **32**
Eastleigh Rd. NN15: Kett 6B **32**
Easton Wlk. NN17: Corby 1F **15**
East Rd. PE8: Ound 4C **40**
East Wlk. NN15: Kett 3C **32**
Eastwood Rd. PE8: Ound 4C **40**
Ebenezer Pl. NN16: Kett 3H **31**
Eckland Lodge Bus. Pk.
NN14: Desb 3A **18**
Edale Grn. NN14: Desb 5A **18**
Eden St. NN16: Kett 3H **31**
Edgar Rd. NN16: Kett 2B **32**
Edgell St. NN16: Kett 3A **32**
Edinburgh Cl. NN14: Roth 5E **25**
Edinburgh Rd. NN16: Kett 2B **32**
Edison Courtyard
NN17: Corby 2D **6**
Edith Rd. NN16: Kett 1C **32**
Edmund St. NN16: Kett 2B **32**
Edward Cl. NN15: Kett 6A **32**
Edward Rd. NN15: Kett 6A **32**
Eider Cl. NN15: Bur L 5E **37**
Eismann Way NN17: Corby 6G **7**
Eleanor Cross 6E **23**
Eliot Cl. NN16: Kett 5A **28**
Elizabeth Rd. NN14: Roth 5E **25**
NN16: Kett 2B **32**
Elizabeth St. NN17: Corby 1C **14**
Elm Ct. NN14: Thrap 3E **39**
Elm Rd. NN15: Kett 4B **32**
Elm Wlk. NN17: Corby 4B **6**
Elton Cl. NN14: Desb 6A **18**
Ennerdale Cl. NN16: Kett 3G **31**
Ennerdale Rd. NN17: Corby 4C **6**
Ensleigh Cl. NN15: Bur L 6G **37**
Enterprise Cl. NN16: Kett 1F **31**
Enterprise Pk. NN17: Corby 4B **8**
Epping Cl. NN15: Bart S 2E **37**
Epsom Wlk. NN18: Corby 4A **14**
Ernest Wright Ho. NN17: Corby 5A **6**
Eskdaill Pl. *NN16: Kett 2H **31***
(off Lindsay St.)
Eskdaill St. NN16: Kett 2H **31**
Eskdale Av. NN17: Corby 6C **6**
Essex Cl. NN17: Corby 1H **13**
Essex Pl. NN15: Kett 1B **36**
Ettrick Cl. NN16: Kett 5G **27**
Eva Rd. NN16: Kett 2C **32**
Everest Ho. *NN17: Corby 1C **14***
(off Everest La.)
Everest La. NN17: Corby 1C **14**
(not continuous)
Evison Ct. *NN14: Roth 5E **25***
(off Evison Rd.)
Evison Rd. NN14: Roth 5E **25**
Exeter St. NN16: Kett 6A **28**
Exmouth Av. NN18: Corby 3D **14**
Express Pk. NN16: Kett 2F **31**
Eyam Cl. NN14: Desb 6A **18**

F

Fairfield Rd. NN14: Ish 6B **36**
Fair La. NN14: Thrap 1F **39**
Fairlight Ct. NN18: Corby 2H **13**
Fairway, The NN15: Kett 5G **31**
Falmer Wlk. NN18: Corby 3H **13**
Falster Cl. NN18: Corby 5G **13**
Faraday Ct. NN14: Thrap 2F **39**
Faraday Gro. NN17: Corby 5E **7**
Farm Cl. NN14: Brigs 5G **17**
Farmfield Cl. NN15: Bur L 3D **36**
Farmstead Rd. NN18: Corby 2G **13**
Farnborough Cl. NN15: Kett 2B **36**
NN18: Corby 6B **14**
Farndale Av. NN17: Corby 6C **6**
Featherbed La. NN18: Lit O 5E **15**
Federation Av. NN14: Desb 1B **24**
Fermyn Cl. NN14: Brigs 4G **17**
Fermyn Pl. NN18: Corby 4G **13**
Fermyn Woods Country Pk. 5H **17**
Fern Dale Cl. NN14: Gedd 6F **23**
Fernie Cl. NN15: Bart S 2E **37**
Field Cotts. NN18: Gt O 1H **21**
Field St. Av. NN16: Kett 2H **31**
Fienedon St. NN15: Bur L 6F **37**
Filey Ct. NN18: Corby 3H **13**
Finch Dr. NN15: Bart S 1E **37**
Finedon Rd. NN15 6F **37**
Fineshade Cl. NN15: Bart S 2E **37**
Fineshade Gro. NN17: Corby 5C **6**
Finland Way NN18: Corby 5G **13**
Fir Rd. NN16: Kett 3B **32**
Fisher PE8: Ound 4B **40**
Fisher Cl. NN14: Thrap 3F **39**
Fishton Cl. NN15: Kett 6A **32**
Fitzwilliam Dr. NN15: Bart S 2E **37**
Fjord Wlk. NN18: Corby 5G **13**
Flatford Cl. NN18: Corby 6B **14**
Fleet St. NN16: Kett 3G **31**
Fleming Rd. NN17: Corby 3E **7**
Flensburg Cl. NN18: Corby 5H **13**
Fletcher Gdns. NN14: Thrap 3E **39**
Fletton Way PE8: Ound 3B **40**
Ford St. NN16: Kett 3A **32**
Forest Ga. Rd. NN17: Corby 6C **6**
Forest Glade NN16: Kett 5A **28**
Forrester Gro. NN14: Thrap 3F **39**
Forstal Cl. NN18: Corby 4B **14**
Foster Cl. NN15: Kett 5F **31**
Foster Ct. NN18: Corby 2C **14**
Fotheringham M. *PE8: Ound 4C **40***
(off East Rd.)
Fotheringhay Ct. NN14: Thrap 2F **39**
Fotheringhay Rd. NN17: Corby 5H **5**
Foundry Wlk. NN14: Thrap 3D **38**
Foxglove Cl. NN18: Corby 5B **14**
Foxlands NN14: Desb 1D **24**
Fox St. NN14: Roth 5E **25**
Foxton Ct. NN15: Kett 5G **31**
Franklin Flds. NN17: Corby 5E **7**
Freeman's La. NN14: Denf 6D **38**
French Dr. NN15: Kett 4C **32**
Front St. NN14: Denf 6D **38**
Fuller St. NN16: Kett 2A **32**
Furlong Rd. NN14: Desb 6E **19**

A-Z Corby & Kettering 43

Furnace Dr.—Kenton Ct.

Furnace Dr. NN14: Thrap 3E 39
Furnace La. NN16: Kett 6F 27
Fyfe Rd. NN17: Corby 5H 5

G

Gables, The NN15: Kett 4H 31
Gainage Cl. NN18: Gt O 6A 14
Gainsborough Av. NN15: Bart S 6E 33
Gainsborough Ct. NN18: Corby 2B 14
Gainsborough Rd. NN18: Corby 4G 13
Gamston Wlk. NN18: Corby 1H 13
Gander Cl. NN17: Weld 6C 8
Gapstile Cl. NN14: Desb 5B 18
Gardens, The LE16: East C 6A 4
NN16: Kett 1G 31
Garfield St. NN15: Kett 5H 31
Garrard Way NN16: Kett 2F 31
Garston Rd. NN18: Gt O 5A 14
Gateford Ct. NN18: Corby 1H 13
Gate La. NN14: Brou 2B 34
Gaultney, The *NN14: Desb* 6C 18
(off Station Rd.)
GEDDINGTON 6F 23
Geddington Rd. NN18: Corby 1F 15
Genner Rd. NN17: Corby 4F 7
George Blackall Ct. *NN17: Corby* 5A 6
(off Keats Way)
George St. NN15: Bur L 4G 37
NN16: Kett 4H 31
NN17: Corby 1C 14
Gibbons Dr. NN14: Roth 4G 25
Gilchrist Av. NN17: Corby 5E 7
Gillingham Rd. NN15: Kett 5F 31
Gipsy La. NN15: Kett 2E 31
Glade Cl. NN15: Bur L 4G 37
Gladstone St. NN14: Desb 6C 18
NN14: Ring 6H 39
NN14: Roth 4F 25
NN16: Kett 3A 32
Glaister Pl. NN16: Kett 3B 32
Glapthorn Rd. PE8: Ound 2A 40
Glastonbury Cl. NN15: Kett 5D 32
Glastonbury Rd. NN18: Corby 1G 13
Glebe Av. NN14: Brou 3B 34
NN15: Kett 5H 31
Glebe Farm NN14: Pytc 5F 35
Glebe Rd. NN15: Bur L 5E 37
Glen Baulk Rd.
NN14: Kett, Tho M 2B 30
Glencoe Dr. NN15: Kett 5C 32
Glendon Rd. NN14: Roth 4F 25
Gleneagles Cl. NN15: Kett 5D 32
Glenshee Cl. NN15: Kett 5C 32
Gloucester Cl. NN16: Kett 3A 32
Gloucester Ct. NN14: Roth 5E 25
Glover Ct. LE16: Cott, Midd 4C 4
Glyndebourne Gdns.
NN18: Corby 3G 13
Goadby's Yd. NN16: Kett 3H 31
Godwin Rd. NN17: Corby 2D 6
Goldsmith Dr. NN17: Corby 5B 6
Gold St. NN14: Desb 6C 18
NN16: Kett 3H 31
(off Newlands)
NN16: Kett 3H 31
(High St.)
Goodhew Cl. NN15: Kett 5F 31
Goodwood Cl. NN18: Lit O 1C 22
Gordon Rd. PE8: Ound 3C 40
Gordon St. NN14: Roth 5F 25
NN16: Kett 3A 32
Gorse Rd. NN16: Kett 1C 32
Gotch Cl. NN15: Bart S 3D 36
Gotch Rd. NN15: Bart S 2D 36
Gough Cl. NN15: Kett 4C 32
Gower Cl. NN15: Kett 1A 36
Grace Ct. NN15: Bur L 6F 37
Grafton PE8: Ound 4B 40
Grafton Dr. NN17: Corby 5H 5
Grafton Rd. NN14: Brigs 6F 17
NN14: Gedd 1F 29
Grafton St. NN16: Kett 1G 31
Granby Cl. NN18: Corby 1H 13
Grange Pl. NN16: Kett 1C 32
Grange Rd. NN14: Brou 2B 34
NN14: Stan 5A 16
NN14: Week 1G 27
NN16: Kett 2G 31
Grange Rd. Bus. Est.
NN14: Gedd 1D 28
Grant Cl. NN15: Kett 6F 31
Grantham Wlk. NN18: Corby 3H 13
Grantown Cl. NN15: Kett 5C 32
Granville St. NN16: Kett 3A 32
Grasmere Rd. NN16: Kett 3F 31
Gray's Cl. NN17: Corby 5C 6
Grays Dr. NN14: Stan 4A 16
Greasley Wlk. NN18: Corby 1H 13
GREAT CRANSLEY 1A 34
Great Folds Rd. NN18: Corby 6F 13
GREAT OAKLEY 5G 13
Great Oakley Meadow Nature Reserve 1G 21
Grebe Cl. NN14: Thrap 1E 39
Green, The NN14: Islip 2C 38
NN14: Wood 6B 38
Greenacre Dr. NN14: Stan 5A 16
Greenbank Av. NN15: Kett 4B 32
Greenbank Ter. NN14: Ring 6H 39
Greenfield Av. NN15: Kett 5F 31
Greenhill Ri. NN18: Corby 3H 13
Greenhill Rd. NN15: Kett 5F 31
Greening Rd. NN14: Roth 3E 25
Greenland Wlk. NN18: Corby 5G 13
Green La. LE16: Sto A 3D 10
NN14: Desb 6A 18
NN14: Ish 6D 36
NN14: Thrap 2E 39
NN16: Kett 3H 31
Greenslade Cl. NN15: Kett 5G 31
Greeve Cl. NN18: Gt O 6A 14
Gregory Wlk. NN18: Corby 3B 14
Grendon Av. NN17: Corby 6H 5
Grenville Cl. NN14: Roth 5G 25
NN17: Corby 5G 5
Gretton Brook Rd.
NN17: Corby 3B 6
Gretton Rd. NN17: Rock 1H 5
NN17: Weld 5C 8
Gretton Rd. Ind. Est.
NN17: Weld 5C 8
Grieg Wlk. NN18: Corby 5G 13
Grimsby Cl. NN18: Corby 3A 14
Grindleford Cl. NN14: Desb 6A 18
Grizedale Cl. NN16: Kett 5G 27
NN17: Corby 5B 6
Grosvenor Cl. NN15: Bart S 2E 37
Grosvenor Rd. NN15: Bart S 2D 36
Grosvenor Way NN15: Bart S 1D 36
Grove, The NN14: Ring 6G 39
NN15: Kett 4H 31
NN18: Corby 1G 15
Grove Rd. NN14: Thrap 3D 38
Grundy Ct. NN15: Kett 5H 31
Gunnell Cl. NN15: Kett 5F 31
Gunthorpe Pl. NN18: Corby 1H 13

H

Hafod Cl. NN18: Gt O 5A 14
Haig Dr. NN15: Kett 4C 32
Halfmoon M. PE8: Ound 4C 40
Halford St. NN14: Thrap 3D 38
Halifax Sq. NN18: Corby 2H 13
Hall Cl. NN15: Kett 5F 31
Hall Hill NN14: Brigs 5G 17
Hall La. LE16: Bring 1A 4
NN15: Kett 4F 31
Halls Cl. NN14: Gedd 6F 23
NN17: Weld 5C 8
Hallwood Rd. NN16: Kett 6A 28
Hamilton Ho. NN18: Corby 2C 14
Ham La. NN14: Ring 5G 39
Hampden Cres. NN16: Kett 2B 32
Handcross Ct. NN18: Corby 3H 13
Hanover Cl. NN15: Bart S 6D 32
Harborough Rd. LE16: Sto A 3C 10
NN14: Desb 2A 18
Harcourt St. NN16: Kett 3A 32
Harden Cl. NN18: Gt O 1G 21
Harding Cl. NN15: Kett 4D 32
Harlech NN18: Corby 4A 14
Harlech Ct. NN14: Thrap 2G 39
Harley Way NN14: Brigs 5H 17
Harpers Cl. NN18: Gt O 1H 21
Harper's Ct. NN14: Brigs 5G 17
Harrington Rd. NN14: Desb 6A 18
NN14: Roth 5D 24
Harris Rd. NN17: Corby 5A 6
Harrogate Ct. NN18: Corby 3H 13
Harry Potter Ho. NN15: Kett 4H 31
Hartley Dr. NN15: Bart S 6E 33
Hartwood Cft. NN16: Kett 5A 28
Harvest Cl. NN15: Bur L 5G 37
Harwood Dr. NN16: Kett 5G 27
Hastings Wlk. NN18: Corby 2H 13
Hatfield Cl. NN18: Corby 4C 14
Hathersage Cl. NN14: Desb 5A 18
Havelock Cotts. PE8: Ound 4C 40
Havelock Ct. NN16: Kett 1A 32
Havelock St. NN14: Desb 6C 18
NN16: Kett 2H 31
Haweswater Rd. NN16: Kett 2E 31
Hawkins Cl. NN14: Roth 4G 25
NN17: Corby 4H 5
Hawson Cl. NN15: Kett 6A 32
Hawthorn Cl. NN15: Bur L 6F 37
Hawthorn Dr. NN14: Thrap 4E 39
Hawthorne Wlk. NN17: Corby 4C 6
Hawthorn Rd. NN15: Bur L 6F 37
NN15: Kett 5H 31
Hawthorns, The NN14: Desb 1E 25
Hay Cl. NN18: Gt O 1H 21
Haynes Rd. NN16: Kett 3B 32
Hazeland Ho. NN14: Desb 6C 18
Hazel Rd. NN15: Kett 4A 32
Hazelwood Ct. *NN16: Kett* 4H 31
(off Hazelwood La.)
Hazelwood La. NN16: Kett 4H 31
Hazelwood Rd. NN17: Corby 6C 6
Headlands NN14: Desb 6E 19
NN15: Brou, Kett 1F 35
Headway NN18: Corby, Gt O 1G 21
Heathcote Gro. NN14: Desb 5A 18
Heather Rd. NN16: Kett 1B 32
Heathfield Wlk. NN18: Corby 3H 13
Heath Way NN15: Bur L 4G 37
Helmsley Way NN18: Corby 3H 13
Hemery Rd. NN15: Kett 5F 31
Hempland Cl. NN18: Gt O 1H 21
Henley Cl. NN15: Bart S 2D 36
Henson Cl. NN16: Kett 6F 27
Henson Way NN16: Kett 1E 31
Hereford Cl. NN14: Desb 5E 19
Herford Cl. NN18: Corby 5F 13
Heritage Ct. NN16: Kett 4H 31
Heritage Way NN17: Corby 3F 7
Hermitage Rd. LE16: Bramp 4A 10
Herne Rd. PE8: Ound 5C 40
Heron Av. NN14: Thrap 1F 39
Heron Cl. NN15: Bur L 5D 36
Hever Cl. NN14: Thrap 2F 39
Hidcote Cl. NN18: Corby 5C 14
Hield Cl. NN18: Gt O 6A 14
Higham Rd. NN15: Bur L 6G 37
Highbrook NN18: Corby 3H 13
Highfield NN14: Wood 5A 38
Highfield Cres. NN15: Kett 1H 35
Highfield Gro. NN17: Corby 6D 6
Highfield Rd. NN14: Thrap 2F 39
NN15: Kett 6H 31
High Hill NN14: Roth 4E 25
High St. LE16: Cott 4C 4
NN14: Brigs 4F 17
NN14: Brou 3A 34
NN14: Denf 6D 38
NN14: Desb 6C 18
NN14: Islip 2C 38
NN14: Pytc 5F 35
NN14: Ring 6G 39
NN14: Roth 4E 25
NN14: Rush 1C 26
NN14: Stan 5A 16
NN14: Thrap 2D 38
NN14: Wood 5B 38
NN15: Bur L 6G 37
NN16: Kett 3H 31
NN17: Corby 1E 15
NN17: Weld 6D 8
Hilda Pl. NN16: Kett 1C 32
Hill, The LE16: Midd 5B 4
Hillcrest Av. NN15: Bur L 6F 37
NN15: Kett 4B 32
Hillcrest Cl. NN14: Thrap 1F 39
Hillfield Rd. PE8: Ound 3A 40
Hillside Av. NN15: Kett 5A 32
Hillside Cres. NN17: Weld 6C 8
Hillside Ter. *NN16: Kett* 3G 31
(off Meadow Rd.)
Hill St. NN16: Kett 2G 31
Hilltop Av. NN14: Desb 5B 18
NN15: Bart S 2D 36
Hilltop Cl. NN14: Desb 5B 18
Hinton Av. NN18: Corby 3G 13
Hinwick Cl. NN15: Kett 2B 36
Hobbs Hill *NN14: Roth* 5E 25
(off Kettering Rd.)
Hockney Av. NN15: Bart S 5E 33
Hodge Way NN16: Kett 3B 32
Hogarth Dr. NN15: Bart S 6E 33
Hogarth Wlk. NN18: Corby 2C 14
Holbein Wlk. NN18: Corby 2B 14
Holdenby NN15: Kett 2A 36
Holdenby Rd. NN15: Kett 2B 36
Holkham Cl. NN18: Corby 5B 14
Hollands Dr. NN15: Bur L 5G 37
Holly La. NN14: Cran 1A 34
Holly Rd. NN16: Kett 1A 32
Holme Cl. LE16: Wilb 2F 11
Holmfirth Wlk. NN18: Corby 3H 13
Holyrood Wlk. NN18: Corby 4A 14
Home Cl. NN18: Gt O 6H 13
Home Ct. NN14: Thrap 2E 39
Home Farm Cl. NN18: Gt O 1H 21
Home Farm Rd. NN14: Stan 5A 16
Honiton Gdns. NN18: Corby 3C 14
Hood Ct. NN17: Corby 5H 5
Hood Wlk. NN15: Kett 5B 32
Hoppet Cl. NN18: Gt O 1G 21
Hoppner Wlk. NN18: Corby 2B 14
Hornbeam Ct. NN14: Desb 6F 19
Horrocks Way NN15: Kett 4D 32
Horselease Cl. NN18: Gt O 1G 21
Horsemarket NN16: Kett 3H 31
Horsham Wlk. NN18: Corby 2H 13
Hortons La. NN14: Thrap 2E 39
Hospital Hill NN14: Roth 4F 25
Hove St. NN18: Corby 2H 13
Howard Av. NN17: Corby 6H 5
Howard St. NN16: Kett 3G 31
Howden Grn. NN14: Desb 5A 18
Howe Cres. NN17: Corby 6G 5
Hoy Wlk. NN17: Corby 4A 6
Hubble Rd. NN17: Corby 4D 6
Hudson Cl. NN18: Corby 4A 14
Humber Wlk. NN17: Corby 4A 6
Hunters Rd. NN17: Corby 4A 8
Huntingdon Rd. NN14: Thrap 2E 39
Hunt St. NN18: Corby 2B 14
Hurst Cl. NN15: Bur L 3G 37
Hutchinson Av. NN14: Brou 4B 34
Huxloe Pl. *NN16: Kett* 3H 31
(off High St.)

I

Ibsen Wlk. NN18: Corby 5G 13
Inham Cl. NN18: Gt O 5A 14
Inkerman Way PE8: Ound 4B 40
Inwood Cl. NN18: Gt O 5A 14
Iona Rd. NN17: Corby 5A 6
Iron Pit Cl. NN18: Corby 2H 15
Ironwood Av. NN14: Desb 5C 18
Irving Gro. NN17: Corby 5C 6
Isebrook Ct. NN15: Bur L 5E 37
Ise Rd. NN15: Kett 4B 32
Ise Vale Av. NN14: Desb 6D 18
Ise Vw. Rd. NN14: Desb 6D 18
ISHAM 6D 36
Isham Rd. NN14: Pytc 5F 35
Islay Wlk. NN17: Corby 5A 6
ISLIP 1C 38
Islip Furnaces Ind. Est.
NN14: Islip 3A 38
Ivydene Ter. NN14: Brou 2A 34
Ivy Rd. NN16: Kett 1B 32

J

Jackson Way NN15: Kett 5F 31
Jamb, The NN17: Corby 1E 15
James Watt Av. NN17: Corby 4E 7
Jasmine Ct. NN16: Kett 6B 28
Jasmine Rd. NN16: Kett 1B 32
Jean Rd. NN16: Kett 2C 32
Jericho PE8: Ound 4C 40
Jesus Hospital NN14: Roth 4F 25
Jetty, The *NN14: Brigs* 4G 17
(off High St.)
Job's Yd. NN16: Kett 3H 31
John Clare Ct. NN16: Kett 5A 28
John Clare Way *NN17: Corby* 5B 6
(off Byron Rd.)
John Smith Av. NN14: Roth 4G 25
John St. NN14: Thrap 2F 39
Jowett Cl. NN15: Kett 5E 33
Jubilee Av. NN18: Corby 2A 14
Jubilee Cl. NN14: Islip 1C 38
Jubilee St. NN14: Roth 5F 25
Jubilee Ter. *NN14: Ish* 6D 36
(off Park Cl.)
Jude's Ct. *NN15: Kett* 4G 31
(off Northampton Rd.)
Judith Rd. NN16: Kett 2B 32
Jura Cl. *NN17: Corby* 5H 5
(off Denford Rd.)
Jutland Way NN16: Kett 3G 31

K

Kane Wlk. NN17: Corby 5C 6
Karlstad Cl. NN18: Corby 5G 13
Kathleen Dr. NN16: Kett 1C 32
Katrine Cl. NN17: Corby 4H 5
Keating Cl. NN15: Bart S 5E 33
Keats Dr. NN16: Kett 5A 28
Keats Way NN17: Corby 5A 6
Keebles Cl. NN14: Stan 5A 16
Keld Cl. NN18: Corby 5B 14
Kelmarsh Rd. NN17: Corby 6A 6
Kelvin Gro. NN17: Corby 6E 7
Kemp Ho. NN17: Corby 2D 6
Kendalls Cl. LE16: Wilb 2F 11
Kenilworth NN18: Corby 4A 14
Kenilworth Dr. NN15: Kett 5D 32
Kenilworth Gdns. NN14: Thrap 2G 39
Kenmore Dr. NN14: Desb 1C 24
Kennel Hill NN14: Brigs 5G 17
Kensington Gdns. NN15: Kett 5G 31
Kensington Wlk. NN18: Corby 4A 14
Kent Cl. NN17: Corby 6A 6
Kenton Ct. NN15: Bart S 5E 33

44 A-Z Corby & Kettering

Nelson Dr.—Rutland St.

Nelson Dr. NN14: Roth 4G **25**
Nelson Rd. NN17: Corby 5H **5**
Nelson St. NN16: Kett 1A **32**
Nene Cl. NN15: Bart S 3D **36**
Nene Cl. NN14: Thrap 2E **39**
Nene Cres. NN17: Corby 4A **6**
Nene Leisure Cen. 3E **39**
Nene Rd. NN15: Bur L 5E **37**
Nene Valley Bus. Pk.
PE8: Ound 4D **40**
Nene Vw. NN14: Islip 1C **38**
PE8: Ound 3B **40**
Nene Way PE8: Ound 2B **40**
Nepcote Cl. NN15: Kett 5B **32**
Netherfield Gro. NN17: Corby 5D **6**
Netherfield Rd. NN15: Kett 6A **32**
Neuville Way NN14: Desb 6B **18**
Neville Ho. *NN17: Corby 1C 14*
(off George St.)
Nevis Cl. NN17: Corby 4A **6**
Newark Dr. NN18: Corby 1H **13**
Newbold Cl. PE8: Ound 3A **40**
Newell Rd. NN14: Ring 6H **39**
Newham Cl. NN14: Roth 4E **25**
New Ho. PE8: Ound 5B **40**
Newlands NN16: Kett 3H **31**
Newland St. NN16: Kett 3H **31**
Newman St. NN15: Bur L 5F **37**
NN16: Kett 3A **32**
Newmarket Cl. NN18: Gt O 6B **14**
New Post Office Sq.
NN17: Corby 1C **14**
New Rd. NN14: Gedd 1E **29**
PE8: Ound 3B **40**
Newstead Ct. NN15: Kett 2A **36**
New St. NN14: Desb 6C **18**
(not continuous)
NN14: Roth 4F **25**
PE8: Ound 4C **40**
NEWTON 5B **22**
Newton Gro. NN17: Corby 4E **7**
Newton Rd. NN14: Newt 5C **22**
NN15: Bart S 2D **36**
New Town NN14: Brigs 4F **17**
Newtown NN14: Wood 5B **38**
Newtown St. NN14: Wood 5B **38**
Nichols St. NN14: Desb 5C **18**
Nine Arches Way NN14: Thrap 2D **38**
Nithsdale Rd. NN17: Corby 6B **6**
Nook, The LE16: Cott 4D **4**
NN17: Corby 1F **15**
Norfolk Cl. NN17: Corby 6A **6**
Norris Cl. NN15: Kett 5E **33**
Norse Wlk. NN18: Corby 5G **13**
Northall St. NN16: Kett 2H **31**
Northam Ct. NN16: Kett 1H **31**
Northampton Rd. NN14: Brou 5A **34**
NN15: Kett 5E **31**
North Av. NN15: Bur L 4F **37**
Northbrook NN18: Corby 3H **13**
Nth. Cape Wlk. NN18: Corby 5G **13**
Northfield Av. NN14: Ring 6H **39**
NN15: Kett 4G **31**
NN16: Kett 2G **31**
Northfield Cl. NN16: Kett 1G **31**
Northfield Rd. NN14: Cran 4B **30**
Nth. Folds Rd. NN18: Corby 6F **13**
North Pk. Dr. NN16: Kett 6A **28**
North St. PE8: Ound 4C **40**
Northumberland Cl. NN15: Kett 1B **36**
Northumberland Rd.
NN15: Kett 1A **36**
Norton Rd. NN17: Corby 6A **6**
Norton St. NN14: Roth 4G **25**
Norway Cl. NN18: Corby 4G **13**
Nunnery Av. NN14: Roth 4E **25**

O

Oak Cl. NN14: Brou 3B **34**
Oakham Cl. NN14: Desb 5B **18**
Oakleas Ri. NN14: Thrap 3E **39**
Oakley Ct. NN18: Corby 6G **13**
Oakley Hay Ind. Est.
NN18: Corby 6F **13**
(not continuous)
Oakley Pond NN18: Gt O 1H **21**
Oakley Rd. NN14: Pipe 2B **20**
NN14: Pipe, Rush 6D **20**
NN17: Corby 2D **14**
NN18: Corby 2G **21**
Oakley St. NN16: Kett 1H **31**
Oak Rd. NN15: Kett 3B **32**
Oaktree Cl. NN14: Desb 5B **18**
Oaktree Ct. *NN16: Kett 4H 31*
(off George St.)
Oathill Ri. NN15: Bur L 5G **37**
Oban Cl. NN15: Kett 5C **32**
Occupation Rd. LE16: Midd 2A **4**
NN17: Corby 6C **6**
PE8: Ound 2C **40**
Octagon, The NN17: Corby 5E **7**
Odeon Bldgs. NN17: Corby 6E **7**
Odeon Cinema 3A **36**
Old Dry La. NN14: Brigs 4F **17**
Oldenburg Rd. NN18: Corby 4F **13**
Old Farm La. NN14: Islip 1C **38**
Oldland Rd. NN18: Corby 4B **14**
Old Rd. NN14: Stan 5A **16**
Ollerton Wlk. NN18: Corby 2H **13**
Ollis Cl. NN17: Corby 5C **6**
Olympic Way NN15: Kett 6F **31**
Orchard Cl. LE16: Wilb 2E **11**
NN14: Desb 6A **18**
NN14: Ring 6H **39**
NN17: Weld 5D **8**
Orchard Ct. NN14: Wood 5A **38**
Orchard Cres. NN16: Kett 1B **32**
Orchard Est. NN14: Pytc 5F **35**
Orchard Way NN14: Thrap 3F **39**
Orchid Cl. *NN14: Desb 5C 18*
(off Burdock Way)
Orion Way NN15: Kett 2H **35**
Orkney Wlk. NN17: Corby 5H **5**
Orlingbury Rd. NN14: Pytc 6F **35**
Orton Rd. NN14: Roth 6D **24**
NN15: Bart S 2D **36**
Osbourne Cl. NN18: Corby 5C **14**
Osiers, The NN14: Desb 1F **25**
Osier Way NN14: Thrap 3D **38**
Oslo Gdns. NN18: Corby 4F **13**
Ostlers Way NN15: Kett 5G **31**
OUNDLE 4B **40**
Oundle Rd. NN14: Thrap 2E **39**
NN17: Weld 5D **8**
Oundle School Swimming Pool
4B **40**
Oval, The NN15: Kett 5H **31**
Ovett Cl. NN15: Kett 5F **31**
Oxford Rd. NN17: Corby 1A **14**
Oxford St. NN14: Roth 3F **25**
NN16: Kett 2G **31**

P

Packer Rd. NN15: Kett 5E **31**
Paddock La. NN14: Desb 6C **18**
Paddock M. NN14: Desb 6C **18**
Paddocks, The NN14: Stan 4B **16**
Pagent Ct. NN15: Kett 6G **31**
Pages Wlk. NN17: Corby 1F **15**
Paradise Av. NN15: Kett 1B **36**
Paradise La. NN15: Kett 1B **36**
Park Av. NN16: Kett 1H **31**
Park Cl. NN14: Ish 6D **36**
Park Lodge NN17: Corby 1C **14**
Park Rd. NN15: Bur L 5F **37**
NN16: Kett 1A **32**
Park Vw. NN14: Thrap 2E **39**
NN16: Kett 1H **31**
Park Wlk. NN14: Brigs 5F **17**
Parsons Gro. NN17: Corby 5E **7**
Pashler Gdns. NN14: Thrap 2E **39**
Patrick Cl. *NN15: Kett 1A 36*
(off Sussex Rd.)
Patrick Ct. NN18: Corby 3B **14**
Patrick Rd. NN15: Kett 1A **36**
NN18: Corby 3B **14**
Pavilion Dr. PE8: Ound 3B **40**
Peacock Dr. NN14: Ring 6H **39**
Peake Cl. LE16: Midd 5B **4**
Peaselands NN14: Desb 5B **18**
Pebbleford Rd. NN15: Kett 5B **32**
Pegasus Ct. NN15: Kett 3A **36**
Peg's La. NN14: Denf 6D **38**
Pembroke Cl. NN14: Thrap 2F **39**
Pendle Av. NN16: Kett 5G **27**
Pendyl Rd. NN14: Desb 2C **18**
Pen Grn. La. NN17: Corby 5E **7**
Pennine Way NN16: Kett 6H **27**
Penrhyn Cl. NN18: Corby 4D **14**
Penrhyn Ct. NN14: Thrap 3F **39**
Perry Cl. NN15: Kett 6G **31**
Petherton Ct. NN16: Kett 2H **31**
Petworth Gdns. NN18: Corby 2H **13**
Pevensey Wlk. NN18: Corby 2H **13**
Pevrel Pl. NN14: Desb 5A **18**
Pexley Ct. PE8: Ound 4A **40**
Phoenix Parkway NN17: Corby 2E **7**
Phoenix Parkway Ind. Est.
NN17: Corby 5F **7**
Phoenix Retail Pk. NN17: Corby 5F **7**
Piggott's La. NN15: Bur L 5G **37**
Pike Rd. NN18: Corby 6G **13**
Pilot Rd. NN17: Corby 6F **7**
Pine Cl. NN14: Desb 1E **25**
Pine Rd. NN15: Kett 4B **32**
Pine Tree Ct. NN14: Islip 1C **38**
Pine Wlk. NN17: Corby 4C **6**
Pinewood Cl. NN16: Kett 5H **27**
Pioneer Av. NN14: Desb 1B **24**
NN15: Bur L 5F **37**
Pipers Cl. NN15: Kett 4A **32**
Piper's Hill NN15: Kett 5A **32**
PIPEWELL 1B **20**
Pipewell Rd.
LE16: East C, Pipe 3A **12**
NN14: Desb 5D **18**
Pipewell Rd. Ind. Est.
NN14: Desb 4D **18**
Playford Cl. NN14: Roth 4H **25**
Pleasant Row NN14: Wood 5B **38**
Plens Nature Reserve, The 5D **18**
Plough Cl. NN14: Roth 4F **25**
Plumpton Ct. NN18: Corby 2H **13**
Podmore Way NN14: Brou 4A **34**
Polegate Ct. NN18: Corby 2H **13**
Pollard St. NN16: Kett 1H **31**
Polwell La. NN15: Bart S 1D **36**
Ponder St. NN14: Roth 4F **25**
Poplar Rd. NN15: Bur L 3G **37**
NN16: Kett 3B **32**
NN17: Corby 4B **6**
Poplar's Farm Rd. NN15: Bart S 6F **33**
Poppyfield Ct. NN14: Thrap 1E **39**
Portree Wlk. NN17: Corby 5A **6**
Post Office Cl. *NN17: Corby 1F 15*
(off Chapel La.)
Pound Cl. NN14: Ring 6H **39**
NN18: Gt O 5H **13**
Prentice Wlk. *NN17: Corby 1F 15*
(off South Rd.)
Preston Ct. NN15: Bur L 4G **37**
Primrose Cl. NN16: Kett 1B **32**
NN18: Corby 5A **14**
Prince Rupert Av. NN14: Desb 6B **18**
Princes Av. NN14: Desb 6D **18**
Princes Ct. *NN16: Kett 2H 31*
(off Princes St.)
Princes St. NN16: Kett 2H **31**
Prince William Rd. PE8: Ound 4A **40**
Princewood Rd. NN17: Corby 3B **6**
Printers Yd. *NN16: Kett 3H 31*
(off Dalkeith Pl.)
NN16: Kett 3H **31**
(Dryland St.)
Priors Ct. NN17: Corby 4B **8**
Priors Haw Rd. NN17: Corby 4B **8**
Priory Ct. NN14: Gedd 1E **29**
Priory M. NN14: Wood 6B **38**
PYTCHLEY 5F **35**
Pytchley Ct. *NN17: Corby 5H 5*
(off Fotheringhay Rd.)
Pytchley La. NN15: Kett 2H **35**
Pytchley Lodge Ind. Est.
NN15: Kett 1A **36**
Pytchley Lodge Rd. NN15: Kett 1H **35**
Pytchley Rd. NN15: Kett 2A **36**
Pywell Ct. NN17: Corby 3H **7**
Pywell Rd. NN17: Corby 3H **7**

Q

Quantock Cl. NN15: Bart S 2E **37**
Quebec Cl. NN18: Corby 4A **14**
Queen Eleanor Rd. NN14: Gedd 6E **23**
Queensberry Rd. NN15: Kett 4H **31**
Queens Cl. LE16: Wilb 2E **11**
Queens Rd. LE16: Wilb 2E **11**
Queen's Sq. *NN17: Corby 2C 14*
(off Cardigan Pl.)
Queen St. NN14: Desb 5D **18**
NN14: Gedd 1E **29**
NN14: Thrap 2F **39**
NN16: Kett 3H **31**
Queensway NN15: Bur L 5E **37**
Quorn Cl. NN15: Bart S 2E **37**

R

Radnor Way NN15: Bart S 2D **36**
Ragsdale St. NN14: Roth 4G **25**
Railside La. NN17: Corby 1E **15**
Railway Cotts. NN18: Gt O 2B **22**
Railway Vw. NN16: Kett 2G **31**
Rainbow Wlk. NN15: Bart S 2D **36**
Raleigh Cl. NN14: Roth 4G **25**
NN17: Corby 5H **5**
Rankine Ho. NN17: Corby 5B **6**
Rannoch Cl. NN15: Kett 5C **32**
Rannoch Way NN17: Corby 4H **5**
Rathlin Cl. NN17: Corby 5H **5**
Raven Dr. NN15: Bart S 1E **37**
Ravenscourt NN17: Corby 5D **6**
Ray Cl. PE8: Ound 2B **40**
Rectory La. NN14: Wood 6B **38**
Rectory Wlk. NN15: Bart S 6D **32**
Redgrave Cl. NN15: Kett 6F **31**
Redwood Cl. NN14: Desb 1E **25**
Regal Dr. NN16: Kett 5A **28**
Regent Cl. NN15: Bur L 5E **37**
Regent Rd. NN15: Bur L 5E **37**
Regent St. NN14: Desb 5D **18**
NN16: Kett 2H **31**
Reigate Wlk. NN18: Corby 4H **13**
(not continuous)
Rendlesham Cl. NN16: Kett 5G **27**
Reservoir Cl. NN14: Stan 4A **16**
Reservoir Rd. NN16: Kett 1H **31**
Reynolds Cl. NN15: Bart S 5E **33**
Reynolds Rd. NN18: Corby 2C **14**
Ribblesdale Av. NN17: Corby 6C **6**
Richard Cl. NN15: Kett 1A **36**
Richmond Av. NN15: Kett 5D **32**
Richmond Rd. NN17: Corby 1C **14**
Ridding Cl. NN18: Corby 4B **14**
Ridge Rd. NN14: Islip 1C **38**
Ridgway Rd. NN15: Bart S 5F **33**
Ridings, The NN14: Desb 5A **18**
Ridley St. NN16: Kett 2G **31**
Riggal Cl. NN14: Brou 4A **34**
Riley Rd. NN16: Kett 1E **31**
RINGSTEAD 6H **39**
Ringstead Cl. NN15: Bart S 2D **36**
NN17: Corby 5H **5**
Ringstead Rd. NN14: Denf 6D **38**
Ripley Rd. LE16: Cott 4D **4**
Ripley Wlk. NN18: Corby 4A **14**
Riverside Cl. PE8: Ound 5C **40**
Riverside Maltings PE8: Ound 3C **40**
Riverside Way NN14: Islip 2C **38**
Roadins Cl. NN15: Kett 6G **31**
Robin Cl. NN15: Bart S 1E **37**
Robinson Cl. NN16: Kett 1F **31**
Robinson Way NN16: Kett 1F **31**
Rochester Cl. NN15: Bart S 6D **32**
Rochester Rd. NN18: Corby 5C **14**
Rock Hill NN14: Roth 4F **25**
ROCKINGHAM 1H **5**
Rockingham Castle 2H **5**
Rockingham Castle Est.
LE16: Rock 2H **5**
Rockingham Cl. NN14: Thrap 2F **39**
Rockingham Hills PE8: Ound 2A **40**
Rockingham M. NN17: Corby 6E **7**
Rockingham Motor Speedway 1A **8**
Rockingham Paddocks
NN16: Kett 5H **27**
Rockingham Rd. LE16: Cott 4D **4**
NN14: Rush 4F **21**
NN16: Kett 6G **27**
NN17: Corby 3A **6**
Rock 'n' Bowl 6H **27**
Rock Rd. PE8: Ound 3B **40**
Rodney Dr. NN17: Corby 5H **5**
Roman Cl. NN17: Weld 5D **8**
Roman Way NN14: Desb 6C **18**
NN14: Thrap 1F **39**
Romney Rd. NN18: Corby 2C **14**
Rose Av. NN17: Weld 5D **8**
Roseberry St. NN16: Kett 3A **32**
Rosebery St. NN14: Ring 6H **39**
NN15: Bur L 6F **37**
Rose Cl. NN14: Brou 2B **34**
NN14: Roth 5G **25**
NN18: Corby 5C **14**
Rose Ct. NN17: Weld 5D **8**
Rosedale Av. NN17: Corby 1C **14**
Rosemount Dr. NN15: Kett 6A **32**
Rose Paddock NN14: Wood 5B **38**
Rose Ter. NN14: Wood 5B **38**
(not continuous)
Rosewood Pl. NN16: Kett 1A **32**
Rossendale Dr. NN15: Bart S 2E **37**
Rossetti Rd. NN18: Corby 2C **14**
ROTHWELL 4G **25**
Rothwell Rd. NN14: Desb 6C **18**
NN14: Kett 6C **26**
NN16: Kett 2F **31**
Roughton Cl. NN15: Kett 1H **35**
Roundhill Rd. NN15: Kett 5H **31**
Rowan Ct. *NN17: Corby 4C 6*
(off Welland Va. Rd.)
Rowell Way PE8: Ound 5D **40**
Rowlett Rd. NN17: Corby 5A **6**
Roxton Cl. NN15: Bart S 2E **37**
Royal Gdns. NN14: Desb 1B **24**
Royce Cl. NN17: Corby 4D **6**
Rubens Wlk. NN18: Corby 2C **14**
Rufford Cl. NN15: Bart S 2E **37**
Rufford Wlk. NN18: Corby 1H **13**
Rushmere Cl. NN14: Islip 1C **38**
RUSHTON 1C **26**
Rushton Rd. LE16: Wilb 2E **11**
NN14: Desb 5D **18**
NN14: Roth 4F **25**
Rushton Triangular Lodge 6A **20**
Russell St. NN16: Kett 3A **32**
Rutherford Ct. NN17: Corby 4F **7**
Rutherglen Rd. NN17: Corby 6D **6**
Ruth Gdns. NN16: Kett 2C **32**
Rutland Cl. NN17: Corby 6H **5**
Rutland Ct. NN14: Desb 5B **18**
Rutland St. NN16: Kett 2A **32**

46 A-Z Corby & Kettering

Tilley Hill Cl. PE8: Ound 2A 40
Timpson Cl. NN16: Kett 6A 28
Tintern Ct. NN15: Kett 5E 33
Tithe Cl. NN14: Ring 6G 39
Todmorden Cl. NN18: Corby 2A 14
Toll Bar Rd. NN14: Islip 2C 38
Toller Pl. NN15: Bart S 1D 36
Toller St. NN16: Kett 3A 32
Toll Ga. Pl. NN18: Corby 1F 15
Top Cl. NN14: Thrap 1G 39
Top End NN14: Pytc 5F 35
Tordoff Pl. NN16: Kett 3H 31
Torksey Cl. NN18: Corby 6G 13
Torridge Cl. NN16: Kett 1F 31
Torridon Ct. NN17: Corby 4A 6
Torville Cres. NN15: Kett 5F 31
Totnes Cl. NN18: Corby 3D 14
Tourist Info. Cen.
  Corby 1C 14
  Kettering 4H 31
  Oundle 4B 40
Towcester Cl. NN16: Lit O 6C 14
Tower Hill Rd. NN18: Corby 2G 13
Trafalgar Rd. NN16: Kett 3G 31
Trailli La. NN14: Wood 5B 38
Treen Cl. NN14: Thrap 2G 39
Trent Cres. NN15: Bur L 6F 37
Trent Rd. NN16: Kett 6G 27
  NN17: Corby 4B 6
Tresham St. NN14: Roth 4F 25
  NN16: Kett 2A 32
Trevithick Rd. NN17: Corby 5G 7
Trinity Cl. NN14: Roth 5E 25
Trinity Rd. NN14: Roth 5D 24
Trinity Wlk. NN18: Corby 3C 14
Tromso Cl. NN17: Corby 5G 13
Tudor Ct. NN16: Kett 3A 32
  (off Alexandra St.)
Tunwell La. NN17: Corby 6F 7
Turner Cl. NN15: Bart S 5E 33
Turner Rd. NN16: Corby 2C 14
Turners Yd. PE8: Ound 4B 40
Tweed Cl. NN15: Bur L 6F 37
Twickenham Ct.
  NN18: Corby 2H 13
Tyler Way NN14: Thrap 3F 39
Tynan Cl. NN15: Kett 5E 33
Tyne Rd. NN17: Corby 4B 6
Tyson Courtyard
  NN18: Corby 6A 8

U

Uist Wlk. NN17: Corby 5A 6
Ullswater Rd. NN16: Kett 3E 31
Underwood Rd. NN14: Roth 4E 25
Union St. NN14: Desb 6C 18
  NN16: Kett 2G 31
Unity St. NN14: Desb 1B 24
Up. Dane NN16: Kett 6A 18
Upperfield Gro. NN17: Corby 5C 6
Up. Steeping NN14: Desb 1D 24
Upper St. NN16: Kett 3H 31
  (off Northall St.)
Uppingham Rd. NN14: Rush 2F 21
  NN17: Corby 6G 5

V

Vale St. NN16: Kett 2G 31
Valley Ri. NN14: Desb 1D 24
Valley Wlk. NN16: Kett 3C 32
Vancouver Cl. NN18: Corby 5H 13
Vara Cl. NN18: Corby 5H 13
Velbert Ho. NN17: Corby 4C 6
Venture Ct. NN17: Corby 4B 8
Vernon Ct. NN16: Kett 6F 27
Vian Way NN17: Corby 5H 5
  (not continuous)
Vickers Cl. NN14: Roth 5H 25

Victoria Ct. NN14: Roth 4F 25
  NN16: Kett 3A 32
  (off Victoria St.)
Victoria Rd. PE8: Ound 3C 40
Victoria St. NN14: Desb 6C 18
  NN15: Bur L 5F 37
  NN16: Kett 3H 31
Viking Cl. NN16: Kett 5A 28
Viking Way NN18: Corby 4F 13
Villa Gdns. NN15: Bur L 6F 37
Vine Cl. PE8: Ound 4C 40
Violet Cl. NN14: Desb 5C 18
  NN18: Corby 5B 14
Violet La. NN14: Glen 4C 26

W

Wadcroft NN16: Kett 3H 31
Wainwirght Av. NN14: Thrap 3E 39
Wakerley Cl. PE8: Ound 4A 40
Walcot Cl. PE8: Ound 2A 40
Wales St. NN14: Roth 4E 25
Walkers La. NN16: Kett 3H 31
Wallis Cres. NN15: Kett 5A 32
Wallis Rd. NN15: Kett 5A 32
Walnut Cl. NN17: Weld 5D 8
Walnut Cres. NN16: Kett 5D 32
Walsingham Av. NN15: Kett 5D 32
Waltham Cl. NN17: Corby 4B 6
Walton Pl. NN18: Corby 1H 13
Wansell Rd. NN17: Corby 5B 8
Wansford Pl. NN17: Corby 5H 5
Wardle Ct. NN16: Kett 2H 31
  (off Princes St.)
Wareham Grn. NN18: Corby 1H 13
  (off Taunton Av.)
WARKTON 1E 33
Warkton Rd. NN14: Wark 1F 33
  NN16: Wark 1F 33
Warkton Way NN17: Corby 5H 5
Warminster Ct. NN18: Corby 6G 5
Warren Bri. PE8: Ound 4A 40
Warren End NN14: Desb 5D 18
Warren Hill NN16: Kett 2E 31
Warren Rd. NN14: Stan 4A 16
Warwick Av. NN14: Stan 4A 16
Warwick Ct. NN15: Kett 5D 32
Warwick Gdns. NN14: Thrap 2G 39
Warwick Way NN17: Corby 1A 14
Washington Ct. NN14: Thrap 1F 39
  NN16: Kett 2B 32
Washington Sq. NN16: Kett 2B 32
Waterhouse Gdns.
  NN15: Bart S 6E 33
Water La. LE16: Cott 5D 4
  NN17: Weld 5C 8
Water Mdw. Cl. NN18: Gt O 6H 13
Watermill Cl. NN14: Desb 6F 19
Water St. NN16: Kett 3A 32
Watson Cl. NN17: Corby 3C 6
  PE8: Ound 2A 40
Watt Av. NN17: Corby 5E 7
Wavell Cl. NN15: Kett 4C 32
Waver Cl. NN18: Corby 4B 14
Waverley Av. NN17: Corby 1E 15
Waverley Rd. NN15: Kett 5B 32
Weaver Cl. NN16: Kett 5H 27
Webb Cl. PE8: Ound 4D 40
Wedgwood Cl. NN14: Desb 6B 18
Wedmore Ct. NN18: Corby 1H 13
WEEKLEY 5D 28
Weekley Glebe Rd. NN16: Kett 6B 28
Weekley Wood La.
  NN16: Week 5C 28
Weinahr Cl. LE16: Wilb 2E 11
Welbeck Ct. NN15: Kett 5D 32
  NN18: Corby 2A 14
WELDON 6D 8
Weldon Nth. Ind. Est.
  NN17: Corby 4C 8
  (not continuous)

Weldon Rd. NN17: Corby 1E 15
Weldon Sth. Ind. Est.
  NN18: Corby 6A 8
Weldon St. NN16: Kett 2A 32
Welford Gro. NN17: Corby 6A 6
Welland Ct. NN14: Desb 6C 18
  NN15: Bur L 5F 37
Welland Rd. NN16: Kett 6G 27
Welland Va. Rd. NN17: Corby 4B 6
Welland Vw. Rd. LE16: Cott 4D 4
Wellingborough Rd.
  NN14: Brou 3A 34
  NN14: Ish 6C 36
  (off Kettering Rd.)
Wellington St. NN16: Kett 2H 31
Wellington Ter. NN14: Islip 2C 38
Wellington Works NN16: Kett 2A 32
  (off Wellington St.)
Wells Cl. NN15: Kett 5F 31
Wells Grn. NN18: Corby 1H 13
Wensleydale Pk. NN17: Corby 5B 6
Wentin Cl. NN18: Gt O 6A 14
Wentworth Dr. PE8: Ound 2A 40
Wesley Cl. NN14: Roth 4F 25
  (off Well Dr.)
Wessex Cl. NN16: Kett 5H 27
West Av. NN15: Bur L 4F 37
Westbury Wlk. NN16: Kett 1H 13
Westcott Way NN17: Corby 1B 14
Westfield Ho. NN16: Kett 3G 31
Westfields NN17: Corby 5C 6
West Furlong NN15: Kett 4F 31
West Glebe Rd. NN17: Corby 5D 6
Westhill Cl. NN15: Kett 4F 31
Westhill Dr. NN15: Kett 4F 31
Westleigh Rd. NN15: Bart S 5F 33
Westley Cl. NN15: Bur L 6F 37
West Lodge Rural Cen. 3E 19
Westminster Dr. NN15: Bart S 6D 32
Westminster Wlk. NN18: Corby 3A 14
Westmorland Dr. NN14: Desb 5E 19
Weston Wlk. NN18: Corby 1A 14
Westover Rd. NN15: Kett 4F 31
West St. NN14: Brou 2A 34
  NN14: Gedd 6E 23
  NN14: Wood 5A 38
  NN16: Kett 4H 31
  PE8: Ound 4B 40
West St. M. PE8: Ound 4B 40
  (off West St.)
West Vw. NN17: Corby 6F 7
Westway NN15: Kett 4F 31
Westwood Wlk. NN18: Corby 2A 14
West Yd. NN14: Islip 1C 38
Weymouth Cl. NN18: Corby 1H 13
Wharfedale Rd. NN17: Corby 4C 6
Wheatfield Dr. NN14: Kett 5G 37
Wheatley Av. NN17: Corby 1D 14
Whitby Cl. NN15: Kett 5D 32
Whiteford Dr. NN15: Kett 6A 32
Whitehill Rd. NN14: Desb 6A 18
Whiteman La. NN14: Roth 4E 25
White Post Ct. NN17: Corby 3C 6
Whitney Rd. NN15: Bur L 6F 37
Whittle Rd. NN17: Corby 5F 7
Whittlesea Ter. NN14: Wood 6B 38
Whitwell Cl. PE8: Ound 4A 40
Whitworth Av. NN17: Corby 4E 7
Wick Cl. NN18: Corby 4B 14
Wicksteed Cl. NN15: Kett 1A 36
Wicksteed Park 6C 32
WILBARSTON 2E 11
Wilbarston Rd. LE16: Sto A 3D 10
Wilby Cl. NN17: Corby 5H 5
Wilkie Cl. NN15: Kett 5F 31
Willetts Cl. NN17: Corby 5C 6
William St. NN15: Bur L 5F 37
  NN16: Kett 1H 31
Willowbrook East Ind. Est.
  NN17: Corby 3H 7
Willow Brook Rd. NN17: Corby 5A 6
Willow Cl. NN14: Desb 6E 19

Willow Herb Wlk. NN14: Desb 5C 18
Willow La. NN14: Stan 5A 16
Willow Rd. NN15: Kett 4A 32
Wilmington Wlk. NN18: Corby 2H 13
Wilson Ter. NN16: Kett 1H 31
Wilton Rd. NN15: Kett 5D 32
Wimbourne Wlk. NN18: Corby 6G 5
Wincanton Ct. NN18: Corby 1H 13
Windermere Rd. NN16: Kett 3F 31
Winding Way NN14: Thrap 2F 39
Windmill Av. NN15: Kett 2B 32
  NN16: Kett 2B 32
Windmill Cl. LE16: Cott 4D 4
Windmill Ct. NN16: Kett 2B 32
  (off Edmund St.)
Windmill Ri. LE16: Cott 4D 4
Windmill Wlk. NN15: Kett 4B 32
Windsor Av. NN14: Desb 1B 24
Windsor Cl. LE16: Wilb 3E 11
Windsor Dr. NN14: Thrap 2F 39
Windsor Gdns. NN16: Kett 2G 31
Windsor Pl. NN17: Corby 2C 14
Wingate Cl. NN15: Kett 4C 32
Winston Dr. NN14: Ish 6B 36
Winterbourne Ct. NN18: Corby 1H 13
Winterburn Ct. NN16: Kett 2E 31
Winthorpe Way NN18: Corby 1H 13
Wold Rd. NN15: Bur L 4H 37
Wolfe Cl. NN18: Corby 4D 32
Wollongong Ho. NN17: Corby 5D 6
Woodfield Gro. NN17: Corby 6C 6
WOODFORD 5B 38
Woodford Cl. NN15: Bart S 2D 36
Woodland Av. NN15: Bart S 1H 21
WOODLAND CAPIO HOSPITAL 6B 26
Woodlands, The NN14: Gedd 6E 23
Woodlands Av. NN17: Corby 4D 6
Woodlands Cl. NN14: Brigs 5G 17
Woodlands Ct. NN16: Kett 1A 32
Woodlands La. NN18: Gt O 1H 21
Woodlands Rd. NN17: Weld 6E 9
Woodlin Cl. PE8: Ound 5A 40
Woodlans M. NN14: Brigs 5G 17
  (off Stable Hill)
Woodnewton Way NN17: Corby 6A 6
Woodside Cl. NN14: Desb 2C 18
Woodside Pk. NN17: Weld 6E 9
Woodstock St. NN15: Bur L 4H 37
Wood St. NN14: Gedd 1F 29
  NN16: Kett 2H 31
  NN17: Corby 1C 14
Woodwell Hill NN14: Desb 1B 24
Woodyard Cl. NN14: Brigs 4G 17
Wordsworth Av. NN17: Corby 4B 6
Wordsworth Rd. NN16: Kett 6A 28
Worksop Gdns. NN18: Corby 1H 13
  (off Clumber Ct.)
Wormleightons Way
  NN14: Gedd 6E 23
  (off West St.)
Worthing Rd. NN18: Corby 2H 13
Wren Cl. NN15: Bart S 1E 37
Wroe Cl. NN18: Gt O 6A 14
Wyatt PE8: Ound 3B 40
Wyatt St. NN16: Kett 3A 32
Wyatt Way PE8: Ound 3A 40
Wyndham Way NN16: Kett 1E 31

Y

Yardley Cl. NN17: Corby 5B 6
Yarrow Gallery 4B 40
Yarwell Cl. NN15: Kett 1A 36
Yateley Dr. NN15: Bart S 2E 37
Yeoman Cl. NN14: Ring 6G 39
Yeomans Ct. NN15: Bur L 5G 37
Yew Cl. NN17: Corby 4C 6
Yew Tree Cl. NN15: Kett 5A 32
York Rd. NN16: Kett 3H 31
  NN18: Corby 2H 13

The representation on the maps of a road, track or footpath is no evidence of the existence of a right of way.

The Grid on this map is the National Grid taken from Ordnance Survey mapping with the permission of the Controller of Her Majesty's Stationery Office.

Copyright of Geographers' A-Z Map Company Ltd.

European Handb

C000284093

GERMAN RAILWAYS

PART 1. LOCOMOTIVES & MULTIPLE UNITS OF DEUTSCHE BAHN

FIFTH EDITION

The complete guide to all Locomotives and
Multiple Units of Deutsche Bahn

Brian Garvin

Published by Platform 5 Publishing Ltd.,
3 Wyvern House, Sark Road, Sheffield S2 4HG, England.

Printed in England by The Lavenham Press Ltd, Lavenham, Suffolk.

ISBN 978 1 909431 03 4

Above: 218 460 is seen shortly after departure from Buchloe with RE32606, the 1051 München Hauptbahnhof to Füssen, whilst in the background 218 488 takes the Memmingen route with RE32796, the 1103 Augsburg Hbf to Hergatz. The date is 3 April 2010. **Robin Ralston**

Front cover: One of the first outings in the new Eintracht Frankfurt livery for 101 110 was IC 2025 from Hamburg Altona to Frankfurt (M). Here the train is seen betwenn Bonn and Köln near Bornheim on 30 August 2012. **Matthias Müller**

Back Cover: 411 053 makes its way along the right bank of the Rhine through Braubach with an ICE service from Dortmund to Wien. This train would usually travel along the left bank of the Rhine but was diverted over the less frequently used route due to engineering work. The famous Marksburg castle can be seen in the background. **Matthias Müller**

CONTENTS

FOREWORD

Can it really be nearly ten years since the previous edition of this book appeared?! It certainly is and much has been happening in Germany since then. Deutsche Bahn was lined up for privatisation but many things began to go wrong once eyes were taken off running a railway and instead concentrated on privatisation. The Berlin S-Bahn once noted for its efficiency and punctuality has been an absolute shambles and this together with other things has put privatisation on hold.

DB Fernverkehr services, especially ICE services, have been hit by quality problems including accident damage putting several ICE sets out of use. A refurbishment programme which has seen the entire ICE 1 fleet completed and work now taking place on the ICE 2 sets as they approach mid-life, has also contributed to the shortage of operational sets. DB Regio has been losing out to private operators but is now fighting back with many new EMUs on order. Problems with the Eisenbahn Bundesamt (EBA) over the new Bombardier Class 442 EMUs prevented them from going into service as planned, but in late 2011 the Nürnberg and Trier based units were allowed into traffic. Many more Class 442s have already been built and started entering service in late 2012. These will soon have an impact on Classes 110 and 143. DB Schenker, like DB Regio, has been losing traffic because of the recession and competition from private operators. It is also fighting back but these factors have seen class totals reduced with many locomotives of Classes 140 and 232 laid up and subsequently scrapped.

The future for DB Fernverkehr will see more ICEs (Class 407) and new IC trains featuring Class 146s and double-deck carriages. DB Regio continues to invest in new EMUs and double-deck carriages and has ordered more Class 146s which will start to replace Class 111s. DB Schenker, having modernised its electric locomotive fleet, has turned its attention to the diesel locomotives with new Class 261s now being delivered which will see off non-modernised 29x types. Some more powerful shunters of Class 265 have also been ordered and will start to enter service in 2013. Meanwhile DB has ordered a new type of locomotive that may be used by any sector. DB Regio was first to take up some of these four-engined TRAXX type diesels (Class 245) however the framework contract will allow other sectors to order some in the future.

In this edition some classes have been reinstated into the main sections. Departmental locomotives such as shed shunters and locomotives belonging to emerging sectors such as DB Netz, DB Fahrweg etc. now find their place in class number order with a note showing the owner when this is not immediately clear.

German Railways Part 2 dealing with private operators, leasing companies and museum lines is in preparation and will appear in 2014. It will incorporate a new format reflecting the current situation where many standard types of locomotive are now in use in the private sector.

It is hoped readers will welcome the appearance of this new edition which is updated to May 2013.

Brian Garvin

AN HISTORICAL BACKGROUND TO GERMANY

After World War II Germany (*Deutschland* in German) was split up by the allies. The Soviets took part of eastern Poland with that country shifting westwards to the "Oder-Neisse Line". The remainder of Germany was divided up with the Soviets getting the eastern part and eastern Berlin and the three Western Allies getting western Berlin and the western part of the country. Eventually the allies grouped their parts together to form the *Bundesrepublik Deutschland* (BRD) which had Bonn as its capital and the eastern zone (Soviet) becoming the *Deutsche Demokratische Republik* (DDR) with East Berlin as its capital. At the end of the 1980s the communist countries started to collapse allowing the unification of the two Germanys which was achieved on 3 October 1990. In effect the DDR applied to join the BRD. The locomotive fleets were merged but passenger and freight traffic in the former East Germany was decimated and consequently many former DR types have been scrapped.

LANGUAGE

The standard language in Germany is, of course, German. However many people can speak very good English, but older people in the former DDR often cannot speak English, as the main foreign language which used to be taught in schools was Russian. The situation is changing rapidly and English speakers should not find too many problems.

GETTING THERE FROM GREAT BRITAIN

By Rail

Eurostar services run daily from London St. Pancras to Brussels Midi taking just over two hours. There are onward connections to Köln (Cologne) by Thalys and DB ICEs calling at Aachen Hbf. If you want to avoid supplements take an IC to Liège or Welkenraedt from where there is a two-hourly local service to Aachen. Eupen has frequent buses which stop outside Aachen Hbf.

By Sea

Stena Line offers a Harwich–Hoek van Holland overnight service. Onward connections are available on the NS via Arnhem/Emmerich or via Hengelo/Bad Bentheim; going via Venlo mean a change of train into a stopping service.

By Air

There are flights from all London airports and many regional airports direct to many German Airports. Berlin, Dresden, Düsseldorf, Frankfurt/Main, Stuttgart and München (Munich) airports are all rail-connected (Bremen is even tram connected!), as are the London airports of Gatwick, Heathrow, Luton and Stansted and the British regional airports at Birmingham and Manchester. Newcastle Airport is served by the Tyne & Wear Metro. The low cost carriers are also useful often serving areas different to the main players.

TICKETS AND PASSES

DB has set fares but there are many discounts available that can be obtained either by purchasing a "Bahncard" or by booking in advance on specific trains with many offers available on the DB website.

There are three Bahncards available, Bahncard 25 costing €100 first class or €50 second class per annum and giving a 25% discount on fares, Bahncard 50 costing €400 first class or €200 second class and giving a 50% discount and Bahncard 100 costing €5000 first class or €3000 second class which is an all-line pass for the year. The Bahncard 50 is available at half-price to children aged 6–17, students aged 18–25 and seniors (over 60).

Sparpreis tickets are quota-controlled and only valid on the trains stated. *Sparpreis 25* gives a 25% discount and requires a 3-day advance purchase. *Sparpreis 50* gives a 50% discount and requires a 3-day advance purchase but is valid only at the weekend, or for a journey involving a Saturday night away.

Without doubt the Lander Tickets and the Schoneswochenende tickets represent good value especially now that some of the former are valid for 1-5 persons and also available at weekends as well. Valid only on Regio services after 09.00. Many are also valid on town trams and buses in "Verbund" areas. Another useful ticket for a long journey is the Quer durch Deutschland ticket valid after 09.00 on Regio services. It pays to shop around. The DB website and www.diebefoerderer.de contain lots of information on validity.

The Platform 5 Publishing magazine *Today's Railways – Europe* has, each spring, a supplementary publication *Rail Pass Guide* which gives details of rover tickets in Germany and other European countries.

ACKNOWLEDGEMENTS

Data for this book has been collected from many sources including magazines, books, internet sites and individuals. The following magazines should be particularly mentioned: Bahn Report, Drehscheibe, Eisenbahn Revue International, Eisenbahn Kurier, Locomotive Club of Great Britain *BULLETIN*, LOK-Report and the Platform 5 Publishing magazine *Today's Railways Europe*. On the internet the websites of Lokrundschau, LOK-Report, Elektrolok, Drehscheibe-online and Revisionsdaten have been particularly useful.

Thanks also to all those people who submitted photographs; those used are individually credited. Special thanks are due to Matthias Müller for supplying an extensive selection of high quality images, many of which have been used in the book.

ORGANISATION OF GERMAN RAILWAYS

EISENBAHNBUNDESAMT (EBA)

This company has a great influence on current events. The Eisenbahn Bundesamt (German Federal Railway Authority) or EBA was set up to cover areas thought not to be part of the new railway companies' remits. It is responsible amongst other things for: the certification of locomotives and rolling stock; the overall supervision of the railways, and is in effect a government department.

DEUTSCHE BAHN AG (DB AG = DB)

The major railways of Germany were nationalised after World War I becoming the *Deutsche Reichsbahn*. After the Second World War the *Bundesrepublik* called its railway system the *Deutsche Bundesbahn* (DB) and the railway of the *Deutsche Demokratische Republik* retained the pre-war name. In this book the pre-war Reichsbahn is referred to as DRG (*Deutsche Reichsbahn Gesellschaft*) whilst the post-war Reichsbahn is referred to as simply DR.

Although split into two systems by the aftermath of the second world war, the DB and DR worked closely together and numbered their loco fleets so that numbers did not clash, so that once Germany was reunited there would be no problem in combining the two systems. For example the DB numbered its new electric locos as E10 whilst the DR had E11. Similarly the DB had E40, E41 and the DR E42. Then in the 1960s came the Berlin Wall and all cooperation came to a halt as the eastern part of the country was sealed off. The real break then came with computerisation when DR adopted a completely different system to the DB. It was no doubt done deliberately just to show that DR was in charge of its own house and was probably ordered from on high.

The combined West German *Deutsche Bundesbahn* (DB) and East German *Deutsche Reichsbahn* (DR) were merged into a new public limited company in 1994 known as *Deutsche Bahn AG*. This company adopted the DB numbering system and most DR stock had been renumbered from 01/01/92 in anticipation of the merger.

DBAG is a holding company for the various "sectors" which are now self-standing subsidiaries the principal ones being as follows:

DB Fahrzeuginstandhaltung GmbH: This company has the major workshops, depots being the responsibility of the respective operating companies.
DB Fernverkehr AG: This is the long distance operator formerly known as DB Reise & Touristik.
DB AutoZug GmbH: This company manages the overnight car sleeper trains and the Niebüll–Westerland car shuttle trains.
DB Regio AG: This is the company responsible for local and regional passenger trains; once the "Nahverkehr" sector. DB Regio has many subsidiaries for particular areas e.g. DB Regionalbahn Rhein-Ruhr GmbH Essen, DB Zug Bus Regionalverkehr Alb Bodensee GmbH, Ulm etc.
S-Bahn Berlin GmbH: A separate company for the Berlin S-Bahn.
S-Bahn Hamburg GmbH: A separate company for the Hamburg S-Bahn.
S-Bahn München GmbH: A separate company for the München S-Bahn.

Userdomer Bäderbahn GmbH: DB Regio formed a separate company to cover the lines on the Island of Usedom.
DB Schenker Rail Deutschland AG: The freight train operator formerly known as Railion and before that DB Cargo.
DB Netz: This is the infrastructure company, the "Network Rail" of Germany. It includes several subsidiaries such as DB Fahrwegdienste GmbH, DB Bahnbaugruppe GmbH the latter having absorbed already Deutsche Gleis- und Tiefbau, GmbH (DGT), Deutsche Bahn Gleisbau GmbH (DBG). Each company has some locomotives which are used nationwide although track depots at Augsburg and Duisburg Wedau do have a fixed allocation.
DB Stations & Service: This company manages the stations, terminals and land.
DB Systemtechnik: The former research and test centres of Halle, Minden and München.

ELECTRIFICATION

Much of the German network is electrified on the overhead system at 15 kV AC 16.7 Hz. This system is also used in Switzerland and Austria, permitting through running of locomotives. Thus DB locos are commonplace in Austria running right over the Brenner Pass to the Italian border. Austrian locos also work deep into Germany. All electric locos and multiple units are assumed to work on the 15 kV AC system unless stated otherwise. The new locomotives of Classes 185 and 189 being dual/multi-voltage allow DB Schenker to work trains through Switzerland to the Italian border, through Denmark into Sweden and into Belgium and the Netherlands. Some electrification is still taking place with Reichenbach to Hof currently in progress and München to Lindau somewhere in the pipeline.

▲ Resplendent in advertising livery for "Bundespolizei", 101 060 awaits departure from Berlin Ostbahnhof at the head of IC-144 to Amsterdam-Schiphol on 04 September 2012. **Matthias Müller**

DB TRAIN SERVICES

These are classified as follows:

IC	Intercity. An interconnecting network between major centres offering a high standard of accommodation.
EC	Eurocity. Similar to IC, but running between different countries.
ICE	Intercity Express. The high-speed Intercity train offering a very high standard of accommodation in new trains.
IRE	Inter Regio Express. The same as RE used in Baden Wüttemberg.
D	Express train (Schnellzug).
RE	Regional Express (semi-fast).
RB	Regionalbahn (local train).
S	S-Bahn (train on suburban network).
NZ	Nacht Zug. Internal overnight trains.
CNL	City Night Line. International overnight services.
EN	Euronacht. International overnight train.

Supplements are payable for travel on ICE, IC and EC; the overnight trains often feature "Global Pricing".

For freight trains DB Schenker has many different classifications; far too many to list individually.

LOCOMOTIVE & MULTIPLE UNIT NUMBERING SYSTEM

The present day DB numbering system can be traced back to that introduced in 1923 when the German railways were nationalised and became the Deutsche Reichsbahn. The system was one that we are now quite used to as it involved having a class number followed by the running number e.g. 01 001. The Reichsbahn grouped its locomotives into definite series. Express passenger locomotives were 01–19, freight locomotives were 50–59 etc. This system was also used for electric locomotives with the addition of an "E" prefix e.g. E04 02. However when it came to diesel locos the class number used was an indication of the horse power and the prefix used was "V" (Verbrennungsmotoren = internal combustion engine). EMUs were "ET" (T = Triebwagen = railcar) whilst DMUs were "VT".

This system remained in use until 1968 when the then DB was one of the first railways in Europe to computerise its locomotive numbers. In the new system the locomotive numbers are divided into three parts, all of which are numeric. The first part is the class number, usually the existing number with an additional digit to denote the type of traction being inserted in front of the former class number. The running number follows which is limited to three digits. This does not cause any problems as far as diesels and electrics are concerned but some steam classes had over 1000 locomotives and new numbers had to be given in some cases. Finally a computer check digit is added at the end of the number.

Examples:

E 10 001	became	110 001-5
V 60 150	"	260 150-8
VT24 624	"	624 624-3

The full breakdown of the traction type digits is:

0	Steam locomotive	5	Battery electric railcar (none now remain in service)
1	Electric locomotive	6	Diesel railcar
2	Diesel locomotive	7	Diesel railbus & departmental railcars
3	Shunting tractors	8	Electric railcar trailers
4	Electric railcars	9	Diesel railcar/railbus trailers

After the running number there is a computer check digit which double checks that all the preceding digits are correct. It is arrived at by multiplying the class and running number digits alternately by 1 and 2. The resulting digits are added together and the sum deducted from the next whole ten gives the check number.

Example 624 624-3

$$
\begin{array}{ll}
 & 6+2+4+6\ +2+4 \\
\times & \underline{1+2+1+2\ +1+2} \\
= & 6+4+4+1+2+2+8 = 27. \\
 & 30-27 = 3.
\end{array}
$$

EUROPEAN VEHICLE NUMBER & VEHICLE KEEPER MARKING

A new development is the European Vehicle Number (EVN). This is a refinement of the former UIC full identification number. Because of open access in Europe it is essential that all traction (and indeed all rolling stock) has a European number. The Vehicle Keeper Marking (VKM) has been deemed necessary because of the large number of railway operators in a country following open access and follows the country code. This has helped to simplify matters in Germany as many private operators had duplicate numbers. Now they have a unique EVN as well!

Taking electric loco 120 151 as an example its full EVN is 91 80 6120 151-6 D-DB which breaks down as follows:

The first digit is a code for a traction unit with the second digit giving the type of traction. In Germany the types are

90. Miscellaneous traction – mostly used for steam locomotives e.g. 90 80 0001 509-3 D-PRESS but also hybrid locomotives.
91. Electric Locomotives faster than 99 km/h e.g. 91 80 6186 336-4 D-DB
92. Diesel locomotives faster than 99 km/h e.g. 92 80 1261 036-8 D-DB
93. High speed EMU e.g. 93 80 5403 027-6 D-DB
94. EMUs e.g. 94 80 0440 106-3 D-AGIL
95. DMUs e.g. 95 80 0650 067-1 D-ODEG
96. Loose trailers (Not used in Germany)
97. Electric shunting locomotives or electric locomotives with maximum speed less than 100 km/h e.g. 97 80 8194 052-7 D-LEG
98. Diesel shunting locomotives or diesel locomotive with maximum speed less than 100 km/h e.g. 98 80 3363 622-2 D-DB
99. Departmental self powered vehicles – includes tamping machines etc. Because of this several DB departmental locomotives have regained their original numbers.

Note that the old UIC railway number (in this case 80 for DB) now stands for the country and not the railway. The railway concerned is indicated at the end as the vehicle keeper. In some cases this might not be a railway but a leasing company.

It will be seen that the old classification, e.g. 120, forms part of the new number. But in years to come there could be a 5120, 7120 etc. (This is already happening with the new Class 442 EMUs which have appeared as 442, 1442 and 2442!) DB in fact chose the extra digit in the classification to keep existing computer check digits the same but this does not apply to all types in particular DMU and EMU. The running number and check digit are next followed by a country code and the VKM.

The full EVN/VKM is shown on the sides of locomotives and vehicles and can be very small as it is a rather long piece of information. For this same reason numbers on the front of locomotives and units only show the basic number without a check digit. As a result of this development, check digits have not been shown in the main lists.

(Of the example VKMs shown above, DB is self explanatory, AGIL is AGILIS one of the new private operators whilst ODEG is Ostdeutsche Eisenbahn Gesellschaft. These codes are used in German Railways Part 2 to identify the various private operators).

9180 6 143 052-9 D-DB

Example of an EVN as applied to 143 052. **Keith Fender**

LAYOUT OF INFORMATION

For each class of vehicle general data and dimensions in metric units are provided. Vehicle lengths are lengths over couplers on buffers. The following standard abbreviations are used:

km/h	kilometres per hour	m	metres
kN	kilonewtons	mm	millimetres
kW	kilowatts		

Builder codes are shown in Appendix 1 on page xxx. For explanation of codes used for accommodation in hauled coaching stock and multiple units see Appendix 2 on page 221.

For each vehicle the number is given in the first column. Where a vehicle has been renumbered the former number is generally shown in parentheses after the current number. Further columns show, respectively, the livery (in bold condensed type), any detail differences, the depot allocation and name where appropriate.

Important note: In multiple unit trains, references to number of engines, traction motors etc. should be understood to be per power car, except for articulated units where the total number in the unit is stated. Weights are in full working order, i.e. with a full tank of fuel etc.

DEPOTS

The changing railway structure has had an effect on depots. Many depots have closed since unification especially in the east where the organisation was in a steam era time warp allocating electric locomotives to numerous little depots etc. Traction fleets are concentrated at fewer and fewer depots with some sectorisation of depots taking place. Baden Württemberg is a good example where Mannheim, an obvious freight depot, had many passenger locos allocated. These have now been moved away to depots reopened by DB Regio in Freiburg and Ludwigshafen. Frankfurt/M S-Bahn units are now based in a new depot adjacent to the main station in what was previously the main postal depot.

The use of the depot abbreviations has declined with the new businesses using the full name (in some cases an amended name) of the depot e.g. NN1 formerly Nürnberg Hbf is now Nürnberg West or even Nürnberg Göstenhof. For the depot code we will continue to use NN1. The depots, once known as a Bahnbetriebswerk (Bw) then became a Betriebeshof (Bh) and are in some cases now a Werk. Most people still refer to the depots as a Bw! One change to the branding of the locomotives is that instead of just "Nürnberg West" the business sector concerned is also shown as two businesses could operate from the same depot.

Some new depots have been built, in the first instance for Fernverkehr to house the new ICE trains. DB Schenker is also into new depots but these are "Kombi" depots – combined depots for locomotives and rolling stock (wagons). In Saarbrücken the old depot has been handed over part to the tramway and part to Euro Cargo Rail. Locomotives still stable there but maintenance is at the new depot at the opposite end of the marshalling yard. Both depots in Nürnberg have been rebuilt. In Köln the existing depots are to be supplemented by three new ones in the next few years; two in the Nippes area (ICE and S-Bahn) and the third at the Deutzerfeld site (DMUs).

A list of depot codes and depots is shown in Appendix 4 on page 222.

MAIN WORKS

The workshops, after several years in limbo in the run up to anticipated privatisation, are now rather firmly based. There have been some closures but Nürnberg once slated for closure is busy refurbishing ICEs and having had workshops modernised now has a secure future performing EMU overhauls. Those remaining are:

Works	Code	Workload
Berlin Schöneweide	BSWSX	Berlin S-Bahn units.
Bremen	HBX	218, 225, 290–295. (Is also the maintenance centre for Bremen area locomotives).

Chemnitz	DCX	Hydraulic transmissions. Part of the works has replaced the old DC depot.
Cottbus	BCSX	232, 233, 234, 290–298, 361–365, 7xx. (But also overhauls electric locomotives as required).
Dessau	LDX	Electric locomotives.
Eberswalde	WEX	Wagons.
Fulda	FFUX	Brake-gear (future uncertain).
Kassel	FKX	Diesel multiple units and carriages.
Krefeld-Oppum	KKROX	Electric multiple units – all types including ICEs.
Meiningen	UMX	Steam locomotives and special work.
Neumünster	ANX	Carriages.
Nürnberg	NNX	ICE2 being refurbished currently but is expected to overhaul EMUs of Classes 423, 440, 442.
Paderborn	EPX	Wagons.
Wittenberge	WWX	Carriages and 708.
Zwickau	DZWX	Wagons.

More and more modern locomotives and rolling stock are being overhauled at depots. These include Hamburg Eidelstedt (101, 401), Magdeburg Rothensee (185), München Hbf. (120, 411).

LIVERIES

The standard livery for all DB locomotives and multiple units is red (verkehrsrot – traffic red). However the Berlin S-Bahn units remain in their traditional colours at the request of Berliners. All ICE trains are white with a red band.

A Advertising livery.
I Inter City, white with a red stripe.
N Non standard livery.
0 Orange.
Y Yellow.

▲ Celebrity 103 184 leads a rake of first class only TEE coaching stock from Dortmund bound for Austria near Oberwinter on 21 April 2011.   **Matthias Müller**

ABBREVIATIONS

Standard abbreviations used in this book are:

Bww	Bahnbetriebeswagenwerke (wagon shop)
CD	České Dráhy (Czech Railways)
CFL	Chemins de Fer Luxembourgois (Luxembourg Railways)
DB	Deutsche Bundesbahn (former German Federal Railway) or Deutsche Bahn AG
DR	Deutsche Reichsbahn (former East German State Railway)
DRG	Deutsche Reichsbahn Gesellschaft (German Railway Company - pre 1945)
CIR ELKE	Computerised Integrated Railroading – Erhöhung der Leistungsfähigkeit im Kernnetz
EBULA	Elektronischer Buchfahrplan & Langsamfahranweisung (Computer display of timetable and speed restrictions)
ETCS	European Train Control System
FS	Ferrovie dello Stato (Italian Railways)
GPS	Global Positioning Satellite System
GSM-R	Global System for Mobile Communications – Rail
INDUSI	Inductive Zugsicherung – signalling warning system
KWS	Konventionelle Wendezeusteuerung. (Original DB push-pull system – pre TDM)
LZB	Linienzugbeeinflussung (cab signalling)
NBS	Neubaustrecke (newly built line – in effect high speed lines)
NS	Nederlandse Spoorwegen (Dutch Railways)
OHLE	Overhead Line Equipment
ÖBB	Österreichische Bundesbahnen (Austrian Federal Railways)
PZB	Punktförmige Zugbeeinflussung
SBB	Schweizerische Bundesbahnen (Swiss Federal Railways)
SIFA	Sicherheitsfahrschalung (deadman's pedal)
SNCB	Société Nationale des Chemins des Fer Belges (Belgian National Railways)
SNCF	Société Nationale des Chemins des Fer Français (French National Railways)
SZ	Slovenske Železnice (Slovenian Railways)
TDM	Time Division Multiplex
WL	Werklok
ZBF	Zugbahnfunk (train radio)
ZWS	Zeitmultiplexe Wendezugsteuerung (time division multiplex push-pull control)

The following codes are used in the lists of locomotives which are common to all classes:

a	automatic coupling
c	CIR ELKE (see above)
m	multiple working fitted
p	push-pull (KWS)
r	push-pull (ZWS/ZDS)

FOREIGN MOTIVE POWER IN GERMANY

Germany has important ports at Hamburg, Bremen and Bremerhaven which attract export/import traffic from/to many parts of Europe as well as for Germany itself. There are also big ports in the adjoining countries especially Belgium (Antwerpen) and The Netherlands (Rotterdam and Amsterdam) which produce lots of traffic going to/from and through Germany. Whilst DB Schenker shares in this traffic there are many private operators involved working through from one country to another. These operators will be found in German Railways Part 2. Obviously foreign motive power reaches the various border points but the following state operators work well into Germany. Under open access arrangement many foreign private companies also work into Germany.

AUSTRIA

Locomotives of Classes 1016, 1116 and 1144 operate well into the southern area of Germany mostly to München but are not unknown in Ingolstadt and Nürnberg. Austrian owned Class 411s (ÖBB 4011) share work with DB units on the Wien – Frankfurt/M route. Class 4024 EMUs reach Rosenheim from Innsbruck.

BELGIUM

SNCB Class 2800 electric locomotives work through from Belgium via Aachen West to Köln (Gremberg) and Duisburg (Rheinhausen) and elsewhere in the Ruhr area.

CZECH REPUBLIC

CD and CD Cargo electric locomotives of Classes 371/372 have workings into Germany getting to Dresden and Leipzig and they are not unknown in Berlin.

DENMARK

DB Schenker Rail Scandinavia Class 3100s work through from Sweden and Denmark to Hamburg (Maschen). Passenger services from Denmark are mostly formed of hired-in DB Class 605s until problems with the Danish IC4 DMUs are resolved.

FRANCE

Thalys TGVs work via Aachen to Köln and the Ruhr area whilst TGV Euroduplex sets work to Frankfurt/M and in due course will also take over from TGV POS sets on workings to Stuttgart and München. SNCF (Akiem) 37000s and 37500s work deep into Germany on freight trains having been seen as far east as Frankfurt/O on the Polish border!

ITALY

FS electric locomotives of Class E412 have been seen in München having worked in on freights via the Brenner route. It is not known whether this is a regular working.

LUXEMBOURG

CFL electric locomotives of Class 4000 work to Trier and along the line to Koblenz on passenger trains soon to be replaced by new CFL dual voltage EMUs. The Class 4000s also work well into Germany on selected freight trains.

NETHERLANDS

NS ICE3s share the work with DB units on Amsterdam to Frankfurt/M trains.

POLAND

PKP electric locomotives work international passenger trains through to Berlin. PKP hired-in multi-voltage locos work through to many areas in Germany with one coal train having PKP motive power through to Ulm! Passenger trains from Wrocław bring PKP diesel locos to Cottbus.

SLOVENIA

SZ electric locomotives of Class 541 (Taurus) have been seen in München having worked in on freights via the Tauern route. It is not known whether this is a regular working.

SWITZERLAND

Swiss Cargo electric locomotives of Classes 423 and 482 can be seen over large areas of Germany many being on hire to private operators. 423s also work into Lindau from Switzerland via Austria. SBB EMUs now operate local services over German lines near Basel and from Konstanz.

▲ 110 511 is the only example of Class 110.3 to have the earlier body style common to Class 110.1, it having been converted from 139 134. Here it is seen waiting for its next duty at Emden Rbf on 5 June 2011. **Matthias Müller**

MAPS OF THE GERMAN RAILWAY NETWORK

KEY TO MAPS

Notes:

The maps on pages 16–24 are not to scale and are a guide both to railways of DB Netz and those of private operators whose stock is detailed in the second part of this book. They should not be used to determine the exact location of any particular line or station.

Whilst we hope these maps will prove very useful to readers of this book, we would refer readers looking for more detailed maps to the comprehensive atlases produced by Schweers and Wall, details of which are below.

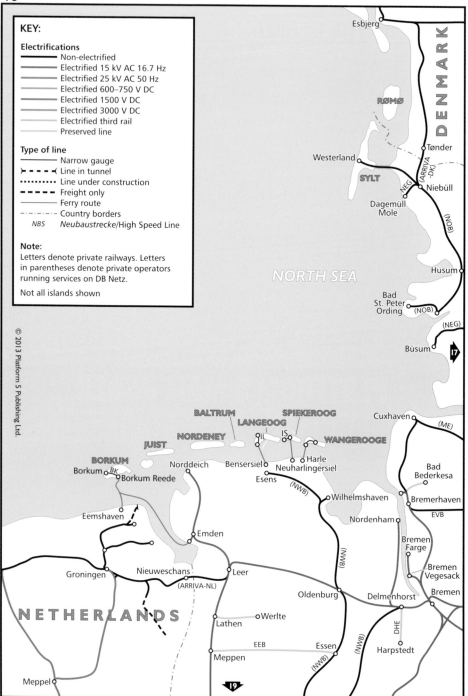

KEY:

Electrifications
- Non-electrified
- Electrified 15 kV AC 16.7 Hz
- Electrified 25 kV AC 50 Hz
- Electrified 600–750 V DC
- Electrified 1500 V DC
- Electrified 3000 V DC
- Electrified third rail
- Preserved line

Type of line
- Narrow gauge
- Line in tunnel
- Line under construction
- Freight only
- Ferry route
- Country borders
- NBS   Neubaustrecke/High Speed Line

Note:
Letters denote private railways. Letters in parentheses denote private operators running services on DB Netz.

Not all islands shown

© 2013 Platform 5 Publishing Ltd.

NORTH SEA

DENMARK

Esbjerg

RØMØ

Tønder

Westerland

SYLT

Niebüll

Dagemüll Mole

(ARRIVA-DK)

NEG

(BON)

Husum

Bad St. Peter Ording

(NOB)

(NEG)

Büsum

17

Cuxhaven

(ME)

BALTRUM

SPIEKEROOG

LANGEOOG

NORDENEY

IL

IS

WANGEROOGE

JUIST

BORKUM

Borkum

BK

Borkum Reede

Norddeich

Benseriel

Harle

Neuharlingersiel

Bad Bederkesa

Esens

(NWB)

Wilhelmshaven

Bremerhaven

EVB

Eemshaven

Nordenham

Emden

Bremen Farge

Groningen

Nieuweschans

Leer

Bremen Vegesack

(ARRIVA-NL)

(NWB)

Oldenburg

Delmenhorst

Bremen

NETHERLANDS

Werlte

Lathen

DHE

EEB

Essen

Harpstedt

Meppen

(NWB)

(NWB)

19

Meppel

Malmö

Simrishamn

Ystad

Trelleborg

BALTIC SEA

© 2013 Platform 5 Publishing Ltd.

Sassnitz

RÜGEN

Sassnitz
Fährhafen

Bergen

Ostseebad Binz

Barth

Putbus   RüKB

Stralsund

(UBB)

Lauterbach
Mole

Göhren

Velgast

Peenemünde

17

Greifswald

USEDOM

UBB

Tessin

Demmin

Züssow

UBB   Wolgast

Seebad Heringsdorf

Swinoujście Centrum

Ueckermünde
Stadthafen

Swinoujście

Lalendorf

(OLA)

Friedland

Trzebież
Szczecińskie

(OLA)

Jatznick

Police

Waren
(Müritz)

Neubrandenburg

(OLA)

(OLA)

Pasewalk

POLAND

ODEG

(ODEG)

Neustrelitz

Prenzlau

Szczecin

Mayenburg

(EGP)

Mirow

Fürstenberg

Poznan →

Wittstock

Rheinsberg
(Mark)

Templin

Passow

Schwedt
(Oder)

Angermünde

(EGP)

Gross
Schönebeck

Neuruppin

Löwenberg
(Mark)

Eberswalde

(ODEG)

NEB

Neustadt-
(Dosse)

21

Kostrzyn

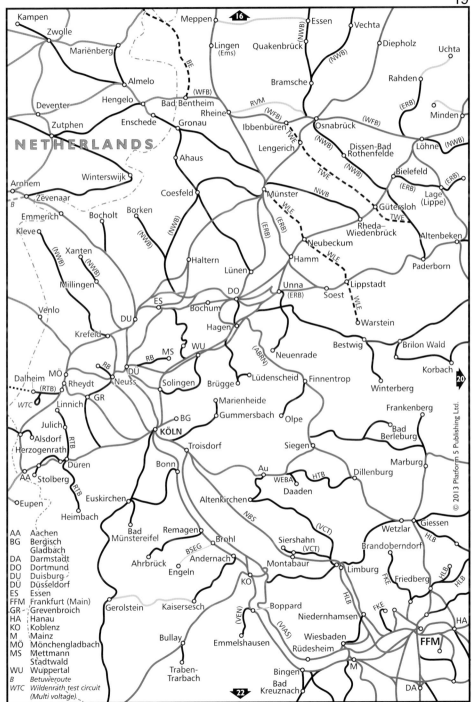

AA   Aachen
BG   Bergisch
       Gladbach
DA   Darmstadt
DO   Dortmund
DU   Duisburg
DÜ   Düsseldorf
ES   Essen
FFM Frankfurt (Main)
GR   Grevenbroich
HA   Hanau
KO   Koblenz
M   Mainz
MÖ   Mönchengladbach
MS   Mettmann
       Stadtwald
WU   Wuppertal
B   Betuweroute
WTC Wildenräth test circuit
       (Multi voltage)

© 2013 Platform 5 Publishing Ltd.

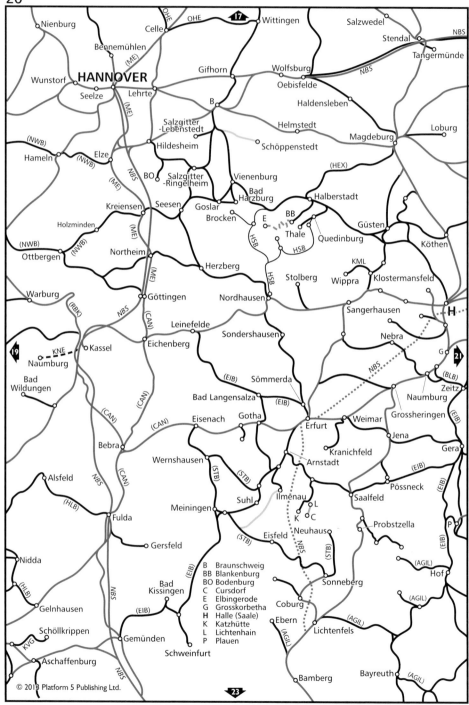

B   Braunschweig
BB   Blankenburg
BO   Bodenburg
C   Cursdorf
E   Elbingerode
G   Grosskorbetha
H   Halle (Saale)
K   Katzhütte
L   Lichtenhain
P   Plauen

© 2018 Platform 5 Publishing Ltd.

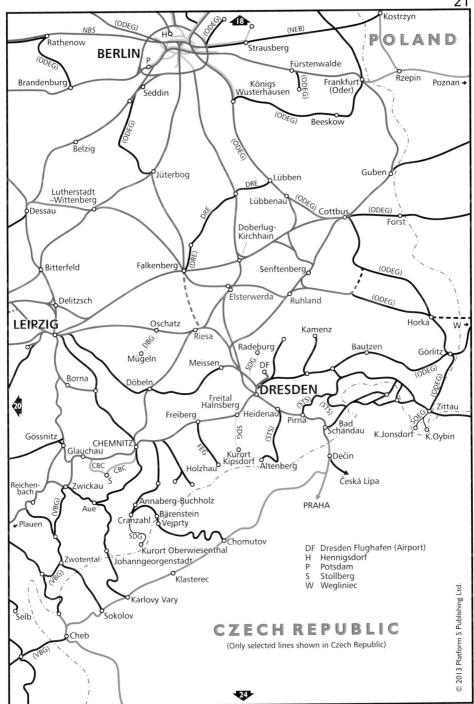

POLAND

Kostrzyn

Rathenow · *NBS* · (ODEG) · H · (ODEG) · **18** · (NEB)
BERLIN · P · Strausberg
Brandenburg · (ODEG) · Fürstenwalde
Seddin · Königs Wusterhausen · Frankfurt (Oder) · Rzepin · Poznan →
(ODEG) · Beeskow

Belzig

Jüterbog · DRE · Lübben · Guben
Lutherstadt–Wittenberg · Lübbenau · (ODEG) · Cottbus · (ODEG)
Dessau · Doberlug-Kirchhain · Forst

Bitterfeld · Falkenberg · (DRE) · Senftenberg · (ODEG)
Delitzsch · Elsterwerda · Ruhland · (ODEG)
LEIPZIG · Oschatz · Riesa · Kamenz · Horka · W →
Mügeln · DBG · Radeburg · Bautzen · Görlitz
Borna · Döbeln · Meissen · SDG · DF · (ODEG)
Freital Halnsberg · **DRESDEN** · (ODEG)
Gössnitz · Freiberg · Heidenau · Pirna · (STS) · Zittau
CHEMNITZ · SDG · Bad Schandau · K.Jonsdorf · SDEG · K.Oybin
Glauchau · CBC · CBC · FEG · Kurort Kipsdorf · (STS) · Dečin
Reichen-bach · S · Holzhau · Altenberg · Česká Lípa
Zwickau · (VBG)
Plauen · Aue · Annaberg-Buchholz · PRAHA
Cranzahl · Bärenstein Vejprty
SDG · Chomutov
Zwotental · Kurort Oberwiesenthal · Johanngeorgenstadt
(VBG) · Klasterec
Selb · Karlovy Vary
Sokolov
Cheb
(VBG)

20

DF	Dresden Flughafen (Airport)
H	Hennigsdorf
P	Potsdam
S	Stollberg
W	Wegliniec

CZECH REPUBLIC
(Only selected lines shown in Czech Republic)

24

22

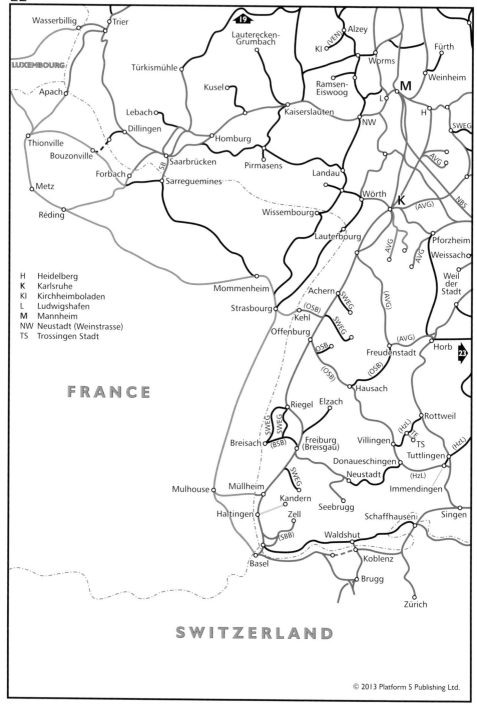

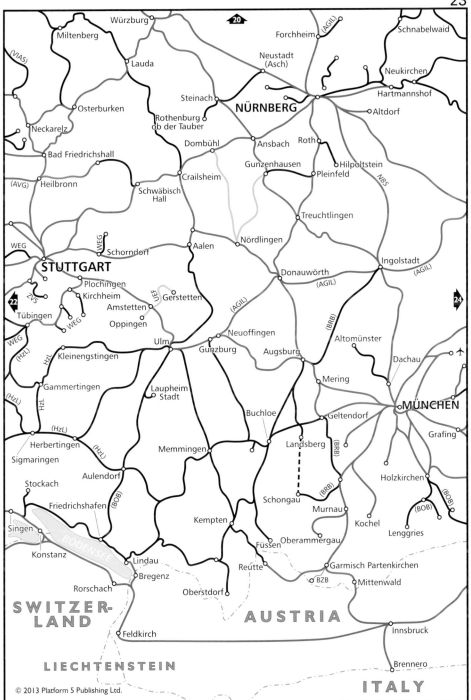

21

Praha
Plzen

Weiden

(VBG)

CZECH REPUBLIC

Waldmünchen

Česká Kubice

Schwandorf

(RBG)

Furth im Wald

(RBG)

Cham   RBG   Lam

Badkötzing

Bodenmais

Bayerisch Eisenstein

(RBG)

Zwiesel

Regensburg

(VBG)

(RBG)

(RBG)

Bogen

(AGIL)

Straubing   Plattling   Grafenau

Neufahrn

Passau

Landshut

Neumark
-St Veit

23

Mühldorf   Simbach

Braunau

Linz

Wien

Burghausen

Garching

Wels

Rosenheim   Stock

Traunstein

Prien   CB

Freilassing

SALZBURG

Aschau   Ruhpolding

(BLB)

AUSTRIA

Berchtesgaden

Kufstein

Wörgl

Graz

Bischofshofen

Schwarzach
St Veit

Villach

Note:
Section from Kufstein to Freilassing
used by ÖBB corridor trains

© 2013 Platform 5 Publishing Ltd.

1. ELECTRIC LOCOMOTIVES

Note: All electric locomotives operate only on the 15 kV 16.7 Hz overhead system unless otherwise stated.

CLASS 101 {.Bo-Bo}

CLASS 101 — Bo-Bo

Class 101 is the work horse of Fernverkehr working EC/IC trains throughout the country often in push-pull mode as well as CNL trains and some overnight fast freights. At one time common in Wien, Austria, 101s rarely get there now but instead can be seen at Innsbrück, Klagenfurt and Graz. Like all the latest locomotives and EMUs, Class 101 features three-phase asynchronous motors and AC drive. Disc brakes are also fitted. Several locomotives carry advertising liveries.

Built: 1996–99.
Builder: ABB Henschel, later Adtranz, Kassel.
One Hour Rating: 6600 kW.
Continuous Rating: 6400 kW.
Maximum Tractive Effort: 300 kN.
Wheel Diameter: 1250 mm.
Weight: 84 tonnes.
Length over Buffers: 19.10 m.
Maximum Speed 220 km/h.
Electric Brake: Rheostatic.

No.	A		No.	A		No.	A	
101 001	A	AH1	101 043		AH1	101 085		AH1
101 002		AH1	101 044		AH1	101 086		AH1
101 003		AH1	101 045		AH1	101 087	A	AH1
101 004		AH1	101 046		AH1	101 088		AH1
101 005		AH1	101 047		AH1	101 089	A	AH1
101 006		AH1	101 048		AH1	101 090		AH1
101 007		AH1	101 049		AH1	101 091		AH1
101 008		AH1	101 050		AH1	101 092		AH1
101 009		AH1	101 051		AH1	101 093		AH1
101 010		AH1	101 052		AH1	101 094		AH1
101 011		AH1	101 053		AH1	101 095		AH1
101 012		AH1	101 054		AH1	101 096		AH1
101 013		AH1	101 055		AH1	101 097		AH1
101 014		AH1	101 056		AH1	101 098		AH1
101 015		AH1	101 057		AH1	101 099		AH1
101 016	A	AH1	101 058		AH1	101 100	A	AH1
101 017		AH1	101 059		AH1	101 101	A	AH1
101 018		AH1	101 060	A	AH1	101 102		AH1
101 019		AH1	101 061		AH1	101 103		AH1
101 020		AH1	101 062		AH1	101 104		AH1
101 021		AH1	101 063		AH1	101 105		AH1
101 022		AH1	101 064		AH1	101 106		AH1
101 023		AH1	101 065		AH1	101 107		AH1
101 024		AH1	101 066		AH1	101 108		AH1
101 025	A	AH1	101 067		AH1	101 109	A	AH1
101 026		AH1	101 068		AH1	101 110	A	AH1
101 027		AH1	101 069		AH1	101 111		AH1
101 028	A	AH1	101 070	A	AH1	101 112		AH1
101 029		AH1	101 071		AH1	101 113		AH1
101 030		AH1	101 072		AH1	101 114		AH1
101 031		AH1	101 073		AH1	101 115		AH1
101 032		AH1	101 074		AH1	101 116		AH1
101 033		AH1	101 075		AH1	101 117		AH1
101 034		AH1	101 076		AH1	101 118	A	AH1
101 035		AH1	101 077		AH1	101 119		AH1
101 036		AH1	101 078		AH1	101 120		AH1
101 037	A	AH1	101 079		AH1	101 121		AH1
101 038		AH1	101 080	A	AH1	101 122		AH1
101 039		AH1	101 081	A	AH1	101 123		AH1
101 040		AH1	101 082		AH1	101 124		AH1
101 041		AH1	101 083	A	AH1	101 125		AH1
101 042	A	AH1	101 084		AH1	101 126		AH1

26

101 127	AH1	101 134	AH1	101 140		AH1
101 128	AH1	101 135	AH1	101 141	A	AH1
101 129	AH1	101 136	AH1	101 142		AH1
101 130	AH1	101 137	AH1	101 143		AH1
101 131	AH1	101 138	AH1	101 144	A	AH1
101 132	AH1	101 139	AH1	101 145		AH1
101 133	AH1					

CLASS 103 — Co-Co

The DB flagship loco of the latter part of the 20th Century, just a few remain in use. 103 222 in use with Systemtecknik and 103 245 have never been withdrawn but 103 113, 184 and 235 were withdrawn and handed over to DB Museum. The museum locomotives have now been taken back as normal traffic locomotives, some special diagrams having been drawn up for them allowing other locomotives to be released. A München locomotive is often used between München and Nürnberg whilst a Frankfurt/M locomotive is now diagrammed to work between Stuttgart and Münster. The locomotives have all been restored back to their former TEE style livery of red and beige.

Built: 1969–74 for DB.
Builder–Mech. Parts: Henschel/Krauss-Maffei/Krupp.
Builder–Elec. Parts: Siemens/AEG-Telefunken/Brown-Boveri.
One Hour Rating: 7780 kW.   **Weight:** 114 tonnes.
Continuous Rating: 7440 kW.   **Length over Buffers:** 19.50 m (20.20 m from 103 216).
Maximum Tractive Effort: 314 kN.   **Maximum Speed** 200 km/h.
Wheel Diameter: 1250 mm.   **Electric Brake:** Rheostatic.

| 103 113 | FGM | 103 222 | STMI | 103 245 | MH1 |
| 103 184 | MH1 | 103 235 | FGM | | |

CLASSES 110, 113 & 115 — Bo-Bo

Originally all Class E10; the standard express passenger locomotive until the arrival of Class 103. Class 113 was previously designated Class 112 but was renumbered when the designation was given to former DR locomotives. Class 110 is with DB Regio except for 110 169 whilst Classes 113 and 115 are with DB Auto Zug. Class 115 is a simple renumbering to show ownership is DB Autozug and not DB Regio! 110 511 is a fairly recent conversion by Dessau works where it performs a support role in case one of its overhauled locomotives fails when out on trials. These classes are definitely on the way out and are being replaced by new EMUs or cascaded Class 111s. Dortmund is to be the last depot with 110s but its locos are still roaming around Nordrheinwestfalen on local services although some are spare for charter services.

Built: 1956–68 for DB.
Builder–Mech. Parts: Henschel/Krauss-Maffei/Krupp.
Builder–Elec. Parts: AEG/Brown Boveri/Siemens.
One Hour Rating: 3700 kW.   **Weight:** 86.4 tonnes (110.1), 86 tonnes (110.3).
Continuous Rating: 3620 kW.   **Length over Buffers:** 16.49 m (110.1), 16.44 m (110.3).
Maximum Tractive Effort: 275 kN.   **Maximum Speed** 150 km/h.
Wheel Diameter: 1250 mm.   **Electric Brake:** Rheostatic.
Non-Standard Livery: N White with red stripes.

Class 110.1. Early Body Design.

115 114			BRG	115 205	BRG	113 267	BRG
115 152			BRG (Z)	110 216	EDO	113 268	BRG
110 169	A	c	STMI	110 235	TS	115 278	BRG
115 198			BRG (Z)	115 261	BRG (Z)		

Class 110.3. Later Body Design. 110 511 was converted from 139 134 and has the early body design.

No.		Code	No.		Code	No.		Code
115 293		BRG (Z)	110 427	p	EDO (Z)	110 468	p	FGM (Z)
110 300		STR (Z)	110 428	p	EDO	110 469	clp	EDO
113 309		BRG	110 432	p	EDO (Z)	110 483		TS (Z)
115 346		BRG	110 438	p	EDO (Z)	110 484		TS (Z)
115 350	cl	BRG	110 441	p	EDO	110 488	l	FGM
110 367	zp	KK2	110 446	p	TS	110 489	clp	EDO (Z)
115 383	cl	BRG	115 448	cl	BRG	110 491	A	EDO
110 406	p	EDO	110 456	p	EDO (Z)	115 509	A clp	BRG
110 416	p	TS (Z)	110 457	p	EDO	110 511	N	LDX
110 418	p	TS	115 459	clp	BRG			

CLASS 111   Bo-Bo

This thyristor locomotive, once used on IC services, is now in the hands of DB Regio. Fitted with ZWS push-pull controls 111s are at home on S-Bahn trains, modern double-deck trains or indeed on trains formed of classic stock. With more and more RE/RB trains changing over to EMU operation it is likely that locomotives will be cascaded to replace Classes 110, 113 and 115 but withdrawals are expected to start in 2013.

Built: 1974–1984 for DB.
Builder–Mech. Parts: Krupp/Krauss-Maffei/Henschel.
Builder–Elec. Parts: Siemens/AEG/Brown Boveri.
One Hour Rating: 3700 kW.   **Weight:** 83 tonnes.
Continuous Rating: 3620 kW.   **Length over Buffers:** 16.75 m.
Maximum Tractive Effort: 295 kN.   **Maximum Speed** 160 (*120) km/h.
Wheel Diameter: 1250 mm.   **Electric Brake:** Rheostatic.

No.		Code	No.		Code	No.	Code
111 005		MH1	111 037		MH1	111 070	FGM
111 006		MH1	111 038		KK2	111 071	MH1
111 007		FGM	111 039	A	MH1	111 073	MH1
111 008		FGM	111 040		MH1	111 074	TS
111 009		KK2	111 041		RL	111 075	TS
111 010		KK2	111 042		RL	111 076	TS
111 011		KK2	111 043		MH1	111 077	TS (Z)
111 012		KK2	111 044		MH1	111 078	TS
111 013		KK2	111 046		MH1	111 079	TS
111 014		KK2	111 047		TS	111 080	TS
111 015		KK2	111 048	l	RF	111 081	HBS
111 016		KK2	111 049	l	MH1	111 082	TS
111 017	A	MH1	111 050	l	RF	111 083	HBS
111 018		RL	111 051	cl	MH1	111 084	HBS
111 019		MH1	111 052	cl	MH1	111 086	FGM
111 020		MH1	111 053	cl	MH1	111 087	HBS
111 021		MH1	111 054	l	RF	111 088	TS
111 022		MH1	111 055	cl	NN1	111 089	HBS
111 023		MH1	111 056	cl	NN1	111 091	HBS
111 024	A	KK2	111 057	c	NN1	111 092	HBS
111 025		MH1	111 058	c	TS	111 093	KK2
111 026		MH1	111 059	l	FGM	111 094	FGM
111 027		MH1	111 060	c	RF	111 095	FGM
111 028		STR	111 061	l	RF	111 096	KK2
111 029		TS	111 062	l	RF	111 097	FGM
111 030		RL	111 063	l	FGM	111 098	FGM
111 031		MH1	111 064	l	RF	111 099	FGM
111 032		RL	111 065	l	MH1	111 100	FGM
111 033		RL	111 066	A l	MH1	111 101	KK2 (Z)
111 035		MH1	111 067	l	MH1	111 102	FGM
111 036		MH1	111 069		RL	111 103	FGM

111 104	FGM	111 131	HBS	111 158	KK2
111 105	FGM	111 132	HBS	111 159	MH1
111 106	NN1	111 133	HBS	111 160	KK2
111 107	NN1	111 134	HBS	111 161	TS
111 108	FGM	111 135	HBS	111 162	TS
111 110	FGM	111 136	HBS	111 163	TS
111 111	KK2	111 137	HBS	111 164	TS
111 112	KK2	111 138	HBS	111 165	TS
111 113	EDO	111 139	HBS	111 166	MH1
111 114	EDO	111 140	HBS	111 167	MH1
111 115	STR	111 141	HBS	111 168	TS
111 116	EDO	111 142	HBS	111 169 A	STR
111 117	EDO	111 143	HBS	111 170	NN1
111 118	EDO	111 144	HBS	111 171	MH1
111 119	KK2	111 145	HBS	111 172	MH1
111 120	KK2	111 146	EDO	111 173	NN1
111 121 A	STR	111 147	KK2	111 174	MH1
111 122	EDO	111 148	MH1	111 175	MH1
111 123	MH1	111 149	EDO	111 176	MH1
111 124	EDO	111 150	EDO	111 177	NN1
111 125	EDO	111 151	EDO	111 178	NN1
111 126	EDO	111 152	EDO	111 179	MH1
111 127	STR	111 153	EDO	111 180	MH1
111 128	EDO	111 155	KK2	111 181	MH1
111 129	EDO	111 156	KK2	111 182	NN1
111 130	NN1	111 157	KK2	111 183	NN1

▲ 111 017 arrives at Lauf West on 19 April 2011 with the 1033 Hersbruck (links Pegnitz) to Forchheim (oberfr). **Robin Ralston**

111 184	NN1	111 199	NN1	111 214	NN1
111 185	NN1	111 200	MH1	111 215	MH1
111 186	NN1	111 201	MH1	111 216	NN1
111 187	NN1	111 202	NN1	111 217	NN1
111 188	FGM	111 203	TS	111 218	NN1
111 189	FGM	111 204	MH1	111 219	NN1
111 190	FGM	111 206	NN1	111 220	NN1 (Z)
111 191	FGM	111 207	NN1	111 221	NN1
111 192	FGM	111 208	NN1	111 222	MH1
111 193	FGM	111 209	TS	111 223	NN1
111 194	FGM	111 210	MH1	111 224	NN1
111 195	FGM	111 211	MH1	111 225	NN1
111 196	FGM	111 212	TS	111 226	NN1
111 197	FGM	111 213	NN1	111 227	NN1
111 198	FGM				

CLASS 112 — Bo-Bo

Class 112 is the express passenger version of Class 143 built after unification. Once used on IC and similar duties the whole class is now with DB Regio often to be seen on trains of double-deck stock sometimes in top & tail mode.

Built: 1992–93 for DR and DB.
Builder: LEW.
One Hour Rating: 4200 kW.
Continuous Rating: 4020 kW.
Maximum Tractive Effort: 248 kN.
Wheel Diameter: 1250 mm.

Former DR Class: 212.
Weight: 82 tonnes.
Length over Buffers: 16.64 m.
Maximum Speed 160 km/h.
Electric Brake: Rheostatic.

112 101	WR	112 131		HBS	112 162		EDO
112 102	BCS	112 132		LMB	112 163		EDO
112 103	WR	112 133		WR	112 164		EDO
112 104	WR	112 134		EDO	112 165		BCS
112 105	BCS	112 136		EDO	112 166		EDO
112 106	WR	112 137		EDO	112 167		AK
112 107	WR	112 138	A	LMB	112 168		AK
112 108	WR	112 139	A	LMB	112 169		LMB
112 109	WR	112 140		AK	112 170		LMB
112 110	BCS	112 141		AK	112 171		AK
112 111	WR	112 142		AK	112 172		AK
112 112	BCS	112 143		AK	112 173		AK
112 113	BCS	112 144		AK	112 174		LMB
112 114	WR	112 145		AK	112 175		AK
112 115	BCS	112 146		AK	112 176		AK
112 116	BCS	112 147		AK	112 177		AK
112 117	WR	112 148		AK	112 178		AK
112 118	WR	112 149		AK	112 179		AK
112 119	WR	112 150		AK	112 180		AK
112 120	WR	112 151		AK	112 181		AK
112 121	WR	112 152		AK	112 182		BCS
112 122	BCS	112 153		AK	112 183		BCS
112 123	BCS	112 154		AK	112 184		BCS
112 124	BCS	112 155		EDO	112 185		BCS
112 125	HBS	112 156		EDO	112 186		WR
112 126	HBS	112 157		EDO	112 187		WR
112 127	HBS	112 158		EDO	112 188		WR
112 128	HBS	112 159		EDO	112 189		WR
112 129	HBS	112 160		EDO	112 190		WR
112 130	HBS	112 161		EDO			

CLASS 114 Bo-Bo

An original DR design. Originally Class 212, then 112, the classification was altered to 114 when the new Class 112s were built. Once concentrated on services in the greater Berlin area, private operators have now taken over some routes with the 2012/13 timetable causing DB to move some to the Frankfurt/M area. 114 009[i] was involved in an accident and has been replaced by fitting its high speed bogies under 143 873. 114 501 is the former departmental 755 025 (112 025) renumbered back into capital stock.

Built: 1990–92 for DR.
Builder: LEW.
One Hour Rating: 4200 kW.
Continuous Rating: 4020 kW.
Maximum Tractive Effort: 248 kN.
Wheel Diameter: 1250 mm.

Former DR Class: 212.
Weight: 82 tonnes.
Length over Buffers: 16.64 m.
Maximum Speed 160 km/h.
Electric Brake: Rheostatic.

114 002	BCS	114 015	LMB	114 030	FGM
114 003	BCS	114 016	FGM	114 031	FGM
114 004	LMB	114 017	BCS	114 032	LMB
114 005	BCS	114 018	FGM	114 033	FGM
114 006	LMB	114 020	FGM	114 034	FGM
114 007	FGM	114 021	FGM	114 035	LMB
114 008	FGM	114 022	FGM	114 036	FGM
114 009[ii]	BCS	114 023	FGM	114 037	FGM
114 010	FGM	114 024	LMB	114 038	FGM
114 011	FGM	114 026	BCS	114 039	LMB
114 012	FGM	114 027	LMB	114 040	BCS
114 013	FGM	114 028	LMB	114 501	STMI
114 014	FGM	114 029	FGM		

▲ 114 005 stands outside Cottbus depot on 28 September 2011. **David Hunt**

CLASS 120 Bo-Bo

Although pre-dating the 101s, Class 120.1 is still used on EC/IC duties all over Germany. Some locomotives are surplus to requirements and act as standby locos but some others have been handed over to DB Regio and modified for Regio use (destination indicator and door controls fitted – Class 120.2). The Rostock locomotives work RE trains to Hamburg. 120.5 locomotives were renumbered to denote their departmental use after the adoption of the European vehicle numbering system.

Built: 1987–88 for DB.
Builder–Mech. Parts: Krupp/Henschel/Krauss-Maffei.
Builder–Elec. Parts: Brown Boveri.
One Hour Rating: 6300 kW.
Continuous Rating: 5600 kW.
Maximum Tractive Effort: 347 kN.
Wheel Diameter: 1250 mm.
Weight: 84 tonnes.
Length over Buffers: 19.40 m.
Maximum Speed 200 km/h.
Electric Brake: Rheostatic.

120 101	MH1	120 122	MH1	120 143	MH1
120 102	MH1	120 123	MH1	120 144	MH1
120 103	MH1	120 124	MH1	120 145	MH1
120 104	MH1	120 125	MH1	120 146	MH1
120 105	MH1	120 126	MH1	120 147	MH1
120 106	MH1	120 127	MH1	120 148	MH1
120 108	MH1	120 130	MH1	120 149	MH1
120 109	MH1	120 131	MH1	120 150	MH1
120 110	MH1	120 132	MH1	120 151	MH1
120 111	MH1	120 133	MH1	120 152	MH1
120 112 A	MH1	120 134	MH1	120 154	MH1
120 113	MH1	120 135	MH1	120 155	MH1
120 114	MH1	120 137	MH1	120 156	MH1
120 115	MH1	120 138	MH1	120 157	MH1
120 118	MH1	120 140	MH1	120 158	MH1 (Z)
120 119	MH1	120 141	MH1	120 159	MH1
120 120	MH1				

120 201	(120 116)	WR	120 205	(120 121)	WR
120 202	(120 129)	WR	120 206	(120 117)	KA
120 203	(120 107)	WR	120 207	(120 136)	KA
120 204	(120 128)	WR	120 208	(120 139)	KA

120 501	(120 153) A	STMI	120 502	(120 160) Y	STMI

CLASS 139 Bo-Bo

Class 139 is a Class 140 fitted with rheostatic brakes. The class was expanded in the 1990s by cascaded 110s being converted for freight use but the class is now in decline. Some have been sold to private operator Lokomotion and others may be sold off to private operators.

Dimensions as for Class 140 below except:

Weight: 86 tonnes.
Electric Brake: Rheostatic.

p Push-pull and multiple-working fitted.

139 132	NN2	139 283		NN2 (Z)	139 314	p	NN2 (Z)
139 172	NN2 (Z)	139 309	p	NN2 (Z)	139 554		NN2 (Z)
139 222	NN2 (Z)	139 311	p	NN2 (Z)	139 557		NN2 (Z)
139 246	NN2 (Z)	139 313	p	NN2 (Z)	139 562		NN2 (Z)
139 262	NN2 (Z)					

CLASS 140 Bo-Bo

This was the standard medium powered freight locomotive of the 1960s. It is now being phased out of service having been replaced by Class 185. Some are likely to see further use with private operators as DB Schenker in a change of heart has started selling off locomotives to private operators! (See German Railways Part 2 for locomotives in private use).

Built: 1957–73 for DB.
Builder–Mech. Parts: Krauss-Maffei.
Builder–Elec. Parts: Siemens.
One Hour Rating: 3700 kW.
Continuous Rating: 3620 kW.
Maximum Tractive Effort: 170 kN.
Wheel Diameter: 1250 mm.

Weight: 83 tonnes.
Length over Buffers: 16.49 m.
Maximum Speed 110 km/h.

m   Multiple working fitted.

140 012	HS (Z)	140 169	HS (Z)	140 291	HS (Z)
140 013	HS (Z)	140 170	HS	140 327	HS (Z)
140 018	HS (Z)	140 172	HS (Z)	140 353	HS (Z)
140 024	HS (Z)	140 184	HS (Z)	140 354	HS (Z)
140 028	HS (Z)	140 214	HS (Z)	140 368	HS (Z)
140 036	HS (Z)	140 217	HS (Z)	140 374	HS (Z)
140 037	HS (Z)	140 218	HS (Z)	140 401	HS (Z)
140 043	HS (Z)	140 261		140 432	HS (Z)

▲ 120 205 approaches Schwerin Hbf with an RE service from Rostock to Hamburg formed of double-deck stock on 18 July 2011.   **Matthias Müller**

140 440	HS (Z)	140 569		HS	140 790	m	RM (Z)
140 450	HS (Z)	140 572		KG (Z)	140 791	m	RM
140 459	HS (Z)	140 585		HS	140 799	m	RM (Z)
140 490	HS (Z)	140 590		KG (Z)	140 805	m	KG (Z)
140 491	HS (Z)	140 600	c	HS	140 806	m	KG (Z)
140 495	HS (Z)	140 621		RM (Z)	140 811	m	KG (Z)
140 501	HS (Z)	140 627		RM (Z)	140 821	m	KG (Z)
140 502	HS (Z)	140 637	c	RM	140 825	m	KG (Z)
140 506	HS (Z)	140 649		RM (Z)	140 833	m	KG (Z)
140 512	HS (Z)	140 656	c	RM (Z)	140 837	m	KG (Z)
140 528	HS	140 677		HS (Z)	140 838	m	KG (Z)
140 535	HS	140 678		RM (Z)	140 843	m	KG
140 537	HS (Z)	140 680		RM (Z)	140 845	m	KG (Z)
140 538	KG (Z)	140 681		HS	140 850	m	KG
140 539	HS	140 716		HS	140 858	m	KG
140 544	KG (Z)	140 728		RM (Z)	140 861	m	KG (Z)

CLASS 143 — Bo-Bo

Originally the standard East German mixed traffic locomotive, unification found them spreading all over Germany. Used by DB Regio they are now too slow for RE and even some RB trains as pathways demand faster locomotives. Mostly replaced by EMUs on S-Bahn duties, scrapping has commenced as they no longer fit in with current plans. Many more locomotives are likely to be withdrawn once the problems with the EMUs of Class 442 are resolved. Several have been sold to DB subsidiaries for freight work for example Mitteldeutsche Eisenbahn Gesellschaft – MEG (See German Railways Part 2).

143 002–370 built 1984–88 and push-pull fitted.
143 801–968 built 1988–89 push-pull and multiple-working fitted.
143 551–662 built 1989–90 and push-pull fitted.
143 969–973 are rebuilds of accident damaged locos from the first series and push-pull and multiple-working fitted.

Built: 1982–90 for DR.
Builder: LEW.
One Hour Rating: 3720 kW.
Continuous Rating: 3540 kW.
Maximum Tractive Effort: 248 kN.
Wheel Diameter: 1250 mm.
Former DR Class: 243.
Weight: 82 tonnes.
Length over Buffers: 16.64 m.
Maximum Speed 120 km/h.
Electric Brake: Rheostatic.

143 660–662 were renumbered from 243 322/096/060.
143 969–973 were renumbered from 243 016/051/099/223/172.

Class 143.0. Standard Design.

143 002		LH2	143 034		LH2	143 062	HBS
143 009		STR	143 036		KD	143 064	FGM
143 011		LH2	143 038		DA	143 065	WR
143 012		TS	143 039		KD	143 066	LH2
143 013		LH2 (Z)	143 040		LL2	143 070	WR
143 015		LH2	143 042	c	RF	143 071	TS
143 017	p	TS	143 043		LH2	143 072	BCS
143 018		STR	143 045		KD	143 073	STR
143 019		FGM	143 047		DA	143 074	LMB (Z)
143 020		LH2	143 050	c	RF	143 075	LH2
143 021		FGM	143 053		LH2	143 076	FGM
143 030		KD	143 055	c	RF	143 078	STR
143 033		DA	143 057		TS	143 083	HBS

▲ A heavy train of steel coil from Oberhausen to Neuwied is seen near Rheinbreitbach on 24 March 2012, hauled by 140 805 and 140 789. **Matthias Müller**

▼ 143 562 awaits departure from Schöna with a local service to Meissen via Dresden on 2 July 2008. **Brian Denton**

143 086		LH2	143 194		STR	143 311		AK			
143 087		DA	143 195	p	TS	143 312	c	RF			
143 089		LH2	143 196		AK	143 313	c	FGM			
143 090	c	STR	143 197		FGM	143 314		AK			
143 091		TS	143 200	p	NN1 (Z)	143 315		TS			
143 092		TS	143 201	p	TS	143 316	c	RF			
143 093		DA	143 205		DA	143 318	p	NN1 (Z)			
143 095		LH2	143 206		HBS	143 319		LH2			
143 098		LH2	143 207		NN1 (Z)	143 321		FGM			
143 100		TS	143 210		WR	143 324		LH2			
143 106		TS	143 212		LH2	143 326		HBS			
143 107		FGM	143 215	p	KD	143 327		LH2			
143 109		TS	143 216		STR	143 330		KD			
143 112		TS	143 218		LH2	143 332	c	RF			
143 113		LMB (Z)	143 220		UE	143 333		BCS			
143 114		STR	143 221		BCS	143 336		KD			
143 116		DA	143 225		LMB	143 337		LH2			
143 119		NN1	143 226		LMB (Z)	143 338		LMB			
143 120		LMB	143 227		FGM	143 339		DA			
143 122		DA	143 228		FGM	143 340		AK			
143 126		DA	143 231		FGM	143 342		DA			
143 129		STR	143 233		WR	143 343		AK			
143 130		LMB	143 238		FGM	143 346		FGM			
143 131		NN1 (Z)	143 239	p	TS	143 347	p	TS			
143 132		FGM	143 241	p	KD	143 348		AK			
143 133		FGM	143 242	p	FGM	143 349		LMB			
143 134		UE	143 243		DA	143 350	c	RF			
143 135		FGM	143 244		DA	143 351		STR			
143 136		HBS	143 247		KD	143 352		AK			
143 137		UE	143 248		FGM	143 354	c	LH2			
143 138		FGM	143 249		LMB (Z)	143 355		DA			
143 139		UE	143 250		WR	143 357		KD			
143 140		TS	143 251		BCS	143 358		KD			
143 141		FGM	143 253	p	NN1 (Z)	143 359		DA			
143 145	c	RF	143 254		BCS	143 360		BCS			
143 146		LMB	143 256		LMB	143 361		UE (Z)			
143 148		NN1 (Z)	143 259		KD	143 362		NN1 (Z)			
143 152		UE	143 263		STR	143 363		LH2			
143 153		UE	143 265	p	TS	143 364	c	RF			
143 155		BCS	143 267		FGM	143 365		BCS			
143 156		LMB	143 270		FGM	143 366		STR			
143 157		DA	143 273		LMB (Z)	143 367		DA			
143 158		FGM	143 274		NN1 (Z)	143 368		DA			
143 159		STR	143 276		AK	143 370		DA			
143 162		HBS	143 278		DA	143 551		LMB (Z)			
143 163		AK	143 280		STR	143 555		TS			
143 166		FGM	143 281		NN1 (Z)	143 556		BCS			
143 168		STR	143 283		UE	143 557		AK			
143 169		UE	143 285		LH2	143 558		UE			
143 170		FGM	143 288		KD	143 559		LMB			
143 171		LMB	143 289		LMB	143 562		UE			
143 173		BCS	143 291		UE	143 563		LH2 (Z)			
143 174		STR	143 292		KD	143 564		WR			
143 175		HBS	143 293		LH2	143 566		BCS			
143 176		TS	143 295		AK	143 567		BCS			
143 177		KD	143 298		KD	143 568		STR			
143 178		UE	143 300		WR	143 569		BCS			
143 180		LH2	143 303		WR	143 570		LH2			
143 181		FGM	143 304		KD	143 572		LH2			
143 185		UE	143 305		BCS	143 574		BCS			
143 189		FGM	143 306		BCS	143 575		TS (Z)			
143 190		LH2	143 307		BCS	143 576		BCS			
143 192		LH2	143 308	c	RF	143 580		FGM			
143 193		WR	143 310		LH2	143 583		KD			

No.		Code	No.		Code	No.		Code
143 585		DA	143 624		NN1	143 642		BCS
143 589		WR	143 625		NN1	143 643		KD
143 591		LMB	143 626		NN1	143 644		FGM
143 595		LH2	143 627		TS (Z)	143 645		TS
143 597		KD	143 628		NN1	143 647		STR
143 598		NN1	143 629		NN1	143 650		LH2
143 601		KD	143 630		UE	143 651		HBS
143 605		KD	143 632		NN1 (Z)	143 653		FGM
143 606		KD	143 634		NN1	143 655		TS
143 610		LH2	143 637		FGM	143 657	c	FGM
143 614		KD	143 639		LH2	143 658		LH2
143 616		AK	143 640	c	RF	143 660		KD
143 621		NN1	143 641		BCS	143 661		STR

Class 143.8. Multiple Working Fitted.

No.		Code	No.		Code	No.		Code
143 802		TS	143 855		KD	143 914		NN1
143 803		FGM	143 856	c	RF	143 917		LH2
143 804	p	TS	143 857		LH2	143 918		LMB (Z)
143 807		UE	143 858		UE	143 919		STR
143 809		BCS	143 859		UE	143 920		TS
143 810	c	RF	143 860		WR	143 922		TS
143 812		BCS	143 861	p	AK (Z)	143 924		TS
143 813	c	STR	143 863		AK	143 925		STR
143 814		DA	143 864		BCS	143 926		LMB
143 816		LH2	143 865		DA (Z)	143 928		LH2
143 818		BCS	143 867		LH2	143 929		LH2 (Z)
143 821		BCS	143 868		BCS	143 930		STR (Z)
143 822	c	LH2	143 870		KD	143 931		BCS
143 823		KD	143 871		LH2	143 932		STR
143 825		STR	143 872		AK	143 933		DA
143 827		TS	143 875		DA	143 934		LH2
143 828		DA	143 878		FGM (Z)	143 935		LH2
143 829		LH2	143 879		LH2	143 939		NN1 (Z)
143 831		LH2	143 880		TS	143 940		LMB (Z)
143 832		LH2	143 881		TS	143 944		LH2
143 834		BCS	143 882		TS	143 947		BCS
143 835	c	STR	143 883		DA	143 948		LMB (Z)
143 837		LH2	143 884		DA	143 949	g	KD
143 839		AK	143 885		DA	143 952		WR
143 840		KD	143 886	p	TS	143 955		BCS (Z)
143 841		WR	143 889		WR	143 957		LH2
143 842		KD	143 891		LH2	143 958	c	STR
143 843		WR	143 893		LH2	143 959		STR
143 844		LH2	143 894		NN1	143 962		NN1 (Z)
143 845		TS	143 896		LH2	143 963		TS
143 846	p	NN1 (Z)	143 899		TS	143 965		TS
143 847	p	NN1 (Z)	143 900		TS	143 966		AK
143 848		BCS	143 903		LH2	143 967		DA
143 849		BCS	143 904		TS	143 968	p	FGM
143 850		LH2	143 905		NN1	143 970		KD
143 852		WR	143 906	c	STR	143 971		FGM
143 853		KD	143 909		DA	143 972	c	RF
143 854		KD	143 910		STR	143 973		DA

CLASS 145 Bo-Bo

This is a medium powered freight locomotive featuring all the latest technology of the time - three phase asynchronous motors, disc brakes and computer controls etc. The locomotive is now recognized as part of the Bombardier TRAXX group. Series production was later changed to a dual-voltage version – Class 185. Locos 145 018/019 were turned out with a "passenger package" being fitted; a destination indicator in the cab, gearing for 160 km/h operation and a driver - passenger communication link as well as door controls. Difficulties with new EMUs for the Hannover area saw 145 031–050 turned out with these fittings as well and used on services in the Hannover area during Expo 2000. The wheel turned full circuit as these "passenger packet" locomotives have recently been working in the Dresden area on Regio services pending deliveries of the new Class 442 EMUs!

Built: 1996–99.
Builders: Adtranz (Hennigsdorf) 001–010; Adtranz Kassel (remainder).
Continuous Rating: 4200 kW. **Weight:** 84 tonnes.
Maximum Tractive Effort: 300 kN. **Length over Buffers:** 18.90 m.
Wheel Diameter: 1250 mm. **Maximum Speed** 140 km/h (*160 km/h).
Electric Brake: Regenerative.

145 001	BSE	145 011		BSE	145 020	BSE
145 002	BSE	145 012		BSE	145 021	BSE
145 003	BSE	145 013ⁱⁱ		BSE	145 022	BSE
145 004	BSE	145 014		BSE	145 023	BSE
145 005	BSE	145 015		BSE	145 024	BSE
145 007	BSE	145 016		BSE	145 025	BSE
145 008	BSE	145 017		BSE	145 026	BSE
145 009	BSE	145 018	*	BSE	145 027	BSE
145 010	BSE	145 019	*	BSE	145 028	BSE

▲ 145 080 passes Lorch in the Rhine valley with a container train bound for Italy on 15 September 2011. **Matthias Müller**

145 029		BSE	145 047	*	BSE	145 064	BSE
145 030		BSE	145 048	*	BSE	145 065	BSE
145 031	*	BSE	145 049	*	BSE	145 066	BSE
145 032	*	BSE	145 050	*	BSE	145 067	BSE
145 033	*	BSE	145 051		BSE	145 068	BSE
145 034	*	BSE	145 052		BSE	145 069	BSE
145 035	*	BSE	145 053		BSE	145 070	BSE
145 036	*	BSE	145 054		BSE	145 071	BSE
145 037	*	BSE	145 055		BSE	145 072	BSE
145 038	*	BSE	145 056		BSE	145 073	BSE
145 039	*	BSE	145 057		BSE	145 074	BSE
145 040	*	BSE	145 058		BSE	145 075	BSE
145 041	*	BSE	145 059		BSE	145 076	BSE
145 042	*	BSE	145 060		BSE	145 077	BSE
145 043	*	BSE	145 061		BSE	145 078	BSE
145 044	*	BSE	145 062		BSE	145 079	BSE
145 045	*	BSE	145 063		BSE	145 080	BSE
145 046	*	BSE					

CLASS 146 — Bo-Bo

This is the Bombardier TRAXX160PAC version for passenger use. DB Regio uses them on modern rakes of push-pull double-deck stock mostly on RE services in their respective areas. Class 146.0 equates to Class 145.0, 146.1 to 185 and 146.2 to 185.2. 146 228 was taken off the 185 production line and is the reason why there is no 185 400! In 2011 DB Fernverkehr ordered a batch of TRAXX160PAC for use on new IC double-deck stock the first of which appeared in September 2012 surprisingly numbered in the 146 5xx series previously used for private locomotives. Subsequently in 2012 DB Regio ordered another batch of 146s most likely as a start to replacing Class 111 which is coming up for 40 years old.

Built: 2001–02 (146.0), 2003–05 (146.1), 2005–07/2013 onwards (146.2), 2012 onwards (146.5).
Builder: Bombardier Kassel.
Continuous Rating: 4200 kW (146.0) 5600 kW others.
Maximum Tractive Effort: 300 kN.　　　　　**Weight:** 84 tonnes.
Wheel Diameter: 1250 mm.　　　　**Length over Buffers:** 18.90 m.
Electric Brake: Regenerative.　　　　**Maximum Speed** 160 km/h.

Class 146.0.

146 001	EDO	146 012	EDO	146 022	EDO
146 002	EDO	146 013	EDO	146 023	EDO
146 003	EDO	146 014	EDO	146 024	EDO
146 004	EDO	146 015	EDO	146 025	EDO
146 005	EDO	146 016	EDO	146 026	EDO
146 006	EDO	146 017	EDO	146 027	EDO
146 007	EDO	146 018	EDO	146 028	EDO
146 008	EDO	146 019	EDO	146 029	EDO
146 009	EDO	146 020	EDO	146 030	EDO
146 010	EDO	146 021	EDO	146 031	EDO
146 011	EDO				

Class 146.1.

146 101	HB	146 112	RF	146 123	HB
146 102	HB	146 113	RF	146 124	HB
146 103	HB	146 114	RF	146 125	HB
146 104	HB	146 115	RF	146 126	HB
146 105	HB	146 116	RF	146 127	HB
146 106	HB	146 117	FGM	146 128	HB
146 107	HB	146 118	FGM	146 129	HB
146 108	HB	146 119	FGM	146 130	HB
146 109	RF	146 120	FGM	146 131	HB
146 110	RF	146 121	FGM	146 132	HB
146 111	RF	146 122	FGM		

Names:

146 110	Müllheim		146 115	Breisgau-Hochschwarzwald
146 113	Ortenaukreis		146 116	Lörrach
146 114	Landkreis Emmendingen			

Class 146.2.

146 201	TS	146 217		TS	146 233		RF
146 202	TS	146 218		TS	146 234		RF
146 203	TS	146 219		TS	146 235	**A**	RF
146 204	TS	146 220	**A**	TS	146 236		RF
146 205	TS	146 221		TS	146 237		RF
146 206	TS	146 222		TS	146 238		RF
146 207	TS	146 223	**A**	TS	146 239		RF
146 208	TS	146 224	**A**	TS	146 240		NN1
146 209	TS	146 225	**A**	TS	146 241		NN1
146 210	TS	146 226	**A**	TS	146 242		NN1
146 211	TS	146 227	**A**	TS	146 243		NN1
146 212	TS	146 228		RF	146 244		NN1
146 213	TS	146 229		RF	146 245		NN1
146 214	TS	146 230		RF	146 246		NN1
146 215	TS	146 231	**A**	RF	146 247		NN1
146 216	TS	146 232		RF			

▲ 146 020 is seen between duties at Dortmund depot on 01 October 2011. **David Hunt**

146 251	146 262	146 273
146 252	146 263	146 274
146 253	146 264	146 275
146 254	146 265	146 276
146 255	146 266	146 277
146 256	146 267	146 278
146 257	146 268	146 279
146 258	146 269	146 280
146 259	146 270	146 281
146 260	146 271	146 282
146 261	146 272	

Names:

146 228 St. Georgen	146 236 Triberg
146 233 Donauschingen	146 237 Karlsruhe

146 551 I	146 560 I	146 569 I
146 552 I	146 561 I	146 570 I
146 553 I	146 562 I	146 571 I
146 554 I	146 563 I	146 572 I
146 555 I	146 564 I	146 573 I
146 556 I	146 565 I	146 574 I
146 557 I	146 566 I	146 575 I
146 558 I	146 567 I	146 576 I
146 559 I	146 568 I	146 577 I

CLASS 151   Co-Co

This 1970s thyristor controlled locomotive has been somewhat overshadowed by the arrival of Classes 185 and 189. Some 151s have lost their auto-couplings to 189s and indeed some of the work as well as 189s have taken over workings on ore trains to Dillingen. 151s no longer have any booked duties into Austria but can be seen all over Germany on heavy freights and intermodal trains. The recession in 2008 saw several examples stored and in 2010 most of them went off for scrap. Those surplus locomotives still in good condition are gathering in the closed marshalling yard at Hamm pending sale or better times. Indeed as this book went to press some locomotives have been sold to RBH Cargo.

Built: 1973–77 for DB.
Builder–Mech. Parts: Krupp.
Builder–Elec. Parts: AEG.
One Hour Rating: 6000 kW.   **Weight:** 126 tonnes.
Continuous Rating: 6470 kW.   **Length over Buffers:** 19.49 m.
Maximum Tractive Effort: 459 kN.   **Maximum Speed** 120 km/h.
Wheel Diameter: 1250 mm.   **Electric Brake:** Rheostatic.
Non-Standard Livery: N Raspberry red.

All multiple working/push-pull fitted.

a   Fitted with automatic couplers for use on heavy iron ore trains.
s   Fitted with Swiss safety equipment (Integra).

151 001	NN2	151 018	NN2 (Z)	151 036	NN2
151 002	NN2	151 020	NN2	151 037	NN2
151 003	NN2	151 021	NN2	151 039	NN2 (Z)
151 005	NN2 (Z)	151 022	NN2	151 040	NN2
151 006	NN2	151 023	NN2	151 041	NN2
151 008	NN2	151 026	NN2	151 042	NN2 (Z)
151 009	NN2 (Z)	151 027	NN2 (Z)	151 043	NN2
151 011	NN2 (Z)	151 028	NN2	151 045	NN2
151 012	NN2	151 029	NN2	151 046	NN2
151 013	NN2 (Z)	151 031	NN2	151 048	NN2
151 015	NN2	151 032	NN2	151 049	NN2
151 016	NN2	151 034	NN2	151 051	NN2 (Z)
151 017	NN2	151 035	NN2	151 052	NN2

151 053		NN2	151 093	a	NN2 (Z)	151 132		NN2
151 055		NN2	151 094		NN2	151 133		NN2
151 056		NN2 (Z)	151 095		NN2	151 134	N	NN2
151 057		NN2 (Z)	151 096		NN2	151 135		NN2
151 058		NN2	151 097		NN2 (Z)	151 136		NN2
151 059		NN2	151 098		NN2 (Z)	151 138		NN2 (Z)
151 060		NN2	151 099		NN2	151 139		NN2
151 061		NN2	151 100		NN2	151 140		NN2
151 062		NN2	151 101		NN2	151 141		NN2
151 063		NN2	151 102	a	NN2	151 142		NN2 (Z)
151 064		NN2	151 103		NN2	151 145	s	NN2 (Z)
151 065		NN2	151 104		NN2	151 146	s	NN2
151 066		NN2	151 105		NN2 (Z)	151 147		NN2
151 067		NN2	151 106	a	NN2	151 148		NN2
151 068		NN2	151 108	a	NN2 (Z)	151 149		NN2
151 069		NN2	151 109		NN2	151 150		NN2
151 070		NN2	151 110	a	NN2	151 153		NN2
151 071		NN2	151 112		NN2	151 155		NN2
151 073		NN2	151 113	a	NN2	151 157		NN2
151 074		NN2 (Z)	151 114	a	NN2 (Z)	151 159		NN2 (Z)
151 075		NN2	151 115	a	NN2 (Z)	151 160		NN2
151 076		NN2	151 116	a	NN2	151 161		NN2
151 077		NN2	151 118	a	NN2 (Z)	151 162		NN2 (Z)
151 078		NN2	151 119	a	NN2	151 163		NN2
151 082		NN2	151 125		NN2	151 164		NN2
151 085		NN2	151 126		NN2	151 165		NN2
151 086	N	NN2	151 128		NN2	151 166		NN2
151 087		NN2	151 129		NN2 (Z)	151 167		NN2 (Z)
151 088		NN2	151 130		NN2	151 168		NN2
151 091	a	NN2 (Z)	151 131		NN2 (Z)	151 169	a	NN2

▲ 151 036 passes alongside the river Rhine shortly after departure from Cologne-Eifeltor with a mixed freight bound for Italy on 2 August 2011. **Matthias Müller**

CLASS 152 Bo-Bo

CLASS 152   Bo-Bo

This class can be traced back to the Siemens experimental Class 127 and is thus part of the Eurosprinter family that have been exported to Spain, Portugal, Greece and Austria. 152 190 is an experiment featuring Insulated Gate Bipolar Transistor (IGBT) converters and was to be loco 152 032 originally. Note the difference in wheel arrangement and weight compared to Class 151 such is progress! About half of the class are allocated to intermodal duties.

Built: 1997–2001.
Builder–Mech. Parts: Krauss Maffei, Siemens/Duewag.
Builder–Elec. Parts: Siemens.
One Hour Rating: 6600 kW.
Continuous Rating: 6400 kW.
Maximum Tractive Effort: 300 kN.
Wheel Diameter: 1250 mm.
Weight: 86 tonnes.
Length over Buffers: 19.58 m.
Maximum Speed 140 km/h.
Electric Brake: Regenerative.

152 001		NN2	152 050	NN2	152 098		NN2
152 002		NN2	152 051	NN2	152 099		NN2
152 003		NN2	152 052	NN2	152 100		NN2
152 004		NN2	152 053	NN2	152 101		NN2
152 005	A	NN2	152 054	NN2	152 102		NN2
152 006		NN2	152 055	NN2	152 103		NN2
152 007		NN2	152 056	NN2	152 104		NN2
152 008		NN2	152 057	NN2	152 105		NN2
152 009		NN2	152 058	NN2	152 106		NN2
152 010		NN2	152 059	NN2	152 107		NN2
152 011		NN2	152 060	NN2	152 108		NN2
152 012		NN2	152 061	NN2	152 109		NN2
152 013		NN2	152 062	NN2	152 110		NN2
152 014		NN2	152 063	NN2	152 111		NN2
152 015		NN2	152 064	NN2	152 112		NN2
152 016		NN2	152 065	NN2	152 113		NN2
152 017		NN2	152 066	NN2	152 114		NN2
152 018		NN2	152 067	NN2	152 115		NN2
152 019		NN2	152 068	NN2	152 116		NN2
152 020		NN2	152 069	NN2	152 117		NN2
152 021		NN2	152 070	NN2	152 118		NN2
152 022		NN2	152 071	NN2	152 119		NN2
152 023		NN2	152 072	NN2	152 120		NN2
152 024		NN2	152 073	NN2	152 121		NN2
152 025		NN2	152 074	NN2	152 122		NN2
152 026		NN2	152 075[II]	NN2	152 123		NN2
152 027[II]		NN2	152 076	NN2	152 124		NN2
152 028		NN2	152 077	NN2	152 125		NN2
152 029		NN2	152 078	NN2	152 126		NN2
152 030		NN2	152 079	NN2	152 127		NN2
152 031		NN2	152 080	NN2	152 128		NN2
152 033		NN2	152 081	NN2	152 129		NN2
152 034		NN2	152 082	NN2	152 130		NN2
152 035		NN2	152 083	NN2	152 131		NN2
152 036		NN2	152 084	NN2	152 132		NN2
152 037		NN2	152 085	NN2	152 133		NN2
152 038		NN2	152 086	NN2	152 134	A	NN2
152 039		NN2	152 087	NN2	152 135	A	NN2
152 040[II]		NN2	152 088	NN2	152 136	A	NN2
152 041		NN2	152 089	NN2	152 137	A	NN2
152 042		NN2	152 090	NN2	152 138	A	NN2
152 043		NN2	152 091	NN2	152 139		NN2
152 044		NN2	152 092	NN2	152 140		NN2
152 045		NN2	152 093	NN2	152 141		NN2 (Z)
152 046		NN2	152 094	NN2	152 142		NN2
152 047		NN2	152 095	NN2	152 143		NN2
152 048		NN2	152 096	NN2	152 144		NN2
152 049		NN2	152 097	NN2	152 145		NN2

▲ 155 068 stands at Engeldorf depot near Leipzig on 1 July 2008. **Brian Denton**

▼ 180 002 Passes through Pirna, south east of Dresden, with a car train from the Czech Republic on 3 July 2008. **Brian Denton**

152 146	NN2	152 155	NN2	152 164	NN2
152 147	NN2	152 156	NN2	152 165	NN2
152 148	NN2	152 157	NN2	152 166	NN2
152 149	NN2	152 158	NN2	152 167	NN2
152 150	NN2	152 159	NN2	152 168	NN2
152 151	NN2	152 160	NN2	152 169	NN2
152 152	NN2	152 161	NN2	152 170	NN2
152 153	NN2	152 162	NN2	152 190	NN2
152 154	NN2	152 163	NN2		

CLASS 155   Co-Co

This former DR thyristor-controlled locomotive pre-dated the general purpose Class 143s. Since 01/01/2006 the class has been concentrated at Berlin Seddin depot but they can turn up anywhere in Germany. Several locomotives have been stored because of the recession whilst some others have been sold to DB subsidiary MEG. (See German Railways Part 2).

Built: 1974–84 for DR.
Builder: LEW.
One Hour Rating: 5400 kW.
Maximum Tractive Effort: 465 kN.
Wheel Diameter: 1250 mm.
Electric Brake: Rheostatic.
Non-Standard Livery: N Raspberry red.

Former DR Class: 250.
Weight: 123 tonnes.
Length over Buffers: 19.60 m.
Maximum Speed 125 km/h.

Note: 155 029/116/212/228/245 were previously 155 185/090/225/193/166 respectively.

155 004	BSE	155 057	BSE (Z)	155 111	BSE
155 006	BSE	155 060	BSE	155 112	BSE
155 007	BSE	155 061	BSE	155 113	BSE
155 008	BSE	155 063	BSE	155 114	BSE
155 009	BSE (Z)	155 065	BSE	155 115	BSE
155 010	BSE	155 066	BSE	155 116[II]	BSE (Z)
155 011	BSE	155 068	BSE	155 117	BSE
155 013	BSE	155 070	BSE	155 118	BSE
155 014	BSE (Z)	155 072	BSE (Z)	155 120	BSE
155 015	BSE	155 073	BSE	155 121	BSE
155 016	BSE	155 075	BSE	155 122	BSE
155 017	BSE	155 077	BSE	155 123	BSE
155 018	BSE (Z)	155 078	BSE (Z)	155 125	BSE
155 019	BSE	155 080	BSE	155 126	BSE
155 020	BSE	155 081	BSE	155 128	BSE
155 023	BSE	155 082	BSE	155 129	BSE (Z)
155 024	BSE (Z)	155 083	BSE	155 130	BSE
155 028	BSE	155 084	BSE	155 131	BSE
155 029[II]	BSE (Z)	155 085	BSE	155 132	BSE
155 030	BSE	155 086	BSE	155 133	BSE
155 031	BSE	155 087	BSE	155 134	BSE
155 032	BSE (Z)	155 089	BSE	155 135	BSE
155 033	BSE	155 091	BSE	155 138	BSE
155 034	BSE (Z)	155 095	BSE	155 139	BSE (Z)
155 035	BSE	155 096	BSE	155 140	BSE
155 036	BSE	155 097	BSE	155 141	BSE
155 037	BSE	155 098	BSE (Z)	155 142	BSE (Z)
155 038	BSE	155 099	BSE	155 146	BSE
155 039	BSE	155 101	BSE	155 147	BSE
155 040	BSE	155 103	BSE	155 148	BSE
155 042	BSE (Z)	155 104	BSE	155 149	BSE
155 043	BSE	155 105	BSE (Z)	155 150	BSE
155 048	BSE (Z)	155 107	BSE	155 151	BSE
155 053	BSE	155 108	BSE	155 152	BSE
155 055	BSE	155 109	BSE	155 154	BSE
155 056	BSE	155 110	BSE	155 157	BSE

155 158	BSE	155 210		BSE (Z)	155 244		BSE
155 159	BSE	155 211		BSE	155 245[II]		BSE
155 161	BSE (Z)	155 212[II]		BSE	155 246		BSE
155 163	BSE	155 213		BSE	155 247		BSE (Z)
155 167	BSE	155 214	N	BSE	155 248		BSE
155 168	BSE (Z)	155 215		BSE (Z)	155 249		BSE (Z)
155 171	BSE	155 216		BSE (Z)	155 251		BSE
155 172	BSE	155 217		BSE (Z)	155 252		BSE
155 175	BSE	155 218		BSE	155 253		BSE
155 178	BSE	155 219	N	BSE	155 255		BSE (Z)
155 180	BSE	155 220		BSE (Z)	155 256		BSE
155 181	BSE	155 221		BSE (Z)	155 257		BSE
155 182	BSE	155 222		BSE	155 259		BSE (Z)
155 183	BSE (Z)	155 223		BSE	155 260		BSE
155 189	BSE	155 224		BSE	155 261		BSE
155 191	BSE	155 228[II]		BSE (Z)	155 262		BSE
155 192	BSE	155 229		BSE	155 263		BSE (Z)
155 194	BSE	155 231		BSE	155 264		BSE
155 196	BSE (Z)	155 232		BSE	155 265		BSE
155 197	BSE	155 234		BSE (Z)	155 266		BSE
155 199	BSE	155 236		BSE (Z)	155 267		BSE
155 201	BSE	155 237		BSE	155 268		BSE (Z)
155 202	BSE	155 238		BSE (Z)	155 269		BSE
155 203	BSE (Z)	155 239		BSE	155 270		BSE (Z)
155 204	BSE	155 240		BSE	155 271		BSE
155 206	BSE	155 241		BSE	155 272		BSE (Z)
155 207	BSE	155 243		BSE	155 273		BSE
155 208	BSE						

▲ 181 218 is seen leading IC 132 from Norddeich Mole to Luxemburg as it passes Winningen in the Mosel valley on 14 May 2012. **Matthias Müller**

CLASS 180   Bo-Bo

This is a dual-voltage locomotive of Czech origin and is in fact the same as CD Class 371/372. They share duties with these locos on workings from Leipzig/Dresden into the Czech Republic. They are gradually being withdrawn as some duties have been taken over by Class 189. Several are stored at Rostock Seehafen.

Built: 1987, 1991 for DR.
Builder: Skoda.
One Hour Rating: 3080 kW.
Maximum Tractive Effort: 141.6 kN.
Wheel Diameter: 1250 mm.
Electric Brake: Rheostatic.
Non-Standard Livery: N Old DR Bordeaux red livery.

Systems: 15 kV AC 16.7 Hz/3000 V DC.
Former DR Class: 230.
Weight: 84 tonnes.
Length over Buffers: 16.08 m.
Maximum Speed 120 km/h.

180 002	DF (Z)	180 010		DF (Z)	180 016	N	DF
180 003	DF (Z)	180 011	N	DF (Z)	180 017		DF
180 006	DF (Z)	180 012		DF	180 018		DF
180 007	DF (Z)	180 013		DF	180 019		DF (Z)
180 008	DF	180 015		DF	180 020	N	DF (Z)
180 009	DF (Z)					

CLASS 181   Bo-Bo

Used for many years on services to and from France, some locomotives have been withdrawn having lost out to TGVs and ICEs. However, there are still a few duties from Frankfurt/M to Strasbourg whilst they still hold down many trains from Koblenz to Trier and Luxembourg for a few more years. (New EMUs have been ordered for Koblenz–Luxembourg services whilst IC trains are likely to be reduced on this route). Sometimes Stuttgart uses the class to work down to Singen whilst the new 2012/13 timetable has a loco working stock transfers north to Dortmund. Another odd working is a weekend IC train to Leipzig.

Built: 1974–75 for DB.
Builder–Mech. Parts: Krupp.
Builder–Elec. Parts: AEG.
One Hour Rating: 3300 (*3240) kW.
Continuous Rating: 3200 (*3000) kW.
Maximum Tractive Effort: 285 kN.
Wheel Diameter: 1250 mm.
Non-Standard Livery: N Blue.

Systems: 15 kV AC 16.7 Hz/25 kV AC 50 Hz.
Weight: 83 tonnes.
Length over Buffers: 17.94 m.
Max. Speed: 160 km/h.
Electric Brake: Rheostatic.

All multiple working/push-pull fitted.

181 201	N	FGM	181 211		FGM	181 219	FGM
181 204		FGM	181 212		FGM (Z)	181 220	FGM
181 205		FGM	181 213		FGM	181 222	FGM (Z)
181 207		FGM	181 214		FGM	181 223	FGM
181 208		FGM (Z)	181 215		FGM	181 224	FGM (Z)
181 209		FGM	181 218		FGM	181 225	FGM (Z)
181 210		FGM					

Names:

181 211 LORRAINE	181 213 SAAR
181 212 LUXEMBOURG	181 214 MOSEL

CLASS 182   Bo-Bo

DB Class 152 did not get authority to work into Austria so part of the order was swapped for some Siemens Taurus locomotives (ÖBB type 1116) which became DB Class 182. So the German freight sector got some 230 km/h dual-voltage locomotives! These are now being switched to DB Regio but really they ought to be with DB Fernverkehr to save that sector hiring in similar locomotives! The main use for the Cottbus locomotives is now on accelerated RE services around Berlin whilst the Dresden ones find use on S-Bahn services! But what a come down for 230 km/h locos!

Built: 2001.
Builder–Mech. Parts: Krauss Maffei, Duewag.
Builder–Elec. Parts: Siemens.
One Hour Rating: 6600 kW.
Continuous Rating: 6400 kW.
Maximum Tractive Effort: 300 kN.
Wheel Diameter: 1250 mm.

Systems: 15 kV AC 16.7 Hz; 25 kV AC 50 Hz.
Weight: 86 tonnes.
Length over Buffers: 19.58 m.
Maximum Speed 230 km/h.
Electric Brake: Rheostatic.

182 001	BCS	182 010	BCS	182 018	DA
182 002	BCS	182 011	BCS	182 019	DA
182 003	BCS	182 012	BCS	182 020	DA
182 004	BCS	182 013 **A**	BCS	182 021	DA
182 005	BCS	182 014	BCS	182 022	DA
182 006	BCS	182 015	BCS	182 023	DA
182 007	BCS	182 016	DA	182 024	UE
182 008	BCS	182 017	DA	182 025	UE
182 009	BCS				

▲ IC2033, the 0732 Hamburg Altona to Frankfurt (Main) Hbf passes Boppard on 23 September 2010 with 182 011 in charge.   **Robin Ralston**

CLASS 185   Bo-Bo

Class 185 is the dual-voltage version of the Bombardier TRAXX family which has virtually replaced Classes 139 and 140. Fittings include ZWS, ZMS, Sifa, ETCS, Ebula, LZB/PZB 90. Up to four locomotives can be operated in multiple. From 185 201 a design variation took place mainly concerning the front end crash protection arrangements. Private operators also use many 185s, details of which appear in German Railways Part 2. When DB Schenker formed an alliance with Green Cargo (Sweden) to form DB Schenker Scandinavia, Green Cargo bought some 185s from DB as part of its input (shown as GC)*, these locomotives being replaced by 185 401-403. It is likely that these latter locomotives may be sold on to another operator. 185 400 is a blank number as a 185 was taken off the production line and turned out as 146 228. Strangely in late 2012 some privately owned locomotives appeared bearing 185 4xx numbers rather than much higher numbers previously used.

Built: 2000–10.
Builder: Bombardier Transportation (Kassel).
Continuous Rating: 5600 kW.
Maximum Tractive Effort: 300 kN.
Wheel Diameter: 1250 mm.

Systems: 15 kV AC 16.7 Hz; 25 kV AC 50 Hz.
Weight: 84 tonnes.
Length over Buffers: 18.90 m.
Maximum Speed 140 km/h.
Electric Brake: Regenerative.

185 020 – 039	Fitted out for working into France.
185 085 – 094	Fitted out for working into Switzerland and Austria (Kornwestheim – Konstanz – Wolfurt).
185 095 – 128	Fitted out for working into Switzerland.
185 321 – 337	DB Schenker Scandinavia locomotives for Hamburg – Denmark – Sweden.
185 338 – 399	Fitted out for working into Austria. (Agreement changed 01/08/12 which excluded earlier locomotives).

185 001	RM	185 038	RM	185 075	RM
185 002	RM	185 039	RM	185 076	RM
185 003	RM	185 040	RM	185 077	RM
185 004	RM	185 041	RM	185 078	RM
185 005	RM	185 042	RM	185 079	RM
185 006	RM	185 043	RM	185 080	RM
185 007	RM	185 044	RM	185 081	RM
185 008	RM	185 045	RM	185 082	RM
185 009	RM	185 046	RM	185 083	RM
185 010	RM	185 047	RM	185 084	RM
185 011	RM	185 048	RM	185 085	RM
185 012	RM	185 049	RM	185 086	RM
185 013	RM	185 050	RM	185 087	RM
185 014	RM	185 051	RM	185 088	RM
185 015	RM	185 052	RM	185 089	RM
185 016	RM	185 053	RM	185 090	A RM
185 017	RM	185 054	RM	185 091	RM
185 018	RM	185 055	RM	185 092	RM
185 019	RM	185 056	RM	185 093	RM
185 020	RM	185 057	RM	185 094	RM
185 021	RM	185 058	RM	185 095	RM
185 022	RM	185 059	RM	185 096	RM
185 023	RM	185 060	RM (Z)	185 097	RM
185 024	RM	185 061	RM	185 098	RM
185 025	RM	185 062	RM	185 099	RM
185 026	RM	185 063	RM	185 100	RM
185 027	RM	185 064	RM	185 101	RM
185 028	RM	185 065	RM	185 102	RM
185 029	RM	185 066	RM	185 103	RM
185 030	RM	185 067	RM	185 104	RM
185 031	RM	185 068	RM	185 105	RM
185 032	RM	185 069	RM	185 106	RM
185 033	RM	185 070	RM	185 107	RM
185 034	RM	185 071	RM	185 108	RM
185 035	RM	185 072	RM	185 109	RM
185 036	RM	185 073	RM	185 110	RM
185 037	RM	185 074	RM	185 111	RM

185 112		RM	185 176		RM	185 240	RM
185 113		RM	185 177		RM	185 241	RM
185 114		RM	185 178		RM	185 242	RM
185 115		RM	185 179		RM	185 243	RM
185 116		RM	185 180		RM	185 244	RM
185 117		RM	185 181		RM	185 245	RM
185 118		RM	185 182		RM	185 246	RM
185 119		RM	185 183		RM	185 247	RM
185 120		RM	185 184		RM	185 248	RM
185 121		RM	185 185		RM	185 249	RM
185 122		RM	185 186		RM	185 250	RM
185 123		RM	185 187		RM	185 251	RM
185 124		RM	185 188		RM	185 252	RM
185 125		RM	185 189		RM	185 253	RM
185 126		RM	185 190		RM	185 254	RM
185 127		RM	185 191		RM	185 255	RM
185 128		RM	185 192		RM	185 256	RM
185 129		RM	185 193		RM	185 257	RM
185 130		RM	185 194		RM	185 258	RM
185 131		RM	185 195		RM	185 259	RM
185 132		RM	185 196		RM	185 260	RM
185 133		RM	185 197		RM	185 261	RM
185 134		RM	185 198		RM	185 262	RM
185 135		RM	185 199		RM	185 263	RM
185 136		RM	185 200		RM	185 264	RM
185 137		RM	185 201		RM	185 265	RM
185 138		RM	185 202		RM	185 266	RM
185 139		RM	185 203		RM	185 267	RM
185 140		RM	185 204		RM	185 268	RM
185 141		RM	185 205		RM	185 269	RM
185 142	A	RM	185 206		RM	185 270	RM
185 143		RM	185 207		RM	185 271	RM
185 144		RM	185 208		RM	185 272	RM
185 145		RM	185 209		RM	185 273	RM
185 146		RM	185 210		RM	185 274	RM
185 147		RM	185 211		RM	185 275	RM
185 148		RM	185 212		RM	185 276	RM
185 149		RM	185 213		RM	185 277	RM
185 150		RM	185 214		RM	185 278	RM
185 151		RM	185 215		RM	185 279	RM
185 152	A	RM	185 216		RM	185 280	RM
185 153		RM	185 217		RM	185 281	RM
185 154		RM	185 218		RM	185 282	RM
185 155		RM	185 219		RM	185 283	RM
185 156		RM	185 220		RM	185 284	RM
185 157		RM	185 221		RM	185 285	RM
185 158		RM	185 222		RM	185 286	RM
185 159		RM	185 223		RM	185 287	RM
185 160		RM	185 224		RM	185 288	RM
185 161		RM	185 225		RM	185 289	RM
185 162		RM	185 226		RM	185 290	RM
185 163		RM	185 227		RM	185 291	RM
185 164		RM	185 228		RM	185 292	RM
185 165		RM	185 229		RM	185 293	RM
185 166		RM	185 230		RM	185 294	RM
185 167		RM	185 231		RM	185 295	RM
185 168		RM	185 232		RM	185 296	RM
185 169		RM	185 233		RM	185 297	RM
185 170		RM	185 234		RM	185 298	RM
185 171		RM	185 235		RM	185 299	RM
185 172		RM	185 236		RM	185 300	RM
185 173		RM	185 237		RM	185 301	RM
185 174		RM	185 238		RM	185 302	RM
185 175		RM	185 239		RM	185 303	RM

185 304	RM	185 337	RM	185 370		RM
185 305	RM	185 338	RM	185 371		RM
185 306	RM	185 339	RM	185 372		RM
185 307	RM	185 340	RM	185 373		RM
185 308	RM	185 341	RM	185 374		RM
185 309	RM	185 342	RM	185 375		RM
185 310	RM	185 343	RM	185 376		RM
185 311	RM	185 344	RM	185 377		RM
185 312	RM	185 345	RM	185 378		RM
185 313	RM	185 346	RM	185 379		RM
185 314	RM	185 347	RM	185 380		RM
185 315	RM	185 348	RM	185 381		RM
185 316	RM	185 349	RM	185 382		RM
185 317	RM	185 350	RM	185 383		RM
185 318	RM	185 351	RM	185 384		RM
185 319	RM	185 352	RM	185 385		RM
185 320	RM	185 353	RM	185 386		RM
185 321	RM	185 354	RM	185 387		RM
185 322	RM	185 355	RM	185 388		RM
185 323	RM	185 356	RM	185 389	A	RM
185 324	RM	185 357	RM	185 390		RM
185 325	RM	185 358	RM	185 391		RM
185 326	RM	185 359	RM	185 392		RM
185 327	RM	185 360	RM	185 393		RM
185 328	RM	185 361	RM	185 394		RM
185 329	RM	185 362	RM	185 395		RM
185 330	RM	185 363	RM	185 396		RM
185 331	RM	185 364	RM	185 397		RM
185 332	GC*	185 365	RM	185 398		RM
185 333	GC*	185 366	RM	185 399	A	RM
185 334	GC*	185 367	RM	185 401		RM
185 335	RM	185 368	RM	185 402		RM
185 336	RM	185 369	RM	185 403		RM

CLASS 186   Bo-Bo

This class is the TRAXX F140MS built for some years by Bombardier but used mostly by private companies until DB Schenker decided it too needed some. The DB locomotives are intended to be used on services into France but few have been reported there! Technical details as Class 185 except that four systems can be used, the extra ones being 1500 V DC and 3000 V DC.

186 321	RM	186 328	RM	186 335	RM
186 322	RM	186 329	RM	186 336	RM
186 323	RM	186 330	RM	186 337	RM
186 324	RM	186 331	RM	186 338	RM
186 325	RM	186 332	RM	186 339	RM
186 326	RM	186 333	RM	186 340	RM
186 327	RM	186 334	RM		

▲ 185 198 hauls a heavy freight through Freilassing, on the border between Germany and Austria, on 24 March 2012. **Raimund Wyhnal**

▼ 189 044 and 189 034 are seen at the head of an empty iron ore train from Dillingen to Rotterdam on 11 April 2012. **Matthias Müller**

CLASS 189 Bo-Bo

The 100 locomotives of this type are intended to work freight trains into Poland, Netherlands, Belgium, Czech Republic and even Italy. They are four-voltage versions of Class 152. The first three locomotives were built in 2002 and underwent tests in Sweden, Czech Republic and elsewhere. The production series followed in 2003, Siemens also building large numbers for its then Dispolok operation as well as other private operators. 189 001–003 were replaced by three later examples in 2003. Getting authority to run in the adjoining countries was a rather painful affair but the class is now seeing widespread use with many locomotives having been cleared for the Netherlands where they haul many trains over the Betouwe route. Some of these are the iron ore trains to Dillingen for which some locomotives have been fitted with heavy duty ("automatic") couplers. A rather strange development was the sale of 189 090–099 to MRCE with the idea of leasing them back but instead MRCE leased the locos to private operators! The latest news about this class concerns those locomotives not cleared for the Netherlands. It was announced in early 2013 that the 32 locomotives concerned will be fitted with Czech and Polish safety systems to allow through running deep into those countries.

Built: 2002–05.
Builder: Siemens.
One Hour Rating: 6600 kW.
Continuous Rating: 6400 kW.
Maximum Tractive Effort: 300 kN.
Wheel Diameter: 1250 mm.

Systems: 15 kV AC 16.7 Hz; 25 kV AC 50 Hz; 1500 V DC; 3000 V DC.
Weight: 86 tonnes.
Length over Buffers: 19.58 m.
Maximum Speed 140 km/h.
Electric Brake: Regenerative.

cz   allowed into Czech Republic Decin area yards.
n   allowed into Netherlands and has white warning panel at each end.

189 001[ll]		NN2	189 031	a n	NN2	189 061			NN2
189 002[ll]		NN2	189 032	a n	NN2	189 062			NN2
189 003[ll]	cz	NN2	189 033	a n	NN2	189 063			NN2
189 004	cz	NN2	189 034	a n	NN2	189 064			NN2
189 005	cz	NN2	189 035	a n	NN2	189 065		n	NN2
189 006	cz	NN2	189 036	a n	NN2	189 066		n	NN2
189 007	cz	NN2	189 037	a n	NN2	189 067		n	NN2
189 008	cz	NN2	189 038	a n	NN2	189 068		n	NN2
189 009	cz	NN2	189 039	a n	NN2	189 069		n	NN2
189 010	cz	NN2	189 040	a n	NN2	189 070		n	NN2
189 011	cz	NN2	189 041	a n	NN2	189 071		n	NN2
189 012	cz	NN2	189 042	a n	NN2	189 072		n	NN2
189 013		NN2	189 043	a n	NN2	189 073		n	NN2
189 014		NN2	189 044	a n	NN2	189 074		n	NN2
189 015		NN2	189 045	a n	NN2	189 075		n	NN2
189 016		NN2	189 046	a n	NN2	189 076		n	NN2
189 017		NN2	189 047	a n	NN2	189 077		n	NN2
189 018		NN2 (Z)	189 048	n	NN2	189 078		n	NN2
189 019		NN2	189 049	n	NN2	189 079		n	NN2
189 020		NN2	189 050	n	NN2	189 080		n	NN2
189 021		NN2	189 051	n	NN2	189 081		n	NN2
189 022		NN2	189 052	n	NN2	189 082		n	NN2
189 023	n	NN2	189 053	n	NN2	189 083		n	NN2
189 024	n	NN2	189 054	n	NN2	189 084		n	NN2
189 025	n	NN2	189 055		NN2	189 085		n	NN2
189 026	n	NN2	189 056		NN2	189 086		n	NN2
189 027	n	NN2	189 057		NN2	189 087		n	NN2
189 028	n	NN2	189 058		NN2	189 088		n	NN2
189 029	n	NN2	189 059		NN2	189 089		n	NN2
189 030	a n	NN2	189 060		NN2	189 100		n	NN2

2. MAIN-LINE DIESEL LOCOMOTIVES

CLASS 202   B-B

At one time there were nearly 900 Class 201/2/4 locomotives but now few are left in DB service. Class 202 belonged to DB Regio with the last examples withdrawn in 2002. Two survive with 202 563 at Meiningen works being a rescue locomotive for overhauled locomotives when out on test and is in a light blue livery. 202 646 belongs to DB Regio Erzgebirgbahn being used to rescue failed DMUs but also used on ballast trains and snowplough duties and retains the old DR Bordeaux red livery. Many withdrawn Class 202s have been modernised at Stendal works and sold to private operators - see German Railways Part 2.

Built: 1964–78 for DR.
Builder: LEW.
Engine: 853 kW.
Transmission: Hydraulic.   **Former DR Class:** 112.
Maximum Tractive Effort: 222 kN.   **Weight:** 64 tonnes.
Wheel Diameter: 1000 mm.   **Length over Buffers:** 14.24 m.
Train Heating: Steam.   **Maximum Speed:** 100 km/h.

202 563	**N**	UMX	202 646	**N**	DC (Z)

CLASS 203   B-B

The former DB Regio workshops at Stendal ended up with over 200 Class 201/202/204 stored there. Realising that the demise of the classes would leave it with no work, the works began to modernise these classes as a local initiative and soon found buyers in the emerging private sector. Such has been the success of these conversions that some DB subsidiaries have now purchased some of these locomotives. First the München S-Bahn hired a locomotive and then bought it. Later DB Bahnbau (DBB) and DB Gleisbau (DGB) purchased some of the 203.3 version; these locomotives now come under DB Netz (DBN). Centrally controlled by DB Netz (DBN) maintenance is undertaken at any convenient depot. For a while DB Regio hired some 203.1 for shunting at Nürnberg Hbf. etc. These have now gone to the private sector although could easily turn up working for DB from time to time!

Built: 1964–78 for DR.
Builder: LEW.
Rebuilt: 2001–2003 by Alstom Locomotive Service, Stendal.
Engine: MTU 12V4000 R10 of 1380 kW (203.0), CAT 3512B DI-TA of 1305 kW (203.3).
Tansmission: Hydraulic.
Maximum Tractive Effort: 206 kN.   **Weight:** 72 tonnes.
Wheel Diameter: 1000 mm.   **Length over buffers:** 14.24 m.
Train Heating: None.   **Maximum Speed:** 100 km/h.
Class Specific Livery: Y   Some Class 203.3 are in a variation of departmental yellow livery with a blue band around the base of the body and a large blue triangle on the front ends.

Class 203/0. MTU engine.

203 002	(202 696)		MH6

Class 203/3. Caterpillar engine.

203 301	(202 675)	**Y**	DBN	203 309	(202 384)	**Y**	DBN
203 302	(202 555)	**Y**	DBN	203 310	(202 334)	**Y**	DBN
203 303	(202 679)	**Y**	DBN	203 311	(202 169)	**Y**	DBN
203 304	(202 416)	**Y**	DBN	203 312	(202 832)	**Y**	DBN
203 305	(202 280)	**Y**	DBN	203 313	(202 825)	**Y**	DBN
203 306	(202 752)	**Y**	DBN	203 314	(202 751)	**Y**	DBN
203 307	(202 685)	**Y**	DBN	203 315	(202 625)	**Y**	DBN
203 308	(202 791)	**Y**	DBN	203 316	(202 672)	**Y**	DBN

CLASS 212   B-B

This class was in effect totally withdrawn by DB Schenker but sectorisation saw other sectors wanting their own locomotives rather than hiring in. Consequently some 212s have been reinstated after overhaul at Cottbus where new MTU engines were fitted and the steam heating boiler was removed. Other 212s have been rebuilt at Stendal in a manner similar to the 202s and have been snapped up by private operators. A larger modernisation has also taken place with some emerging from Stendal as Class 214. Some locomotives were converted to Class 714 in the old system and have now been given EVNs that show the old 212 number. As these locomotives still carry 212 numbers they are shown there. All of the Class 212s remaining with DB are in use with DB Netz. Where given, the allocations are nominal as locomotives needing attention often get sent to the nearest depot available. More locomotives are expected to change to a yellow livery in due course. Locos with new engines are with Fahrwegdienste the other two are with DB Bahnbau Gruppe.

Built: 1962–65 for DB.
Builder: MaK/Jung/Deutz/Henschel.
Engine: MTU MB 12V652 TA/MAN V6 V 18/21 TL. * MTU 8V4000 R41.
Power: 1005 kW (1350 hp).
Transmission: Hydraulic. Voith L216 rs.
Maximum Tractive Effort: 183 kN.   **Weight:** 62 tonnes.
Wheel Diameter: 950 mm.   **Length over Buffers:** 12.30 m.
Train Heating: None.   **Maximum Speed:** 100 km/h.
Non-Standard Livery: N 212 093 is in old DB purple red livery.
           212 329 is in old DB turquoise & beige livery.

All multiple working fitted.

212 034		*	TK	212 265		*	TK	212 317		*	TK
212 036		*	TK	212 274		*	TK	212 323		*	TK
212 093	N	*	TK	212 298		*	TK	212 329	N	*	TK
212 094		*	TK	212 306	Y		MAOB	212 347		*	TK
212 097	Y		EDEF	212 310		*	TK			

CLASS 213   B-B

These locomotives are 212s with different gearing and hydrodynamic brakes for use on steep lines. They worked for many years from Koblenz and latterly from Hof. Their duties were all taken over by DMUs and the class withdrawn. Subsequently some locos have been acquired by DB Netz for use by DB Bahnbau Gruppe whilst others are in use by private operators - see German Railways Part 2.

Built: 1965–66 for DB.
Builder: MaK.
Engine: MTU MB 12V652 TA.
Power: 1005 kW (1350 hp).
Transmission: Hydraulic. Voith L620B rs.
Maximum Tractive Effort: 194 kN.   **Weight:** 63 tonnes.
Wheel Diameter: 950 mm.   **Length over Buffers:** 12.30 m.
Train Heating: Steam (if still fitted).   **Maximum Speed:** 100 km/h.

213 332	Y		MAOB	213 333	Y		MAOB	213 336	Y		MAOB (Z)
213 337	Y		MAOB (Z)					

CLASS 215 B-B

DB Autozug acquired these locomotives for working its trains between Niebüll and Westerland (Sylt). All are now out of service with most stored at Chemnitz works where they await sale or scrapping. Amazingly they have never been officially withdrawn and remain in stock!

Built: 1968–69 for DB.
Builder: Krupp/MaK/Henschel/Krauss-Maffei.
Engine: MTU MB 16V 652 TB or MAN 12 V 956 TB.
Power: 1400 kW (1900 hp) or 1840 kW (2400 hp).
Transmission: Hydraulic. Voith L820 rs or MTU K252 SU.
Maximum Tractive Effort: 245 kN.   **Weight:** 79–80 tonnes.
Wheel Diameter: 1000 mm.   **Length over Buffers:** 16.40 m.
Train Heating: Steam.   **Maximum Speed:** 140 km/h.

All multiple working fitted.

215 901	(215 034)	ANB (Z)		215 908	(215 062)	ANB (Z)
215 902	(215 035)	ANB (Z)		215 909	(215 064)	ANB (Z)
215 903	(215 036)	ANB (Z)		215 910	(215 096)	ANB (Z)
215 904	(215 046)	ANB (Z)		215 911	(215 115)	ANB (Z)
215 905	(215 047)	ANB (Z)		215 912	(215 123)	ANB (Z)
215 906	(215 048)	ANB (Z)		215 913	(215 127)	ANB (Z)
215 907	(215 056)	ANB (Z)		215 914	(215 139)	ANB (Z)

▲ Due to an engine failure on 719 101, the track testing train is being piloted by 203 305 and 203 311 on 4 June 2010. They are seen at Braubach on the right bank of the Rhine, with the famous Marksburg castle in the background.   **Matthias Müller**

CLASS 217 B-B

This is basically a Class 216 (all now withdrawn) fitted with an electric train supply but surprisingly ended up working for the freight sector. 217 001/002 were used by the research department until recently. Most locomotives are now stored at München Nord Rbf their duties in the Mühldorf area having been taken over by Class 247. 217 002 has been sold to Bahntouristik Express and is still in former TEE livery.

Built: 1965–66 for DB.
Builder: Krupp.
Engine: MTU MB 16V 652 TB10.
Power: 1415 kW (1900 hp). Also 375 kW (500 hp) auxiliary engine.
Transmission: Hydraulic. Voith L820 WS rs/MTU K252.
Maximum Tractive Effort: 245 kN. | **Weight:** 79–81.5 tonnes.
Wheel Diameter: 1000 mm. | **Length over Buffers:** 16.40 m.
Train Heating: Electric. | **Maximum Speed:** 120 km/h.

All multiple working fitted.

217 012	MMF (Z)	217 015	MMF (Z)	217 017	MMF (Z)
217 019	MMF (Z)	217 021	MMF (Z)		

CLASS 218 B-B

Most of this class is used by DB Regio and its subsidiaries on push-pull services but some are hired in by DB Fernverkehr and used on EC/IC trains in some areas (eg. München–Lindau). Those allocated to Niebüll are used by DB Autozug on car shuttles to Westerland. The 218.8 series are DB Fernverkehr rescue locos with numbers allocated according to their original construction batch number. ZWS controls are being fitted to locomotives currently passing through Bremen works so some push-pull work is envisaged for these locos for some years to come. Continuing deliveries of new DMUs and loss of services to private operators as well as more electrification (München–Lindau) will mean further reallocations or indeed withdrawals. Locomotives 218 329, 330 and 339 have been fitted with Caterpillar 3516B HD engines for assessment. Overhauls of 218 002–218 298 have now ceased. A large number of locomotives are stored at Bremen works and Hamm pending sale. 218 002-218 011 were recently running as Class 225 but the authorities insisted that as they had not been rebuilt they should revert to their original numbers! These locomotives belong to DB Schenker for freight use. During 2011 DB placed a framework contract with Bombardier for a new class of diesel locomotive (Class 245). These locos are likely to replace all the remaining 218s within a few years.

Built: 1968–79 for DB.
Builder: Krupp/MaK/Henschel/Krauss-Maffei.
Engine: MTU MA 12V 956 TB 10 (*12V 956 TB 11, §Pielstick 16 PA 4V 200, †MTU MA 12V956 TBG11, ‡MTU 16V 4000R40 of 2000 kW).
Power: 1840 kW (2500 hp) (*§2061 kW (3000 hp)).
Transmission: Hydraulic. Voith L820 rs.
Maximum Tractive Effort: 245 kN. | **Weight:** 76.5–78.5 tonnes.
Wheel Diameter: 1000 mm. | **Length over Buffers:** 16.40 m.
Train Heating: Electric. | **Maximum Speed:** 140 km/h.
Non-Standard Livery: N 218 105 TEE Livery (Red/Beige); 218 387 Old DB purple red livery (Purpurrot).

All multiple working fitted.

218 002	(225 802)		TK	218 006	(225 806)	TK (Z)
218 003	(225 803)	‡	TK (Z)	218 009	(225 807)	TU
218 005	(225 805)	‡	TK (Z)	218 011	(225 811)	TK (Z)

218 101		FGM (Z)	218 157		ANB (Z)	218 203	†	MKP (Z)
218 102		FF	218 158		AL (Z)	218 204	*	TU (Z)
218 105	N	NAH	218 161		TU (Z)	218 205	*	MKP (Z)
218 108		FGM (Z)	218 163		TU (Z)	218 208		RK
218 128		AL (Z)	218 164		TU (Z)	218 214	†	MKP (Z)
218 139		RK	218 184		ANB (Z)	218 219	*	MKP (Z)
218 153		MKP (Z)	218 191		TP	218 220	*	ANB (Z)
218 155		FGM (Z)	218 201	*	MKP (Z)	218 223	*	MKP (Z)
218 156		TU (Z)	218 202	*	MKP (Z)	218 224	‡	MKP (Z)

Number			Code	Number			Code	Number			Code
218 241		*	TU (Z)	218 387	N	*	FK	218 446		*	FGM
218 249			RK	218 389		*	FNB	218 447		*	HBS
218 261	Y		MAOB	218 390		‡	LL1	218 448		*	HBS
218 271			NRH (Z)	218 391	Y	*	MAOB	218 449		*	KK2
218 272			RK	218 392	Y		BSE	218 450		*	HBS
218 287	Y		MAOB	218 393		‡	MKP (Z)	218 451		*	HBS
218 304	Y	*	MAOB	218 396		*	RHL	218 452		*	HBS
218 307		‡	ANB	218 397		*	ANB	218 453		*	AK
218 308		*	FGM (Z)	218 399		*	STMI	218 454		*	MKP
218 311		*	ANB	218 400			MMF	218 455		‡	HBS
218 313		*	ANB	218 401		‡	MMF	218 456		‡	TU
218 314		*	ANB	218 402			MMF	218 457		‡	MKP
218 315		‡	ANB	218 403		‡	MMF	218 458		‡	MKP
218 319		*	ANB	218 404		*	MMF	218 459		‡	MKP
218 321		‡	ANB	218 405			MMF	218 460		‡	MKP
218 322		‡	ANB	218 406			TU	218 461		‡	MKP
218 323		§	AL (Z)	218 407		*	AK	218 462		‡	MKP
218 324		‡	MMF (Z)	218 408		*	TU	218 463		‡	MMF
218 326		§	TU	218 409		*	TU	218 464		*	TU
218 329		§	AK	218 410		*	TU	218 465		‡	MMF
218 330		§	AK	218 411		*	SKL	218 466		‡	MMF
218 333		‡	AK	218 412		*	SKL	218 467		‡	MKP
218 334		§	AL (Z)	218 413		*	AK	218 468		‡	LL1 (Z)
218 339		§	AK	218 414		*	SKL	218 469		‡	MKP
218 340		*	ANB	218 415		*	FGM	218 470		*	HBS
218 341		*	ANB	218 416		‡	MMF	218 471		‡	MKP
218 342		*	ANB	218 417		*	FGM	218 472		*	MKP
218 343		*	RHL	218 418			MMF	218 473		*	HBS
218 345		‡	ANB	218 419		‡	MMF	218 474		*	HBS
218 346		‡	MKP (Z)	218 420		*	FGM	218 475		‡	MKP
218 347		‡	AL (Z)	218 421		‡	MMF	218 476		*	TU
218 349		‡	AL (Z)	218 422		t	MMF	218 477	Y	*	FGM
218 350		‡	MMF (Z)	218 423		‡	MMF	218 478		*	FGM (Z)
218 351		†	TU (Z)	218 424		*	SKL	218 479		*	MMF (Z)
218 353		†	MMF (Z)	218 425		*	SKL	218 480		*	RK
218 355		*	AL (Z)	218 426		*	MMF	218 481		*	TU
218 356		*	MMF	218 427		§	TU	218 482		*	FGM (Z)
218 359		*	ANB	218 428		‡	MMF	218 483		*	RK
218 360		‡	MMF (Z)	218 429		§	FGM	218 484		*	RK
218 362		*	ANB	218 430		§	MMF	218 485		‡	MKP (Z)
218 363		*	ANB	218 431		‡	TU	218 486		§	MKP
218 364		*	ANB	218 432		‡	TU	218 487		‡	AL
218 366		*	ANB	218 433		‡	MMF	218 488		‡	MKP
218 369		*	ANB	218 434		‡	TU	218 489		‡	MKP
218 371		*	ANB	218 435		‡	MKP	218 490		‡	MKP
218 372		*	ANB	218 436		‡	TU	218 491		‡	TU
218 374		*	ANB (Z)	218 437		*	MMF	218 492		‡	MKP
218 376		*	ANB	218 438		‡	TU	218 493		‡	MKP
218 377		*	AL (Z)	218 439		*	TU	218 494		‡	TU
218 378		*	ANB (Z)	218 440		*	MMF	218 495		‡	TU
218 379		*	ANB	218 442		*	TU	218 496		†	TU
218 380		*	ANB	218 443		*	TU	218 497		†	FGM
218 381		*	ANB	218 444		*	MMF	218 498		§	MMF
218 385		*	ANB	218 445		*	MMF	218 499		§	TU
218 386		*	ANB								

Number		Code	Number		Code
218 810	(218 159)	FGM	218 832	(218 357)	BRG
218 812	(218 188)	BRG	218 833	(218 383)	FGM
218 813	(218 189)	FGM	218 834	(218 367)	BRG
218 822	(218 231)	FGM (Z)	218 835	(218 370)	BRG
218 824	(218 233)	FGM	218 836	(218 388)	AN
218 825	(218 237)	FGM	218 837	(218 303)	BRG
218 830	(218 305)	FGM	218 838	(218 373)	FGM
218 831	(218 394)	BRG	218 839	(218 317)	BRG

CLASS 225 B-B

Previously Class 215, the classification of those locomotives in the freight sector was changed to denote their different use. As can be seen several are in store and more are likely to be displaced with the arrival of Class 265 Gravita 15BB.

Built: 1968–69 for DB.
Builder: Krupp/MaK/Henschel/Krauss-Maffei.
Engine: MTU MB 16V 652 TB (*MAN 12 V 956 TB).
Power: 1400 kW (1900 hp) (*1840 kW (2400 hp)).
Transmission: Hydraulic. Voith L820 rs or MTU K252 SU.
Maximum Tractive Effort: 245 kN.   **Weight:** 79–80 tonnes.
Wheel Diameter: 1000 mm.   **Length over Buffers:** 16.40 m.
Train Heating: None.   **Maximum Speed:** 140 km/h.

All multiple working fitted.

b   Fitted with Belgian safety equipment.
e   Fitted with electric train heating.

225 001	*	FMB (Z)	225 020		EOB (Z)	225 051		EOB (Z)
225 003	*	FMB (Z)	225 021		HO	225 073		HO
225 004	*	FMB (Z)	225 023	b	MMF	225 081	*	FMB (Z)
225 005	*	FMB (Z)	225 024	*b	EOB	225 082		TK (Z)
225 008	*	TK	225 025	b	FMB	225 094		FMB (Z)
225 009	*	FMB	225 027	*b	HO	225 099		FMB (Z)
225 010	*	MMF (Z)	225 028	*b	HO (Z)	225 100		FMB (Z)
225 011		MMF	225 029	b	HO (Z)	225 101		MMF (Z)
225 015		FMB	225 030	*e	MMF (Z)	225 109		FMB
225 017		EOB (Z)	225 031	e	MMF	225 117		EOB
225 018		EOB (Z)	225 032	e	MMF			

▲ 218 105 in TEE red and beige livery is seen propelling a weekday only commuter train from Bonn to Rheinbach near Witterschlick on 20 April 2011. **Matthias Müller**

CLASS 229 C-C

The whole class was withdrawn by 2001 but some have been reinstated after having been purchased by DB Bahnbau for use on engineering trains. Some other 229s have gone to MEG - see German Railways Part 2.

Rebuilt: 1992–93 by Krupp, Essen.
Engine: 2480 kW.
Transmission: Hydraulic.
Maximum Tractive Effort: 276 kN.
Wheel Diameter: 1000 mm.
Train Heating: Electric.

Former DR Class: 119.
Weight: 96 tonnes.
Length over Buffers: 19.46 m.
Maximum Speed: 140 km/h.

229 100	Y	DBN	229 147	Y	DBN	229 181	Y	DBN
229 126	Y	DBN						

CLASS 232 Co-Co

Once there were over 1100 Soviet built diesels on the DR but fewer than half this number survive and they are Classes 232, 233, 234 and 241 (Classes 220, 230, 231, 242 having gone). Class 232 was built specifically for the eastern bloc countries and featured an electric train supply. As inherited, Class 232 was a mixed traffic locomotive but now the class is dedicated to freight work. Built like a Soviet tank these locomotives are quite powerful and DB found them quite useful resulting in many being moved to the west part of the country at Oberhausen where one 232 could replace two Class 216s in multiple. Because of the recession and loss of freight traffic, many locomotives are in store at places such as Mukran, Eisenach and Saalfeld. The 232.9s are fitted out for working into the Netherlands and have a white warning panel on the front. Several locomotives have been sold to DB Schenker subsidiaries in other countries such as Poland (East West Railways) only to be hired back for work in Germany!

Built: 1973–82 for DR.
Builder: October Revolution Locomotive Works, Voroshilovgrad, USSR.
Engine: Kolomna 16-cylinder 5D49 (*2-5D49M).
Power: 2200 kW (2950 hp). (*2950 kW engine).
Transmission: Electric.
Maximum Tractive Effort: 340 kN.
Wheel Diameter: 1050 mm.
Train Heating: Electric.
Non-Standard Livery: N These locomotives are hired from East West Railways (EWR) are in a red and white livery.

Former DR Class: 132.
Weight: 123 tonnes.
Length over Buffers: 20.62 m.
Maximum Speed: 140 km/h.

All locomotives now fitted for multiple working.

232 005	N	WRS	232 259	EOB	232 413		BSE
232 093		LH1	232 262	LH1	232 426		NN2
232 109		EOB	232 280	NN2	232 428		WRS
232 117		NN2	232 283	EOB	232 448		LH1 (Z)
232 131		LH1	232 301	WRS (Z)	232 457		NN2 (Z)
232 187		LH1 (Z)	232 330	LH1	232 461		BSE (Z)
232 195		LH1 (Z)	232 347	HO	232 469		LH1
232 201		EOB	232 349	LH1 (Z)	232 472		NN2 (Z)
232 202		WRS (Z)	232 350	WRS (Z)	232 484	N	WRS
232 209		BSE	232 358	LH1	232 488		US (Z)
232 230		LH1	232 359	NN2	232 495		DF (Z)
232 238		NN2 (Z)	232 363	NN2 (Z)	232 498		LH1
232 240		DF	232 378	WRS (Z)	232 502		EOB
232 241		EOB	232 379	WRS (Z)	232 524		TK
232 252		WRS	232 384	LH1	232 527		NN2
232 254		LH1	232 388	TK	232 528		NN2 (Z)
232 255		LH1	232 401	N	WRS	232 529		LH1 (Z)

232 530		WRS (Z)	232 583	EOB	232 668		LH1
232 531	N	WRS	232 587	LH1	232 669		LH1 (Z)
232 534		NN2	232 589	NN2	232 673		LH1 (Z)
232 535		LH1	232 592	TK	232 675		LH1
232 553		LH1 (Z)	232 601	MMF	232 686		NN2 (Z)
232 561		EOB	232 609	NN2	232 691		DF (Z)
232 567	N	WRS	232 618	NN2	232 693		BSE
232 568		EOB	232 635	TK	232 703		TK
232 569		LH1	232 654	EOB	232 704		DF
232 571		BSE	232 665	DF			

232 800	(232 237)	*	LH1 (Z)	232 905	(232 423)	BSE
232 901	(232 072)		BSE	232 906	(232 504)	BSE
232 902	(232 161)		NN2 (Z)	232 908[II]	(232 699)	BSE
232 903	(232 170)		HO (Z)	232 909	(232 657)	BSE
232 904	(232 320)		EOB			

▲ 232 905 runs light engine through Duisburg-Wanheim on 13 September 2011. Note the white warning panel on the front of the locomotive for working into the Netherlands. **Matthias Müller**

CLASS 233 Co-Co

In the middle 1990s several Class 232 locomotives were experimentally fitted with new engines built by MaK, Caterpillar, Kolomna and Krupp, with Kolomna winning as 64 locos were modified with this new engine by Cottbus works and reclassified as Class 233. These are an updated version of the previous engine with higher efficiency and cleaner exhaust etc. The recession has seen may locomotives stored with only about half the class in use by late 2012. Some locomotives are stored at Hamm and Chemnitz. Details as Class 232 except:

Engine: Kolomna 16-cylinder 12D49.

233 040	LH1	233 306	LH1	233 547	BSE (Z)
233 043	MMF (Z)	233 314	LH1	233 562	LH1 (Z)
233 076	LH1 (Z)	233 321	BSE	233 572	LH1
233 112	BSE	233 322	LH1	233 586	NN2 (Z)
233 118	NN2 (Z)	233 326	LMR (Z)	233 588	NN2
233 127	BSE	233 367	NN2	233 594	MMF (Z)
233 151	NN2 (Z)	233 373	NN2	233 596	LH1 (Z)
233 176	NN2	233 441	BSE (Z)	233 616	LMR
233 179	LH1 (Z)	233 450	LH1	233 622	LMR (Z)
233 204	LH1 (Z)	233 451	MMF (Z)	232 625	LH1 (Z)
233 206	LH1 (Z)	233 452	NN2	233 636	BSE
233 217	LH1	233 458	NN2 (Z)	233 643	MMF (Z)
233 219	LH1	233 478	BSE	233 652	LH1 (Z)
233 232	NN2	233 486	LH1	233 662	MMF (Z)
233 233	BSE	233 493	BSE (Z)	233 683	LH1
233 249	BSE (Z)	233 510	NN2	233 689	NN2 (Z)
233 264	LH1 (Z)	233 511	NN2	233 696	BSE (Z)
233 281	BSE (Z)	233 515	BSE (Z)	233 698	NN2
233 285	LH1	233 521	LH1	233 702	BSE (Z)
233 288	LH1	233 525	BSE	233 705	LMR (Z)
233 289	MMF (Z)	233 536	LH1 (Z)	233 709	HO
233 295	NN2 (Z)				

CLASS 234 Co-Co

This class is a modified Class 232 re-geared for fast passenger work. Some locomotives are also fitted with ZWS for push-pull passenger train use. Most of the duties for this class have been superseded by DMUs. The two active locos are based in Berlin as back up locomotives for DB Fernverkehr, principally to cover for dual-voltage locos working to Poland.

Built: 1973–82 for DR.
Builder: October Revolution Locomotive Works, Voroshilovgrad, USSR.
Engine: Kolomna 16-cylinder 5D49.
Power: 2200 kW (2950 hp).
Transmission: Electric. | **Former DR Class:** 132.
Maximum Tractive Effort: 340 kN. | **Weight:** 123 tonnes.
Wheel Diameter: 1050 mm. | **Length over Buffers:** 20.62 m.
Train Heating: Electric. | **Maximum Speed:** 140 km/h.

234 144	r	BSE (Z)	234 278	r	BRG	234 551	r	BSE (Z)
234 242	r	BRG	234 468	r	BSE (Z)			

CLASS 241 Co-Co

Several Class 232s were given a bigger engine for working heavy trains in the Rühr area with some working through to steelworks in the Netherlands for which purpose the locos involved have been fitted with Dutch ATB. These workings have now ceased. The 241.8s were used on similar workings into Belgium (Aachen–Montzen) but electrification of the route made them surplus (These locos were restricted to 60 km/h in Belgium as they were not fitted with the Belgian safety system "Memor").

Built: 1973–82 for DR.
Builder: October Revolution Locomotive Works, Voroshilovgrad, USSR.
Engine: 2-5D49M.
Power: 2940 kW (4000 hp).
Transmission: Electric.
Maximum Tractive Effort: 340 kN.
Wheel Diameter: 1050 mm.
Train Heating: Electric.

Former DR Class: 132.
Weight: 123 tonnes.
Length over Buffers: 20.62 m.
Maximum Speed: 100 km/h.

241 008	(232 008)	EOB		241 801	(232 580)	LH1 (Z)
241 338	(232 338)	LH1		241 802	(232 706)	LH1 (Z)
241 353	(232 353)	EOB		241 803	(232 558)	LH1 (Z)
241 449	(232 449)	EOB		241 804	(232 483)	LH1 (Z)
241 697	(232 697)	EOB		241 805	(232 284)	LH1 (Z)

▲ Brand new 245 003 is on show at Innotrans 2012 in Berlin on 21 September 2012. These locomotives are expected to enter service during 2013.

Brian Garvin

CLASS 245 {Bo-Bo}

This is the new diesel version of the TRAXX family (P160 DE ME) featuring four "industrial" type engines as found in road vehicles etc. The idea being that when maximum power is needed all four engines will be used but as the going gets easier engines will shut down with possibly only one in use sometimes. Computers will control the engines in use and help to even out engine hours. There are obvious fuel savings involved. A framework contract for 200 locos is involved with DB Regio coming in first with an order for 20 locos which will replace Class 218 on passenger work. Erected at Kassel the bodies come from Wrocław in Poland, bogies are from Siegen, whilst Hennigsdorf and Mannheim are involved in the electrical components all being other Bombardier plants.

Built: 2012–
Builder: Bombardier Kassel.
Engine: 4 x Caterpillar C18 564 kW.
Power: 564–2256 kW.
Transmission: Electric.
Maximum Tractive Effort: 300 kN.
Wheel Diameter: 1250 mm.
Train Heating: Electric.
Braking: Electric 150 kN, dynamic 1600 kW.
Weight: 83 tonnes.
Length over Buffers: 18.90 m.
Maximum Speed: 160 km/h.

245 001	(MKP)	245 008	(MMF)	245 015	(MMF)
245 002	(MKP)	245 009	(MMF)	245 016	(FGM)
245 003	(MKP)	245 010	(MMF)	245 017	(FGM)
245 004	(MKP)	245 011	(MMF)	245 018	(FGM)
245 005	(MKP)	245 012	(MMF)	245 019	(FGM)
245 006	(MKP)	245 013	(MMF)	245 020	(FGM)
245 007	(MKP)	245 014	(MMF)		

CLASS 247 {Co-Co}

Class 247 or 266 that is the question! When DB Schenker bought English Welsh and Scottish Railway it also inherited Euro Cargo Rail and with it a batch of EMD JT42CWRM - a modernised EWS Class 66 which was given the French classification 77000. As 186s were replacing diesels in France, DB Schenker transferred some 247s to its operations in Germany. The main visual difference to the earlier Class 66s is the air conditioning pod on the cab roof. The former Railion had some 66s which were classified as 266 but surprisingly DB gave the ECR locomotives Class 247 only for the EBA to allocate Class 266! DB Schenker officially renumbered the locomotives as 266.4xx but all locomotives still carry Class 247 DB numbers and 266 EVNs! There are two centres of operation - Mühldorf where pairs of 217/218s have been released and the Ruhr area where 225s and 232s have been replaced.

Built: 2007–08.
Builder: EMD London, Ontario, Canada (Model JT42CWRM).
Engine: General Motors 12N-710G3B-EC two stroke.
Power: 2385 kW at 904 rpm.
Transmission: Electric.
Maximum Tractive Effort: 260 kN.
Wheel Diameter: 1120 mm.
Train Heating: None.
Weight: 127 tonnes.
Length over Buffers: 21.35 m.
Maximum Speed: 120 km/h
Non-Standard Livery: N All Class 247s retain their Euro Cargo Rail grey livery with front end yellow warning panels.

247 011	N	HBH	247 041	N	EOB	247 051	N	MMF
247 016	N	EOB	247 042	N	EOB	247 052	N	MMF
247 020	N	HBH	247 043	N	MMF	247 053	N	MMF
247 026	N	EOB	247 044	N	MMF	247 054	N	MMF
247 029	N	EOB	247 045	N	MMF	247 055	N	MMF
247 031	N	EOB	247 046	N	MMF	247 056	N	MMF
247 034	N	EOB	247 047	N	MMF	247 057	N	MMF
247 035	N	EOB	247 048	N	MMF	247 058	N	MMF
247 038	N	EOB	247 049	N	MMF	247 059	N	MMF
247 039	N	EOB	247 050	N	MMF	247 060	N	MMF

▲ When DB purchased the British freight operator EWS it also acquired its French subsidiary Euro Cargo Rail and consequently became the owner of a batch of Class 247 locomotives, a modernised version of the EWS Class 66. Some of these locos now see operation in Germany but retain their ECR silver livery with front end yellow warning panels. Here 247 052 is seen with a long tank train at Pirach on the line between Burghausen and Mühldorf on 10 May 2011. **Quintus Vosman**

▼ Gravita 10BB 261 035 is seen paused at Hamburg-Süd, part of the huge Hamburg docks complex, on 12 May 2012. **Matthias Müller**

CLASS 261 B-B

This new class is being delivered to replace non-modernised locomotives of Classes 290 291, 295 and 298. DB has surprisingly ordered 130 of these locomotives from Voith, the firm only having started locomotive production in 2008. The type is known as "Gravita 10BB". The first ten locomotives were numbered as Class 260 as they lacked particle filters and after being used for driver training were returned to Voith. Consequently Class 261 starts at 261 011. Whether the first ten locomotives will be retrofitted remains to be seen. Interestingly the first locomotives delivered to Mainz Bischofsheim have been noted working in the Limburg area reportedly replacing Class 225s in the Westerwald area.

Built: 2010–13
Builder: Voith Turbo Lokomotivtechnik GmbH & Co KG, Kiel.
Engine: MTU 8V 4000 R3.
Power: 1000 kW.
Transmission: Hydraulic, L4r4zseU2.
Maximum Tractive Effort: 337 kN.
Wheel Diameter: 1000 mm.
Train Heating: None.

Weight: 80 tonnes.
Length over Buffers: 15.72 m.
Maximum Speed: 100 km/h.

261 011	LH1	261 044	LH1	261 077	AM
261 012	LMR	261 045	LH1	261 078	FMB
261 013	LMR	261 046	LH1	261 079	FMB
261 014	LMR	261 047	LH1	261 080	FMB
261 015	LH1	261 048	LH1	261 081	LH1
261 016	LH1	261 049	AM	261 082	LH1
261 017	AM	261 050	AM	261 083	HS
261 018	LH1	261 051	FMB	261 084	HS
261 019	LH1	261 052	FMB	261 085	EOB
261 020	LH1	261 053	FMB	261 086	EOB
261 021	LH1	261 054	FMB	261 087	LH1
261 022	HS	261 055	AM	261 088	LH1
261 023	LH1	261 056	FMB	261 089	LH1
261 024	LH1	261 057	FMB	261 090	LH1
261 025	LH1	261 058	FMB	261 091	AM
261 026	LH1	261 059	FMB	261 092	AM
261 027	AM	261 060	LH1	261 093	LH1
261 028	AM	261 061	LH1	261 094	LH1
261 029	AM	261 062	LH1	261 095	LH1
261 030	AM	261 063	LH1	261 096	AM
261 031	FMB	261 064	LH1	261 097	AM
261 032	HS	261 065	LH1	261 098	AM
261 033	AM	261 066	LH1	261 099	AM
261 034	AM	261 067	AM	261 100	AM
261 035	AM	261 068	HS	261 101	EOB
261 036	AM	261 069	AM	261 102	EOB
261 037	AM	261 070	HS	261 103	AM
261 038	AM	261 071	HS	261 104	AM
261 039	FMB	261 072	HS	261 105	EOB
261 040	AM	261 073	HS	261 106	EOB
261 041	LH1	261 074	HS	261 107	EOB
261 042	LH1	261 075	HS	261 108	EOB
261 043	LH1	261 076	HS	261 109	EOB

CLASS 265 B-B

Yet another new class ordered by DB Schenker. This is the more powerful Gravita locomotive - the Gravita 15BB. The first ten locomotives were received at the beginning of 2013 and distributed around the system where no doubt they will start to replace Classes 225 and 232.

Built: 2012–13.
Builder: Voith Turbo Lokomotivtechnik GmbH & Co KG, Kiel.
Engine: MTU 12V4000R43.
Power: 1500 kW.
Transmission: Hydraulic, L5r4zseU2.
Maximum Tractive Effort: 317–330 kN.
Wheel Diameter: 1000 mm.
Train Heating: None.

Weight: 84–90 tonnes.
Length over Buffers: 16.90 m.
Maximum Speed: 100 km/h.

265 001	FMB	265 012		FMB	265 022
265 002	LH1	265 013			265 023
265 003	HS	265 014			265 024
265 004	EOB	265 015			265 025
265 005	FMB	265 016			265 026
265 006	EOB	265 017			265 027
265 007	HS	265 018			265 028
265 008	LH1	265 019			265 029
265 009	FMB	265 020			265 030
265 010	HS	265 021			265 031
265 011	EOB				

▲ 265 011 and 265 004 haul a train of steel slabs from Duisburg HKM (Hüttenwerke Krupp Mannesmann) to Hohenlimburg, seen here passing Oberhausen West, on 5 June 2013. **Matthias Müller**

CLASS 290   B-B

This is the heavy duty shunting and trip locomotive of the old DB. Since 1996 many have been converted to operate under remote radio control (Class 294) and thus can be driverless allowing the duties of shunter and driver to be combined. Some Class 290s are fitted with hump shunting radio control. This allows the hump tower to take control of the loco when hump shunting to allow better co-ordination between point setting and train movement. 290 625/26/77/90 at München Nord are such locos and these have been given altered liveries to denote this being fitted with yellow/black chevrons and flashing lights. However a further renumbering saw locomotives fitted with an MTU 8V 4000 R1 engine which is more efficient and meets modern emission standards etc. At the same time other improvements were made to enable these locomotives to last another 10–15 years. Upon completion the running number was increased by 500. Conversions from Class 290 to 294 recently stopped with the arrival of Class 261. Most early locomotives that have not been modernised are now in store or have been sold to private operators.

Built: 1964–74 for DB.
Builder: MaK/Jung/Deutz/Henschel.
Engine: MTU MB 16V 652 TA 10 (290.0) MTU 8V 4000 R1 (290.5).
Power: 820 kW (1100 hp).
Transmission: Hydraulic. Voith L206 rs.   **Weight:** 78.8(*77) tonnes.
Maximum Tractive Effort: 241 kN.   **Length over Buffers:** 14.32 (*14.00) m.
Wheel Diameter: 1100 mm.   **Maximum Speed:** 80 (*70) km/h.
Non-Standard Livery: N 290 371 is a designated museum locomotive and is in original purple red livery.

f funk = radio control for hump shunting.

No.		Livery	No.		Livery	No.		Livery
290 003	*	WRS (Z)	290 520		TK	290 570		LH1 (Z)
290 008	*	DZW (Z)	290 521		SSR (Z)	290 591		BSE
290 189	f	LH1 (Z)	290 522		AM	290 592		NN2 (Z)
290 371	N	LH1	290 524		WRS	290 621		NN2
290 504		WRS	290 525		DF	290 625	f	MH1 (Z)
290 505		LH1	290 526		DF	290 626	f	MH1
290 506	*	US (Z)	290 527		BSE	290 632		AM
290 507	*	LH1 (Z)	290 531		US (Z)	290 633		TK
290 509	*	KG (Z)	290 532		WRS	290 636		BSE
290 510		WRS	290 533		AM	290 637		LH1 (Z)
290 511	*	NN2	290 557		MIH	290 639		TK
290 512	*	US (Z)	290 561		WRS	290 641		NN2
290 513	*	US (Z)	290 562		BSE	290 677	f	MH1
290 514	*	NN2 (Z)	290 564		LH1 (Z)	290 678		NN2
290 515	*	US (Z)	290 565		BSE	290 679		NN2
290 516	*	AM (Z)	290 566		DF (Z)	290 688		MH1
290 517	*	DF (Z)	290 567		LH1 (Z)	290 690	f	MH1
290 519	*	NN2	290 569		AM			

CLASS 291   B-B

Slightly more powerful than the Class 290, most 291s operate at North Sea ports such as Bremen, Bremerhaven, Hamburg on freight tripping and shunting associated with the ports. Those rebuilt with remote radio controls are now Class 295. Most early locomotives that have not been modernised are now in store or have been sold to private operators.

Built: 1965–78 for DB.
Builder: MaK/Jung/Deutz/Henschel.
Engine: MTU MB 16V 652 TA 10.
Power: 820 kW (1100 hp).
Transmission: Hydraulic. Voith L26 rsb.   **Weight:** 78 tonnes.
Maximum Tractive Effort: 245 kN.   **Length over Buffers:** 14.00 m.
Wheel Diameter: 1100 mm.   **Maximum Speed:** 90 km/h.

No.	Livery	No.	Livery	No.	Livery
291 010	AM (Z)	291 034	AM (Z)	291 038	AM
291 011	WRS (Z)	291 035	WRS (Z)	291 901	WRS
291 032	AM (Z)	291 036	AM	291 902	WRS (Z)
291 033	AM	291 037	AM (Z)	291 903	WRS (Z)

CLASS 294 B-B

These locomotives are Class 290 fitted with remote radio controls. Many locomotives have been further modified with new MTU engines with 500 being added to the running number. All locos fitted with the radio controls have new automatic couplings. In 2000 ten locomotives were modified for multiple working at either end of a train via radio transmission. These locomotives become class 294.90x later being renumbered to 294.95x. For technical details see Class 290.

Class 294.0 Standard design.

294 154	EOB (Z)	294 634	LH1	294 703	KG
294 571	FMB	294 635	NN2	294 704	TK
294 572	HS	294 638	RHL	294 705	RM
294 573	RM	294 640	MIH	294 706	KG
294 574	HS	294 642	HB	294 707	EOB
294 575	MIH	294 643	FMB	294 708	MH1
294 576	LMR	294 644	FB	294 710	MH1
294 577	FB	294 645	LH1	294 711	FMB
294 578	FB	294 646	FMB	294 712	MIH
294 579	FB	294 647	NN2	294 713	EOB
294 580	NN2	294 648	NN2	294 714	HS
294 581	HS	294 649	EOB	294 715	KG
294 582	RO	294 650	NN2	294 716	TK
294 583	FMB	294 651	SSR	294 717	NN2
294 584	EHGV	294 653	LH1	294 718	EHGV
294 585	FMB	294 655	HS	294 719	KG
294 586	FMB	294 656	FB	294 720	KG
294 587	NN2	294 657	KG	294 721	TK
294 588	RO	294 658	SSR	294 722	EHGV
294 589	RM	294 659	FB	294 723	EHGV
294 590	HS	294 660	NN2 (Z)	294 724	HO
294 593	FMB	294 661	MH1	294 725	KG
294 594	RO	294 662	DZW	294 726	KG (Z)
294 595	RM	294 663	LH1	294 727	EOB
294 597	HS	294 664	TU	294 728	TK
294 598	NN2	294 665	FMB	294 729	NN2
294 599	NN2	294 667	EOB	294 730	RM
294 600	RO	294 668	LH1	294 731	EHGV
294 601	NN2	294 669	KG	294 732	RM
294 602	LMR	294 670	KG	294 733	SSR
294 603	HO	294 671	EHGV	294 734	MIH
294 604	EHGV	294 672	HB	294 735	FMB
294 605	HS	294 673	HO	294 736	FMB
294 606	MIH	294 674	EOB	294 737	FMB
294 607	FB	294 675	KG	294 738	LH1
294 608	FMB	294 676	NN2	294 739	FMB
294 609	TK	294 680	EHGV	294 740	RM
294 610	RO	294 681	TK	294 741	SSR
294 612	NN2	294 682	KG	294 742	EHGV
294 613	RM	294 683	RM	294 743	EHGV
294 614	EOB	294 684	FB	294 744	TK
294 615	DZW (Z)	294 685	NN2	294 745	NN2
294 616	RHL	294 686	FMB	294 746	RM
294 617	RHL	294 687	NN2	294 747	NN2
294 618	RHL	294 691	HO	294 748	LH1
294 619	NN2	294 692	KG	294 749	TK
294 620	TK	294 693	EOB	294 750	NN2
294 622	RO	294 694	EOB	294 751	RM
294 623	FB	294 695	MIH	294 752	RM
294 624	MMF	294 696	EHGV	294 753	NN2
294 628	FB	294 698	HB	294 754	US
294 629	RM	294 700	EOB	294 755	FB
294 630	EOB	294 701	MH1	294 756	FMB
294 631	SSR	294 702	LH1	294 757	RM

No.	Code	No.	Code	No.	Code
294 758	KG	294 809	MMF	294 857	EOB
294 759	TK	294 810	NN2	294 858	SSR
294 760	NN2	294 811	TK	294 859	FB
294 761	HB	294 812	RM	294 860	EOB
294 762	NN2	294 813	EHGV	294 861	EOB
294 763	RM	294 814	MIH	294 862	FMB
294 764	SSR	294 815	TK	294 863	TK
294 765	NN2	294 816	NN2	294 864	MIH
294 766	MH1	294 817	MH1	294 865	EHGV
294 767	MMF	294 818	FMB	294 866	EHGV
294 768	MH1	294 819	FB	294 867	MIH
294 769	EOB	294 820	LMR	294 868	RO
294 770	HO	294 821	SSR	294 869	RM
294 771	EHGV	294 822	FMB	294 870	HS
294 772	EHGV	294 823	SSR	294 872	FMB
294 773	EOB	294 824	TK	294 873	FB
294 774	HS	294 825	HB	294 874	EHGV
294 775	RM	294 826	MIH	294 875	SSR
294 776	RM	294 827	LH1	294 876	SSR
294 777	KG	294 828	FMB	294 877	RM
294 778	MIH	294 829	HS	294 878	HO
294 779	TK	294 830	EOB	294 879	HO
294 780	EHGV	294 831	EOB	294 880	KG
294 781	TK	294 832	KG	294 881	EOB
294 782	EOB	294 833	TK	294 882	EHGV
294 783	EHGV	294 834	TK	294 883	RM
294 785	EHGV	294 835	TK	294 885	RM
294 786	RO	294 836	MIH	294 886	EHGV
294 787	HO	294 837	FMB	294 887	MIH
294 788	TK	294 838	SSR	294 888	EOB
294 789	EOB	294 839	HO	294 889	DZW
294 790	KG (Z)	294 840	FMB	294 890	EOB
294 791	EOB	294 841	HS	294 891	EOB
294 792	EOB	294 842	TK	294 892	HS
294 793	EOB (Z)	294 843	RM	294 893	KG
294 794	EHGV	294 844	SSR	294 895	LH1
294 795	RM	294 845	KG	294 896	EOB
294 797	MIH	294 846	HS	294 897	EOB
294 798	EOB	294 847	EHGV	294 898	NN2
294 799	NN2	294 848	EOB	294 899	FMB
294 800	EHGV	294 849	MIH	294 901[II]	FMB
294 801	KG	294 850	EHGV	294 902[II]	NN2
294 802	FMB	294 851	TK	294 903[II]	EHGV
294 803	EOB	294 852	EOB	294 904[II]	MIH
294 804	MH1	294 853	EOB	294 905[II]	LH1
294 805	RM	294 854	SSR	294 906[II]	EOB
294 806	EOB	294 855	EOB	294 907[II]	DZW
294 807	KG	294 856	HB	294 908[II]	KG
294 808	FMB				

Class 294.9 Fitted with radio-controlled multiple working.

No.		Code	No.		Code
294 951	(294 197)	HS	294 956	(290 152)	HS
294 952	(294 296)	HS	294 957	(290 199)	HS
294 953	(290 209)	HS	294 958	(290 400)	HS
294 954	(290 394)	HS	294 959	(290 384)	HS
294 955	(290 111)	HS	294 960	(290 166)	HS

CLASS 295 — B-B

These are Class 291s fitted with the remote radio controls and automatic couplers. For technical details see Class 291.

295 001	HBH	295 049	HB	295 076	HO (Z)
295 002	HBH	295 050	HB (Z)	295 077	HB
295 003	HBH	295 051	HB	295 078	HS
295 004	HBH	295 052	HB	295 079	HB (Z)
295 005	HB	295 053	HBH (Z)	295 080	HB (Z)
295 006	HB	295 054	AM	295 082	HB (Z)
295 007	HB	295 055	HB (Z)	295 083	AM (Z)
295 012	AM	295 056	HB (Z)	295 085	HB (Z)
295 013	HO (Z)	295 058	HS	295 086	AM (Z)
295 016	AM	295 059	HB	295 087	AM
295 018	AM	295 060	AM (Z)	295 088	AM (Z)
295 019	AM	295 062	AM	295 089	HB
295 021	AM	295 063	AM (Z)	295 090	AM (Z)
295 022	HB	295 065	AM (Z)	295 091	HBH
295 023	AM	295 066	AM (Z)	295 092	HB
295 039	HBH (Z)	295 067	HB (Z)	295 093	HO
295 040	HB	295 068	AM (Z)	295 094	HB
295 041	HB	295 069	HB (Z)	295 095	HB (Z)
295 042	AM	295 070	AM (Z)	295 096	HO (Z)
295 043	HB	295 071	HB	295 097	HB
295 044	HB	295 072	HO (Z)	295 098	AM (Z)
295 046	AM (Z)	295 074	HB	295 099	AM (Z)
295 047	HBH (Z)	295 075	AM (Z)	295 100	HB

▲ 294-663 pauses between duties as yard pilot at Grosskorbetha on 1 July 2008.   **Brian Denton**

CLASS 296   B-B

These locomotives are former Class 290s fitted with remote control not only from staff nearby but full remote control from a hump tower in a manner similar to the 290s at München. However the 296s have new engines but were given a new class number rather than being in the 290.5 series.

296 023	HS	296 042	KG	296 052	KG
296 028	AM	296 043	RM	296 053	KG
296 029	HS	296 044	HS	296 054	HS
296 030	AM	296 045	EHGV	296 055	EHGV
296 034	RM	296 046	EHGV	296 056	RM
296 037	AM	296 047	AM	296 058	HS
296 038	RM	296 048	AM	296 059	KG
296 039	RM	296 049	HS	296 060	HS
296 040	KG	296 050	KG	296 063	RM
296 041	AM	296 051	KG	296 068	BSE

CLASS 298   B-B

This is the old DR equivalent of Classes 290/1. Many were built as heavy duty shunters (298.3 or V100.4) but others were converted from Class 201 (298.0–2). All have subsequently been fitted with remote radio controls but as the whole class was to be converted in a short period no renumbering took place. Automatic couplers were fitted when converted. The 298.0 are all now stored with many having gone to Stendal works for modernisation and sale to private operators. All 298.3 have been rebuilt with a Caterpillar engine.

Rebuilt: 1978 RAW Stendal.
Engine: 736 kW. (298.0), 773 kW Caterpillar AT DI –TA 3508 (298.3 except locos in "Z" status).
Transmission: Hydraulic.   **Former DR Class:** 108 (298.0–2), 111 (298.3).
Maximum Tractive Effort: **Weight:** 63.7 tonnes.
Wheel Diameter: 1000 mm.   **Length over Buffers:** 14.24 m.
Train Heating: None.   **Maximum Speed:** 60 km/h.

Class 298/0. Rebuilt from Class 201 keeping same serial number.

298 058	BSN (Z)	298 080	BSE (Z)	298 155	BSE (Z)
298 069	BSE (Z)	298 104	BSE (Z)		

Class 298/3. Rebuilt from Class 293, adding 300 to serial number.

298 301	BSN (Z)	298 315	BSE	298 327	BSE
298 302	BSE	298 316	BSE	298 328	BSE
298 303	BSE	298 317	BSE	298 329	BSE
298 304	BSN (Z)	298 318	WRS	298 330	BSE
298 305	LMR (Z)	298 319	BSE	298 331	BSE
298 306	WRS	298 320	BSE	298 332	LH1 (Z)
298 307	BSE	298 321	DF	298 333	LH1 (Z)
298 308	BSE	298 322	BSE	298 334	BSE
298 309	WRS	298 323	DF	298 335	BSE
298 310	BSE	298 324	LMR	298 336	BSE
298 312	WRS	298 325	BSE	298 337	BSE
298 313	BSE	298 326	DF		

3. DIESEL SHUNTING LOCOMOTIVES

3.1. STANDARD GAUGE

In this section the code 'D' denotes a locomotive in departmental use. (Shed and wagon pilots, DB Netz depot pilots etc.)

CLASS 310   B

These are the only survivors of the former DR Köf series having been retained as departmental shunters.

Built: 1933–34. for DR.
Builder: Orenstein & Koppel & BMAG.
Engine: 6KVD 145.   **Former DR Class:** 100
Power: 192 kW.   **Transmission:** Mechanical.
Non-Standard Livery: N 310 279 light blue, remainder black.

| 310 279 | **N** | D | UMX | | 310 631 | **N** | D | BRG | | 310 734 | **N** | | US |

CLASS 311   B

This class was the post war small shunting locomotive in East Germany. Just one locomotive of this class remains in departmental use at Meiningen works.

Built: 1962 for DR.
Builder: LKM.
Engine: 6KVD 18/15-1 SRW.   **Former DR Class:** 101.
Power: 132 kW.   **Transmission:** Hydraulic.
Non-Standard Livery: N light blue.

| 311 632 | **N** | D | UMX |

CLASS 312   B

Another former DR class with a slightly more powerful engine than Class 311. All those that remain are now in departmental use.

Built: 1967–71 for DR.
Builder: LKM.
Engine: 6KVD 18/15-1 SRW.   **Former DR Class:** 102.
Power: 162 kW.   **Transmission:** Hydraulic.

Class 312/0.

Maximum Tractive Effort: 80 kN.   **Weight:** 24 tonnes.
Wheel Diameter: 1000 mm.   **Maximum Speed:** 55 km/h.
Length over Buffers: 6.94 m.
Non-Standard Livery: N 312 021 Blue; 312 039 Red and white.

| 312 021 | **N** | D | BCS | | 312 039 | **N** | D | LL1 |

Class 312/1.

Maximum Tractive Effort: 71 kN.   **Weight:** 24.3 tonnes.
Wheel Diameter: 1000 mm.   **Maximum Speed:** 40 km/h.
Length over Buffers: 8.00 m.
Non-Standard Livery: N 312 139 light blue; 312 153/179 red with broad yellow bands; 312 244 orange.

| 312 139 | **N** | D | WWX | | 312 179 | **N** | D | WM | | 312 244 | **N** | D | LL1 |
| 312 153 | **N** | D | WM | | | | | |

CLASSES 322, 323 & 324   B

These are former DB Köf type shunters retained for departmental use.

Built: 1953–60 for DB.
Builder: Gmeinder/Jung.
Engine: Kaeble GN 130s / KHD A6M 517/617.
Power: 95 kW (128 hp).
Transmission: Hydraulic.   **Weight:** 16 tonnes.
Maximum Tractive Effort: 47 kN. **Length over Buffers:** 6.45 m.
Wheel Diameter: 850 mm.   **Maximum Speed:** 30 (322), 45 (323) km/h.
Non-Standard Livery: N All locomotives retain original DB red livery.

322 641	**N**	D	TU	323 627	**N**	D	EHGV	323 818	**N**	D	FMB
323 260	**N**		HHL	323 729	**N**	D	TK (Z)	324 023	**N**	D	HBX

▲ 335-113 takes a break from its duties as pilot at Mühldorf on 21 October 2010. The auto coupler fitted to this locomotive can clearly be seen between the buffers.   **Brian Denton**

CLASS 332 B

This class is the West German 1950s updated version of the pre-war Köf. Once totalling over 300 locos, those that remain are in departmental use whilst others have found further use with private operators.

Built: 1959–66 for DB.
Builder: Gmeinder/Jung/Orenstein & Koppel.
Engine: MWM RHS 518A/Kaeble MD 140.
Power: 179 kW (240 hp).
Transmission: Hydraulic. **Weight:** 20 tonnes.
Maximum Tractive Effort: 55 kN. **Length over Buffers:** 7.83 m.
Wheel Diameter: 950 mm. **Maximum Speed:** 45 km/h.
Non-Standard Livery: N 332 298 Turquoise and beige.

332 013	Y		MAOB	332 182			MAOB	332 259			MAOB
332 022		D	TU	332 199		D	MIH (Z)	332 260		D	STR
332 058		D	STMH	332 220		D	NN1	332 263		D	NN1
332 062			MAOB	332 221		D	MKP	332 281		D	EDO
332 064		D	ANX	332 245		D	NHO	332 294		D	EHGV
332 078				332 255		D	TS	332 298	N	D	TU
332 081		D	RM								

CLASSES 333 & 335 B

This is the West German 1960s version of the Köf. Class 335 are 333s converted to remote radio control and fitted with automatic couplers. With changing freight needs the radio control has been removed from some locos and these are now 333.5.

Built: 1967–78 for DB.
Builder: Gmeinder/Jung/Orenstein & Koppel.
Engine: MWM RHS 518A/Kaeble MD 140.
Power: 179 kW (240 hp).
Transmission: Hydraulic. **Weight:** 24 tonnes.
Maximum Tractive Effort: 80 kN. **Length over Buffers:** 7.83 m.
Wheel Diameter: 950 mm. **Maximum Speed:** 45 km/h
Non-Standard Livery: N 335 124/125/200/214 raspberry red and white; 335 128 turquoise and beige.

*   Modified front end appearance with circular fan visible.
AZ   DB Autozug.

333 104			AOP	335 082		D	EOB	335 133		*	LH1
333 117		D	MAOB	335 090			KG	335 134		D	SSR
333 145	Y		EDEF	335 103		*	STR	335 135		*D	FGM
335 006			WRS	333 104		D	AOH	335 136		*	AM
335 007			FK	335 105		*	KG	335 137		*	KG
335 009			FK	335 107		*	KG	335 138		*	KG
335 011			MH1	335 109		*	AM	335 140		*	RO (Z)
335 013			FK	335 111			ANX	335 141		*	NN2
335 024		D	DCX	335 112		*	MKP	335 142		*	RM
335 026		D	KG	335 113		D	MMF	335 144		*	KG
335 027			KG	335 114		D	LMR	335 150		*	STR
333 028		D	AOH	335 116		*	MKP	335 152		*	RM
335 029		D	RB	335 118		*	RO	335 153		*	WRS
335 030			FMB	335 120		*	AM	335 154		*	NN2
335 033			MIH (Z)	335 121		*	RO	335 155		*	MIH
335 036			KG	335 122		*	RO	335 156		*	NN2
333 045		D	STMI	335 124	N	*	MKP	335 157		*	STR (Z)
335 047		D	WRS	335 125	N	*	TK	335 160		*	EOB
335 054		D	MIH (Z)	335 126		D	HBR	335 161		D	LDX
335 066		D	MH1	335 128	N	*	LH1	335 163			KG
335 072		D	BCSX	335 129		*	AM	335 164		*	RO
335 079			EOB	335 131		*	TK	335 167		D	SSR

335 175		D	BSE	335 227	D	HS	333 570	D	NN2
335 177		*	RM	335 228	D	AHBIU	333 647	D	RM
335 185		D	KG	335 229	D	BSE	333 649	*	KG
335 186		D	HBR	335 232	D	HBR	333 651	D	RO
335 200	N	*D	FGM	335 234	D	AM	333 668	D	RO
335 207		D	WM	335 236	D	KG	333 669	D	BCS
335 210		D	AM	335 238	D	Lohnde	333 670	D	WR
335 213		D	HS	335 244	D	HO	333 671	D	BCSX
335 214	N	AZ	BSE (Z)	335 248	D	HS	333 673	D	BCS
335 220			EDEF	335 249	D	LH1	333 676	D	NNX
335 221		D	MKP	335 251	D	HBR	333 679	*	EOB (Z)
335 224		D	RM	333 525	D	LOHNDE			

CLASSES 345 & 346   **D**

These classes were the standard DR shunting locomotive. When more than 1000 Class 346 were built the number series then went to Class 345. The remaining examples with DB are in departmental use. 346 995 is DB Autozug pilot at Berlin Warsehauerstrasse.

Built: 1959–82 for DR.
Builder: LKM.
Engine: 12KVD21SVW of 478 kW.
Transmission: Hydraulic.
Maximum Tractive Effort: 175 kN (198 kN 346 201–999).
Wheel Diameter: 1100 mm.
Length over Buffers: 10.88 m.

Former DR Class: 105 & 106.
Weight: 55 tonnes. (60 tonnes 346 201–999).
Maximum Speed: 60 km/h.

345 021	Y		EDEF	346 811	Y	D	WRS	346 995	Y	AZ	BSE
346 464	Y	D	LE								

▲ 362 904 is busy on shunting duties at München Hauptbahnhof on 23 September 2012.
Matthias Müller

CLASS 347

D

These are Class 345 and 346 locomotives converted to 5 foot gauge for working at the train ferry berth at Sassnitz-Mukran.

| 347 036 | WRS (Z) | 347 140 | WRS (Z) | 347 141 | WRS (Z) |

CLASSES 362 & 364

C

Formerly Class 260, Class 360 was adopted when the locomotives were downgraded to shunting tractors. Along came radio controls so another new class number 364 was allocated. Class 362 is the last reclassification when the locomotives were fitted with Caterpillar engines.

Built: 1956–61 for DB.
Builder: Krupp/MaK/Jung/Krauss-Maffei/Deutz/Henschel/Esslingen/Gmeinder.
Engine: MTU GTO6/GTO6A/MB 12V 493 AZ (Class 364), Caterpillar 3412 E D1-TTA (Class 362).
Power: 485 kW (650 hp). **Weight:** 48–49.5 tonnes.
Transmission: Hydraulic. Voith L27z Ub/L37z Ub/L217.
Maximum Tractive Effort: 122 kN. **Length over Buffers:** 10.45 m.
Wheel Diameter: 1250 mm. **Maximum Speed:** 60 km/h.
Non-Standard Livery: N 364 533/858 purple red; 364 776 turquoise and beige.

362 362			LH1	362 560		FMB	362 805		AM
363 378		·	DF	362 564		SSH	362 845		MIH
362 382			MMF	362 568		LH1	362 849		NN2
362 385			TK	362 571		DF	362 852		HB
362 388			DF	362 574		AM	362 853		LH1
362 389			AM	362 582		EOB	362 855		DF
362 390		D	EOB	362 587		LH1	362 856		LH1
362 391			LH1	362 589		SSR	364 858	N	TU
362 400			MIH	362 592		TK	362 863		BSE
362 401			BSN (Z)	362 594		WRS	362 872		MIH
362 406			LH1	362 596		DF	362 873		MIH
362 410			BSE (Z)	362 597		HS	362 875		MIH
362 412			FK (Z)	362 598		NN2	362 878		RM
362 415			KG	362 600		DF	362 888		MIH
362 419			HS	362 605		HB	362 892		AM
362 423			BSE	362 612		DF	362 896		WRS
362 427			MIH (Z)	362 614		DF	362 900		WRS
364 447		D	SSR	362 748		AM (Z)	362 903		LH1
362 448			HS	362 754		EOB (Z)	362 904		MIH
362 502		D	SSR	362 755		WRS (Z)	364 906		FB (Z)
362 509			DF	362 756		MH1	362 910		HS (Z)
362 510			TK	362 757		WRS	362 911		DF (Z)
362 517			DF	362 761		NN2 (Z)	362 916	D	BSE
362 523			AM	362 766		EOB (Z)	362 919		WRS (Z)
362 526			BSE (Z)	364 767	D	RM	362 921		LH1
364 533	N		TU	362 768		MMF	362 926		LH1
362 538			DF	362 769		AM	362 937		DF (Z)
362 540			KG	364 776	N D	MMF	362 938		LH1
362 544			FMB (Z)	364 779		RO (Z)	362 939		KG
362 547			KG	362 780		BSE	362 940		BSE
362 550			MIH (Z)	362 791		BSE	362 941		BSE
362 551			DF	362 797		AM	362 942		EOB
362 558			NN2	362 799		AM (Z)	362 943		LH1
362 559			AM						

CLASSES 363 & 365 C

A modified Class 360 for use in areas where heavy trains are found (steel, coal etc). These locos are ballasted to give greater adhesion for shunting these heavy trains. Reclassified 365 when radio controls were fitted and another class number (363) was given when Caterpillar engines were fitted.

Built: 1955–64 for DB.
Builder: Krupp/MaK/Henschel/Krauss-Maffei/Esslingen.
Engine: MTU GTO6/GTO6A (Class 365), Caterpillar 3412 E D1-TTA (Class 363).
Power: 485 kW (650 hp). **Weight:** 53 tonnes.
Transmission: Hydraulic. Volith L27z Ub/L37z Ub/L217.
Maximum Tractive Effort: 138 kN. **Length over Buffers:** 10.45 m.
Wheel Diameter: 1250 mm. **Maximum Speed:** 60 km/h.
Non-Standard Livery: N 365 143 Turquoise and beige.

363 036		MIH	363 172		RM	363 440	LH1
363 042		BSE	363 176		MMF	363 441	KG
363 044		RM	363 177		NN2 (Z)	363 444	EHGV
363 103		TK	363 178		EHGV	363 445	KG
365 104		MIH	363 179		MH1	363 446	BSE
363 105		MIH (Z)	363 182		HS	363 622	AM
363 106		DF	363 185		HB	363 625	TK
363 107		MMF (Z)	363 186		TK (Z)	363 626	HB
363 110		TK	363 187		TK	363 628	RHL
363 111		HS	363 188		DF	363 631	LH1
363 112		TK	363 189		KG	363 632	AM (Z)
363 113		SSR	363 190		NN2	363 635	AM
363 114		LH1	363 191		EHGV	363 649	RM
363 115		FMB	363 192		NN2	363 650	AM
363 116		FMB	363 193		TK	363 651	KG
363 117		RM	363 194		RHL	363 652	EHGV
363 118		MH1	363 195		NN2	363 654	MH1
363 121		DF (Z)	363 196		TK (Z)	363 655	LH1
363 122		TK	363 198		TK	363 658	RM
363 124		BSE	363 199		NN2	363 660	EOB
363 128		MH1	363 200		FMB (Z)	363 662	SSR
363 132		BSE	363 201		BSE	363 664	BSE
363 133		MH1	363 205		TK	363 665	MH1
363 134		HS (Z)	363 206		EOB	363 669	MH1
363 135		MH1	363 207		NRH (Z)	363 676	AM
363 136		BSE	363 209		RM	363 677	LH1
363 137		KG	363 210		EOB	363 678	MMF
363 139		TK	363 211		FMB	363 679	FMB
363 141		TK	363 212		NN2 (Z)	363 680	SSR (Z)
365 143	N	TU	363 215		AM	363 681	TK
363 146		HS	363 216		AM	363 682	AM (Z)
363 147		EOB	363 218		FMB	365 683	TU
363 149		LH1	363 219		FMB	363 684	HB (Z)
363 150		TK	363 220		RM	363 685	TK (Z)
363 151		LH1	363 223		HB	363 686	LH1
363 152		RM (Z)	363 224		EHGV	363 691	EHGV
363 153		SSR	363 230		MH1	363 692	TK
363 154		SSR	363 231		MIH	363 696	LH1
363 155		MH1 (Z)	363 235		DF	363 699	FMB
363 156		DZW	363 238		DF	363 701	FMB
363 160		HB	363 240		SSR	363 702	EOB
363 163		BSE	363 241		MH1	363 703	LH1
363 165		BSN	363 424		LH1	363 704	MH1
363 166		NN2	363 425		AM	363 706	MH1
363 167		TK	363 436		TK	363 707	FMB
363 168		NN2 (Z)	363 437		MIH	363 708	MH1
363 169		RM	363 438		HE (Z)	363 709	AM (Z)
363 171		FMB (Z)	363 439		MH1	363 710	MH1

363 711	MH1	363 810	AM	363 826		FMB	
363 713	MH1	363 811	BSE	363 827		MH1	
363 719	TK	363 814	NN2	363 829		FMB	
363 720	KG	363 816	BSE	363 830		AM	
363 722	RM	363 817	AM	363 831		TK	
363 724	HS	363 819	MH1	363 832		FMB	
363 726	AM	363 820	EHGV	363 834		AM	
363 736	AM (Z)	363 821	BSE	363 836	D	MKP	
363 737	LH1	363 823	FMB (Z)	363 837		FMB (Z)	
363 739	EOB	363 824	EHGV	363 840		MH1	
363 809	AM						

CLASS 381   Bo

These battery electric shunting locomotives were all withdrawn from capital stock but remain in departmental use.

Built: 1936–38.
Builder Mechanical Parts: Windhoff.
Builder Electrical Parts: AEG/Siemens.
Length over Buffers: 6.45 m.

381 005	D	KK2	381 018	D	LDX	381 020	D	FMB

▲ Class 363 is a modified Class 360, now fitted with a Caterpillar engine. 363 182 is seen at Seelze depot on 30 September 2011.
David Hunt

CLASS 382   Bo

This battery electric shunting engine is used on the Hamburg S-Bahn as a depot shunter.

Built: 1953 for DB.
Builder Mechanical Parts: Gmeinder.
Builder Electrical Parts: Kiepe.
Length over Buffers: 6.43 m.
Weight: 21 tonnes.
Maximum Speed: 30km/h.

382 001   D   AOH

3.2. NARROW GAUGE

The island of Wangerooge has a narrow gauge railway which was part of the old DB and surprisingly has never been privatised as were lines in the East after unification. It now comes under DB Fernverkehr! (Being the successor to the old Reise & Touristik).

399 105/6   C

Since unification, many industries in the former DDR have closed down and consequently many former industrial locomotives have come on the market. DB acquired these two from a steelworks in Helbra. They were built in Romania and are the manufacturer's type L18H.

Built: 1989.
Builder: U23A.
Engine: D2156HMN8 (MAN design built under licence).
Power: 132 kW (180 hp).   **Gauge:** 1000 mm.
Transmission: Hydraulic.   **Weight:** 16.5 tonnes.
Maximum Tractive Effort: 50 kN.   **Length over Buffers:** 5.40 m.
Wheel Diameter: **Maximum Speed:** 28 km/h.

399 105-6   HWG | 399 106-4   HWG

399 107/8   C

These two new locomotives for the DB metre gauge line allowed older locos 399 101–104 to be withdrawn.

Built: 1999.
Builder: Schöma (Type CFL 150 DCL).
Engine: KHD BF6M1013CP.
Power: 166 kW.   **Gauge:** 1000 mm.
Transmission: Hydraulic.   **Weight:** 16 tonnes.
Maximum Tractive Effort: 50 kN   **Length over Buffers:** 6.597 m.
Wheel Diameter: **Maximum Speed:** 20 km/h.

399 107-2   HWG | 399 108-0   HWG

4. INTER-CITY EXPRESS (ICE)

The Inter City Express was introduced in 1989 when the first ICE1 sets were built following some years of running a prototype train. These followed high speed train practice in Europe by have powerful locomotives either end of a rake of carriages. ICE2 was different being a half set with a driving trailer at one end. The next version was supposed to be ICE2-2 but in fact came out as a completely different train, ICE3, which had powered axles throughout the train and was a true EMU. It was produced in various versions – 403, 406, 411 and 415 (q.v.). Now Class 407 is about to appear and after that an ICx is being prepared which will be an ICE platform with many different train formations. On 09/07/2008 an ICE3 derailed at Köln Hbf caused by a defective axle. The problems with wheels and axles caused examinations at depots to be at more frequent intervals resulting in more units under maintenance than plans allowed. New axles and wheels are now being provided which hopefully will bring back some sort of normality.

The Principal ICE Routes are shown below together with the usual type used on that route. In each case only the core route is shown. Route 20 trains from Hamburg may start back from Kiel whilst at the other end of the route at Basel some may run through to Interlaken etc.

ICE 10	Berlin Ostbhf – Hamm – Düsseldorf/Köln	ICE 2
ICE 11	Berlin Ostbhf – Braunschweig – Kassel – Frankfurt/M – Stuttgart – München	ICE 1
ICE 12	Berlin Ostbhf – Braunschweig – Kassel – Frankfurt/M – Basel	ICE 1
ICE 20	Hamburg Altona – Kassel – Frankfurt/M – Basel	ICE 1
ICE 22	Hamburg Altona – Kassel – Frankfurt/M – Stuttgart	ICE 1
ICE 25	Hamburg Altona/Bremen – Hannover - Kassel – Würzburg – Nürnberg – München	ICE 1 & 2
ICE 28	Hamburg Altona – Berlin – Leipzig – Nürnberg – München	ICE T
ICE 31	Hamburg Altona – Ruhr – Köln – Koblenz – Frankfurt/M	ICE 1
ICE 41	Essen – Köln – Frankfurt/M – Würzburg – Nürnberg – München	ICE 3
ICE 42	Dortmund – Köln – Frankfurt/M – Stuttgart – München	ICE 3
ICE 43	Dortmund – Köln – Frankfurt/M – Basel	ICE 3
ICE 45	Köln – Wiesbaden – Mannheim – Stuttgart	ICE 3
ICE 49	Köln – Frankfurt/M	ICE 3
ICE 50	Dresden – Leipzig – Frankfurt/M – Wiesbaden	ICE T
ICE 75	Berlin – Hamburg – København	ICE TD
ICE 76	Berlin – Hamburg – Århus	ICE TD
ICE 78	Frankfurt/M – Köln – Oberhausen – Amsterdam	ICE 3M
ICE 79	Frankfurt/M – Köln – Brussels	ICE 3M
ICE 82	Frankfurt/M – Saarbrücken – Paris	ICE 3M
ICE 91	Frankfurt/M – Nürnberg – Wien	ICE T

CLASS 401   ICE1

Originally each train had a power car on each end with a variable number of trailers in between. With the introduction of the other types of ICEs the trailers on Class 401 sets have now been standardised with 12 trailers being the norm. In 2005 the mid-life refurbishment started or as DB calls it "Redesign". Each set was internally stripped of seats and fittings at the Hamburg base. The trains were then sent to Nürnberg works for their "redesign". Apart from new fittings the major change has seen a first class carriage altered to second class (Class 802.7) and the second class seats in the service car have been altered to first class and the carriage relocated in the train. All vehicles have had their generous seat pitch reduced so that five extra seats have been added to first class vehicles and eight to the second class ones. Electrical equipment on the power cars has been improved and new bogie frames provided. Braking and air conditioning have been thoroughly overhauled. Laptop points have been provided. The telephone compartments have been removed in this age of the mobile telephone. After the reformations caused by all this work it was thought the sets would be stable, but there continue to be alterations but surprisingly not with the sets that work into Switzerland. The formations shown were as reported towards the end of 2012 when no doubt the end of year peak needed as many trains in service as possible.

The terrible accident at Eschede saw set 51 mostly destroyed. 401 020 was written off after fire damage and was replaced by 401 019 which in turn was later replaced by the spare power car from set 51 (401 051). 401 573 is in effect now a new vehicle; having been damaged it received parts from withdrawn vehicles including 401 551. The aftermath of the Eschede accident saw all sets have their set numbers stencilled above all the bogies.

The use of ICE1 sets has changed little since introduction. Their base remains at Hamburg and their main route is still over the North–South high speed line. Sets 62–71 were cleared for working in Austria; it is not clear whether this now applies following refurbishment. Sets 72–90 are cleared for working in Switzerland. The class is not allowed on the Köln–Frankfurt/M high speed line.

POWER CARS:

Built: 1989–93.
Builder–Mech. Parts: Krauss-Maffei, Krupp, Thyssen-Henschel.
Builder–Elec. Parts: ABB, AEG, Siemens.
Wheel Arrangement: Bo-Bo.
Control System: Thyristor with oil-cooled rectifiers (sets 1–20), GTO thyristor (sets 52–90).
Maximum Rating: 4800 kW (6400 hp).
Weight: 80 tonnes (Sets 1–20), 77 tonnes (Sets 52–90).
Traction Motors: Three-phase asynchronous motors as on Class 120.
Length over Couplers: 20.56 m.
Max. Speed: 280 km/h.
Livery: White with red stripe.

TRAILER CARS:

Length over Couplers: 26.40 m.

▲ Now over 20 years old but still synonymous with premium high speed services in Germany, ICE 1 set number 16 passes underneath rather a threatening sky at Bornheim between Bonn and Köln on 11 April 2012. **Matthias Müller**

CLASS 801.0. A (TFso).

Builders: Duewag, Waggon-Union, ABB/Henschel.
Weight: 52 tonnes.   **Accommodation:** 56/– 1T.

CLASS 801.4. A (TFso).

Builders: Duewag, Waggon-Union, ABB/Henschel.
Weight: 52 tonnes.   **Accommodation:** 56/– 1T.

CLASS 801.8. A (TFso).

Builders: Waggon-Union, ABB/Henschel.
Weight: 52 tonnes.   **Accommodation:** 56/– 1T.

CLASS 802.0. B (TSso).

Builders: Duewag, LHB.
Weight: 53 tonnes.   **Accommodation:** –/71 2T.

CLASS 802.3. B (TSso).

Builders: Duewag, LHB, MBB, MAN.
Weight: 53 tonnes.   **Accommodation:** –/71 2T.

CLASS 802.6. B (TSso).

Builders: MBB, MAN.
Weight: 53 tonnes.   **Accommodation:** –/71 2T.

CLASS 802.7. B (TSso).

Rebuilt from Class 801.4 carriages.

Builders: Duewag, Waggon-Union, ABB/Henschel. Rebuilt at Nürnberg works.
Weight: 53 tonnes.   **Accommodation:** –/71 1T

CLASS 802.8. B (TSso).

Builders: MBB, MAN.
Weight: 53 tonnes.   **Accommodation:** –/71 2T.

CLASS 802.9. B (TSso).

26 extra vehicles built as part of ICE2 order as there were insufficient second class carriages.

Built: 1996–97.
Builders:
Weight: 53 tonnes.   **Accommodation:** –/74 2T

CLASS 803.1. B (TSO) with special facilities (Service car).

Builders: Duewag.
Weight: 53 tonnes.
Accommodation: 36/– 1TD, conference room and conductor's compartment.

CLASS 804. Bord Restaurant. These cars have a restaurant, a kitchen, a bar and bar seating. They are noticeable by their raised roofs, a design feature which has not been perpetuated in future builds.

Builders: Waggon-Union, ABB/Henschel.
Weight: 56 tonnes.   **Accommodation:** 24 restaurant + 16 bar.

For formations, see pages 84–85.

Spare cars:

401 011   401 055   401 057   401 061   401 516
801 007   801 069   801 070   801 833   801 840
802 011   802 076   802 098   802 626   802 828   802 836   802 906   802 915
803 139
804 026   804 034   804 037

Names:

These are carried on the side of the trailer car nearest to the locomotive; consequently the names are shown against the set numbers.

01	Giessen	56	Freilassing
02	Flensburg	57	Landshut
04	Mühldorf a. Inn	58	Gütersloh
05	Offenbach am Main	59	Bad Oldesloh
06	Plattling	60	Mühlheim (Ruhr)
07	Freilassing	61	Bebra
08	Lichtenfels	62	Geisenheim/Rheingau
09	Aschaffenburg	67	Garmisch Partenkirchen
10	Gelsenkirchen	68	Crailsheim
11	Nürnberg	69	Worms
12	Memmingen	73	Trimmerdorfer Strand
13	Frankenthal (Pfalz)	74	Zürich
14	Friedrichshafen	76	Bremen
15	Regensburg	77	Basel
16	Pforzheim	78	Bremerhaven
17	Itzehoe	80	Castrop-Rauxel
19	Osnabrück	84	Bruchsal
20	Lüneburg	85	Hildesheim
52	Hanau	87	Fulda
53	Neumünster	88	Rüdesheim am Rhein
54	Heppenheim an der Bergstrasse	90	Ludwigshafen am Rhein
55	Rosenheim		

▲ ICE3 set number 354, headed by 403 054, stands at Köln Hauptbahnhof on 30 June 2010.

Keith Fender

01	401 001	802 031	802 631	802 411	802 053	802 058	802 703	802 393	804 027
02	401 002	802 844	802 653	802 412	802 092	802 093	802 714	802 008	804 013
03	401 003	802 860	802 627	802 372	802 027	802 063	802 901	802 057	804 046
04	401 004	802 843	802 617	802 317	802 318	802 341	802 918	802 039	804 004
05	401 005	802 815	802 612	802 361	802 368	802 375	802 902	802 040	804 016
06	401 006	802 806	802 602	802 329	802 309	802 036	802 718	802 807	804 039
07	401 007	802 816	802 610	802 327	802 326	802 383	802 701	802 316	803 128
08	401 008	802 813	802 618	802 449	802 380	802 051	802 052	802 071	804 028
09	401 009	802 614	802 315	802 306	802 379	802 307	802 022	802 044	804 012
10	401 010	802 328	802 624	802 047	802 055	802 046	802 922	802 333	804 042
11									
12	401 012	802 810	802 606	802 301	802 304	802 026	802 909	802 365	804 018
13	401 013	802 804	802 605	802 371	802 322	802 430	802 343	802 384	804 014
14	401 014	802 803	802 603	802 369	802 360	802 342	802 029	802 034	804 001
15	401 015	802 834	802 629	802 350	802 007	802 012	802 917	802 817	804 015
16	401 016	802 382	802 370	802 064	802 325	802 394	802 914	802 408	804 011
17	401 017	802 835	802 635	802 351	802 010	802 420	802 921	802 042	804 017
18	401 018	802 809	802 611	802 312	802 109	802 035	802 313	802 033	804 020
19	401 051	802 811	802 615	802 314	802 363	802 023	802 016	802 321	804 036
20	401 019	802 859	802 634	802 366	802 396	802 074	802 908	802 024	804 003
51									
52	401 052	802 852	802 620	802 395	802 337	802 336	802 903	802 072	804 038
53	401 053	802 818	802 623	802 075	802 407	802 401	802 070	802 073	804 029
54	401 054	802 824	802 616	802 378	802 305	802 302	802 367	802 406	804 049
55		802 830	802 632	802 303	802 335	802 320	802 926	802 066	804 033
56	401 056	802 826	802 607	802 364	802 377	802 362	802 025	802 049	804 006
57	401 555	802 825	802 644	802 416	802 451	802 415	802 005	802 402	806 043
58	401 058	802 814	802 619	802 381	802 608	802 458	802 919	802 827	804 007
59	401 059	802 838	802 640	802 400	802 018	802 445	802 920	802 021	804 035
60	401 060	802 801	802 625	802 334	802 065	802 056	802 911	802 387	804 005
61	401 511	802 832	802 630	802 398	802 399	802 003	802 002	802 001	804 031
62	401 062	802 850	802 628	802 339	802 338	802 094		802 015	804 047
63	401 063	802 819	802 601	802 389	802 388	802 332	802 904	802 062	804 024
64	401 064	802 831	802 643	802 349	802 385	802 006	802 913	802 347	804 030
65	401 065	802 802	802 631	802 085	802 077	802 078	802 910	802 020	804 025
66	401 066	802 833	802 637	802 324	802 356	802 355	802 916	802 354	802 022
67	401 067	802 840	802 633	802 081	802 082	802 080	802 905	802 344	804 040
68	401 068	802 841	802 638	802 410	802 049	802 083	802 925	802 084	804 019
69	402 045	802 821	802 604	802 391	802 392	802 004	802 068	802 086	804 023
70	401 070	802 842	802 642	802 433	802 067	802 038	802 924	802 087	804 041
71	401 071	802 823	802 641	802 359	802 079	802 017	802 345	802 028	
72	401 072	802 856	802 622	802 386	802 330	802 060	802 059	802 331	804 021
73	401 073	802 829	802 645	802 447	802 413	802 358	802 712	802 353	804 044
74	401 074	802 845	802 654	802 434	802 454	802 437	802 709	802 050	804 054
75	401 075	802 846	802 647	802 421	802 405	802 422	802 923	802 425	804 008
76	401 076	802 849	802 648	802 424	802 423	802 450	802 707	802 308	804 048
77	401 077	802 839	802 650	802 428	802 089	802 429	802 706	802 048	804 050
78	401 078	802 812	802 652	802 432	802 431	802 091	802 715	802 414	804 052
79	401 079	802 848	802 659	802 442	802 443	802 444	802 710	802 069	804 059
80	401 080	802 822	802 636	802 009	802 346	802 097	802 711	802 061	804 032
81	401 081	802 847	802 646	802 448	802 419	802 417	802 907	802 310	804 045
82	401 082	802 858	802 660	802 457	802 323	802 041	802 716	802 446	804 060
83	401 083	802 853	802 651	802 453	802 404	802 090	802 702	802 032	804 002
84	401 084	802 855	802 657	802 348	802 352	802 438	802 704	802 390	804 051
85	401 085	802 851	802 613	802 319	802 376	802 397	802 043	802 452	804 009
86	401 086	802 820	802 656	802 455	802 439	802 096	802 912	802 013	804 057
87	401 087	802 805	802 658	802 440	802 456	802 441	802 705	802 030	804 055
88	401 088	802 854	802 655	802 435	802 436	802 095	802 717	802 054	804 056
89	401 089	802 857	802 649	802 426	802 088	802 427	802 713	802 045	804 053
90	401 090	802 837	802 639	802 418	802 357	802 014	802 708	802 403	804 058

803 101	801 096	801 434	801 834	401 501	I	AH1
803 157	801 427	801 428	801 852	401 502	I	AH1
803 121	801 410	801 012	801 817	401 503	I	AH1
803 115	801 018	801 412	801 812	401 504	I	AH1
803 109	801 019	801 017	801 820	401 505	I	AH1
803 117	801 027	801 436	801 843	401 506	I	AH1
801 049	801 050	801 805	401 507		I	AH1
803 129	801 052	801 051	801 803	401 508	I	AH1
803 104	801 031	801 001	801 809	401 509	I	AH1
803 123	801 002	801 037	801 824	401 510	I	AH1
803 119	801 030	801 036	801 821	401 512	I	AH1
803 120	801 035	801 034	801 819	401 513	I	AH1
803 106	801 011	801 005	801 802	401 514	I	AH1
803 138	801 405	801 414	801 836	401 515	I	AH1
803 102	801 013	801 409	801 805	401 069	I	AH1
803 105	801 061	801 087	801 801	401 517	I	AH1
803 110	801 010	801 055	801 807	401 518	I	AH1
803 113	801 023	801 058	801 811	401 519	I	AH1
803 107	801 004	801 033	801 816	401 520	I	AH1
803 116	801 026	801 029	801 814	401 552	I	AH1
803 134	801 072	801 059	801 832	401 001	I	AH1
803 114	801 025	801 032	801 818	401 554	I	AH1
803 133		801 403			I	AH1
803 103	801 003	801 401	801 813	401 556	I	AH1
803 143	801 435	801 022	801 837	401 557	I	AH1
803 125	801 047	801 046	801 826	401 558	I	AH1
803 137	801 008	801 076	801 838	401 559	I	AH1
803 124	801 044	801 043	801 825	401 560	I	AH1
803 135	801 063	801 064	801 830	401 561	I	AH1
803 112	801 065	801 067	801 804	401 562	I	AH1
803 136	801 073	801 074	801 839	401 563	I	AH1
803 130	801 068	801 423	801 857	401 564	I	AH1
803 131	801 066	801 028	801 831	401 565	I	AH1
803 122	801 040	801 041	801 823	401 566	I	AH1
803 141	801 080	801 079	801 841	401 567	I	AH1
803 132	801 062	801 082	801 828	401 568	I	AH1
803 126	801 042	801 048	801 827	401 569	I	AH1
803 142	801 095	801 433	801 842	401 570	I	AH1
803 140	801 078	801 077	801 835	401 571	I	AH1
803 118	801 038	801 039	801 822	401 572	I	AH1
803 144	801 071	801 094	801 844	401 573	I	AH1
803 146	801 093	801 429	801 853	401 574	I	AH1
803 148	801 098	801 438	801 846	401 575	I	AH1
803 149	801 408	801 024	801 847	401 576	I	AH1
803 151	801 425	801 086	801 849	401 577	I	AH1
803 154	801 092	801 091	801 851	401 578	I	AH1
803 155	801 085	801 407	801 858	401 579	I	AH1
803 159	801 056	801 411	801 810	401 580	I	AH1
803 145	801 084	801 083	801 845	401 581	I	AH1
803 160	801 053	801 054	801 860	401 582	I	AH1
803 152	801 090	801 417	801 850	401 583	I	AH1
803 156	801 057	801 006	801 856	401 584	I	AH1
803 111	801 020	801 016	801 808	401 585	I	AH1
803 153	801 060	801 081	801 855	401 586	I	AH1
803 147	801 045	801 015	801 829	401 587	I	AH1
803 158	801 431	801 430	801 854	401 588	I	AH1
803 150	801 089	801 088	801 848	401 589	I	AH1
803 127	801 075	801 416	801 859	401 590	I	AH1

CLASS 402 ICE2

As already stated these trains are formed as half sets with a power car at one end being matched by a driving trailer at the other end. Two units in multiple form a "full-train". To ease coupling arrangements at stations the trains are fitted with Scharfenberg couplers. When introduced the units were allocated to and commissioned at a new ICE depot alongside MH1 depot but given a separate identity – München Süd with the adjoining depot becoming München West. In June 2000 all these units were transferred to a new depot in Berlin from where most trains then operated. They work from Berlin to the Ruhr area and Köln splitting at Hamm with a portion going via Essen to Düsseldorf and another going via Wuppertal to Köln and Bonn. Trains from Hamburg and Bremen combine in Hannover and then go on to Kassel, Würzburg and München.

After the refurbishment of the ICE1 trains the ICE2 trains were taken in to Nürnberg works for similar treatment. The train formations remain the same. The children's play area has been reduced and a cloakroom area replaced by seating allowing an extra 13 second class seats per set, but the data that follows is that prior to refurbishment.

POWER CARS:

Built: 1996–97.
Builder–Mech. Parts: Krauss Maffei, SFT Krupp.
Builder–Elec. Parts: Siemens.
Wheel Arrangement: Bo-Bo.
Continuous Rating: 4800 kW.
Maximum Tractive Effort: 300 kN.
Wheel Diameter: 1250 mm.
Length over Couplers: 20.56 m.

Weight: 78 tonnes.
Maximum Speed: 300 km/h.

TRAILER CARS

Length over Couplers: 26.40 m.

Class 805.0. A (FO).

Builders: DWA, LHB.
Weight: 45 tonnes.
Accommodation: 52/– 1T.

Class 805.3. A (FO).

Builder: MAN.
Weight: 45 tonnes.
Accommodation: 53/– 2T.

Class 806.0. B (TSO).

Builder: Duewag.
Weight: 46 tonnes.
Accommodation: –/63 2T 1W + children's area.

Class 806.3. B (TSO).

Builder: Duewag.
Weight: 46 tonnes.
Accommodation: –/74 2T.

Class 806.6. B (TSO).

Builders: Duewag/LHB.
Weight: 46 tonnes.
Accommodation: –/74 2T.

Class 807. WR (RU) Restaurant car with conductor's compartment.

Builder: LHB.
Weight: 51 tonnes.
Accommodation: 23 chairs, conductor's office 1TD.

Class 808. B (DTSO) Driving trailer second.

Builders: MAN/Adtranz.
Weight: 53 tonnes.
Accommodation: –/52 1T.

201	402 001	805 306	805 004	807 020	806 024	806 310	806 620	808 001	I	BRG
202	402 002	805 314	805 001	807 016	806 028	806 303	806 635	808 002	I	BRG
203	402 003	805 304	805 006	807 025	806 026	806 306	806 639	808 003	I	BRG
204	402 004	805 340	805 032	807 004	806 038	806 307	806 638	808 004	I	BRG
205	402 005	805 331	805 033	807 033	806 029	806 333	806 602	808 005	I	BRG
206	402 046	805 311	805 011	807 017	806 013	806 319	806 604	808 006	I	BRG

207	402 007	805 302	805 041	807 018	806 018	806 318	806 644	808 007	I	BRG
208	402 008	805 308	805 008	807 005	806 011	806 311	806 641	808 008	I	BRG
209	402 009	805 313	805 013	807 031	806 017	806 314	806 603	808 009	I	BRG
210	402 010		805 014	807 032	806 021	806 312	806 605	808 010	I	BRG
211	402 011	805 312	805 010	807 029	806 010	806 324	806 643	808 011	I	BRG
212	402 012	805 309	805 009	807 027	806 001	806 313	806 642	808 012	I	BRG
213	402 013	805 318	805 017	807 041	806 002	806 328	806 601	808 013	I	BRG
214	402 014	805 341	805 037	807 030	806 035	806 335	806 625	808 014	I	BRG
215	402 015	805 342	805 012	807 044	806 041	806 341	806 630	808 045	I	BRG
216	402 016	805 339	805 042	807 043	806 042	806 342	806 637	808 016	I	BRG
217	402 017	805 336	805 026	807 003	806 037	806 337	806 627	808 017	I	BRG
218	402 018	805 303	805 040	807 015	806 015	806 338	806 626	808 018	I	BRG
219	402 019	805 319	805 019	807 023	806 005	806 301	806 614	808 019	I	BRG
220	402 020	805 320	805 020	807 012	806 004	806 302	806 608	808 020	I	BRG
221	402 021	805 321	805 021	807 013	806 006	806 329	806 611	808 021	I	BRG
222	402 022	805 322	805 022	807 014	806 007	806 320	806 610	808 022	I	BRG
223	402 023	805 337	805 003	807 011	806 027	806 327	806 619	808 023	I	BRG
224	402 024	805 328	805 030	807 028	806 040	806 340	806 618	808 024	I	BRG
225	402 025	805 330	805 031	807 038	806 025	806 332	806 609	808 025	I	BRG
226	402 026	805 329	805 027	807 037	806 030	806 317	806 636	808 026	I	BRG
227	402 027	805 333	805 036	807 039	806 034	806 330	806 623	808 027	I	BRG
228	402 006	805 334	805 035	807 040	806 032	806 334	806 621	808 028	I	BRG
229	402 029	805 325	805 028	807 026	806 039	806 339	806 629	808 029	I	BRG
230	402 030	805 305	805 007	807 007	806 008	806 309	806 640	808 030	I	BRG
231	402 031	805 307	805 024	807 021	806 012	806 308	806 612	808 031	I	BRG
232	402 032	805 335	805 038	807 001	806 036	806 336	806 624	808 032	I	BRG
233	402 033	805 327	805 005	807 002	806 020	806 305	806 615	808 033	I	BRG
234	402 034	805 324	805 023	807 035	806 019	806 322	806 616	808 034	I	BRG
235	402 035	805 332	805 034	807 034	806 031	806 331	806 622	808 035	I	BRG
236	402 036	805 316	805 018	807 042	806 003	806 321	806 631	808 036	I	BRG
237	402 037	805 343	805 043	807 009	806 043	806 343	806 632	808 037	I	BRG
238	402 038	805 323	805 025	807 008	806 014	806 316	806 613	808 038	I	BRG
239	402 039	805 317	805 016	807 006	806 023	806 325	806 607	808 039	I	BRG
240	402 040	805 315	805 015	807 036	806 033	806 326	806 606	808 040	I	BRG
241	402 041	805 301	805 002	807 022	806 009	806 304	806 634	808 041	I	BRG
242	402 042	805 326	805 039	807 019	806 016	806 323	806 617	808 042	I	BRG
243	402 043	805 344	805 044	807 010	806 044	806 344	806 633	808 043	I	BRG
244	402 044	805 338	805 029	807 024	806 022	806 315	806 628	808 044	I	BRG
Spare	402 028	805 310						808 015	I	BRG

Names:

201	Rheinsberg	223	Schwerin
202	Wuppertal	224	Bielefeld
203	Cottbus/Chósebuz	225	Oldenburg (Oldb)
204	Bielefeld	226	Lutherstadt Wittenberg
205	Zwickau	227	Ludwiglust
206	Magdeburg	228	Altenburg
207	Stendal	229	Templin
208	Bonn	230	Delitzsch
209	Riesa	231	Brandenburg an der Havel
210	Fontanestadt	232	Frankfurt (Oder)
211	Uelzen	233	Ulm
212	Potsdam	234	Minden (Westfalen)
213	Nauen	235	Görlitz
214	Hamm (Westfalen)	236	Jüterbog
215	Bitterfeld	237	Neustrelitz
216	Dessau	238	Saarbrücken
217	Bergen auf Rügen	239	Essen
218	Braunschweig	240	Bochum
219	Hagen	241	Bad Hersfeld
220	Meiningen	242	Quedlinburg
221	Lubbenau/Spreewald	243	Bautzen
222	Eberswalde	244	Koblenz

CLASS 403 ICE3

The ICE3 sets marked a new generation of ICE trains where the power was spread throughout the train. The trains feature all the latest in technology with three-phase asynchronous motors for traction. The passenger accommodation features: electronic seat reservation details shown above each seat; electronic destination indicators at carriage doorways; video and audio facilities, etc. With the power spread through the train the classification of vehicles was altered and all are now class 403 although technically some vehicles which are not powered should be an 8xx, but as they carry vital electrical equipment for the rest of the train they are counted as power cars. In these latest series of ICE trains the first class cars are always 0xx, 1xx, 2xx; the service car/bar-car is 3xx and the second class cars are 5xx, 6xx, 7xx, and 8xx. The 0xx and 5xx are always the driving cars. ICE3s cover workings over the Köln– Frankfurt/M high speed line. The trains also have set numbers in the 3xx series shown on the body sides above the bogies. From about 2002 seat pitch has been reduced allowing more seats per vehicle to be provided but at the expense of some seats not being alongside a window.

A + A + A + R + BD + B + B + B (DMFO–TFO–MFO–TRUB–TSO–MSO–TSO–DMSO).

Built: 1998–2002; 2004–05 (403 051-63).
Builder–Elec. Parts: Siemens.
Wheel Arrangement: Bo-Bo + 2-2 + Bo-Bo + 2-2 + 2-2 + Bo-Bo + 2-2 + Bo-Bo.
Continuous Rating: 8000 kW.
Maximum Tractive Effort: 300 kN.
Wheel Diameter: 1250 mm.
Train Weight: 409 tonnes.
Length over Couplers: 200 metres (driving car 25.675 m, intermediate cars 24.775 m).
Maximum Speed: 330 km/h.

Class 403.0. A (DMFO).

Builder–Mech. Parts: Adtranz (Nürnberg).
Weight: 51 tonnes.   **Accommodation:** 50/–.

Class 403.1. A (TFO) with transformer.

Builder–Mech. Parts: Siemens.
Weight: 55 tonnes.   **Accommodation:** 48/– 2T.

Class 403.2. A (MFO).

Builder–Mech. Parts: Siemens.
Weight: 50 tonnes.   **Accommodation:** 74/– 2T.

Class 403.3. R (TRUB).

Builders–Mech. Parts: Alstom/LHB.
Weight: 51 tonnes.   **Accommodation:** 24 chairs + service point.

Class 403.8. B (TSO).

Builders–Mech. Parts: Bombardier/DWA Ammendorf.
Weight: 47 tonnes.   **Accommodation:** –/56 1TD.

Class 403.7. B (MSO).

Builder–Mech. Parts: Siemens.
Weight: 50 tonnes.   **Accommodation:** –/74 2T.

Class 403.6. B (TSO) with transformer.

Builders–Mech. Parts: Bombardier/DWA Ammendorf.
Weight: 54 tonnes.   **Accommodation:** –/74 2T

Class 403.5. B (DMSO).

Builder–Mech. Parts: Adtranz (Nürnberg).
Weight: 51 tonnes.   **Accommodation:** –/68.

301	403 001	403 101	403 201	403 301	403 801	403 701	403 601	403 501	I	MH1
302	403 002	403 102	403 202	403 302	403 802	403 702	403 602	403 502	I	MH1
303	403 003	403 103	403 203	403 303	403 803	403 703	403 603	403 503	I	MH1
304	403 022	403 104	403 204	403 304	403 804	403 704	403 604	403 504	I	MH1
305	403 005	403 105	403 205	403 305	403 805	403 705	403 605	403 505	I	MH1

306	403 006	403 106	403 206	403 306	403 806	403 706	403 606	403 506	I	MH1
307	403 007	403 107	403 207	403 307	403 807	403 707	403 607	403 507	I	MH1
308	403 008	403 108	403 208	403 308	403 808	403 708	403 608	403 508	I	MH1
309	403 009	403 109	403 209	403 309	403 809	403 709	403 609	403 509	I	MH1
310	403 010	403 110	403 221	403 310	403 810	403 710	403 610	403 510	I	MH1
311	403 011	403 111	403 211	403 311	403 811	403 711	403 611	403 511	I	MH1
312	403 012	403 112	403 212	403 312	403 821	403 712	403 612	403 512	I	MH1
313	403 013	403 113	403 213	403 313	403 813	403 713	403 613	403 513	I	MH1
314	403 019	403 119	403 225	403 325	403 823	403 714	403 614	403 514	I	MH1
315	403 015	403 115	403 215	403 315	403 815	403 715	403 615	403 515	I	MH1
316	403 016	403 116	403 210	403 316	403 816	403 716	403 616	403 516	I	MH1
317	403 017	403 117	403 217	403 317	403 817	403 717	403 617	403 517	I	MH1
318	403 018	403 118	403 218	403 318	403 818	403 718	403 618	403 518	I	MH1
319	403 014	403 131	403 219	403 319	403 819	403 719	403 619	403 519	I	MH1
320	403 020	403 121	403 220	403 320	403 820	403 720	403 621	403 520	I	MH1
321	403 021	403 120	403 216	403 331	403 812	403 721	403 620	403 521	I	MH1
322	403 004	403 122	403 222	403 322	403 822	403 722	403 622	403 522	I	MH1
323	403 023	403 123	403 223	403 314	403 814	403 723	403 623	403 523	I	MH1
324	403 024	403 124	403 224	403 324	403 824	403 724	403 624	403 524	I	MH1
325	403 025	403 125	403 214	403 321	403 825	403 725	403 625	403 525	I	MH1
326	403 026	403 126	403 226	403 323	403 826	403 726	403 626	403 526	I	MH1
327	403 027	403 127	403 227	403 327	403 827	403 727	403 627	403 527	I	MH1
328	403 028	403 128	403 228	403 328	403 828	403 728	403 628	403 528	I	MH1
329	403 029	403 129	403 229	403 329	403 829	403 729	403 629	403 529	I	MH1
330	403 030	403 130	403 230	403 330	403 830	403 730	403 630	403 530	I	MH1
331	403 031	403 114	403 231	403 326	403 812	403 731	403 631	403 531	I	MH1
332	403 032	403 132	403 232	403 332	403 832	403 732	403 632	403 532	I	MH1
333	403 033	403 133	403 233	403 333	403 833	403 733	403 633	403 533	I	MH1
334	403 034	403 134	403 234	403 334	403 834	403 734	403 634	403 534	I	MH1
335	403 035	403 135	403 235	403 335	403 835	403 735	403 635	403 535	I	MH1
336	403 036	403 136	403 236	403 336	403 836	403 736	403 636	403 536	I	MH1
337	403 037	403 137	403 237	403 337	403 837	403 737	403 637	403 537	I	MH1
351	403 051	403 151	403 251	403 351	403 851	403 751	403 651	403 551	I	MH1
352	403 052	403 152	403 252	403 352	403 852	403 752	403 652	403 552	I	MH1
353	403 053	403 153	403 253	403 353	403 853	403 753	403 653	403 553	I	MH1
354	403 054	403 154	403 254	403 354	403 854	403 754	403 654	403 554	I	MH1
355	403 055	403 155	403 255	403 355	403 855	403 755	403 655	403 555	I	MH1
356	403 056	403 156	403 256	403 356	403 856	403 756	403 656	403 556	I	MH1
357	403 057	403 157	403 257	403 357	403 857	403 757	403 657	403 557	I	MH1
358	403 058	403 158	403 258	403 358	403 858	403 758	403 658	403 558	I	MH1
359	403 059	403 159	403 259	403 359	403 859	403 759	403 659	403 559	I	MH1
360	403 060	403 160	403 260	403 360	403 860	403 760	403 660	403 560	I	MH1
361	403 061	403 161	403 261	403 361	403 861	403 761	403 661	403 561	I	MH1
362	403 062	403 162	403 262	403 362	403 862	403 762	403 662	403 562	I	MH1
363	403 063	403 163	403 263	403 363	403 863	403 763	403 663	403 563	I	MH1

Names:

301	Freiburg im Breisgau	318	Münster Westf.
302	Hansestadt Lübeck	319	Duisburg
303	Dortmund	321	Krefeld
304	München	322	Solingen
305	Baden-Baden	325	Ravensburg
307	Oberhausen	328	Aachen
310	Wolfsburg	330	Göttingen
311	Wiesbaden	331	Westerland/Sylt
312	Montabaur	332	Augsburg
313	Treuchtlingen	334	Offenburg
316	Siegburg	336	Ingolstadt
317	Recklinghausen	337	Stuttgart

CLASS 406 ICE3M

These multi-voltage sets were built to enable through services to operate off the Frankfurt/M–Köln high speed line into The Netherlands, Belgium and even Frankfurt/M to France with a new ICE depot being built at Frankfurt-Griesheim to service them. DB pantographs are fitted to the 406.1 and 406.6 vehicles, DC pantographs (for NS, SNCB/NMBS and SNCF) are fitted to the 406.2 and 406.7 vehicles whilst AC pantographs (for SBB, SNCB and SNCF) are fitted to the 406.3 and 406.8 vehicles.

A + A + B + R + BD + B + B + B (DMFO–TFO–MSO–TRUB–TSO–MSO–TSO–DMSO).

Built: 1998–2001.
Systems: 15 kV AC 16.7 Hz, 25 kV AC 50 Hz, 1500 V DC.
Wheel Arrangement: Bo-Bo + 2-2 + Bo-Bo + 2-2 + 2-2 + Bo-Bo + 2-2 + Bo-Bo.
Continuous Rating: 8000 kW.
Maximum Tractive Effort: 300 kN.
Wheel Diameter: 1250 mm.
Train Weight: 409 tonnes.
Length over Couplers: 200 m (driving car 25.675 m, intermediate cars 24.775 m).
Maximum Speed: 330 km/h (AC), 220 km/h (DC).

Class 406.0. A (DMFO).

Builder–Mech. Parts: Adtranz (Nürnberg).
Weight: 51 tonnes.   **Accommodation:** 49/–

Class 406.1. A (TFO) with transformer.

Builder–Mech. Parts: Siemens.
Weight: 55 tonnes.   **Accommodation:** 46/– 2T.

Class 406.2. B (MSO).

Builder–Mech. Parts: Siemens.
Weight: 50 tonnes.   **Accommodation:** –/61 2T.

Class 406.3. R (TRUB).

Builders–Mech. Parts: Alstom/LHB.
Weight: 51 tonnes.   **Accommodation:** 24 chairs + service point.

Class 406.8. B (TSO).

Builders–Mech. Parts: Bombardier/DWA Ammendorf.
Weight: 47 tonnes.   **Accommodation:** –/54 1TD.

Class 406.7. B (MSO).

Builder–Mech. Parts: Siemens.
Weight: 50 tonnes.   **Accommodation:** –/74 2T.

Class 406.6. B (TSO) with transformer.

Builders–Mech. Parts: Bombardier/DWA Ammendorf.
Weight: 54 tonnes.   **Accommodation:** –/72 2T

Class 406.5. B (DMSO).

Builder–Mech. Parts: Adtranz (Nürnberg).
Weight: 51 tonnes.   **Accommodation:** –/64.

4601	406 001	406 101	406 201	406 301	406 801	406 701	406 601	406 501	I	FGM
4602	406 002	406 102	406 202	406 302	406 802	406 702	406 602	406 502	I	FGM
4603	406 003	406 103	406 203	406 303	406 803	406 703	406 603	406 503	I	FGM
4604	406 004	406 104	406 204	406 304	406 804	406 704	406 604	406 504	I	FGM
4607	406 007	406 107	406 207	406 307	406 807	406 707	406 607	406 507	I	FGM
4610	406 010	406 110	406 210	406 310	406 810	406 710	406 610	406 510	I	FGM
4611	406 011	406 111	406 211	406 311	406 811	406 711	406 611	406 511	I	FGM
4651	406 051	406 151	406 251	406 351	406 851	406 751	406 651	406 551	I	LD
4652	406 052	406 152	406 252	406 352	406 852	406 752	406 652	406 552	I	LD
4653	406 053	406 153	406 253	406 353	406 853	406 753	406 653	406 553	I	LD
4654	406 054	406 154	406 254	406 354	406 854	406 754	406 681	406 581	I	FGM
4680	406 080	406 180	406 280	406 380	406 880	406 780	406 680	406 580	I	FGM

4681	406 081	406 181	406 281	406 381	406 881	406 781			I	FGM (Z)
4682	406 082	406 182	406 282	406 382	406 882	406 782	406 682	406 582	I	FGM
4683	406 083	406 183	406 283	406 383	406 883	406 783	406 683	406 583	I	FGM
4684	406 084	406 184	406 284	406 384	406 884	406 784	406 684	406 584	I	FGM
4685	406 085	406 185	406 285	406 385	406 885	406 785	406 685	406 585	I	FGM

Damaged   406 554 406 654

Names:

4603	Mannheim	4611	Düsseldorf
4605	Würzburg	4612	Montabaur
4606	Limburg an der Lahn	4613	Schwäbisch Hall
4607	Hannover	4651	Amsterdam
4609	Köln	4652	Arnhem
4610	Frankfurt(Main)	4653	Utrecht

▲ **407 002**, one of the multi-voltage Velaro D variant of ICE, was used on a test run from Mönchengladbach-Rheydt to München on 19 April 2011. It is pictured near Bad Breisig on the left bank of the Rhine. **Matthias Müller**

CLASS 407 ICE M/VELARO D

15 more multi-voltage ICE3 (406) were ordered from Siemens in November 2007 for service from December 2011. Just like previous orders the run on order has turned into a new type – Class 407! The trains are based on the Siemens Velaro model which has been exported (Spain, China, Russia) and thus this type is Velaro – D (D= Deutschland). Although only 15 sets were initially ordered there will in fact be 17 as an extra one was later ordered to make up for an accident damaged 406 whilst another extra one is being provided by Siemens as compensation for late delivery. The sets are intended to strengthen the fleet for working into other countries with one of the first services expected to be a new Frankfurt/M to southern France. However commissioning is behind schedule and instead of entering service in December 2011 the first units are not expected in service now until sometime in 2013. Like the 406s the units are intended to work into France, Belgium and possibly the UK in due course. 407s are expected to be able to work in multiple with Classes 403 and 406. A change to previous ICEs is that the 407 is a Siemens product whereas all previous sets have been constructed by consortia. Certain equipment is now located on the roof (e.g. air conditioning). Each train has four independent converters with one converter feeding four traction motors. Any failure of one converter will not affect the other three thus a train could continue with 75% traction power. Low level three phase asynchronous motors with cage rotors are provided but it is understood that set 17 will have synchronous motors and in effect be another test bed unit. Weights are unknown as Siemens could only quote a weight for the complete train. The set numbers will be 7xx not 47xx as originally planned.

A + A + AR + B + B + B + B + B (DMFO–TFO–MRFO–TSO–TSO–MSO–TSO–DMSO).

Built: 2009–12.
Builder: Siemens.
Systems: 15 kV AC 16.7 Hz, 25 kV AC 50 Hz, 1500 V, 3000V DC.
Wheel Arrangement: Bo-Bo + 2-2 + Bo-Bo + 2-2 + 2-2 + Bo-Bo + 2-2 + Bo-Bo.
Continuous Rating: 8000 kW (AC), 4200kW (DC).
Maximum Tractive Effort: 300 kN.
Wheel Diameter: 1250 mm.
Train Weight: 454 tonnes.
Length over Couplers: 200.72 m (Driving cars 25.735 m, intermediate cars 24.175 m).
Maximum Speed: 320 km/h (AC), 220 km/h (DC).
Width: 2.924 m.
Total Accommodation: 460 (111F, 333S, 16 in Bistro).

Class 407.0. A (DMFO).
Weight: **Accommodation:** 42/–
One door per side.

Class 407.1. A (TFO) with transformer.
Weight: **Accommodation:** 51/– 2T (24 seats quiet area).
One door per side, 24 quiet seats. DC Pantograph.

Class 407.2. AR (MRFO).
Weight: **Accommodation:** 18/– 2T (+ 16 seats in Bistro).
Two doors per side.

Class 407.3. B (TSO).
Weight: **Accommodation:** –/45 2T (1 disabled, 1 staff).
One door per side, staff offices, AC Pantograph.

Class 407.8. B (TSO).
Weight: **Accommodation:** –/76 2T.
One door per side, AC Pantograph.

Class 407.7. B (MSO) with rectifier.
Weight: **Accommodation:** –/76 2T.
Two doors per side.

Class 407.6. B (TSO) with transformer.
Weight: **Accommodation:** –/72 2T.
One door per side, quiet coach, DC pantograph.

Class 407.5. B (DMSO).
Weight: **Accommodation:** –/64.
One door per side.

701	407 001	407 101	407 201	407 301	407 801	407 701	407 601	407 501	I (FGM)
702	407 002	407 102	407 202	407 302	407 802	407 702	407 602	407 502	I (FGM)
703	407 003	407 103	407 203	407 303	407 803	407 703	407 603	407 503	I (FGM)
704	407 004	407 104	407 204	407 304	407 804	407 704	407 604	407 504	I (FGM)
705	407 005	407 105	407 205	407 305	407 805	407 705	407 605	407 505	I (FGM)
706	407 006	407 106	407 206	407 306	407 806	407 706	407 606	407 506	I (FGM)
707	407 007	407 107	407 207	407 307	407 807	407 707	407 607	407 507	I (FGM)
708	407 008	407 108	407 208	407 308	407 808	407 708	407 608	407 508	I (FGM)
709	407 009	407 109	407 209	407 309	407 809	407 709	407 609	407 509	I (FGM)
710	407 010	407 110	407 210	407 310	407 810	407 710	407 610	407 510	I (FGM)
711	407 011	407 111	407 211	407 311	407 811	407 711	407 611	407 511	I (FGM)
712	407 012	407 112	407 212	407 312	407 812	407 712	407 612	407 512	I (FGM)
713	407 013	407 113	407 213	407 313	407 813	407 713	407 613	407 513	I (FGM)
714	407 014	407 114	407 214	407 314	407 814	407 714	407 614	407 514	I (FGM)
715	407 015	407 115	407 215	407 315	407 815	407 715	407 615	407 515	I (FGM)
716	407 016	407 116	407 216	407 316	407 816	407 716	407 616	407 516	I (FGM)
717	407 017	407 117	407 217	407 317	407 817	407 717	407 617	407 517	I (FGM)

CLASS 410   ICE-S

Class 410 is an ICE experimental set, ICE-S where the "S" is understood to stand for Schnellfahrstreckendienst. The two power cars were part of the Class 402 production run built in 1997 but intended for experimental use. Originally based at the München Technical Centre and maintained by MH1 the set is now based in Minden and maintained in Berlin.

Class 410.1. Power cars built by Krauss Maffei/Siemens.
Class 810. 101 built by MAN, 102 built by Duewag.

    410 101 810 101 810 102 410 102 I BRG

▲ Although nominally a 4-car set, the Class 410 experimental ICE is a highly versatile unit that can be strengthened by the addition of spare trailer cars to suit the needs of the particular test being undertaken. It is seen here in strengthened form on Austria's new high-speed Westbahn on 28 August 2012.   **Raimund Wyhnal**

CLASS 411 ICE-T

These tilting ICE-3 sets come in two versions. Class 411 is a seven-car set and Class 415 is a five-car set. The 411s feature a restaurant car whereas the 415s have a bistro. The units are intended for running not only over the newly built high speed lines but also over old lines with curves hence the decision to fit tilt. In January 2004 vehicles 411 706 and 411 806 were burnt out in the sidings at Leipzig. The other vehicles are now spares. In the winter of 2006/07 some 411s had their intermediate carriages swapped with Class 415 so that 7-car trains could run into Switzerland (q.v.). About the same time three 411s were sold to Austrian Federal Railways for their share of the revised services into Austria which were to be 411s working Frankfurt/M to Wien. For completeness they are included here.

The driving coaches are interesting in that the driver's position is centrally located and immediately behind is a lounge with a full view through the driving cab. Set numbers are carried above the bogies – 11xx.

A + AB + R + BD + B + B + B (DTFO–MCO–MRUB (MRSB*)–TSO–MSO–MSO–DTSO).

Built: 1998–2000, 2004–05 (*1151 onwards ICE-T2 with extra seating).
Builders–Mech. Parts: Bombardier/DWA (Ammendorf and Görlitz) (trailers), Siemens (power cars).
Builder–Elec. Parts: Siemens.
Wheel Arrangement: 2-2 + 1A-A1 + 1A-A1 + 2-2 + 1A-A1 + 1A-A1 + 2-2.
Traction Motors: 2 x 500 kW.
Continuous Rating: 1000 kW.
Length over Couplers: 185 m (driving car 27.45 m, intermediate cars 25.90 m).
Wheel Diameter: 890 mm.
Maximum Speed: 230 km/h.
Tilt: FIAT, hydraulic.

Class 411.0. A (DTFO) with transformer.

Weight: 56 tonnes.   **Accommodation:** 41/– (*43/–).

Class 411.1. B (MCO).

Weight: 53 tonnes.   **Accommodation:** 12/47 2T.

Class 411.2. R (MRUB).

Weight: 55 tonnes.   **Accommodation:** 24 restaurant with bar and children's compartment including –/6.

Class 411.2*. BR (MRSB).

Weight: 59 tonnes.   **Accommodation:** –/14 with children's compartment and bistro with 14 bar seats.

Class 411.8. B (TSO).

Weight: 47 tonnes.   **Accommodation:** –/64(3) 2T (*–/68(3) 2T).

Class 411.7. B (MSO).

Weight: 53 (*55)tonnes.   **Accommodation:** –/62 2T (*–/68 2T) with
service point.

Class 411.6. B (MSO).

Weight: 52 (*53) tonnes.   **Accommodation:** –/62 1W 1TD 1T (*–/67 1W 1TD 1T).

Class 411.5. B (DTSO) with transformer.

Weight: 56 tonnes.   **Accommodation:** –/63 (*–/66).

1101-1132. ICE-T.

1101	411 001	411 101	411 201	411 801	411 701	411 601	411 501	I	MH1
1102	411 002	411 102	411 206	411 802	411 702	411 602	411 502	I	MH1
1103	411 003	411 104	411 203	411 803	411 703	411 603	411 503	I	MH1
1104	411 006	411 103	411 204	411 804	411 704	411 604	411 504	I	MH1
1105	411 005	411 105	411 205	411 805	411 705	411 605	411 505	I	MH1
1107	411 007	411 107	411 207	411 807	411 707	411 607	411 507	I	MH1
1108	411 008	411 108	411 208	411 808	411 708	411 608	411 508	I	MH1
1109	411 009	411 109	411 209	411 820	411 709	411 609	411 509	I	MH1

1110	411 010	411 110	411 210	411 810	411 710	411 610	411 510	I	MH1
1111	411 011	411 111	411 211	411 811	411 711	411 611	411 511	I	MH1
1112	411 012	411 112	411 212	411 812	411 712	411 612	411 512	I	MH1
1113	411 013	411 113	411 213	411 813	411 713	411 613	411 513	I	MH1
1117	411 017	411 117	411 217	411 817	411 717	411 617	411 517	I	MH1
1118	411 018	411 118	411 218	411 818	411 718	411 618	411 518	I	MH1
1119	411 019	411 119	411 219	411 819	411 719	411 619	411 519	I	MH1
1125	411 004	411 125	411 225	411 825	411 725	411 625	411 525	I	MH1
1126	411 026	411 126	411 202	411 826	411 726	411 626	411 526	I	MH1
1127	411 027	411 127	411 227	411 827	411 727	411 627	411 527	I	MH1
1128	411 028	411 128	411 228	411 828	411 728	411 628	411 528	I	MH1
1129	411 029	411 129	411 226	411 829	411 729	411 629	411 529	I	MH1
1130	411 030	411 130	411 230	411 830	411 730	411 630	411 530	I	MH1
1131	411 031	411 131	411 231	411 831	411 731	411 631	411 531	I	MH1
1132	411 032	411 132	411 232	411 832	411 732	411 632	411 532	I	MH1

Names:

1101	Neustadt/Weinstrasse	1117	Erlangen
1102	Neubrandenburg	1118	Plauen (Vogtland)
1103	Paderborn	1119	Meissen
1104	Erfurt	1125	Arnstadt
1105	Dresden	1126	Leipzig
1107	Pirna	1127	Weimar
1108	Berlin	1128	Reutlingen
1109	Güstrow	1129	Kiel
1110	Naumburg/Saale	1130	Jena
1111	Hansestadt Wismar	1131	Trier
1112	Freie und Hansestadt Hamburg	1132	Wittenberge
1113	Hansestadt Stralsund		

▲ Class 411 set number 1158 passes through Kaub with a diverted ICE service from Dortmund to Wien on 15 September 2011. The train is seen unusually travelling along the right bank of the Rhine, the usual route via the left bank having been closed for engineering work. **Matthias Müller**

1151–1178. ICE-T2.

1151	411 051	411 151	411 251	411 851	411 751	411 651	411 551	I	MH1
1152	411 052	411 152	411 252	411 852	411 752	411 652	411 552	I	MH1
1153	411 053	411 153	411 253	411 853	411 753	411 653	411 553	I	MH1
1154	411 054	411 154	411 254	411 854	411 754	411 654	411 554	I	MH1
1155	411 071	411 155	411 255	411 855	411 755	411 655	411 555	I	MH1
1156	411 056	411 156	411 256	411 856	411 756	411 656	411 556	I	MH1
1157	411 057	411 157	411 257	411 857	411 757	411 657	411 557	I	MH1
1158	411 058	411 158	411 258	411 858	411 758	411 658	411 558	I	MH1
1159	411 059	411 159	411 259	411 859	411 759	411 659	411 559	I	MH1
1160	411 060	411 160	411 260	411 860	411 760	411 660	411 560	I	MH1
1161	411 061	411 161	411 261	411 861	411 761	411 661	411 561	I	MH1
1162	411 062	411 162	411 262	411 862	411 762	411 662	411 562	I	MH1
1163	411 063	411 163	411 263	411 863	411 763	411 663	411 563	I	MH1
1164	411 064	411 164	411 264	411 864	411 764	411 664	411 564	I	MH1
1165	411 065	411 165	411 265	411 865	411 765	411 665	411 565	I	MH1
1166	411 066	411 166	411 266	411 866	411 766	411 666	411 566	I	MH1
1167	411 067	411 167	411 267	411 867	411 767	411 667	411 567	I	MH1
1168	411 068	411 168	411 268	411 868	411 768	411 668	411 568	I	MH1
1169	411 069	411 169	411 269	411 869	411 769	411 669	411 569	I	MH1
1170	411 070	411 170	411 270	411 870	411 770	411 670	411 570	I	MH1
1171	411 055	411 171	411 271	411 871	411 771	411 671	411 571	I	MH1
1172	411 072	411 172	411 272	411 872	411 772	411 672	411 592	I	MH1
1173	411 073	411 173	411 273	411 873	411 773	411 673	411 573	I	MH1
1174	411 074	411 174	411 274	411 874	411 774	411 674	411 574	I	MH1
1175	411 075	411 175	411 275	411 875	411 775	411 675	411 575	I	MH1
1176	411 076	411 176	411 276	411 876	411 776	411 676	411 576	I	MH1
1177	411 077	411 177	411 277	411 877	411 777	411 677	411 577	I	MH1
1178	411 078	411 178	411 278	411 878	411 778	411 678	411 578	I	MH1
1180	411 080	411 120	411 220	411 821	411 720	411 620	411 580	I	MH1
1181	411 081	411 121	411 221	411 809	411 721	411 621	411 581	I	MH1
1182	411 082	411 122	411 229	411 822	411 722	411 622	411 582	I	MH1
1183	411 083	411 123	411 223	411 823	411 723	411 623	411 583	I	MH1
1184	411 084	411 124	411 224	411 824	411 724	411 624	411 584	I	MH1
1190	411 090	411 190	411 290	411 890	411 790	411 690	411 590	I	MH1
1191	411 091	411 191	411 291	411 891	411 791	411 691	411 591	I	MH1
1192	411 092	411 192	411 292	411 892	411 792	411 606	411 506	I	MH1
Spare		411 025	411 106	411 222	411 592	411 692			

Sets 1180–84 formed from 415 080–84.
Sets 1190–92 formed from 411 014–16.

Names:

1151	Elsterwerda	1167	Traunstein
1152	Travemünde	1169	Tutzing
1153	Ilmenau	1171	Oschatz
1154	Sonneberg	1172	Bamberg
1156	Waren (Müritz)	1173	Halle (Saale)
1157	Innsbruck	1175	Villingen - Schwenningen
1158	Falkenberg/Elster	1176	Coburg
1159	Passau	1177	Rathenow
1160	Markt Holzkirchen	1178	Ostseebad Warnemünde
1161	Andernach	1180	Darmstadt
1162	Vaihingen an der Enz	1181	Horb am Neckar
1163	Ostseebad Binz	1182	Mainz
1164	Rödental	1183	Oberursel (Taunus)
1165	Bad Oeynhausen	1184	Kaiserslautern
1166	Bingen am Rhein		

CLASS 415 ICE-T

These are similar to Class 411 but are only five car sets and some feature a Swiss pantograph as the units are for working into Switzerland on the Stuttgart–Horb–Singen–Zürich services – a well known route for plenty of curves! Sets 415 080–085 are for working into Switzerland and besides a Swiss pantograph also have Swiss safety systems fitted. Set numbers are carried above the bogies e.g. 1501. In the winter of 2006/07 some intermediate carriages from 411s were swapped with those in 415s; the Swiss trains needed strengthening and as all the Swiss equipment was on the driving trailers this was deemed the easiest solution. These units no longer work from Stuttgart to Zürich as problems with the main ICE3 fleet caused them to be used elsewhere and their intended workings changed to loco-hauled IC trains.

A + BR + B + B + B (DTFO–MRSB–MSO–MSO–DTSO).

Built: 1998–99.
Builders–Mech. Parts: Bombardier/DWA (Ammendorf and Görlitz) (trailers), Siemens (power cars).
Builder–Elec. Parts: Siemens.
Wheel Arrangement: 2-2 + 1A-A1 + 1A-A1 + 1A-A1 + 2-2.
Traction Motors: 6 x 500 kW.
Continuous Rating: 3000 kW.
Length over Couplers: 130 m (driving car 27.45 m, intermediate cars 25.90 m).
Wheel Diameter: 890 mm.
Maximum Speed: 230 km/h.
Tilt: FIAT, hydraulic.

Class 411.5. A (DTFO) with transformer.

Weight: 56 tonnes.   **Accommodation:** 41/–.

Class 415.1. BR (MRSB).

Weight: 53 tonnes.   **Accommodation:** –/22 with children's compartment and bistro with 14 bar seats.

Class 415.7. R (MSO).

Weight: 53 tonnes.   **Accommodation:** –/62 1T with service point.

Class 415.6. B (MSO).

Weight: 52 tonnes.   **Accommodation:** –/62 1W 1TD 1T.

Class 415.5. B (DTSO) with transformer.

Weight: 56 tonnes.   **Accommodation:** –/63.

1501	415 001	415 101	415 701	415 601	415 501	I	FGM
1502	415 002	415 102	415 702	415 602	415 502	I	FGM
1503	415 003	415 103	415 703	415 603	415 503	I	FGM
1504	415 004	415 104	415 704	415 604	415 504	I	FGM
1505	415 005	415 105	415 705	415 605	415 505	I	FGM
1506	415 006	415 106	415 706	415 606	415 506	I	FGM
1520	415 020	415 180	415 780	415 680	415 520	I	FGM
1521	415 021	415 181	415 781	415 681	415 521	I	FGM
1522	415 022	415 182	415 782	415 682	415 522	I	FGM
1523	415 023	415 183	415 783	415 683	415 523	I	FGM
1524	415 024	415 184	415 784	415 684	415 524	I	FGM

Sets 1520–1524 formed from 411 020–024.

Names:

1501	Eisenach	1520	Gotha
1502	Karlsruhe	1521	Homburg
1503	Altenbeken	1522	Torgau
1504	Heidelberg	1523	Hansestadt Greifswald
1505	Marburg (Lahn)	1524	Hansestadt Rostock

5. ELECTRIC MULTIPLE UNITS

CLASS 420   3-CAR UNITS

First introduced for S-Bahn services around München in time for the 1972 Olympics the class later spread to Stuttgart and Frankfurt/M and for a while also in the Rühr. Large numbers of units have now been withdrawn. The most recent units were only built in the 1990s so the class will be around for a while yet, Stuttgart having recently refurbished some of its units. It is now expected that when Stuttgart gets its new Class 430s the best of its 420s will be transferred to Frankfurt/M to replace the older 420s there. These in turn will be replaced by later deliveries of Class 430. Sets 420 400/16 were modernised as ET420 Plus prototypes but nothing further has been heard of this project. Set 420 391 has been created from vehicles previously 420 241, 421 241 and 420 710. 421 411^{II} and 421 412^{II} were previously 421 401 and 421 403. 420 912^{II} was previously 421 903.

B + AB + B (DMSO–MCO–DMSO (non-gangwayed)).

Built: 1969–96.
Builders–Mech. Parts: Linke-Hoffmann-Busch/Messerschmitt-Bölkow-Blohm/Orenstein & Koppel/Uerdingen/Waggon-Union.
Builders–Elec. Parts: AEG/Brown-Boveri/Siemens.
Wheel Arrangement: Bo-Bo + Bo-Bo + Bo-Bo.
Traction Motors: 4 x 200 kW.
Accommodation: –/63 + 17/49 + –/65.
Weight: 44 + 41 + 44 tonnes.   **Maximum Speed:** 120 km/h.
Length over Couplers: 23.30 + 20.80 + 23.30 m.

420 233	421 233	420 733	FF (Z)	420 313	421 313	420 813	FF
420 257	421 257	420 757	FF (Z)	420 314	421 314	420 814	FF
420 261	421 261	420 761	FF	420 316	421 316	420 816	FF
420 264	421 264	420 764	FF	420 317	421 317	420 817	FF
420 265	421 265	420 765	FF	420 318	421 318	420 818	FF
420 266	421 266	420 766	FF	420 321	421 321	420 821	FF
420 267	421 267	420 767	FF	420 323	421 323	420 823	FF
420 271	421 271	420 771	FF	420 324	421 324	420 824	FF
420 272	421 272	420 772	FF	420 325	421 325	420 825	FF
420 276	421 276	420 776	FF	420 326	421 326	420 826	FF
420 278	421 278	420 778	FF	420 331	421 331	420 831	FF
420 280	421 280	420 780	FF	420 333	421 333	420 833	FF
420 282	421 282	420 782	FF	420 337	421 337	420 837	FF
420 284	421 284	420 784	FF (Z)	420 338	421 338	420 838	FF
420 285	421 285	420 785	FF	420 344	421 344	420 844	FF
420 286	421 286	420 786	FF	420 349	421 349	420 849	FF
420 287	421 287	420 787	FF	420 350	421 350	420 850	FF
420 288	421 288	420 788	FF	420 356	421 356	420 856	FF
420 289	421 289	420 789	FF	420 360	421 360	420 860	FF
420 290	421 290	420 790	FF	420 363	421 363	420 863	FF
420 292	421 292	420 792	FF	420 367	421 367	420 867	FF
420 293	421 293	420 793	FF	420 377	421 377	420 877	FF
420 294	421 294	420 794	FF	420 378	421 378	420 878	FF
420 295	421 295	420 795	FF	420 384	421 384	420 884	FF
420 297	421 297	420 797	FF	420 385	421 385	420 885	FF
420 298	421 298	420 798	FF	420 386	421 386	420 886	FF
420 301	421 301	420 801	FF	420 388	421 388	420 888	FF
420 302	421 302	420 802	FF	420 389	421 389	420 889	FF
420 303	421 303	420 803	FF	420 391	421 391	420 891	FF
420 305	421 305	420 805	FF (Z)	420 400	421 400	420 900	TP
420 306	421 306	420 806	FF	420 401	421 411^I	420 901	TP
420 307	421 307	420 807	FF (Z)	420 402	421 402	420 902	TP
420 308	421 308	420 808	FF	420 403	421 412^I	420 912^I	TP
420 309	421 309	420 809	FF	420 404	421 404	420 904	TP
420 310	421 310	420 810	FF (Z)	420 405	421 405	420 905	TP
420 311	421 311	420 811	FF (Z)	420 406	421 406	420 906	TP

420 407	421 407	420 907	TP	420 449	421 449	420 949	TP
420 408	421 408	420 908	TP	420 450	421 450	420 950	TP
420 409	421 409	420 909	TP	420 451	421 451	420 951	TP
420 410	421 410	420 910	TP	420 452	421 452	420 952	TP
420 411	421 411ᴵᴵ	420 911	TP	420 453	421 453	420 953	TP
420 412	421 412ᴵᴵ	420 912ᴵᴵ	TP	420 454	421 454	420 954	TP
420 413	421 413	420 913	TP	420 455	421 455	420 955	TP
420 414	421 414	420 914	TP	420 456	421 456	420 956	TP
420 415	421 415	420 915	TP	420 457	421 457	420 957	TP
420 416	421 416	420 916	TP	420 458	421 458	420 958	TP
420 417	421 417	420 917	TP	420 459	421 459	420 959	TP
420 418	421 418	420 918	TP	420 460	421 460	420 960	TP
420 419	421 419	420 919	TP	420 461	421 461	420 961	TP
420 420	421 420	420 920	TP	420 462	421 462	420 962	TP
420 421	421 421	420 921	TP	420 463	421 463	420 963	TP
420 422	421 422	420 922	TP	420 464	421 464	420 964	TP
420 423	421 423	420 923	TP	420 465	421 465	420 965	TP
420 424	421 424	420 924	TP	420 466	421 466	420 966	TP
420 425	421 425	420 925	FF	420 467	421 467	420 967	TP
420 426	421 426	420 926	TP	420 468	421 468	420 968	TP
420 427	421 427	420 927	TP	420 469	421 469	420 969	TP
420 428	421 428	420 928	FF	420 470	421 470	420 970	TP
420 429	421 429	420 929	FF	420 471	421 471	420 971	TP
420 430	421 430	420 930	FF	420 472	421 472	420 972	TP
420 431	421 431	420 931	TP	420 473	421 473	420 973	TP
420 432	421 432	420 932	TP	420 474	421 474	420 974	TP
420 433	421 433	420 933	TP	420 475	421 475	420 975	TP
420 434	421 434	420 934	TP	420 476	421 476	420 976	TP
420 435	421 435	420 935	TP	420 477	421 477	420 977	TP
420 436	421 436	420 936	TP	420 478	421 478	420 978	TP
420 437	421 437	420 937	TP	420 479	421 479	420 979	TP
420 438	421 438	420 938	TP	420 480	421 480	420 980	TP
420 439	421 439	420 939	TP	420 481	421 481	420 981	TP
420 440	421 440	420 940	TP	420 482	421 482	420 982	TP
420 441	421 441	420 941	TP	420 483	421 483	420 983	TP
420 442	421 442	420 942	TP	420 484	421 484	420 984	TP
420 443	421 443	420 943	TP	420 485	421 485	420 985	TP
420 444	421 444	420 944	TP	420 486	421 486	420 986	TP
420 445	421 445	420 945	TP	420 487	421 487	420 987	TP
420 446	421 446	420 946	TP	420 488	421 488	420 988	TP
420 447	421 447	420 947	TP	420 489	421 489	420 989	TP
420 448	421 448	420 948	TP				

Names:

420 271	HOFHEIM-AM-TAUNUS		420 293	LUDWIGSBURG
420 272	HOCHHEIM		420 305	STADT PLOCHINGEN
420 276	ESCHBORN		420 331	KREIS LUDWIGSBURG
420 278	OBERURSEL		420 333	WAIBLINGEN
420 280	KARBEN		420 337	UNTERTÜRKHEIM
420 282	KRIFTEL		420 338	BÖBLINGEN
420 284	HÖCHST		420 385	BIETIGHEIM-BISSENGEN
420 285	MAINZ		420 389	BAD CANSTATT
420 286	NIEDERJOSBACH		420 416	LEONBERG
420 287	DORTELWEIL		420 438	STADT LEONBERG
420 288	RÖDELHEIM			

CLASS 422   4-SECTION ARTICULATED UNITS

This class can be regarded as a follow on to Class 423 for which the number series was all but complete. DB Regio Nordrheinwestfalen ordered 78 units in 2005 for services on the Rhein-Ruhr S-Bahn. There was an option for 72 more units but this was not taken up although 84 units have been built. The original order was shared between Alstom and Bombardier with originally 27 trains being erected at the Bombardier plant in Hennigsdorf and 51 at the Alstom plant in Salzgitter. Electrical equipment came from Bombardier in Mannheim with Bombardier Siegen providing the bogies for the articulation whilst Alstom provided the 156 end bogies. The Verkehrsverbund Rhein-Ruhr was going to order another 116 sets but changed its mind and decided to wait to see the results from Class 430. However with some of the S-Bahn lines being offered up for franchising it was later decided to cancel any further orders pending the results of the franchise competition. Like other new EMUs the Class 422 has had its "teething problems". In particular software problems with the on board computers especially those concerned with Automatic Train Protection (in this case Ebicab 500 PZB) were brought to light after two instances of signals being passed at danger. The EBA reduced the maximum speed to 100 km/h and insisted on two drivers in the cab! This led to many train services being covered by Class 143 and classic S-Bahn stock. All the problems were sorted by a software update. Another change from Class 423 concerns the unpowered bogie which on the 423s was unbraked. On the 422 it is braked and also has supplementary magnetic brakes.

AB + B + B + AB (DMCO–TSO–TSO–DMCO).

Built: 2007–10.
Builder–Mech. Parts: Alstom.
Builder–Elec. Parts: Bombardier.
Wheel Arrangement: Bo-Bo-2-Bo-Bo.
Traction Motors: 8 x 293 kW three phase asynchronous motors per set.
Accommodation: 8/40 + –/48 + –/48 + 8/40.
Weight: 112 tonnes.
Length over Couplers: 69.43 m.
Width: 3.02 m.   **Maximum Speed:** 140 km/h.
Wheel Diameter: 850 mm.   **Floor Height:** 1025 mm.

422 001	432 001	432 501	422 501	EE
422 002	432 002	432 502	422 502	EE
422 003	432 003	432 503	422 503	EE
422 004	432 004	432 504	422 504	EE
422 005	432 005	432 505	422 505	EE
422 006	432 006	432 506	422 506	EE
422 007	432 007	432 507	422 507	EE
422 008	432 008	432 508	422 508	EE
422 009	432 009	432 509	422 509	EE
422 010	432 010	432 510	422 510	EE
422 011	432 011	432 511	422 511	EE
422 012	432 012	432 512	422 512	EE
422 013	432 013	432 513	422 513	EE
422 014	432 014	432 514	422 514	EE
422 015	432 015	432 515	422 515	EE
422 016	432 016	432 516	422 516	EE
422 017	432 017	432 517	422 517	KD
422 018	432 018	432 518	422 518	KD
422 019	432 019	432 519	422 519	KD
422 020	432 020	432 520	422 520	KD
422 021	432 021	432 521	422 521	KD
422 022	432 022	432 522	422 522	KD
422 023	432 023	432 523	422 523	KD
422 024	432 024	432 524	422 524	KD
422 025	432 025	432 525	422 525	KD
422 026	432 026	432 526	422 526	KD
422 027	432 027	432 527	422 527	KD
422 028	432 028	432 528	422 528	KD
422 029	432 029	432 529	422 529	KD
422 030	432 030	432 530	422 530	KD
422 031	432 031	432 531	422 531	KD

422 032	432 032	432 532	422 532	KD
422 033	432 033	432 533	422 533	KD
422 034	432 034	432 534	422 534	KD
422 035	432 035	432 535	422 535	EE
422 036	432 036	432 536	422 536	EE
422 037	432 037	432 537	422 537	EE
422 038	432 038	432 538	422 538	EE
422 039	432 039	432 539	422 539	EE
422 040	432 040	432 540	422 540	EE
422 041	432 041	432 541	422 541	EE
422 042	432 042	432 542	422 542	EE
422 043	432 043	432 543	422 543	EE
422 044	432 044	432 544	422 544	EE
422 045	432 045	432 545	422 545	KD
422 046	432 046	432 546	422 546	KD
422 047	432 047	432 547	422 547	KD
422 048	432 048	432 548	422 548	KD
422 049	432 049	432 549	422 549	KD
422 050	432 050	432 550	422 550	KD
422 051	432 051	432 551	422 551	KD
422 052	432 052	432 552	422 552	KD
422 053	432 053	432 553	422 553	KD
422 054	432 054	432 554	422 554	KD
422 055	432 055	432 555	422 555	KD
422 056	432 056	432 556	422 556	KD
422 057	432 057	432 557	422 557	KD
422 058	432 058	432 558	422 558	KD
422 059	432 059	432 559	422 559	KD
422 060	432 060	432 560	422 560	KD
422 061	432 061	432 561	422 561	KD
422 062	432 062	432 562	422 562	KD
422 063	432 063	432 563	422 563	KD
422 064	432 064	432 564	422 564	KD
422 065	432 065	432 565	422 565	KD
422 066	432 066	432 566	422 566	KD
422 067	432 067	432 567	422 567	KD
422 068	432 068	432 568	422 568	KD
422 069	432 069	432 569	422 569	EE
422 070	432 070	432 570	422 570	EE
422 071	432 071	432 571	422 571	EE
422 072	432 072	432 572	422 572	EE
422 073	432 073	432 573	422 573	EE
422 074	432 074	432 574	422 574	EE
422 075	432 075	432 575	422 575	EE
422 076	432 076	432 576	422 576	EE
422 077	432 077	432 577	422 577	EE
422 078	432 078	432 578	422 578	EE
422 079	432 079	432 579	422 579	EE
422 080	432 080	432 580	422 580	EE
422 081	432 081	432 581	422 581	EE
422 082	432 082	432 582	422 582	EE
422 083	432 083	432 583	422 583	EE
422 084	432 084	432 584	422 584	EE

Names:

422 009	Dortmund		422 082	Hilden
422 079	Haltern am See		422 083	Düsseldorf
422 081	Solingen		422 084	Essen

CLASS 423   4-SECTION ARTICULATED UNITS

Introduced in 1998 this class was the first of a new generation of S-Bahn unit intended to replace Class 420/421 in the München and Stuttgart areas, and provide new services in the Köln and Ruhr areas. Three-phase asynchronous motors are used with water cooled rectifiers. Another break with the previous units is the use of articulation to reduce weight and length of the train. There are three sets of doors per carriage which feature an aluminium alloy body which is wider than the bodies of units of Classes 424, 425 and 426. LCD display units inside and outside are provided for passenger information. The München area units have LZB fitted so that closer intervals can be worked along the core section of the city route from München Hbf to München Ostbahhof. Set 423 025 has been withdrawn after accident damage. There have been problems with these units especially in autumn which has led to additional braking being provided and sanding equipment.

AB + B + B + AB (DMCO–TSO–TSO–DMCO).

Built: 1998–2004.
Builder–Mech. Parts: Alstom LHB.
Builder–Elec. Parts: Adtranz.
Wheel Arrangement: Bo-Bo-2-Bo-Bo.
Traction Motors: 8 x 295 kW three phase asynchronous motors per set.
Accommodation: 8/40 + –/48 + –/48 + 8/40.
Weight: 105 tonnes.
Length over Couplers: 18.24 + 15.46 + 15.46 + 18.24 m.
Width: 3.02 m.   **Maximum Speed:** 140 km/h.
Wheel Diameter: 850 mm.   **Floor Height:** 995 mm.

423 001	433 001	433 501	423 501	TP
423 002	433 002	433 502	423 502	TP
423 003	433 003	433 503	423 503	TP
423 004	433 004	433 504	423 504	TP
423 005	433 005	433 505	423 505	TP
423 006	433 006	433 506	423 506	TP
423 007	433 007	433 507	423 507	TP
423 008	433 008	433 508	423 508	TP
423 009	433 009	433 509	423 509	TP
423 010	433 010	433 510	423 510	TP
423 011	433 011	433 511	423 511	TP
423 012	433 012	433 512	423 512	TP
423 013	433 013	433 513	423 513	TP
423 014	433 014	433 514	423 514	TP
423 015	433 015	433 515	423 515	TP
423 016	433 016	433 516	423 516	TP
423 017	433 017	433 517	423 517	TP
423 018	433 018	433 518	423 518	TP
423 019	433 019	433 519	423 519	TP
423 020	433 020	433 520	423 520	TP
423 021	433 021	433 521	423 521	TP
423 022	433 022	433 522	423 522	TP
423 023	433 023	433 523	423 523	TP
423 024	433 024	433 524	423 524	TP
423 026	433 026	433 526	423 526	TP
423 027	433 027	433 527	423 527	TP
423 028	433 028	433 528	423 528	TP
423 029	433 029	433 529	423 529	TP
423 030	433 030	433 530	423 530	TP
423 031	433 031	433 531	423 531	TP
423 032	433 032	433 532	423 532	TP
423 033	433 033	433 533	423 533	TP
423 034	433 034	433 534	423 534	KK2
423 035	433 035	433 535	423 535	KK2
423 036	433 036	433 536	423 536	KK2
423 037	433 037	433 537	423 537	KK2
423 038	433 038	433 538	423 538	KK2
423 039	433 039	433 539	423 539	KK2

423 040	433 040	433 540	423 540	KK2
423 041	433 041	433 541	423 541	KK2
423 042	433 042	433 542	423 542	KK2
423 043	433 043	433 543	423 543	KK2
423 044	433 044	433 544	423 544	KK2
423 045	433 045	433 545	423 545	KK2
423 046	433 046	433 546	423 546	KK2
423 047	433 047	433 547	423 547	KK2
423 048	433 048	433 548	423 548	KK2
423 049	433 049	433 549	423 549	KK2
423 050	433 050	433 550	423 550	KK2
423 051	433 051	433 551	423 551	KK2
423 052	433 052	433 552	423 552	KK2
423 053	433 053	433 553	423 553	KK2
423 054	433 054	433 554	423 554	KK2
423 055	433 055	433 555	423 555	KK2
423 056	433 056	433 556	423 556	KK2
423 057	433 057	433 557	423 557	KK2
423 058	433 058	433 558	423 558	MH6
423 059	433 059	433 559	423 559	MH6
423 060	433 060	433 560	423 560	MH6

▲ 420 939 heads a 6-car empty rake heading for Plochingen depot near Stuttgart Oberturkheim on 23 September 2011. **Brian Garvin**

423 061	433 061	433 561	423 561	MH6
423 062	433 062	433 562	423 562	MH6
423 063	433 063	433 563	423 563	MH6
423 064	433 064	433 564	423 564	MH6
423 065	433 065	433 565	423 565	MH6
423 066	433 066	433 566	423 566	MH6
423 067	433 067	433 567	423 567	MH6
423 068	433 068	433 568	423 568	MH6
423 069	433 069	433 569	423 569	MH6
423 070	433 070	433 570	423 570	MH6
423 071	433 071	433 571	423 571	MH6
423 072	433 072	433 572	423 572	MH6
423 073	433 073	433 573	423 573	MH6
423 074	433 074	433 574	423 574	MH6
423 075	433 075	433 575	423 575	MH6
423 076	433 076	433 576	423 576	MH6
423 077	433 077	433 577	423 577	MH6
423 078	433 078	433 578	423 578	MH6
423 079	433 079	433 579	423 579	MH6
423 080	433 080	433 580	423 580	MH6
423 081	433 081	433 581	423 581	MH6
423 082	433 082	433 582	423 582	MH6
423 083	433 083	433 583	423 583	MH6
423 084	433 084	433 584	423 584	MH6
423 085	433 085	433 585	423 585	MH6
423 086	433 086	433 586	423 586	MH6
423 087	433 087	433 587	423 587	MH6
423 088	433 088	433 588	423 588	MH6
423 089	433 089	433 589	423 589	MH6
423 090	433 090	433 590	423 590	MH6
423 091	433 091	433 591	423 591	MH6
423 092	433 092	433 592	423 592	MH6
423 093	433 093	433 593	423 593	MH6
423 094	433 094	433 594	423 594	MH6
423 095	433 095	433 595	423 595	MH6
423 096	433 096	433 596	423 596	MH6
423 097	433 097	433 597	423 597	MH6
423 098	433 098	433 598	423 598	MH6
423 099	433 099	433 599	423 599	MH6
423 100	433 100	433 600	423 600	MH6
423 101	433 101	433 601	423 601	MH6
423 102	433 102	433 602	423 602	MH6
423 103	433 103	433 603	423 603	MH6
423 104	433 104	433 604	423 604	MH6
423 105	433 105	433 605	423 605	MH6
423 106	433 106	433 606	423 606	MH6
423 107	433 107	433 607	423 607	MH6
423 108	433 108	433 608	423 608	MH6
423 109	433 109	433 609	423 609	MH6
423 110	433 110	433 610	423 610	MH6
423 111	433 111	433 611	423 611	MH6
423 112	433 112	433 612	423 612	MH6
423 113	433 113	433 613	423 613	MH6
423 114	433 114	433 614	423 614	MH6
423 115	433 115	433 615	423 615	MH6
423 116	433 116	433 616	423 616	MH6
423 117	433 117	433 617	423 617	MH6
423 118	433 118	433 618	423 618	MH6
423 119	433 119	433 619	423 619	MH6
423 120	433 120	433 620	423 620	MH6
423 121	433 121	433 621	423 621	MH6
423 122	433 122	433 622	423 622	MH6
423 123	433 123	433 623	423 623	MH6
423 124	433 124	433 624	423 624	MH6

423 125	433 125	433 625	423 625	MH6
423 126	433 126	433 626	423 626	MH6
423 127	433 127	433 627	423 627	MH6
423 128	433 128	433 628	423 628	MH6
423 129	433 129	433 629	423 629	MH6
423 130	433 130	433 630	423 630	MH6
423 131	433 131	433 631	423 631	MH6
423 132	433 132	433 632	423 632	MH6
423 133	433 133	433 633	423 633	MH6
423 134	433 134	433 634	423 634	MH6
423 135	433 135	433 635	423 635	MH6
423 136	433 136	433 636	423 636	MH6
423 137	433 137	433 637	423 637	MH6
423 138	433 138	433 638	423 638	MH6
423 139	433 139	433 639	423 639	MH6
423 140	433 140	433 640	423 640	MH6
423 141	433 141	433 641	423 641	MH6
423 142	433 142	433 642	423 642	MH6
423 143	433 143	433 643	423 643	MH6
423 144	433 144	433 644	423 644	MH6
423 145	433 145	433 645	423 645	MH6
423 146	433 146	433 646	423 646	MH6
423 147	433 147	433 647	423 647	MH6
423 148	433 148	433 648	423 648	MH6
423 149	433 149	433 649	423 649	MH6
423 150	433 150	433 650	423 650	MH6
423 151	433 151	433 651	423 651	MH6
423 152	433 152	433 652	423 652	MH6
423 153	433 153	433 653	423 653	MH6
423 154	433 154	433 654	423 654	MH6
423 155	433 155	433 655	423 655	MH6
423 156	433 156	433 656	423 656	MH6
423 157	433 157	433 657	423 657	MH6
423 158	433 158	433 658	423 658	MH6
423 159	433 159	433 659	423 659	MH6
423 160	433 160	433 660	423 660	MH6
423 161	433 161	433 661	423 661	MH6
423 162	433 162	433 662	423 662	MH6
423 163	433 163	433 663	423 663	MH6
423 164	433 164	433 664	423 664	MH6
423 165	433 165	433 665	423 665	MH6
423 166	433 166	433 666	423 666	MH6
423 167	433 167	433 667	423 667	MH6
423 168	433 168	433 668	423 668	MH6
423 169	433 169	433 669	423 669	MH6
423 170	433 170	433 670	423 670	MH6
423 171	433 171	433 671	423 671	MH6
423 172	433 172	433 672	423 672	MH6
423 173	433 173	433 673	423 673	MH6
423 174	433 174	433 674	423 674	MH6
423 175	433 175	433 675	423 675	MH6
423 176	433 176	433 676	423 676	MH6
423 177	433 177	433 677	423 677	MH6
423 178	433 178	433 678	423 678	MH6
423 179	433 179	433 679	423 679	MH6
423 180	433 180	433 680	423 680	MH6
423 181	433 181	433 681	423 681	MH6
423 182	433 182	433 682	423 682	MH6
423 183	433 183	433 683	423 683	MH6
423 184	433 184	433 684	423 684	MH6
423 185	433 185	433 685	423 685	MH6
423 186	433 186	433 686	423 686	MH6
423 187	433 187	433 687	423 687	MH6
423 188	433 188	433 688	423 688	MH6

423 189	433 189	433 689	423 689	MH6
423 190	433 190	433 690	423 690	MH6
423 191	433 191	433 691	423 691	MH6
423 192	433 192	433 692	423 692	KK2
423 193	433 193	433 693	423 693	KK2
423 194	433 194	433 694	423 694	KK2
423 195	433 195	433 695	423 695	KK2
423 196	433 196	433 696	423 696	KK2
423 197	433 197	433 697	423 697	KK2
423 198	433 198	433 698	423 698	KK2
423 199	433 199	433 699	423 699	KK2
423 200	433 200	433 700	423 700	MH6
423 201	433 201	433 701	423 701	MH6
423 202	433 202	433 702	423 702	MH6
423 203	433 203	433 703	423 703	MH6
423 204	433 204	433 704	423 704	MH6
423 205	433 205	433 705	423 705	MH6
423 206	433 206	433 706	423 706	MH6

▲ Units 423 095 and 423 090 with vehicle 423 595 leading are seen at Rheinbreitbach between Bonn and Koblenz, with an empty stock movement from Krefeld-Oppum to München on 12 August 2012.   **Matthias Müller**

423 207	433 207	433 707	423 707	MH6
423 208	433 208	433 708	423 708	MH6
423 209	433 209	433 709	423 709	MH6
423 210	433 210	433 710	423 710	MH6
423 211	433 211	433 711	423 711	MH6
423 212	433 212	433 712	423 712	MH6
423 213	433 213	433 713	423 713	MH6
423 214	433 214	433 714	423 714	MH6
423 215	433 215	433 715	423 715	MH6
423 216	433 216	433 716	423 716	MH6
423 217	433 217	433 717	423 717	MH6
423 218	433 218	433 718	423 718	MH6
423 219	433 219	433 719	423 719	MH6
423 220	433 220	433 720	423 720	MH6
423 221	433 221	433 721	423 721	MH6
423 222	433 222	433 722	423 722	MH6
423 223	433 223	433 723	423 723	MH6
423 224	433 224	433 724	423 724	MH6
423 225	433 225	433 725	423 725	MH6
423 226	433 226	433 726	423 726	MH6
423 227	433 227	433 727	423 727	MH6
423 228	433 228	433 728	423 728	MH6
423 229	433 229	433 729	423 729	MH6
423 230	433 230	433 730	423 730	MH6
423 231	433 231	433 731	423 731	MH6
423 232	433 232	433 732	423 732	MH6
423 233	433 233	433 733	423 733	MH6
423 234	433 234	433 734	423 734	MH6
423 235	433 235	433 735	423 735	MH6
423 236	433 236	433 736	423 736	MH6
423 237	433 237	433 737	423 737	MH6
423 238	433 238	433 738	423 738	MH6
423 239	433 239	433 739	423 739	MH6
423 240	433 240	433 740	423 740	MH6
423 241	433 241	433 741	423 741	MH6
423 242	433 242	433 742	423 742	MH6
423 243	433 243	433 743	423 743	MH6
423 244	433 244	433 744	423 744	MH6
423 245	433 245	433 745	423 745	KK2
423 246	433 246	433 746	423 746	KK2
423 247	433 247	433 747	423 747	KD
423 248	433 248	433 748	423 748	KD
423 249	433 249	433 749	423 749	KD
423 250	433 250	433 750	423 750	KD
423 251	433 251	433 751	423 751	KD
423 252	433 252	433 752	423 752	KD
423 253	433 253	433 753	423 753	KD
423 254	433 254	433 754	423 754	KD
423 255	433 255	433 755	423 755	KD
423 256	433 256	433 756	423 756	KD
423 257	433 257	433 757	423 757	KD
423 258	433 258	433 758	423 758	KD
423 259	433 259	433 759	423 759	KD
423 260	433 260	433 760	423 760	KD
423 261	433 261	433 761	423 761	KD
423 262	433 262	433 762	423 762	KD
423 263	433 263	433 763	423 763	KD
423 264	433 264	433 764	423 764	MH6
423 265	433 265	433 765	423 765	MH6
423 266	433 266	433 766	423 766	MH6
423 267	433 267	433 767	423 767	MH6
423 268	433 268	433 768	423 768	MH6
423 269	433 269	433 769	423 769	MH6
423 270	433 270	433 770	423 770	MH6

423 271	433 271	433 771	423 771	MH6
423 272	433 272	433 772	423 772	MH6
423 273	433 273	433 773	423 773	MH6
423 274	433 274	433 774	423 774	MH6
423 275	433 275	433 775	423 775	MH6
423 276	433 276	433 776	423 776	MH6
423 277	433 277	433 777	423 777	MH6
423 278	433 278	433 778	423 778	MH6
423 279	433 279	433 779	423 779	MH6
423 280	433 280	433 780	423 780	MH6
423 281	433 281	433 781	423 781	MH6
423 282	433 282	433 782	423 782	MH6
423 283	433 283	433 783	423 783	MH6
423 284	433 284	433 784	423 784	MH6
423 285	433 285	433 785	423 785	MH6
423 286	433 286	433 786	423 786	MH6
423 287	433 287	433 787	423 787	MH6
423 288	433 288	433 788	423 788	MH6
423 289	433 289	433 789	423 789	MH6
423 290	433 290	433 790	423 790	KD
423 291	433 291	433 791	423 791	KD
423 292	433 292	433 792	423 792	KD
423 293	433 293	433 793	423 793	KD
423 294	433 294	433 794	423 794	KD
423 295	433 295	433 795	423 795	KD
423 296	433 296	433 796	423 796	KD
423 297	433 297	433 797	423 797	KD
423 298	433 298	433 798	423 798	KD
423 299	433 299	433 799	423 799	KD
423 300	433 300	433 800	423 800	KD
423 301	433 301	433 801	423 801	FF
423 302	433 302	433 802	423 802	FF
423 303	433 303	433 803	423 803	FF
423 304	433 304	433 804	423 804	FF
423 305	433 305	433 805	423 805	FF
423 306	433 306	433 806	423 806	TP
423 307	433 307	433 807	423 807	TP
423 308	433 308	433 808	423 808	TP
423 309	433 309	433 809	423 809	TP
423 310	433 310	433 810	423 810	TP
423 311	433 311	433 811	423 811	TP
423 312	433 312	433 812	423 812	MH6
423 313	433 313	433 813	423 813	MH6
423 314	433 314	433 814	423 814	MH6
423 315	433 315	433 815	423 815	MH6
423 316	433 316	433 816	423 816	MH6
423 317	433 317	433 817	423 817	MH6
423 318	433 318	433 818	423 818	MH6
423 319	433 319	433 819	423 819	MH6
423 320	433 320	433 820	423 820	MH6
423 321	433 321	433 821	423 821	MH6
423 322	433 322	433 822	423 822	TP
423 323	433 323	433 823	423 823	TP
423 324	433 324	433 824	423 824	TP
423 325	433 325	433 825	423 825	FF
423 326	433 326	433 826	423 826	FF
423 327	433 327	433 827	423 827	FF
423 328	433 328	433 828	423 828	FF
423 329	433 329	433 829	423 829	FF
423 330	433 330	433 830	423 830	FF
423 331	433 331	433 831	423 831	FF
423 332	433 332	433 832	423 832	FF
423 333	433 333	433 833	423 833	FF
423 334	433 334	433 834	423 834	FF

423 335	433 335	433 835	423 835	TP
423 336	433 336	433 836	423 836	TP
423 337	433 337	433 837	423 837	TP
423 338	433 338	433 838	423 838	TP
423 339	433 339	433 839	423 839	TP
423 340	433 340	433 840	423 840	TP
423 341	433 341	433 841	423 841	TP
423 342	433 342	433 842	423 842	TP
423 343	433 343	433 843	423 843	TP
423 344	433 344	433 844	423 844	TP
423 345	433 345	433 845	423 845	TP
423 346	433 346	433 846	423 846	TP
423 347	433 347	433 847	423 847	MH6
423 348	433 348	433 848	423 848	MH6
423 349	433 349	433 849	423 849	MH6
423 350	433 350	433 850	423 850	MH6
423 351	433 351	433 851	423 851	MH6
423 352	433 352	433 852	423 852	MH6
423 353	433 353	433 853	423 853	MH6
423 354	433 354	433 854	423 854	MH6
423 355	433 355	433 855	423 855	MH6
423 356	433 356	433 856	423 856	MH6
423 357	433 357	433 857	423 857	MH6
423 358	433 358	433 858	423 858	MH6
423 359	433 359	433 859	423 859	MH6
423 360	433 360	433 860	423 860	MH6
423 361	433 361	433 861	423 861	MH6
423 362	433 362	433 862	423 862	MH6
423 363	433 363	433 863	423 863	MH6
423 364	433 364	433 864	423 864	MH6
423 365	433 365	433 865	423 865	MH6
423 366	433 366	433 866	423 866	MH6
423 367	433 367	433 867	423 867	TP
423 368	433 368	433 868	423 868	TP
423 369	433 369	433 869	423 869	TP
423 370	433 370	433 870	423 870	TP
423 371	433 371	433 871	423 871	TP
423 372	433 372	433 872	423 872	FF
423 373	433 373	433 873	423 873	FF
423 374	433 374	433 874	423 874	FF
423 375	433 375	433 875	423 875	FF
423 376	433 376	433 876	423 876	FF
423 377	433 377	433 877	423 877	FF
423 378	433 378	433 878	423 878	FF
423 379	433 379	433 879	423 879	FF
423 380	433 380	433 880	423 880	FF
423 381	433 381	433 881	423 881	FF
423 382	433 382	433 882	423 882	FF
423 383	433 383	433 883	423 883	FF
423 384	433 384	433 884	423 884	FF
423 385	433 385	433 885	423 885	FF
423 386	433 386	433 886	423 886	FF
423 387	433 387	433 887	423 887	FF
423 388	433 388	433 888	423 888	FF
423 389	433 389	433 889	423 889	FF
423 390	433 390	433 890	423 890	FF
423 391	433 391	433 891	423 891	FF
423 392	433 392	433 892	423 892	FF
423 393	433 393	433 893	423 893	FF
423 394	433 394	433 894	423 894	FF
423 395	433 395	433 895	423 895	FF
423 396	433 396	433 896	423 896	FF
423 397	433 397	433 897	423 897	FF
423 398	433 398	433 898	423 898	FF

423 399	433 399	433 899	423 899	FF	
423 400	433 400	433 900	423 900	FF	
423 401	433 401	433 901	423 901	FF	
423 402	433 402	433 902	423 902	FF	
423 403	433 403	433 903	423 903	FF	
423 404	433 404	433 904	423 904	FF	
423 405	433 405	433 905	423 905	FF	
423 406	433 406	433 906	423 906	FF	
423 407	433 407	433 907	423 907	FF	
423 408	433 408	433 908	423 908	FF	
423 409	433 409	433 909	423 909	FF	
423 410	433 410	433 910	423 910	FF	
423 411	433 411	433 911	423 911	FF	
423 412	433 412	433 912	423 912	FF	
423 413	433 413	433 913	423 913	FF	
423 414	433 414	433 914	423 914	FF	
423 415	433 415	433 915	423 915	FF	
423 416	433 416	433 916	423 916	FF	
423 417	433 417	433 917	423 917	FF	
423 418	433 418	433 918	423 918	FF	
423 419	433 419	433 919	423 919	FF	
423 420	433 420	433 920	423 920	FF	
423 421	433 421	433 921	423 921	FF	
423 422	433 422	433 922	423 922	FF	
423 423	433 423	433 923	423 923	FF	
423 424	433 424	433 924	423 924	FF	
423 425	433 425	433 925	423 925	FF	
423 426	433 426	433 926	423 926	FF	
423 427	433 427	433 927	423 927	FF	
423 428	433 428	433 928	423 928	FF	
423 429	433 429	433 929	423 929	FF	
423 430	433 430	433 930	423 930	FF	
423 431	433 431	433 931	423 931	FF	
423 432	433 432	433 932	423 932	FF	
423 433	433 433	433 933	423 933	FF	
423 434	433 434	433 934	423 934	FF	
423 435	433 435	433 935	423 935	FF	
423 436	433 436	433 936	423 936	FF	
423 437	433 437	433 937	423 937	FF	
423 438	433 438	433 938	423 938	FF	
423 439	433 439	433 939	423 939	FF	
423 440	433 440	433 940	423 940	FF	
423 441	433 441	433 941	423 941	FF	
423 442	433 442	433 942	423 942	FF	
423 443	433 443	433 943	423 943	FF	
423 444	433 444	433 944	423 944	FF	
423 445	433 445	433 945	423 945	FF	
423 446	433 446	433 946	423 946	FF	
423 447	433 447	433 947	423 947	FF	
423 448	433 448	433 948	423 948	FF	
423 449	433 449	433 949	423 949	FF	
423 450	433 450	433 950	423 950	FF	
423 451	433 451	433 951	423 951	FF	
423 452	433 452	433 952	423 952	FF	
423 453	433 453	433 953	423 953	FF	Heusenstamm
423 454	433 454	433 954	423 954	FF	
423 455	433 455	433 955	423 955	FF	
423 456	433 456	433 956	423 956	FF	
423 457	433 457	433 957	423 957	MH6	
423 458	433 458	433 958	423 958	MH6	
423 459	433 459	433 959	423 959	MH6	
423 460	433 460	433 960	423 960	MH6	
423 461	433 461	433 961	423 961	TP	
423 462	433 462	433 962	423 962	TP	

CLASS 424 4-SECTION ARTICULATED UNITS

These articulated units are a variant of Class 425 (below) for duties around Hannover. They have a lower maximum speed and have small extensions which stick out under the doors at stations instead of the folding steps on Class 425.

AB + B + B + AB (DMCO–TSO–TSO–DMCO).

Built: 1998–99.
Builders–Mech. Parts: Bombardier/DWA Ammendorf; Siemens.
Builder–Elec. Parts: Adtranz Hennigsdorf.
Wheel Arrangement: Bo-Bo-2-Bo-Bo.
Traction Motors: 8 x 295 kW three phase asynchronous motors per set.
Accommodation: 12/24(14) + –/56 + –/56 + 12/16(16) 1TD.
Weight: 35 + 21 + 21 + 36 tonnes.
Length over Couplers: 18.24 + 15.46 + 15.46 + 18.24 m.
Width: 2.84 m. **Maximum Speed:** 140 km/h.
Wheel Diameter: 850 mm. **Floor Height:** 798 mm.

424 001	434 001	434 501	424 501	HHL	Burgdorf
424 002	434 002	434 502	424 502	HHL	Bückeburg
424 003	434 003	434 503	424 503	HHL	
424 004	434 004	434 504	424 504	HHL	Lehrte
424 005	434 005	434 505	424 505	HHL	Wedemark
424 006	434 006	434 506	424 506	HHL	Neustadt am Rübenberge
424 007	434 007	434 507	424 507	HHL	Bad Nenndorf
424 008	434 008	434 508	424 508	HHL	
424 009	434 009	434 509	424 509	HHL	
424 010	434 010	434 510	424 510	HHL	Stadthagen
424 011	434 011	434 511	424 511	HHL	
424 012	434 012	434 512	424 512	HHL	
424 013	434 013	434 513	424 513	HHL	
424 014	434 014	434 514	424 514	HHL	Springe
424 015	434 015	434 515	424 515	HHL	
424 016	434 016	434 516	424 516	HHL	
424 017	434 017	434 517	424 517	HHL	Bad Münder am Deister
424 018	434 018	434 518	424 518	HHL	Stadt Celle
424 019	434 019	434 519	424 519	HHL	Stadt Minden
424 020	434 020	434 520	424 520	HHL	
424 021	434 021	434 521	424 521	HHL	Wunstorf
424 022	434 022	434 522	424 522	HHL	
424 023	434 023	434 523	424 523	HHL	Stadt Seelze
424 024	434 024	434 524	424 524	HHL	Stadt Nienburg
424 025	434 025	434 525	424 525	HHL	
424 026	434 026	434 526	424 526	HHL	Landeshauptstadt Hannover
424 027	434 027	434 527	424 527	HHL	
424 028	434 028	434 528	424 528	HHL	
424 029	434 029	434 529	424 529	HHL	
424 030	434 030	434 530	424 530	HHL	
424 031	434 031	434 531	424 531	HHL	
424 032	434 032	434 532	424 532	HHL	Fürstenbad Pyrmont
424 033	434 033	434 533	424 533	HHL	Rattenfängerstadt Hameln
424 034	434 034	434 534	424 534	HHL	
424 035	434 035	434 535	424 535	HHL	Häste
424 036	434 036	434 536	424 536	HHL	
424 037	434 037	434 537	424 537	HHL	Stadt Langenhagen
424 038	434 038	434 538	424 538	HHL	Stadt Barsinghausen
424 039	434 039	434 539	424 539	HHL	
424 040	434 040	434 540	424 540	HHL	

▲ Having just departed from Köln Messe station, a pair of Class 425 units head for a dive-under in the adjacent network of lines on 27 July 2011. 425 092 is bringing up the rear. **Antony Guppy**

CLASS 425 — 4-SECTION ARTICULATED UNITS

These units are the new standard DB local EMU for what can be called "outer suburban" or regional services. They differ from Class 423 in that they are narrower and have only two sets of doors per carriage side provided. Other features include regenerative braking, Scharfenberg couplers and controlled emission toilets. Most units are with DB Regio but the units at Ludwigshafen belong to S-Bahn Rhein-Neckar whilst those at Hannover are with S-Bahn Hannover.

AB + B + B + AB (DMCO–TSO–TSO–DMCO).

Built: 1999–2004.
Builders–Mech. Parts: Bombardier/DWA Ammendorf, Siemens.
Builder–Elec. Parts: Adtranz Hennigsdorf.
Wheel Arrangement: Bo-Bo-2-Bo-Bo.
Traction Motors: 8 x 293 kW three phase asynchronous motors per set.
Accommodation: 12/24(14) + –/56 + –/56 + 12/16(16) 1TD.
Weight: 35 + 21 + 21 + 36 tonnes.
Length over Couplers: 18.24 + 15.46 + 15.46 + 18.24 m.
Width: 2.84 m.   **Maximum Speed:** 160 km/h.
Wheel Diameter: 850 mm.   **Floor Height:** 798 mm.

Class 425.0.

425 001	435 001	435 501	425 501	LMB
425 002	435 002	435 502	425 502	LMB
425 003	435 003	435 503	425 503	LMB
425 004	435 004	435 504	425 504	LMB
425 005	435 005	435 505	425 505	LMB
425 006	435 006	435 506	425 506	LMB
425 007	435 007	435 507	425 507	LMB
425 008	435 008	435 508	425 508	LMB
425 009	435 009	435 509	425 509	LMB
425 010	435 010	435 510	425 510	LMB
425 011	435 011	435 511	425 511	LMB
425 012	435 012	435 512	425 512	LMB
425 013	435 013	435 513	425 513	FF
425 014	435 014	435 514	425 514	FF
425 015	435 015	435 515	425 515	FF
425 016	435 016	435 516	425 516	FF
425 017	435 017	435 517	425 517	FF
425 018	435 018	435 518	425 518	FF
425 019	435 019	435 519	425 519	EMST
425 020	435 020	435 520	425 520	EMST
425 021	435 021	435 521	425 521	EMST
425 022	435 022	435 522	425 522	EMST
425 023	435 023	435 523	425 523	KK2
425 024	435 024	435 524	425 524	EMST
425 025	435 025	435 525	425 525	EMST
425 026	435 026	435 526	425 526	EMST
425 027	435 027	435 527	425 527	EMST
425 028	435 028	435 528	425 528	KK2
425 029	435 029	435 529	425 529	EMST
425 030	435 030	435 530	425 530	KK2
425 031	435 031	435 531	425 531	KK2
425 032	435 032	435 532	425 532	KK2
425 033	435 033	435 533	425 533	KK2
425 034	435 034	435 534	425 534	KK2
425 035	435 035	435 535	425 535	KK2
425 036	435 036	435 536	425 536	EMST
425 037	435 037	435 537	425 537	KK2
425 038	435 038	435 538	425 538	KK2
425 039	435 039	435 539	425 539	KK2
425 040	435 040	435 540	425 540	KK2
425 041	435 041	435 541	425 541	EMST

425 042	435 042	435 542	425 542	FF	
425 043	435 043	435 543	425 543	FF	
425 044	435 044	435 544	425 544	MH6	
425 045	435 045	435 545	425 545	MH6	
425 046	435 046	435 546	425 546	MH6	Traunstein
425 047	435 047	435 547	425 547	MH6	
425 048	435 048	435 548	425 548	RL	Bad Aibling
425 049	435 049	435 549	425 549	RL	
425 050	435 050	435 550	425 550	FF	
425 051	435 051	435 551	425 551	FF	
425 052	435 052	435 552	425 552	MH6	Weilheim
425 053	435 053	435 553	425 553	FF	
425 054	435 054	435 554	425 554	KK2	
425 055	435 055	435 555	425 555	EE	
425 056	435 056	435 556	425 556	EE	
425 057	435 057	435 557	425 557	EE	
425 058	435 058	435 558	425 558	EE	
425 059	435 059	435 559	425 559	EE	
425 060	435 060	435 560	425 560	EE	
425 061	435 061	435 561	425 561	EE	
425 062	435 062	435 562	425 562	EE	
425 063	435 063	435 563	425 563	EE	
425 064	435 064	435 564	425 564	EE	
425 065	435 065	435 565	425 565	EE	
425 066	435 066	435 566	425 566	EE	
425 067	435 067	435 567	425 567	EE	
425 068	435 068	435 568	425 568	EMST	
425 069	435 069	435 569	425 569	EE	
425 070	435 070	435 570	425 570	EE	
425 071	435 071	435 571	425 571	EMST	
425 072	435 072	435 572	425 572	EE	
425 073	435 073	435 573	425 573	EE	
425 074	435 074	435 574	425 574	EE	
425 075	435 075	435 575	425 575	EE	
425 076	435 076	435 576	425 576	EE	
425 077	435 077	435 577	425 577	EE	
425 078	435 078	435 578	425 578	EE	
425 079	435 079	435 579	425 579	EE	
425 080	435 080	435 580	425 580	EMST	
425 081	435 081	435 581	425 581	EMST	
425 082	435 082	435 582	425 582	EE	
425 083	435 083	435 583	425 583	EE	
425 084	435 084	435 584	425 584	RL	
425 085	435 085	435 585	425 585	MH6	
425 086	435 086	435 586	425 586	RL	
425 087	435 087	435 587	425 587	FF	
425 088	435 088	435 588	425 588	RL	
425 089	435 089	435 589	425 589	FF	
425 090	435 090	435 590	425 590	STR	Saarlouis
425 091	435 091	435 591	425 591	KK2	
425 092	435 092	435 592	425 592	KK2	
425 093	435 093	435 593	425 593	KK2	
425 094	435 094	435 594	425 594	KK2	
425 095	435 095	435 595	425 595	KK2	
425 096	435 096	435 596	425 596	KK2	
425 097	435 097	435 597	425 597	KK2	
425 098	435 098	435 598	425 598	KK2	
425 099	435 099	435 599	425 599	KK2	
425 100	435 100	435 600	425 600	KK2	
425 101	435 101	435 601	425 601	KK2	
425 102	435 102	435 602	425 602	KK2	
425 103	435 103	435 603	425 603	KK2	
425 104	435 104	435 604	425 604	EMST	
425 105	435 105	435 605	425 605	KK2	

425 106	435 106	435 606	425 606	KK2	
425 107	435 107	435 607	425 607	KK2	
425 108	435 108	435 608	425 608	KK2	
425 109	435 109	435 609	425 609	RL	
425 110	435 110	435 610	425 610	RL	
425 111	435 111	435 611	425 611	RL	
425 112	435 112	435 612	425 612	STR	
425 113	435 113	435 613	425 613	RL	
425 114	435 114	435 614	425 614	RL	
425 115	435 115	435 615	425 615	RL	
425 116	435 116	435 616	425 616	RL	
425 117	435 117	435 617	425 617	RL	
425 118	435 118	435 618	425 618	RL	
425 119	435 119	435 619	425 619	RL	
425 120	435 120	435 620	425 620	RL	
425 121	435 121	435 621	425 621	RL	
425 122	435 122	435 622	425 622	RL	
425 123	435 123	435 623	425 623	RL	
425 124	435 124	435 624	425 624	RL	
425 125	435 125	435 625	425 625	MH6	
425 126	435 126	435 626	425 626	MH6	Markt Bruckmühl
425 127	435 127	435 627	425 627	STR	
425 128	435 128	435 628	425 628	STR	
425 129	435 129	435 629	425 629	STR	
425 130	435 130	435 630	425 630	STR	
425 131	435 131	435 631	425 631	STR	
425 132	435 132	435 632	425 632	STR	Homburg
425 133	435 133	435 633	425 633	STR	
425 134	435 134	435 634	425 634	STR	
425 135	435 135	435 635	425 635	STR	
425 136	435 136	435 636	425 636	STR	
425 137	435 137	435 637	425 637	STR	
425 138	435 138	435 638	425 638	STR	Merzig
425 139	435 139	435 639	425 639	STR	
425 140	435 140	435 640	425 640	STR	
425 141	435 141	435 641	425 641	STR	
425 142	435 142	435 642	425 642	STR	Türkismühle
425 143	435 143	435 643	425 643	MH6	
425 144	435 144	435 644	425 644	MH6	
425 145	435 145	435 645	425 645	MH6	
425 146	435 146	435 646	425 646	MH6	Gemeinde Feldkirchen-Westerham
425 147	435 147	435 647	425 647	MH6	
425 148	435 148	435 648	425 648	MH6	
425 149	435 149	435 649	425 649	MH6	
425 150	435 150	435 650	425 650	HHL	
425 151	435 151	435 651	425 651	HHL	
425 152	435 152	435 652	425 652	HHL	Hannover Airport Line
425 153	435 153	435 653	425 653	HHL	
425 154	435 154	435 654	425 654	HHL	
425 155	435 155	435 655	425 655	HHL	Hannover Airport
425 156	435 156	435 656	425 656	RL	

Class 425.2. New units for S-Bahn Rhein–Neckar.
These units are similar to Class 425.0, but the maximum speed is 140 km/h.

425 201	435 201	435 701	425 701	RL	Mosbach
425 202	435 202	435 702	425 702	RL	Neustadt an der Weinstrasse
425 203	435 203	435 703	425 703	RL	Wiesloch Walldorf
425 204	435 204	435 704	425 704	RL	Hassloch
425 205	435 205	435 705	425 705	RL	Germersheim
425 206	435 206	435 706	425 706	RL	Mannheim
425 207	435 207	435 707	425 707	RL	Ludwigshafen am Rhein
425 208	435 208	435 708	425 708	RL	Eberbach am Neckar
425 209	435 209	435 709	425 709	RL	Speyer
425 210	435 210	435 710	425 710	RL	Heidelberg

425 211	435 211	435 711	425 711	RL	Bruchsal
425 212	435 212	435 712	425 712	RL	Kaiserslautern
425 213	435 213	435 713	425 713	RL	
425 214	435 214	435 714	425 714	RL	
425 215	435 215	435 715	425 715	RL	
425 216	435 216	435 716	425 716	RL	
425 217	435 217	435 717	425 717	RL	
425 218	435 218	435 718	425 718	RL	
425 219	435 219	435 719	425 719	RL	
425 220	435 220	435 720	425 720	RL	
425 221	435 221	435 721	425 721	RL	
425 222	435 222	435 722	425 722	RL	
425 223	435 223	435 723	425 723	RL	
425 224	435 224	435 724	425 724	RL	
425 225	435 225	435 725	425 725	RL	
425 226	435 226	435 726	425 726	RL	
425 227	435 227	435 727	425 727	RL	
425 228	435 228	435 728	425 728	RL	
425 229	435 229	435 729	425 729	RL	
425 230	435 230	435 730	425 730	RL	
425 231	435 231	435 731	425 731	RL	
425 232	435 232	435 732	425 732	RL	

▲ 426 036 and 426 031 form an RB service from Koblenz to Cochem near Pommern in the Mosel valley on 29 September 2011. **Matthias Müller**

425 233	435 233	435 733	425 733	RL	
425 234	435 234	435 734	425 734	RL	
425 235	435 235	435 735	425 735	RL	
425 236	435 236	435 736	425 736	RL	
425 237	435 237	435 737	425 737	RL	
425 238	435 238	435 738	425 738	RL	
425 239	435 239	435 739	425 739	RL	
425 240	435 240	435 740	425 740	RL	
425 250	435 250	435 750	425 750	RL	
425 251	435 251	435 751	425 751	RL	
425 252	435 252	435 752	425 752	RL	
425 253	435 253	435 753	425 753	RL	
425 254	435 254	435 754	425 754	RL	
425 255	435 255	435 755	425 755	RL	
425 256	435 256	435 756	425 756	RL	
425 257	435 257	435 757	425 757	RL	
425 258	435 258	435 758	425 758	RL	
425 259	435 259	435 759	425 759	RL	
425 260	435 260	435 760	425 760	RL	
425 261	435 261	435 761	425 761	RL	
425 262	435 262	435 762	425 762	RL	
425 263	435 263	435 763	425 763	RL	
425 264	435 264	435 764	425 764	RL	
425 265	435 265	435 765	425 765	RL	
425 266	435 266	435 766	425 766	RL	
425 267	435 267	435 767	425 767	RL	
425 268	435 268	435 768	425 768	RL	
425 269	435 269	435 769	425 769	RL	
425 271	435 271	435 771	425 771	HHL	Laatzen
425 272	435 272	435 772	425 772	HHL	Sehnde
425 273	435 273	435 773	425 773	HHL	
425 274	435 274	435 774	425 774	HHL	
425 275	435 275	435 775	425 775	HHL	
425 276	435 276	435 776	425 776	HHL	
425 277	435 277	435 777	425 777	HHL	
425 278	435 278	435 778	425 778	HHL	
425 279	435 279	435 779	425 779	HHL	
425 280	435 280	435 780	425 780	HHL	
425 281	435 281	435 781	425 781	HHL	Hildesheim
425 282	435 282	435 782	425 782	HHL	
425 283	435 283	435 783	425 783	HHL	

Class 425.3. New units for S-Bahn Rhein-Neckar and Rheinland Pfalz–Saarland.
These units are similar to Class 425.0, but the maximum speed is 140 km/h.

425 301	435 301	435 801	425 801	RL	
425 302	435 301	435 801	425 802	TP	
425 303	435 301	435 801	425 803	TP	
425 304	435 301	435 801	425 804	TP	
425 305	435 301	435 801	425 805	TP	
425 306	435 301	435 801	425 806	TP	
425 307	435 301	435 801	425 807	TP	
425 308	435 301	435 801	425 808	TP	
425 309	435 301	435 801	425 809	TP	
425 310	435 301	435 801	425 810	TP	
425 311	435 301	435 801	425 811	TP	
425 312	435 301	435 801	425 812	TP	
425 313	435 301	435 801	425 813	TP	
425 314	435 301	435 801	425 814	TP	
425 315	435 301	435 801	425 815	HBS	Hude (Old)
425 316	435 301	435 801	425 816	HBS	Stadt Wolfsburg
425 317	435 301	435 801	425 817	HBS	Elsfleth
425 318	435 301	435 801	425 818	HBS	Brake (Unterweser)
425 319	435 301	435 801	425 819	HBS	Berne
425 320	435 301	435 801	425 820	HBS	Nordenham

CLASS 426 2-SECTION ARTICULATED UNITS

These sets are two-car versions of Class 425 and have similar features.

AB + B (DMCO–DMSO).

Built: 1999–2002.
Builders–Mech. Parts: Bombardier/DWA Ammendorf; Siemens/Duewag.
Builder–Elec. Parts: Adtranz Hennigsdorf.
Wheel Arrangement: Bo-2-Bo.
Traction Motors: 4 x 293 kW three phase asynchronous motors per set.
Accommodation: 12/16(16) 1TD + –/40(14).
Weight: 35 + 35 tonnes.
Length over Couplers: 18.245 + 18.245 m.
Width: 2.84 m. **Maximum Speed:** 160 km/h.
Wheel Diameter: 850 mm. **Floor Height:** 798 mm.

426 001	426 501	FF		426 023	426 523	STR	
426 002	426 502	FF		426 024	426 524	EMST	
426 003	426 503	FF		426 025	426 525	EMST	
426 004	426 504	STR		426 026	426 526	EMST	
426 005	426 505	STR		426 027	426 527	EMST	
426 006	426 506	STR		426 028	426 528	MH6	
426 007	426 507	STR		426 029	426 529	MH6	
426 008	426 508	STR		426 030	426 530	MH6	
426 009	426 509	TP		426 031	426 531	MH6	
426 010	426 510	TP		426 032	426 532	MH6	
426 011	426 511	TP		426 033	426 533	MH6	
426 012	426 512	TP		426 034	426 534	MH6	
426 013	426 513	TP		426 035	426 535	MH6	
426 014	426 514	TP		426 036	426 536	STR	
426 015	426 515	STR		426 037	426 537	STR	
426 016	426 516	STR		426 038	426 538	STR	
426 017	426 517	STR		426 039	426 539	STR	
426 018	426 518	STR		426 040	426 540	STR	
426 019	426 519	STR		426 041	426 541	STR	
426 020	426 520	STR		426 042	426 542	STR	
426 021	426 521	STR		426 043	426 543	STR	
426 022	426 522	STR					

Names:

426 004	Wahlhausen		426 036	Rohrbach
426 005	Limbach		426 037	Illingen
426 006	Oberlinxweiler		426 039	Wemmetsweiler
426 007	Kirkel		426 040	Namborn
426 008	Besseringen		426 041	Rentrisch
426 028	Tirol		426 042	Hofeld
426 029	Reutte		426 043	Miederlinxweiler
426 030	Oberammergau			

CLASS 1428   4-SECTION ARTICULATED UNITS

In 2012 DB Regio NRW ordered 14 FLIRT EMUs from Stadler to be based at Münster most likely as replacements for the 425s working from there on RB42/RE42 services. These are to be FLIRT 3 sets slightly modified from earlier versions to meet new European TSI and crash standards (EN 15227). These lightweight sets are aluminium and feature all the latest fittings expected these days – air conditioned, two vacuum toilets (one disabled), three multi-purpose areas, information displays, laptop sockets, CCTV etc and automatic couplings. At time of going to press full details of the numbering had not been announced; details will appear in the Platform 5 magazine *TODAY'S RAILWAY'S EUROPE* when known.

AB + B +B + B (DMCOL- TSO–TSOL -DMSO).

Built: 2014
Builders–Mech. Parts: Stadler.
Builder–Elec. Parts:
Wheel Arrangement: Bo-2-2-2-Bo.
Traction Motors: 4 x 500 kW.
Accommodation: 24/201. 2T (1 disabled).
Weight: 132.9 tonnes.   **Wheel Diameter:** 920 mm, (powered), 760 mm (unpowered).
Length over Couplers: 74.70m.   **Maximum Speed:** 160 km/h.
Width: 2.88 m.   **Floor Height:** 780 mm.

1428 001	1828	1828	1428 501	(EMS)
1428 002	1828	1828	1428 502	(EMS)
1428 003	1828	1828	1428 503	(EMS)
1428 004	1828	1828	1428 504	(EMS)
1428 005	1828	1828	1428 505	(EMS)
1428 006	1828	1828	1428 506	(EMS)
1428 007	1828	1828	1428 507	(EMS)
1428 008	1828	1828	1428 508	(EMS)
1428 009	1828	1828	1428 509	(EMS)
1428 010	1828	1828	1428 510	(EMS)
1428 011	1828	1828	1428 511	(EMS)
1428 012	1828	1828	1428 512	(EMS)
1428 013	1828	1828	1428 513	(EMS)
1428 014	1828	1828	1428 514	(EMS)

▲ 429 030 is seen working an RE service from Stralsund to Sassnitz near Rambin on the island of Rügen on 23 May 2010. Car 429 530 is leading.   **Matthias Müller**

CLASS 429.0   5-SECTION ARTICULATED UNITS

These units are the well liked Stadler FLIRT low floor articulated EMUs originally designated Class 427 by DB. The class number was changed by the EBA from 01/01/09 to 429 when European numbering came along so the DB sets were given running numbers following those sets already with private operators. Like other Stadler products these EMUs are fine sets but surprisingly only have one set of doors per carriage. Air conditioned, disabled toilet, multi-purpose area (tip up seats and catering machines) in fact everything you would expect to find on a modern unit (including plugs for laptops). All five sets are allocated to Rostock and work Rostock–Stralsund–Sassnitz/Ostseebad Binz.

AB + B + B + B + AB (DMCO–TSO–TSO-TSO–DMCO).

Built: 2007.
Builder–Mech. Parts: Stadler
Builder–Elec. Parts:
Wheel Arrangement: Bo-2-2-2-2-Bo.
Traction Motors: 4 x 500 kW three phase asynchronous motors per set.
Accommodation: Total 15F/225S plus 33 tip up.
Weight: 145 tonnes.
Length over Couplers: **Maximum Speed:** 160 km/h.
Width: 2.88 m.   **Floor Height:** 600 mm. (90%), 1120 mm (10%).
Wheel Diameter: 860 mm (Powered), 750 mm (non-powered).

429 026	829 026	829 326	829 626	429 526	WR	
429 027	829 027	829 327	829 627	429 527	WR	
429 028	829 028	829 328	829 628	429 528	WR	Hansestadt Stralsund
429 029	829 029	829 329	829 629	429 529	WR	
429 030	829 030	829 330	829 630	429 530	WR	

CLASS 429.1   5-SECTION ARTICULATED UNITS

DB Regio has ordered 28 five car articulated emus from Stadler for services in Rheinland Pfalz. Like other units from this builder aluminium construction provides a lightweight unit which is fitted out with air conditioning, vacuum toilets, laptop sockets, CCTV, etc. The design is modified from the earlier version to meet new European TSI and crash standards. Each vehicle has one set of doors per side except the middle vehicle which has none. Full numbering details have not been announced and when known will appear in the Platform 5 magazine *TODAY'S RAILWAYS EUROPE.*

B + B + B + B + AB (DMSO- TSOL-TSO-TSOL-DMCO)

Built: 2013–14.
Builders–Mech. Parts: Stadler.
Builder–Elec. Parts:
Wheel Arrangement: Bo-2-2-2-2-Bo.
Traction Motors: 4 x 500 kW
Accommodation: 21/249, 2T (1 disabled).
Weight: circa 156 tonnes.   **Wheel Diameter:** 920 mm, (powered), 760 mm (unpowered).
Length over Couplers: 90.800m.   **Maximum Speed:** 160 km/h.
Width: 2.88 m.   **Floor Height:** 780/1200 mm, (low/high).

429 100	829	829	829	429 600	(STR)
429 101	829	829	829	429 601	(STR)
429 102	829	829	829	429 602	(STR)
429 103	829	829	829	429 603	(STR)
429 104	829	829	829	429 604	(STR)
429 105	829	829	829	429 605	(STR)
429 106	829	829	829	429 606	(STR)
429 107	829	829	829	429 607	(STR)
429 108	829	829	829	429 608	(STR)
429 109	829	829	829	429 609	(STR)
429 110	829	829	829	429 610	(STR)
429 111	829	829	829	429 611	(STR)

429 112	829	829	829	429 612	(STR)
429 113	829	829	829	429 613	(STR)
429 114	829	829	829	429 614	(STR)
429 115	829	829	829	429 615	(STR)
429 116	829	829	829	429 616	(STR)
429 117	829	829	829	429 617	(STR)
429 118	829	829	829	429 618	(STR)
429 119	829	829	829	429 619	(STR)
429 120	829	829	829	429 620	(STR)
429 121	829	829	829	429 621	(STR)
429 122	829	829	829	429 622	(STR)
429 123	829	829	829	429 623	(STR)
429 124	829	829	829	429 624	(STR)
429 125	829	829	829	429 625	(STR)
429 126	829	829	829	429 626	(STR)
429 127	829	829	829	429 627	(STR)

CLASS 430　　　　　　　　4-SECTION ARTICULATED UNITS

Class 430 is yet another S-Bahn unit, this time for the Stuttgart system. 83 sets have been ordered to replace the remaining Class 420s on the Stuttgart system. 29 sets are to be built by Alstom in Salzgitter and 54 by Bombardier in Aachen. The first sets have already been built and testing is taking place with a view to entry into service in 2013. Subsequently DB ordered a few extra sets for Stuttgart incorporating them into a new order for the Rhein-Ruhr area but the Rhein-Ruhr area cancelled their units! However the Rhein Main area has since ordered 90 sets which will replace the remaining Class 420s there.

AB + B + B + AB (DMCO–TSO–TSO–DMCO).

Built: 2011–
Builder–Mech. Parts: Alstom.
Builder–Elec. Parts: Bombardier.
Wheel Arrangement: Bo-Bo-2-Bo-Bo.
Traction Motors: 8 x 295 kW three phase asynchronous motors per set.
Accommodation: 8/40 + –/48 + –/48 + 8/40.
Weight: 119 tonnes.
Length over Couplers: 15.14 + 14.894 + 14.894 + 15.14 m.
Width: 3.03 m.　　　　　　　　　　　　　**Maximum Speed:** 140 km/h.
Wheel Diameter:　　　　　　　　　　　**Floor Height:** 1025 mm.

430 001	431 001	431 501	430 501	(TP)
430 002	431 002	431 502	430 502	(TP)
430 003	431 003	431 503	430 503	(TP)
430 004	431 004	431 504	430 504	(TP)
430 005	431 005	431 505	430 505	(TP)
430 006	431 006	431 506	430 506	(TP)
430 007	431 007	431 507	430 507	(TP)
430 008	431 008	431 508	430 508	(TP)
430 009	431 009	431 509	430 509	TP
430 010	431 010	431 510	430 510	(TP)
430 011	431 011	431 511	430 511	(TP)
430 012	431 012	431 512	430 512	(TP)
430 013	431 013	431 513	430 513	(TP)
430 014	431 014	431 514	430 514	(TP)
430 015	431 015	431 515	430 515	TP
430 016	431 016	431 516	430 516	(TP)
430 017	431 017	431 517	430 517	(TP)
430 018	431 018	431 518	430 518	(TP)
430 019	431 019	431 519	430 519	(TP)
430 020	431 020	431 520	430 520	TP
430 021	431 021	431 521	430 521	TP
430 022	431 022	431 522	430 522	TP
430 023	431 023	431 523	430 523	TP
430 024	431 024	431 524	430 524	(TP)

430 025	431 025	431 525	430 525	(TP)
430 026	431 026	431 526	430 526	TP
430 027	431 027	431 527	430 527	(TP)
430 028	431 028	431 528	430 528	TP
430 029	431 029	431 529	430 529	(TP)
430 030	431 030	431 530	430 530	(TP)
430 031	431 031	431 531	430 531	(TP)
430 032	431 032	431 532	430 532	(TP)
430 033	431 033	431 533	430 533	(TP)
430 034	431 034	431 534	430 534	(TP)
430 035	431 035	431 535	430 535	(TP)
430 036	431 036	431 536	430 536	(TP)
430 037	431 037	431 537	430 537	(TP)
430 038	431 038	431 538	430 538	(TP)
430 039	431 039	431 539	430 539	(TP)
430 040	431 040	431 540	430 540	(TP)
430 041	431 041	431 541	430 541	(TP)
430 042	431 042	431 542	430 542	(TP)
430 043	431 043	431 543	430 543	(TP)
430 044	431 044	431 544	430 544	(TP)
430 045	431 045	431 545	430 545	(TP)
430 046	431 046	431 546	430 546	(TP)
430 047	431 047	431 547	430 547	(TP)
430 048	431 048	431 548	430 548	(TP)
430 049	431 049	431 549	430 549	(TP)
430 050	431 050	431 550	430 550	(TP)

▲ 440 203, one of the 5-section variants of Class 440, is seen near Marling whilst forming an RB service from Freising to Landshut on 16 July 2010. **Matthias Müller**

430 051	431 051	431 551	430 551	(TP)
430 052	431 052	431 552	430 552	(TP)
430 053	431 053	431 553	430 553	(TP)
430 054	431 054	431 554	430 554	(TP)
430 055	431 055	431 555	430 555	(TP)
430 056	431 056	431 556	430 556	(TP)
430 057	431 057	431 557	430 557	(TP)
430 058	431 058	431 558	430 558	(TP)
430 059	431 059	431 559	430 559	(TP)
430 060	431 060	431 560	430 560	(TP)
430 061	431 061	431 561	430 561	(TP)
430 062	431 062	431 562	430 562	(TP)
430 063	431 063	431 563	430 563	(TP)
430 064	431 064	431 564	430 564	(TP)
430 065	431 065	431 565	430 565	(TP)
430 066	431 066	431 566	430 566	(TP)
430 067	431 067	431 567	430 567	(TP)
430 068	431 068	431 568	430 568	(TP)
430 069	431 069	431 569	430 569	(TP)
430 070	431 070	431 570	430 570	(TP)
430 071	431 071	431 571	430 571	(TP)
430 072	431 072	431 572	430 572	(TP)
430 073	431 073	431 573	430 573	(TP)
430 074	431 074	431 574	430 574	(TP)
430 075	431 075	431 575	430 575	(TP)
430 076	431 076	431 576	430 576	(TP)
430 077	431 077	431 577	430 577	(TP)
430 078	431 078	431 578	430 578	(TP)
430 079	431 079	431 579	430 579	(TP)
430 080	431 080	431 580	430 580	(TP)
430 081	431 081	431 581	430 581	(TP)
430 082	431 082	431 582	430 582	(TP)
430 083	431 083	431 583	430 583	(TP)
430 084	431 084	431 584	430 584	(TP)
430 085	431 085	431 585	430 585	(TP)
430 086	431 086	431 586	430 586	(TP)
430 087	431 087	431 587	430 587	(TP)
430 101	431 101	431 601	430 601	(FF)
430 102	431 102	431 602	430 602	(FF)
430 103	431 103	431 603	430 603	(FF)
430 104	431 104	431 604	430 604	(FF)
430 105	431 105	431 605	430 605	(FF)
430 106	431 106	431 606	430 606	(FF)
430 107	431 107	431 607	430 607	(FF)
430 108	431 108	431 608	430 608	(FF)
430 109	431 109	431 609	430 609	(FF)
430 110	431 110	431 610	430 610	(FF)
430 111	431 111	431 611	430 611	(FF)
430 112	431 112	431 612	430 612	(FF)
430 113	431 113	431 613	430 613	(FF)
430 114	431 114	431 614	430 614	(FF)
430 115	431 115	431 615	430 615	(FF)
430 116	431 116	431 616	430 616	(FF)
430 117	431 117	431 617	430 617	(FF)
430 118	431 118	431 618	430 618	(FF)
430 119	431 119	431 619	430 619	(FF)
430 120	431 120	431 620	430 620	(FF)
430 121	431 121	431 621	430 621	(FF)
430 122	431 122	431 622	430 622	(FF)
430 123	431 123	431 623	430 623	(FF)
430 124	431 124	431 624	430 624	(FF)
430 125	431 125	431 625	430 625	(FF)
430 126	431 126	431 626	430 626	(FF)

430 127	431 127	431 627	430 627	(FF)
430 128	431 128	431 628	430 628	(FF)
430 129	431 129	431 629	430 629	(FF)
430 130	431 130	431 630	430 630	(FF)
430 131	431 131	431 631	430 631	(FF)
430 132	431 132	431 632	430 632	(FF)
430 133	431 133	431 633	430 633	(FF)
430 134	431 134	431 634	430 634	(FF)
430 135	431 135	431 635	430 635	(FF)
430 136	431 136	431 636	430 636	(FF)
430 137	431 137	431 637	430 637	(FF)
430 138	431 138	431 638	430 638	(FF)
430 139	431 139	431 639	430 639	(FF)
430 140	431 140	431 640	430 640	(FF)
430 141	431 141	431 641	430 641	(FF)
430 142	431 142	431 642	430 642	(FF)
430 143	431 143	431 643	430 643	(FF)
430 144	431 144	431 644	430 644	(FF)
430 145	431 145	431 645	430 645	(FF)
430 146	431 146	431 646	430 646	(FF)
430 147	431 147	431 647	430 647	(FF)
430 148	431 148	431 648	430 648	(FF)
430 149	431 149	431 649	430 649	(FF)
430 150	431 150	431 650	430 650	(FF)
430 151	431 151	431 651	430 651	(FF)
430 152	431 152	431 652	430 652	(FF)
430 153	431 153	431 653	430 653	(FF)
430 154	431 154	431 654	430 654	(FF)
430 155	431 155	431 655	430 655	(FF)
430 156	431 156	431 656	430 656	(FF)
430 157	431 157	431 657	430 657	(FF)
430 158	431 158	431 658	430 658	(FF)
430 159	431 159	431 659	430 659	(FF)
430 160	431 160	431 660	430 660	(FF)
430 161	431 161	431 661	430 661	(FF)
430 162	431 162	431 662	430 662	(FF)
430 163	431 163	431 663	430 663	(FF)
430 164	431 164	431 664	430 664	(FF)
430 165	431 165	431 665	430 665	(FF)
430 166	431 166	431 666	430 666	(FF)
430 167	431 167	431 667	430 667	(FF)
430 168	431 168	431 668	430 668	(FF)
430 169	431 169	431 669	430 669	(FF)
430 170	431 170	431 670	430 670	(FF)
430 171	431 171	431 671	430 671	(FF)
430 172	431 172	431 672	430 672	(FF)
430 173	431 173	431 673	430 673	(FF)
430 174	431 174	431 674	430 674	(FF)
430 175	431 175	431 675	430 675	(FF)
430 176	431 176	431 676	430 676	(FF)
430 177	431 177	431 677	430 677	(FF)
430 178	431 178	431 678	430 678	(FF)
430 179	431 179	431 679	430 679	(FF)
430 180	431 180	431 680	430 680	(FF)
430 181	431 181	431 681	430 681	(FF)
430 182	431 182	431 682	430 682	(FF)
430 183	431 183	431 683	430 683	(FF)
430 184	431 184	431 684	430 684	(FF)
430 185	431 185	431 685	430 685	(FF)
430 186	431 186	431 686	430 686	(FF)
430 187	431 187	431 687	430 687	(FF)
430 188	431 188	431 688	430 688	(FF)
430 189	431 189	431 689	430 689	(FF)
430 190	431 190	431 690	430 690	(FF)

CLASS 440   3, 4 & 5-SECTION ARTICULATED UNITS

Class 440 is known as the Alstom Coradia Continental incorporating ideas learnt from the Class 618 LIREX experimental DMU. Just like Bombardier, Alstom is offering its latest product in 2, 3, 4, and 5-car versions. A big change is that to accomplish the low floor, a lot of electrical equipment is on the roof! In 2006 DB Regio ordered 26 3-car, 48 4-car and 6 5-car sets for various services around Augsburg, München, Nürnberg and Würzburg. The 440 has also been ordered by private operators Agilis and Nord West Bahn, details of which appear in German Railways Part 2. The driving cars have differing lengths, sets being "short" or "long". All DB sets so far are "short". Teething problems ensued with air-conditioning, toilets and couplings. The EBA had its own concerns which also helped to delay entry into service of the units. The problems overcome, the Augsburg area units entered service in December 2009 one year late.

CLASS 440.0   4-SECTION ARTICULATED UNITS

For its *E-Netz Augsburg*, DB Regio ordered 37 4-section 440s so that services from München via Augsburg to Treutchlingen and Ulm could be improved. Using EMUs the *"Fugger Express"* as the new service is called allowed trains from München to split at Augsburg for the above destinations. 440 002 experienced a fire with some roof equipment whilst standing in Augsburg on 23/06/09 but was back in service by the end of that year. Later DB Regio ordered five more sets for the Würzburg area and six sets for München – Passau.

AB + B + B + AB (DMCO–TSO–TSO–DMCO).

Built: 2008–10.
Builder–Mech. Parts: Alstom
Builder–Elec. Parts:
Wheel Arrangement: Bo-Bo-2-Bo-Bo.
Traction Motors: 8 x 360 kW three phase asynchronous motors per set.
Accommodation: 8/40 + –/48 + –/48 + 8/40.
Weight: 140 tonnes.
Length over Couplers: 70.90 m.
Width: 2.92 m.   **Maximum Speed:** 160 km/h.
Wheel Diameter: 850 mm.   **Floor height:** 600 mm (entrance), 730 mm (saloons).

440 001	441 001	441 501	440 501	MH6
440 002	441 002	441 502	440 502	MH6
440 003	441 003	441 503	440 503	MH6
440 004	441 004	441 504	440 504	MH6
440 005	441 005	441 505	440 505	MH6
440 006	441 006	441 506	440 506	MH6
440 007	441 007	441 507	440 507	MH6
440 008	441 008	441 508	440 508	MH6
440 009	441 009	441 509	440 509	MH6
440 010	441 010	441 510	440 510	MH6
440 011	441 011	441 511	440 511	MH6
440 012	441 012	441 512	440 512	MH6
440 013	441 013	441 513	440 513	MH6
440 014	441 014	441 514	440 514	MH6
440 015	441 015	441 515	440 515	MH6
440 016	441 016	441 516	440 516	MH6
440 017	441 017	441 517	440 517	MH6
440 018	441 018	441 518	440 518	MH6
440 019	441 019	441 519	440 519	MH6
440 020	441 020	441 520	440 520	MH6
440 021	441 021	441 521	440 521	MH6
440 022	441 022	441 522	440 522	MH6
440 023	441 023	441 523	440 523	MH6
440 024	441 024	441 524	440 524	MH6
440 025	441 025	441 525	440 525	MH6
440 026	441 026	441 526	440 526	MH6

440 027	441 027	441 527	440 527	MH6	
440 028	441 028	441 528	440 528	MH6	
440 029	441 029	441 529	440 529	MH6	
440 030	441 030	441 530	440 530	MH6	
440 031	441 031	441 531	440 531	MH6	
440 032	441 032	441 532	440 532	MH6	
440 033	441 033	441 533	440 533	MH6	
440 034	441 034	441 534	440 534	MH6	
440 035	441 035	441 535	440 535	MH6	
440 036	441 036	441 536	440 536	MH6	
440 037	441 037	441 537	440 537	MH6	
440 038	441 038	441 538	440 538	NWH	
440 039	441 039	441 539	440 539	NWH	
440 040	441 040	441 540	440 540	NWH	
440 041	441 041	441 541	440 541	NWH	
440 042	441 042	441 542	440 542	NWH	
440 043	441 043	441 543	440 543	MH6	
440 044	441 044	441 544	440 544	MH6	Plattling
440 045	441 045	441 545	440 545	MH6	
440 046	441 046	441 546	440 546	MH6	
440 047	441 047	441 547	440 547	MH6	
440 048	441 048	441 548	440 548	MH6	

▲ 3-section Class 440, 440 309 works local service RB 58041, the 1157 from Jossa to Würzburg Hauptbahnhof on 16 March 2012, seen near Himmelstadt. **Matthias Müller**

CLASS 440.2   5-SECTION ARTICULATED UNITS

These five section sets were ordered by DB Regio for the *Donau–Isar Express* service *(DIEX)* which is the name given to the RE service from München to Passau. A mixture of 4 and 5 section units was ordered.

AB + B + B + B + AB (DMCO–TSO–TSO–TSO–DMCO).

Built: 2009–10.
Builder–Mech. Parts: Alstom.
Builder–Elec. Parts:
Wheel Arrangement: Bo-Bo-2-2-Bo-Bo.
Traction Motors: 8 x 360 kW three phase asynchronous motors per set.
Accommodation: 24F/266S per set.
Weight:
Length over Couplers: 87.90 m.
Width: 2.92 m.   **Maximum Speed:** 160 km/h.
Wheel Diameter: 850 mm.   **Floor Height:** 600 mm (entrance), 730 mm (saloons).

440 201	441 201	841 201	441 701	440 701	MH6	
440 202	441 202	841 202	441 702	440 702	MH6	
440 203	441 203	841 203	441 703	440 703	MH6	Passau
440 204	441 204	841 204	441 704	440 704	MH6	
440 205	441 205	841 205	441 705	440 705	MH6	
440 206	441 206	841 206	441 706	440 706	NWH	

CLASS 440.3   3-SECTION ARTICULATED UNITS

The third type of Coradia Continental ordered by DB Regio is a three section train for services based on Würzburg. Although allocated there at the moment, when the new depot in Nürnberg opens it is fully expected they will be located there. Routes covered include Nürnberg–Würzburg, Nürnberg–Aisch and from Würzburg to Kitzingen, Bamberg and Treutchlingen. The DB units are short sets whilst Nord West Bahn has ordered some long sets.

AB + B + AB (DMCO–TSO–DMCO).

Built: 2008–2010, 2012–2014.
Builder–Mech. Parts: Alstom.
Builder–Elec. Parts:
Wheel Arrangement: Bo-2-Bo-Bo.
Traction Motors: 6 x 360 kW three phase asynchronous motors per set.
Accommodation:
Weight: 112 tonnes.
Length over Couplers: 54.50 m.
Width: 2.92 m.   **Maximum Speed:** 160 km/h.
Wheel Diameter: 850 mm.   **Floor Height:** 600 mm (entrance), 730 mm (saloons).

440 301	441 801	440 801	NWH	440 314	441 814	440 814	NWH
440 302	441 802	440 802	NWH	440 315	441 815	440 815	NWH
440 303	441 803	440 803	NWH	440 316	441 816	440 816	NWH
440 304	441 804	440 804	NWH	440 317	441 817	440 817	NWH
440 305	441 805	440 805	NWH	440 318	441 818	440 818	NWH
440 306	441 806	440 806	NWH	440 319	441 819	440 819	NWH
440 307	441 807	440 807	NWH	440 320	441 820	440 820	NWH
440 308	441 808	440 808	NWH	440 321	441 821	440 821	NWH
440 309	441 809	440 809	NWH	440 322	441 822	440 822	NWH
440 310	441 810	440 810	NWH	440 323	441 823	440 823	NWH
440 311	441 811	440 811	NWH	440 324	441 824	440 824	NWH
440 312	441 812	440 812	NWH	440 325	441 825	440 825	NWH
440 313	441 813	440 813	NWH	440 326	441 826	440 826	NWH

CLASS 1440 3-SECTION ARTICULATED UNITS

DB Regio Nordrheinwestfalen has ordered from Alstom 28 3-car emus to operate on S5 and S8 services As the design has been updated to meet the new European TSI and crash standards these units have been given the 1440 classification but full details were still awaited as this book went to press.

Built: 2014–
Builder–Mech. Parts: Alstom
Builder–Elec. Parts:
Wheel Arrangement:
Traction Motors:
Accommodation:
Weight:
Length over Couplers:
Width:
Wheel Diameter:

Maximum Speed:
Floor Height:

1440 300	1441 300	1440 800	(KD)	1440 314	1441 314	1440 814	(KD)
1440 301	1441 301	1440 801	(KD)	1440 315	1441 315	1440 815	(KD)
1440 302	1441 302	1440 802	(KD)	1440 316	1441 316	1440 816	(KD)
1440 303	1441 303	1440 803	(KD)	1440 317	1441 317	1440 817	(KD)
1440 304	1441 304	1440 804	(KD)	1440 318	1441 318	1440 818	(KD)
1440 305	1441 305	1440 805	(KD)	1440 319	1441 319	1440 819	(KD)
1440 306	1441 306	1440 806	(KD)	1440 320	1441 320	1440 820	(KD)
1440 307	1441 307	1440 807	(KD)	1440 321	1441 321	1440 821	(KD)
1440 308	1441 308	1440 808	(KD)	1440 322	1441 322	1440 822	(KD)
1440 309	1441 309	1440 809	(KD)	1440 323	1441 323	1440 823	(KD)
1440 310	1441 310	1440 810	(KD)	1440 324	1441 324	1440 824	(KD)
1440 311	1441 311	1440 811	(KD)	1440 325	1441 325	1440 825	(KD)
1440 312	1441 312	1440 812	(KD)	1440 326	1441 326	1440 826	(KD)
1440 313	1441 313	1440 813	(KD)	1440 327	1441 327	1440 827	(KD)

CLASS 442 2, 3, 4 & 5-SECTION ARTICULATED UNITS

This class is the Talent 2 – Bombardier's new EMU train offered in various versions. It is an updated version of the Talent EMUs delivered to Austria but has been bedevilled with problems. Whilst the first units were being built regulations were changed which the EBA insisted had to apply to these new units. A dispute situation arose but construction never stopped. DB Regio had entered a framework contract for up to 321 EMUs ordering the first sets in 2007 followed by more and more with the total being 295 at the end of 2011. The first 4-car unit appeared at Innotrans in Berlin in 2008 but by late 2011 no units had entered traffic (over 100 built!). There are reports that Bombardier itself had to dismantle (scrap?) some sets as construction defects were found. In March 2011 the EBA authorised the sets for Nürnberg to enter traffic but not in multiple and not to exceed 140 km/h. DB Regio refused to accept these conditions. In July 2011 the EBA agreed for the Nürnberg sets to run in multiple but still restricted to 140 km/h. DB Regio would not accept the units as they had ordered sets for 160 km/h! Meanwhile there had been other problems as these units also had the Ebicab 500 safety system as on the Ruhr 430s where problems had been encountered so all the 442s had to have software updates. During autumn 2011 the EBA authorised the 4-car sets for Nürnberg and Trier to run without restriction but there was no clearance for the other versions. In late autumn 2011 some of the 4-car sets were seen to be on driver training duties at Trier, Aachen, Berlin, Cottbus and Nürnberg and in 2012 units were slowly authorised for service in those areas.

CLASS 442.0   2-SECTION ARTICULATED UNITS

DB Regio having won some franchise contracts ordered new 2-car EMUs from Bombardier for use around Trier, Cottbus and München. Because of the problems outlined above none had entered service in late 2011 making those for Trier and Cottbus two years late. Those for München might actually enter service on time – December 2013!

AB + B (DMCO–DMSO).

Built: 2008–09.
Builder–Mech. Parts: Bombardier.
Builder–Elec. Parts: Bombardier.
Wheel Arrangement: Bo-2-Bo.
Traction Motors: 4 x 505 kW three phase asynchronous motors per set.
Accommodation: 8/46 + 0/45 plus 10 tip up.
Weight:
Length over Couplers: 20.05 + 20.05 m.
Width: 2.926 m.   **Maximum Speed:** 160 km/h.
Wheel Diameter: 850 mm.   **Floor Height:** 800 mm (entrance), 695/1250 (saloons).

442 001	442 501	STR		442 007	442 507	BCS
442 002	442 502	(STR)		442 008	442 508	BCS
442 003	442 503	STR		442 009	442 509	(MH6)
442 004	442 504	STR		442 010	442 510	(MH6)
442 005	442 505	STR		442 011	442 511	(MH6)
442 006	442 506	BCS				

CLASS 442.1   3-SECTION ARTICULATED UNITS

As part of the framework contract with Bombardier DB Regio ordered several batches of 3-car sets as follows; Rhein-Sieg Express (3 for December 2010); Saxonia Dresden–Leipzig (4 for June 2011); E-Netz Franken (5 for December 2011); Mittelhessen Express (6 for December 2011); Berlin/Brandenburg (26 for December 2011/12), Elbe-Elster Netz (8 for June 2013) and S-Bahn Leipzig/Halle (36 for December 2013). As mentioned above acceptance problems have delayed entrance into service. For these units the design has already been updated as they have the latest form of anti climb buffers whereas the 442.2 has not.

AB + B (DMCO–DMSO).

Built: 2009–
Builder–Mech. Parts: Bombardier.
Builder–Elec. Parts: Bombardier.
Wheel Arrangement: Bo-2-Bo.
Traction Motors: 4 x 505 kW three phase asynchronous motors per set.
Accommodation: 8/46 + 0/45 plus 10 tip up.
Weight:
Length over Couplers: 20.05 + 20.05 m.
Width: 2.926 m.   **Maximum Speed:** 160 km/h.
Wheel Diameter: 850 mm.   **Floor Height:** 800 mm (entrance), 695/1250 (saloons).

442 101	843 101	442 601	KA		442 116	843 116	442 616	DA
442 102	843 102	442 602	KA		442 117	843 117	442 617	(DA)
442 103	843 103	442 603	KA		442 118	843 118	442 618	DA
442 104	843 104	442 604	NN1		442 119	843 119	442 619	BLO
442 105	843 105	442 605	NN1		442 120	843 120	442 620	BLO
442 106	843 106	442 606	NN1		442 121	843 121	442 621	BLO
442 107	843 107	442 607	NN1		442 122	843 122	442 622	BLO
442 108	843 108	442 608	NN1		442 123	843 123	442 623	BLO
442 109	843 109	442 609	FGM		442 124	843 124	442 624	BLO
442 110	843 110	442 610	FGM		442 125	843 125	442 625	BLO
442 111	843 111	442 611	(FGM)		442 126	843 126	442 626	BLO
442 112	843 112	442 612	(FGM)		442 127	843 127	442 627	BCS
442 113	843 113	442 613	(FGM)		442 128	843 128	442 628	BCS
442 114	843 114	442 614	(FGM)		442 129	843 129	442 629	BLO
442 115	843 115	442 615	DA		442 130	843 130	442 630	BLO

442 131	843 131	442 631	BLO
442 132	843 132	442 632	(BLO)
442 133	843 133	442 633	BLO
442 134	843 134	442 634	BLO
442 135	843 135	442 635	BLO
442 136	843 136	442 636	BLO
442 137	843 137	442 637	BLO
442 138	843 138	442 638	BLO
442 139	843 139	442 639	BLO
442 140	843 140	442 640	BLO
442 141	843 141	442 641	BLO
442 142	843 142	442 642	BCS
442 143	843 143	442 643	BCS
442 144	843 144	442 644	BCS
442 145	843 145	442 645	
442 146	843 146	442 646	
442 147	843 147	442 647	
442 148	843 148	442 648	
442 149	843 149	442 649	
442 150	843 150	442 650	
442 151	843 151	442 651	
442 152	843 152	442 652	
442 153	843 153	442 653	
442 154	843 154	442 654	
442 155	843 155	442 655	
442 156	843 156	442 656	
442 157	843 157	442 657	
442 158	843 158	442 658	
442 159	843 159	442 659	

442 160	843 160	442 660
442 161	843 161	442 661
442 162	843 162	442 662
442 163	843 163	442 663
442 164	843 164	442 664
442 165	843 165	442 665
442 166	843 166	442 666
442 167	843 167	442 667
442 168	843 168	442 668
442 169	843 169	442 669
442 170	843 170	442 670
442 171	843 171	442 671
442 172	843 172	442 672
442 173	843 173	442 673
442 174	843 174	442 674
442 175	843 175	442 675
442 176	843 176	442 676
442 177	843 177	442 677
442 178	843 178	442 678
442 179	843 179	442 679
442 180	843 180	442 680
442 181	843 181	442 681
442 182	843 182	442 682
442 183	843 183	442 683
442 184	843 184	442 684
442 185	843 185	442 685
442 186	843 186	442 686
442 187	843 187	442 687
442 188	843 188	442 688

Names:

442 119   Potsdam Park Sanssouci

▲ 442 128 calls at Saarmund whilst working RB28825, the 1701 Berlin-Schönefeld Flughafen to Potsdam Griebnitzsee on 4 September 2012.   **Matthias Müller**

CLASS 442.2   4-SECTION ARTICULATED UNITS

The first Talent 2 to appear was a 4-car set for the Nürnberg S-Bahn, 442 212 being exhibited at Innotrans in Berlin in 2008. Over 100 sets have been ordered meaning that the allocated numbers are insufficient as 5-car sets are numbered from 442 301. The new EVN system of numbering means that subsequent builds will be Class 1442 or 2442 etc. Those areas getting the new units are: Mosel (8 due 2009); Cottbus (3 due 2009); Nürnberg (42 due December 2010); Rhein-Sieg Express (10 due December 2010); E-Netz Franken (9 due December 2011); Mittelhessen Express (16 due December 2011); München area (34 due December 2013) and S-Bahn Leipzig/Halle (15 due December 2013). As mentioned above acceptance problems have delayed entrance into service but things were getting back on track by late 2012.

AB + B + B (DMCO–TSO-TSO-DMSO).

Built: 2008–
Builder–Mech. Parts: Bombardier.
Builder–Elec. Parts: Bombardier.
Wheel Arrangement: Bo-2-Bo-2-Bo.
Traction Motors: 6 x 505 kW three phase asynchronous motors per set.
Accommodation:
Weight:
Length over Couplers: 20.05 + 16.10 + 16.10 + 20.05 m.
Width: 2.926 m.   **Maximum Speed:** 160 km/h.
Wheel Diameter: 850 mm.   **Floor Height:** 800 mm (entrance), 695/1250 (saloons).
Non-Standard Livery: N Silver and dark grey, green doors.

(+) Withdrawn before delivery! – Returned to Builder.

442 200	443 200	443 700	442 700	STR	
442 201	443 201	443 701	442 701	(+)	
442 202	443 202	443 702	442 702	STR	
442 203	443 203	443 703	442 703	STR	
442 204	443 204	443 704	442 704	STR	
442 205	443 205	443 705	442 705	(STR)	
442 206	443 206	443 706	442 706	STR	
442 207	443 207	443 707	442 707	(STR)	
442 208	443 208	443 708	442 708	(STR)	
442 209	443 209	443 709	442 709	BCS	
442 210	443 210	443 710	442 710	BCS	
442 211	443 211	443 711	442 711	BCS	
442 212	443 212	443 712	442 712	(+)	
442 213	443 213	443 713	442 713	(+)	
442 214	443 214	443 714	442 714	(+)	
442 215	443 215	443 715	442 715	(+)	
442 216	443 216	443 716	442 716	(+)	
442 217	443 217	443 717	442 717	NN1	Hartmannshof
442 218	443 218	443 718	442 718	NN1	Neumarkt i. d. Oberpflalz
442 219	443 219	443 719	442 719	NN1	Röthenbach a.d. Pegnitz
442 220	443 220	443 720	442 720	NN1	
442 221	443 221	443 721	442 721	NN1	
442 222	443 222	443 722	442 722	NN1	
442 223	443 223	443 723	442 723	NN1	
442 224	443 224	443 724	442 724	NN1	
442 225	443 225	443 725	442 725	NN1	
442 226	443 226	443 726	442 726	NN1	
442 227	443 227	443 727	442 727	NN1	
442 228	443 228	443 728	442 728	NN1	
442 229	443 229	443 729	442 729	NN1	
442 230	443 230	443 730	442 730	NN1	
442 231	443 231	443 731	442 731	NN1	
442 232	443 232	443 732	442 732	NN1	
442 233	443 233	443 733	442 733	NN1	
442 234	443 234	443 734	442 734	NN1	
442 235	443 235	443 735	442 735	NN1	
442 236	443 236	443 736	442 736	NN1	

442 237	443 237	443 737	442 737		NN1
442 238	443 238	443 738	442 738		NN1
442 239	443 239	443 739	442 739		NN1
442 240	443 240	443 740	442 740		NN1
442 241	443 241	443 741	442 741		NN1
442 242	443 242	443 742	442 742		NN1
442 243	443 243	443 743	442 743		NN1
442 244	443 244	443 744	442 744		NN1
442 245	443 245	443 745	442 745		NN1
442 246	443 246	443 746	442 746		NN1
442 247	443 247	443 747	442 747		NN1
442 248	443 248	443 748	442 748		NN1
442 249	443 249	443 749	442 749		NN1
442 250	443 250	443 750	442 750		NN1
442 251	443 251	443 751	442 751		NN1
442 252	443 252	443 752	442 752		NN1
442 253	443 253	443 753	442 753		NN1
442 254	443 254	443 754	442 754		KA
442 255	443 255	443 755	442 755		KA
442 256	443 256	443 756	442 756		KA
442 257	443 257	443 757	442 757		KA
442 258	443 258	443 758	442 758		KA
442 259	443 259	443 759	442 759		KA
442 260	443 260	443 760	442 760		KA
442 261	443 261	443 761	442 761		KA
442 262	443 262	443 762	442 762		KA
442 263	443 263	443 763	442 763		KA
442 264	443 264	443 764	442 764		NN1
442 265	443 265	443 765	442 765		NN1
442 266	443 266	443 766	442 766		NN1
442 267	443 267	443 767	442 767		NN1
442 268	443 268	443 768	442 768		NN1
442 269	443 269	443 769	442 769		NN1
442 270	443 270	443 770	442 770		NN1
442 271	443 271	443 771	442 771		NN1
442 272	443 272	443 772	442 772		NN1
442 273	443 273	443 773	442 773		NN1
442 274	443 274	443 774	442 774		NN1
442 275	443 275	443 775	442 775		NN1
442 276	443 276	443 776	442 776		NN1
442 277	443 277	443 777	442 777		NN1
442 278	443 278	443 778	442 778		FGM
442 279	443 279	443 779	442 779		FGM
442 280	443 280	443 780	442 780		FGM
442 281	443 281	443 781	442 781		FGM
442 282	443 282	443 782	442 782		FGM
442 283	443 283	443 783	442 783		FGM
442 284	443 284	443 784	442 784		FGM
442 285	443 285	443 785	442 785		FGM
442 286	443 286	443 786	442 786		FGM
442 287	443 287	443 787	442 787		FGM
442 288	443 288	443 788	442 788		FGM
442 289	443 289	443 789	442 789		FGM
442 290	443 290	443 790	442 790		FGM
442 291	443 291	443 791	442 791		FGM
442 292	443 292	443 792	442 792		FGM
442 293	443 293	443 793	442 793		(FGM)
1442 200	1443 200	1443 200	1442 700	N	(LH2)
1442 201	1443 201	1443 201	1442 701	N	(LH2)
1442 202	1443 202	1443 202	1442 702	N	(LH2)
1442 203	1443 203	1443 203	1442 703	N	(LH2)
1442 204	1443 204	1443 204	1442 704	N	(LH2)
1442 205	1443 205	1443 205	1442 705	N	(LH2)

1442 206	1443 206	1443 206	1442 706	**N**	(LH2)
1442 207	1443 207	1443 207	1442 707	**N**	(LH2)
1442 208	1443 208	1443 208	1442 708	**N**	(LH2)
1442 209	1443 209	1443 209	1442 709	**N**	(LH2)
1442 210	1443 210	1443 210	1442 710	**N**	(LH2)
1442 211	1443 211	1443 211	1442 711	**N**	(LH2)
1442 212	1443 212	1443 212	1442 712	**N**	(LH2)
1442 213	1443 213	1443 213	1442 713	**N**	(LH2)
1442 214	1443 214	1443 214	1442 714	**N**	(LH2)
2442 200	2443 200	2443 700	2442 700		(MH2)
2442 201	2443 201	2443 701	2442 701		(MH2)
2442 202	2443 202	2443 702	2442 702		MH2
2442 203	2443 203	2443 703	2442 703		MH2
2442 204	2443 204	2443 704	2442 704		MH2
2442 205	2443 205	2443 705	2442 705		MH2
2442 206	2443 206	2443 706	2442 706		(MH2)
2442 207	2443 207	2443 707	2442 707		(MH2)
2442 208	2443 208	2443 708	2442 708		(MH2)
2442 209	2443 209	2443 709	2442 709		(MH2)
2442 210	2443 210	2443 710	2442 710		(MH2)
2442 211	2443 211	2443 711	2442 711		(MH2)
2442 212	2443 212	2443 712	2442 712		(MH2)
2442 213	2443 213	2443 713	2442 713		MH2
2442 214	2443 214	2443 714	2442 714		MH2
2442 215	2443 215	2443 715	2442 715		(MH2)
2442 216	2443 216	2443 716	2442 716		MH2
2442 217	2443 217	2443 717	2442 717		MH2
2442 218	2443 218	2443 718	2442 718		MH2
2442 219	2443 219	2443 719	2442 719		MH2

▲ 442 200 passes underneath the A61 motorway bridge near Winningen whilst working an RB service through the Mosel valley from Trier to Koblenz on 16 September 2012. **Matthias Müller**

2442 220	2443 220	2443 720	2442 720	(MH2)
2442 221	2443 221	2443 721	2442 721	(MH2)
2442 222	2443 222	2443 722	2442 722	MH2
2442 223	2443 223	2443 723	2442 723	(MH2)
2442 224	2443 224	2443 724	2442 724	MH2
2442 225	2443 225	2443 725	2442 725	(MH2)
2442 226	2443 226	2443 726	2442 726	(MH2)
2442 227	2443 227	2443 727	2442 727	(MH2)
2442 228	2443 228	2443 728	2442 728	(MH2)
2442 229	2443 229	2443 729	2442 729	(MH2)
2442 230	2443 230	2443 730	2442 730	(MH2)
2442 231	2443 231	2443 731	2442 731	(MH2)
2442 232	2443 232	2443 732	2442 732	(MH2)
2442 233	2443 233	2443 733	2442 733	(MH2)

CLASS 442.3   5-SECTION ARTICULATED UNITS

59 sets have been ordered for the following areas: Rhein-Sieg Express (2 due December 2010); Saxonia Dresden–Leipzig (4 due June 2011); E-Netz Franken (8 due December 2011); Berlin area (22 due December 2011/12) and Rostock area (23 due December 2012). Apart from the Rostock area units most others had entered service during 2012.

AB + B (DMCO–DMSO).

Built: 2009–
Builder–Mech. Parts: Bombardier.
Builder–Elec. Parts: Bombardier.
Wheel Arrangement: Bo-2-Bo-2-2-Bo.
Traction Motors: 6 x 505 kW three phase asynchronous motors per set.
Accommodation:
Weight:
Length over Couplers: 20.05 + 16.10 + 16.10 +16.10 + 20.05 m.
Width: 2.926 m.   **Maximum Speed:** 160 km/h.
Wheel Diameter: 850 mm.   **Floor Height:** 800 mm (entrance), 695/1250 (saloons).

442 301	843 301	443 301	443 801	442 801	KA
442 302	843 302	443 302	443 802	442 802	KA
442 303	843 303	443 303	443 803	442 803	NN1
442 304	843 304	443 304	443 804	442 804	NN1
442 305	843 305	443 305	443 805	442 805	NN1
442 306	843 306	443 306	443 806	442 806	NN1
442 307	843 307	443 307	443 807	442 807	NN1
442 308	843 308	443 308	443 808	442 808	NN1
442 309	843 309	443 309	443 809	442 809	NN1
442 310	843 310	443 310	443 810	442 810	NN1
442 311	843 311	443 311	443 811	442 811	DA
442 312	843 312	443 312	443 812	442 812	DA
442 313	843 313	443 313	443 813	442 813	DA
442 314	843 314	443 314	443 814	442 814	DA
442 315	843 315	443 315	443 815	442 815	BLO
442 316	843 316	443 316	443 816	442 816	BLO
442 317	843 317	443 317	443 817	442 817	BLO
442 318	843 318	443 318	443 818	442 818	BLO
442 319	843 319	443 319	443 819	442 819	BLO
442 320	843 320	443 320	443 820	442 820	BLO
442 321	843 321	443 321	443 821	442 821	BLO
442 322	843 322	443 322	443 822	442 822	BLO
442 323	843 323	443 323	443 823	442 823	BLO
442 324	843 324	443 324	443 824	442 824	BLO
442 325	843 325	443 325	443 825	442 825	BLO
442 326	843 326	443 326	443 826	442 826	BLO
442 327	843 327	443 327	443 827	442 827	BLO
442 328	843 328	443 328	443 828	442 828	BLO
442 329	843 329	443 329	443 829	442 829	BLO

442 330	843 330	443 330	443 830	442 830	BLO
442 331	843 331	443 331	443 831	442 831	BLO
442 332	843 332	443 332	443 832	442 832	BLO
442 333	843 333	443 333	443 833	442 833	BLO
442 334	843 334	443 334	443 834	442 834	BLO
442 335	843 335	443 335	443 835	442 835	BLO
442 336	843 336	443 336	443 836	442 836	BLO
442 337	843 337	443 337	443 837	442 837	(WR)
442 338	843 338	443 338	443 838	442 838	(WR)
442 339	843 339	443 339	443 839	442 839	(WR)
442 340	843 340	443 340	443 840	442 840	(WR)
442 341	843 341	443 341	443 841	442 841	(WR)
442 342	843 342	443 342	443 842	442 842	(WR)
442 343	843 343	443 343	443 843	442 843	(WR)
442 344	843 344	443 344	443 844	442 844	(WR)
442 345	843 345	443 345	443 845	442 845	(WR)
442 346	843 346	443 346	443 846	442 846	(WR)
442 347	843 347	443 347	443 847	442 847	(WR)
442 348	843 348	443 348	443 848	442 848	(WR)
442 349	843 349	443 349	443 849	442 849	(WR)
442 350	843 350	443 350	443 850	442 850	(WR)
442 351	843 351	443 351	443 851	442 851	(WR)
442 352	843 352	443 352	443 852	442 852	(WR)
442 353	843 353	443 353	443 853	442 853	(WR)
442 354	843 354	443 354	443 854	442 854	(WR)
442 355	843 355	443 355	443 855	442 855	(WR)
442 356	843 356	443 356	443 856	442 856	(WR)
442 357	843 357	443 357	443 857	442 857	(WR)
442 358	843 358	443 358	443 858	442 858	(WR)
442 359	843 359	443 359	443 859	442 859	(WR)

▲ Class 472 is the oldest type of unit still in daily use on the Hamburg S-Bahn. Unit 472 042, with vehicle 472 542 leading, heads a six-car formation into Hamburg Hauptbahnhof on 17 August 2012. **Keith Fender**

CLASS 1445 BOMBARDIER TWINDEXX VARIO 4-CAR EMU

DB Regio has ordered two batches of double deck EMUs from Bombardier. In 1997/8 Bombardier built a 3-car double deck EMU known then as a "Meridian" train. It did not catch on in the Dresden area and is understood to have been returned to the builder. But now a much improved version has caught on with 16 ordered for Schleswig Holstein (services from Hamburg to Kiel/ Flensburg) and 12 more ordered for the Main-Spessart area. Two power cars will sandwich two trailers; automatic couplers will allow quick coupling/uncoupling at Neumünster for the Hamburg trains. Full details of the units had not been received as this book went to press. The numbering is also uncertain as early press releases referred to these units as 445s but this designation now applies to Stadler built units for the Berlin area! The Hamburg trains are expected to be in service for the December 2014 timetable. The trains will be built at Görlitz with bogies from Siegen and electrical gear from Västerås in Sweden; Mitrac 1000 propulsion/ control system.

Built: 2014
Builders–Mech. Parts: Bombardier.
Builder–Elec. Parts: Bombardier.
Wheel Arrangement:
Traction Motors: 4 x 575 = 2300 kW.
Accommodation: Spessart trains 25/400.
Weight:
Length over Couplers: 25.30 m (Power cars).
Width:

Wheel Diameter:
Maximum Speed: 160 km/h.

▲ Hamburg S-Bahn unit 474 055 is seen bringing up the rear of a six-car service bound for Hamburg Altona. The unit has just left Hamburg Hauptbahnhof on 17 August 2012. **Keith Fender**

CLASS 450

DB owns some trams! DB financed some of the vehicles for the Karlsruhe S-Bahn service which are worked by the Albtalbahn. The vehicles are numbered in the Albtalbahn series but carry in addition the DB logo and DB numbers. Further details are in German Railways Part 2.

450 001	RK	450 004	RK
450 003	RK	450 005	RK

CLASS 472   HAMBURG S-BAHN 3-CAR UNITS

This class is now getting old; it is expected that replacements will soon be ordered with perhaps 60 new sets replacing them. Even more new sets may be ordered to allow for expansion of services.

B + A + B (DMSO–MFO–DMSO (non-gangwayed)).

Built: 1974–84.
Builders-Mech. Parts: Linke-Hofmann-Busch/Messerschmitt-Bölkow-Blohm.
Builder–Elec. Parts: Brown-Boveri.
Electrification System: 1200 V DC bottom contact third rail.
Wheel Arrangement: Bo-Bo + Bo-Bo + Bo-Bo.
Traction Motors: 4 x 125 kW per power car.
Accommodation: –/65 + 66/– + –/65.   **Length over Couplers:** 65.82 m.
Weight: 40 + 34 + 40 tonnes.   **Maximum Speed:** 100 km/h.

w   Windows in ends of all vehicles.

472 001	473 001	472 501		AOP		472 035	473 035	472 535	w	AOP
472 002	473 002	472 502		AOP		472 036	473 036	472 536	w	AOP
472 003	473 003	472 503		AOP		472 037	473 037	472 537	w	AOP
472 004	473 004	472 504		AOP		472 038	473 038	472 538	w	AOP
472 005	473 005	472 505		AOP		472 039	473 039	472 539	w	AOP
472 009	473 009	472 509		AOP		472 040	473 040	472 540	w	AOP
472 012	473 012	472 512		AOP		472 041	473 041	472 541	w	AOP
472 013	473 013	472 513		AOP		472 042	473 042	472 542	w	AOP
472 014	473 014	472 514		AOP		472 043	473 043	472 543	w	AOP
472 015	473 015	472 515		AOP		472 044	473 044	472 544	w	AOP
472 016	473 016	472 516		AOP		472 045	473 045	472 545	w	AOP
472 017	473 017	472 517		AOP		472 046	473 046	472 546	w	AOP
472 018	473 018	472 518		AOP		472 047	473 047	472 547	w	AOP
472 019	473 019	472 519		AOP		472 048	473 048	472 548	w	AOP
472 020	473 020	472 520		AOP		472 049	473 049	472 549	w	AOP
472 023	473 023	472 523		AOP		472 050	473 050	472 550	w	AOP
472 024	473 024	472 524		AOP		472 053	473 053	472 553	w	AOP
472 025	473 025	472 525		AOP		472 054	473 054	472 554	w	AOP
472 026	473 026	472 526		AOP		472 055	473 055	472 555	w	AOP
472 027	473 027	472 527		AOP		472 056	473 056	472 556	w	AOP
472 028	473 028	472 528		AOP		472 057	473 057	472 557	w	AOP
472 029	473 029	472 529		AOP		472 058	473 058	472 558	w	AOP
472 030	473 030	472 530		AOP		472 059	473 059	472 559	w	AOP
472 031	473 031	472 531		AOP		472 060	473 060	472 560	w	AOP
472 032	473 032	472 532	w	AOP		472 061	473 061	472 561	w	AOP
472 033	473 033	472 533	w	AOP		472 062	473 062	472 562	w	AOP
472 034	473 034	472 534	w	AOP						

CLASS 474   HAMBURG S-BAHN 3-CAR UNITS

These units allowed Classes 470 (1959–70) and 471 (1939–1958) to be withdrawn. Like other modern units three-phase asynchronous motors are provided as are water cooled GTO thyristors and Scharfenberg couplers. Some units have been rebuilt as dual-voltage for the S-Bahn service to Stade where the line was already electrified at 15 kV AC. To get a head start nine additional units were built as dual voltage and their entry into service allowed older units to go into works for conversion. 474 104–112 are the new sets whilst 474 113–145 are converted from 474 059–091. Technically speaking all the dual-voltage sets should have been given a new class number!

Built: 1996–2001, 2006.
Builder–Mech. Parts: LHB later Alstom/LHB.
Builder–Elec. Parts: ABB Henschel (Later Adtranz, Kassel).
Electrification System: 1200 V DC bottom contact third rail and 15 kV AC (d).
Wheel Arrangement: Bo-Bo + 2-2 + Bo-Bo.
Traction Motors: 4 x 115 kW.
Accommodation: –/71 + –/66 + –/71.   **Length over Couplers:** 22.895 + 19.77 + 22.895 m.
Weight: 102 tonnes.   **Maximum Speed:** 100 km/h.

d   Dual voltage

474 001	874 001	474 501	AOP	474 044	874 044	474 544		AOP
474 002	874 002	474 502	AOP	474 045	874 045	474 545		AOP
474 003	874 003	474 503	AOP	474 046	874 046	474 546		AOP
474 004	874 004	474 504	AOP	474 047	874 047	474 547		AOP
474 005	874 005	474 505	AOP	474 048	874 048	474 548		AOP
474 006	874 006	474 506	AOP	474 049	874 049	474 549		AOP
474 007	874 007	474 507	AOP	474 050	874 050	474 550		AOP
474 008	874 008	474 508	AOP	474 051	874 051	474 551		AOP
474 009	874 009	474 509	AOP	474 052	874 052	474 552		AOP
474 010	874 010	474 510	AOP	474 053	874 053	474 553		AOP
474 011	874 011	474 511	AOP	474 054	874 054	474 554		AOP
474 012	874 012	474 512	AOP	474 055	874 055	474 555		AOP
474 013	874 013	474 513	AOP	474 056	874 056	474 556		AOP
474 014	874 014	474 514	AOP	474 057	874 057	474 557		AOP
474 015	874 015	474 515	AOP	474 058	874 058	474 558		AOP
474 016	874 016	474 516	AOP	474 092	874 092	474 592		AOP
474 017	874 017	474 517	AOP	474 093	874 093	474 593		AOP
474 018	874 018	474 518	AOP	474 094	874 094	474 594		AOP
474 019	874 019	474 519	AOP	474 095	874 095	474 595		AOP
474 020	874 020	474 520	AOP	474 096	874 096	474 596		AOP
474 021	874 021	474 521	AOP	474 097	874 097	474 597		AOP
474 022	874 022	474 522	AOP	474 098	874 098	474 598		AOP
474 023	874 023	474 523	AOP	474 099	874 099	474 599		AOP
474 024	874 024	474 524	AOP	474 100	874 100	474 600		AOP
474 025	874 025	474 525	AOP	474 101	874 101	474 601		AOP
474 026	874 026	474 526	AOP	474 102	874 102	474 602		AOP
474 027	874 027	474 527	AOP	474 103	874 103	474 603		AOP
474 028	874 028	474 528	AOP	474 104	874 104	474 604	d	AOP
474 029	874 029	474 529	AOP	474 105	874 105	474 605	d	AOP
474 030	874 030	474 530	AOP	474 106	874 106	474 606	d	AOP
474 031	874 031	474 531	AOP	474 107	874 107	474 607	d	AOP
474 032	874 032	474 532	AOP	474 108	874 108	474 608	d	AOP
474 033	874 033	474 533	AOP	474 109	874 109	474 609	d	AOP
474 034	874 034	474 534	AOP	474 110	874 110	474 610	d	AOP
474 035	874 035	474 535	AOP	474 111	874 111	474 611	d	AOP
474 036	874 036	474 536	AOP	474 112	874 112	474 612	d	AOP
474 037	874 037	474 537	AOP	474 113	874 113	474 613	d	AOP
474 038	874 038	474 538	AOP	474 114	874 114	474 614	d	AOP
474 039	874 039	474 539	AOP	474 115	874 115	474 615	d	AOP
474 040	874 040	474 540	AOP	474 116	874 116	474 616	d	AOP
474 041	874 041	474 541	AOP	474 117	874 117	474 617	d	AOP
474 042	874 042	474 542	AOP	474 118	874 118	474 618	d	AOP
474 043	874 043	474 543	AOP	474 119	874 119	474 619	d	AOP

474 120	874 120	474 620	d	AOP		474 133	874 133	474 633	d	AOP
474 121	874 121	474 621	d	AOP		474 134	874 134	474 634	d	AOP
474 122	874 122	474 622	d	AOP		474 135	874 135	474 635	d	AOP
474 123	874 123	474 623	d	AOP		474 136	874 136	474 636	d	AOP
474 124	874 124	474 624	d	AOP		474 137	874 137	474 637	d	AOP
474 125	874 125	474 625	d	AOP		474 138	874 138	474 638	d	AOP
474 126	874 126	474 626	d	AOP		474 139	874 139	474 639	d	AOP
474 127	874 127	474 627	d	AOP		474 140	874 140	474 640	d	AOP
474 128	874 128	474 628	d	AOP		474 141	874 141	474 641	d	AOP
474 129	874 129	474 629	d	AOP		474 142	874 142	474 642	d	AOP
474 130	874 130	474 630	d	AOP		474 143	874 143	474 643	d	AOP
474 131	874 131	474 631	d	AOP		474 144	874 144	474 644	d	AOP
474 132	874 132	474 632	d	AOP		474 145	874 145	474 645	d	AOP

CLASS 479.2   SINGLE CAR

These units operate on an isolated line which runs from Lichtenhain to Cursdorf in Thüringen, which is part of the Oberweissbacher Bergbahn, an odd funicular which runs in open country from Obstfelderschmiede to Lichtenhain. Opened in 1923, the line received modernised vehicles in the 1980s. The Berlin S-Bahn workshops did the rebuilding and used a lot of S-Bahn equipment. A visit to this line and its funicular connection to the rest of the DB network is a must!

Built: 1981.
Builder: RAW Schöneweide.
Electrification System: 600 V DC overhead.
Wheel Arrangement: A-A.
Traction Motors: 2 x 60 kW.   **Former DR Class:** 279.2.
Accommodation: –/24.   **Length over Couplers:** 11.5 m.
Weight: 14.4 tonnes.   **Maximum Speed:** 50 km/h.

Originally Class ET 188.

| 479 201 | US | | 479 203 | US | | 479 205 | US |

▲ Wearing their distinctive red & ochre livery, Berlin S-Bahn sets 480 074/058/061 enter Berlin Schöneweide station with an S9 train heading for Berlin-Schönefeld Flughafen on 25 November 2011.   **Brian Garvin**

BERLIN S-BAHN

The Berlin S-Bahn is a third-rail 800 V DC system and was operated by the DR. The part of the S-Bahn which operated solely in the former West Berlin was transferred to the former West Berlin Transport Authority (the BVG) in 1984, but the whole operation is now a subsidiary of the DB. The BVG received the very oldest units to operate its part of the system, and in 1987 took delivery of some new units of Class 480. The DR also ordered new units, now known as Class 485, but these were of much more spartan design. Upon unification plans that had gathered dust on shelves for years were brought out and the task started of restoring the S-Bahn to its former glory. Routes that had been cut or abandoned were restored to use. Many of the S-Bahn units were from the 1940s and were over 50 years old so new S-Bahn units were needed and the Class 481/2 sets were decided upon as the new standard.

The Berliners refer to 8-car trains as *Vollzüge* (full trains), and thus a four-car train is known as a *Halbzüg* (half-train) and a two-car unit is known as a *Viertelzüg* (quarter-train). Since most units consist of a power car and a non-driving trailer, the smallest train which can be operated is a four-car. However, the inner units of a six or eight-car train can face either direction. Units consisting of two power cars (Class 480) and driving motor/driving trailer can, of course, operate as a 2-car train.

In recent years the Berlin S-Bahn has been in a mess. When privatisation was the way forward several depots and workshops were closed as an efficiency measure but train availability dropped and some serious maintenance problems ensued. Train services had to be reorganised and many trains ran with short formations. The end result was that privatisation plans were dropped and some depots and workshops reopened and only recently has availability got back to normal levels but only after many withdrawn sets were reinstated and overhauled at Dessau and/or Wittenberge workshops as Schöneweide works could not cope.

Having got their trains back up to strength Berliners still have bad journeys having to put up with rebuilding works, especially the major works taking place between Ostkreuz and Ostbahnhof which will be going on for many years yet.

Livery: Red and ochre

CLASS 480 2-CAR UNITS

Units to BVG design. 480 001–004 were prototypes and have been withdrawn. 480 009 was scrapped after an accident as were 480 053 and 480 573. Set 480 025 was burnt out in 2000 and 480 554 was scrapped after hitting a tree in 2002. 480 554[II] has been renumbered from 480 553 and 480 573[II] has presumably been renumbered from 480 509.

B + B (DMSO–DMSO) Non-gangwayed.

Built: 1986–94.
Builders–Mech. Parts: Waggon-Union, ABB Henschel, AEG Hennigsdorf.
Builders–Elec. Parts: AEG, Siemens.
Wheel Arrangement: Bo-Bo + Bo-Bo.
Traction Motors: 4 x 90 kW three-phase asynchronous motors per power car.
Accommodation: –/44 + – /44.   **Length over Couplers:** 18.40 + 18.40 m.
Weight: 30 + 30 tonnes.   **Maximum Speed:** 100 km/h.

480 005	480 505	BGA		480 021	480 521	BGA
480 006	480 506	BGA		480 022	480 522	BGA
480 007	480 507	BGA		480 023	480 523	BGA
480 008	480 508	BGA		480 026	480 526	BGA
480 009	480 509	BGA		480 027	480 527	BGA
480 011	480 511	BGA		480 028	480 528	BGA
480 013	480 513	BGA		480 029	480 529	BGA
480 014	480 514	BGA		480 030	480 530	BGA
480 015	480 515	BGA		480 032	480 532	BGA
480 016	480 516	BGA		480 033	480 533	BGA
480 017	480 517	BGA		480 034	480 534	BGA
480 018	480 518	BGA		480 035	480 535	BGA
480 019	480 519	BGA		480 036	480 536	BGA

480 037	480 537	BGA	480 063	480 563	BGA
480 038	480 538	BGA	480 064	480 564	BGA
480 040	480 540	BGA	480 065	480 565	BGA
480 041	480 541	BGA	480 066	480 566	BGA
480 042	480 542	BGA	480 067	480 567	BGA
480 044	480 544	BGA	480 068	480 568	BGA
480 045	480 545	BGA	480 069	480 569	BGA
480 046	480 546	BGA	480 071	480 571	BGA
480 047	480 547	BGA	480 072	480 572	BGA
480 048	480 548	BGA	480 073	480 573[II]	BGA
480 049	480 549	BGA	480 074	480 574	BGA
480 051	480 551	BGA	480 075	480 575	BGA
480 052	480 552	BGA	480 076	480 576	BGA
480 054	480 554[II]	BGA	480 077	480 577	BGA
480 055	480 555	BGA	480 078	480 578	BGA
480 056	480 556	BGA	480 079	480 579	BGA
480 057	480 557	BGA	480 080	480 580	BGA
480 058	480 558	BGA	480 081	480 581	BGA
480 059	480 559	BGA	480 082	480 582	BGA
480 060	480 560	BGA	480 083	480 583	BGA
480 061	480 561	BGA	480 084	480 584	BGA
480 062	480 562	BGA	480 085	480 585	BGA

▲ Berlin S-Bahn unit 481 017 leads a four-car S9 train to Berlin-Schönefeld Flughafen, approaching Berlin Landsberger Allee on 2 October 2010. **Matthias Müller**

CLASS 481   2-CAR BERLIN S-BAHN UNITS

Following the unification of Germany the S-Bahn network of Berlin could also be brought back under unified control and the many sections that had lain dormant for many years could be reactivated. It was obvious large numbers of new S-Bahn units would be required consequently some 500 units of Class 481/2 were ordered. They have now replaced all pre-war units. In recent years this class has been plagued with problems causing many sets to be taken out of service resulting in withdrawn and stored units of other classes being reinstated and overhauled.

B + AB (DMSO–MCO) Non-gangwayed.

Built: 1995–2004.
Builders: Adtranz Hennigsdorf, Bombardier/DWA Ammendorf.
Wheel Arrangement: Bo-2 + Bo-Bo
Traction Motors: One 200 kW and two 200 kW.
Accommodation: –/30 (14) + 12/38.   **Length over Couplers:** 18.40 m + 18.40 m.
Weight: 31 + 28 tonnes.   **Maximum Speed:** 100 km/h.

481 001	482 001	BWS		481 048	482 048	BWS
481 002	482 002	BWS		481 049	482 049	BGA
481 003	482 003	BWS		481 050	482 050	BGA
481 004	482 004	BWS		481 051	482 051	BWS
481 005	482 005	BWS		481 052	482 052	BWS
481 006	482 006	BWS		481 053	482 053	BWS
481 007	482 007	BWS		481 054	482 054	BWS
481 008	482 008	BWS		481 055	482 055	BWS
481 009	482 009	BWS		481 056	482 056	BWS
481 010	482 010	BWS		481 057	482 057	BWS
481 011	482 011	BWS		481 058	482 058	BWS
481 012	482 012	BWS		481 059	482 059	BWS
481 013	482 013	BWS		481 060	482 060	BWS
481 014	482 014	BWS		481 061	482 061	BWS
481 015	482 015	BWS		481 062	482 062	BWS
481 016	482 016	BWS		481 063	482 063	BWS
481 017	482 017	BWS		481 064	482 064	BWS
481 018	482 018	BWS		481 065	482 065	BWS
481 019	482 019	BWS		481 066	482 066	BWS
481 020	482 020	BWS		481 067	482 067	BWS
481 021	482 021	BWS		481 068	482 068	BWS
481 022	482 022	BWS		481 069	482 069	BWS
481 023	482 023	BWS		481 070	482 070	BWS
481 024	482 024	BWS		481 071	482 071	BWS
481 025	482 025	BWS		481 072	482 072	BWS
481 026	482 026	BWS		481 073	482 073	BWS
481 027	482 027	BWS		481 074	482 074	BWS
481 028	482 028	BWS		481 075	482 075	BWS
481 029	482 029	BWS		481 076	482 076	BWS
481 030	482 030	BWS		481 077	482 077	BWS
481 031	482 031	BWS		481 078	482 078	BWS
481 032	482 032	BWS		481 079	482 079	BWS
481 033	482 033	BWS		481 080	482 080	BWS
481 034	482 034	BGA		481 081	482 081	BWS
481 035	482 035	BWS		481 082	482 082	BWS
481 036	482 036	BWS		481 083	482 083	BWS
481 037	482 037	BWS		481 084	482 084	BWS
481 038	482 038	BWS		481 085	482 085	BWS
481 039	482 039	BWS		481 086	482 086	BWS
481 040	482 040	BWS		481 087	482 087	BWS
481 041	482 041	BWS		481 088	482 088	BWS
481 042	482 042	BWS		481 089	482 089	BWS
481 043	482 043	BGA		481 090	482 090	BWS
481 044	482 044	BWS		481 091	482 091	BWS
481 045	482 045	BWS		481 092	482 092	BWS
481 046	482 046	BWS		481 093	482 093	BWS
481 047	482 047	BWS		481 094	482 094	BWS

481 095	482 095	BWS	481 159	482 159	BWS
481 096	482 096	BWS	481 160	482 160	BWS
481 097	482 097	BWS	481 161	482 161	BWS
481 098	482 098	BWS	481 162	482 162	BWS
481 099	482 099	BWS	481 163	482 163	BWS
481 100	482 100	BWS	481 164	482 164	BWS
481 101	482 101	BWS	481 165	482 165	BWS
481 102	482 102	BWS	481 166	482 166	BWS
481 103	482 103	BWS	481 167	482 167	BWS
481 104	482 104	BWS	481 168	482 168	BWS
481 105	482 105	BWS	481 169	482 169	BWS
481 106	482 106	BWS	481 170	482 170	BWS
481 107	482 107	BWS	481 171	482 171	BWS
481 108	482 108	BWS	481 172	482 172	BWS
481 109	482 109	BWS	481 173	482 173	BWS
481 110	482 110	BWS	481 174	482 174	BWS
481 111	482 111	BWS	481 175	482 175	BWS
481 112	482 112	BWS	481 176	482 176	BWS
481 113	482 113	BWS	481 177	482 177	BWS
481 114	482 114	BWS	481 178	482 178	BWS
481 115	482 115	BWS	481 179	482 179	BWS
481 116	482 116	BWS	481 180	482 180	BWS
481 117	482 117	BWS	481 181	482 181	BWS
481 118	482 118	BWS	481 182	482 182	BWS
481 119	482 119	BWS	481 183	482 183	BWS
481 120	482 120	BWS	481 184	482 184	BWS
481 121	482 121	BWS	481 185	482 185	BWS
481 122	482 122	BWS	481 186	482 186	BWS
481 123	482 123	BWS	481 187	482 187	BWS
481 124	482 124	BWS	481 188	482 188	BWS
481 125	482 125	BWS	481 189	482 189	BWS
481 126	482 126	BWS	481 190	482 190	BWS
481 127	482 127	BWS	481 191	482 191	BWS
481 128	482 128	BWS	481 192	482 192	BWS
481 129	482 129	BWS	481 193	482 193	BWS
481 130	482 130	BWS	481 194	482 194	BWS
481 131	482 131	BWS	481 195	482 195	BWS
481 132	482 132	BWS	481 196	482 196	BWS
481 133	482 133	BWS	481 197	482 197	BWS
481 134	482 134	BWS	481 198	482 198	BWS
481 135	482 135	BWS	481 199	482 199	BWS
481 136	482 136	BWS	481 200	482 200	BWS
481 137	482 137	BWS	481 201	482 201	BWS
481 138	482 138	BWS	481 202	482 202	BWS
481 139	482 139	BWS	481 203	482 203	BWS
481 140	482 140	BWS	481 204	482 204	BWS
481 141	482 141	BWS	481 205	482 205	BWS
481 142	482 142	BWS	481 206	482 206	BWS
481 143	482 143	BWS	481 207	482 207	BWS
481 144	482 144	BWS	481 208	482 208	BWS
481 145	482 145	BWS	481 209	482 209	BWS
481 146	482 146	BWS	481 210	482 210	BWS
481 147	482 147	BWS	481 211	482 211	BWS
481 148	482 148	BWS	481 212	482 212	BWS
481 149	482 149	BWS	481 213	482 213	BWS
481 150	482 150	BWS	481 214	482 214	BWS
481 151	482 151	BWS	481 215	482 215	BWS
481 152	482 152	BWS	481 216	482 216	BWS
481 153	482 153	BWS	481 217	482 217	BWS
481 154	482 154	BWS	481 218	482 218	BWS
481 155	482 155	BWS	481 219	482 219	BWS
481 156	482 156	BWS	481 220	482 220	BWS
481 157	482 157	BWS	481 221	482 221	BWS
481 158	482 158	BWS	481 222	482 222	BWS

481 223	482 223	BWS	481 248	482 248	BWS
481 224	482 224	BWS	481 249	482 249	BWS
481 225	482 225	BWS	481 250	482 250	BWS
481 226	482 226	BWS	481 251	482 251	BWS
481 227	482 227	BWS	481 252	482 252	BWS
481 228	482 228	BWS	481 253	482 253	BWS
481 229	482 229	BWS	481 254	482 254	BWS
481 230	482 230	BWS	481 255	482 255	BWS
481 231	482 231	BWS	481 256	482 256	BWS
481 232	482 232	BWS	481 257	482 257	BWS
481 233	482 233	BWS	481 258	482 258	BWS
481 234	482 234	BWS	481 259	482 259	BWS
481 235	482 235	BWS	481 260	482 260	BWS
481 236	482 236	BWS	481 261	482 261	BWS
481 237	482 237	BWS	481 262	482 262	BWS
481 238	482 238	BWS	481 263	482 263	BWS
481 239	482 239	BWS	481 264	482 264	BWS
481 240	482 240	BWS	481 265	482 265	BWS
481 241	482 241	BWS	481 266	482 266	BWS
481 242	482 242	BWS	481 267	482 267	BWS
481 243	482 243	BWS	481 268	482 268	BWS
481 244	482 244	BWS	481 269	482 269	BWS
481 245	482 245	BWS	481 270	482 270	BWS
481 246	482 246	BWS	481 271	482 271	BWS
481 247	482 247	BWS	481 272	482 272	BWS

▲ 485 048 pauses at Berlin Ostbahnhof on 10 September 2009, whilst in charge of an S7 service to Ahrensfelde.
Keith Fender

481 273	482 273	BWS	481 337	482 337	BGA
481 274	482 274	BWS	481 338	482 338	BGA
481 275	482 275	BWS	481 339	482 339	BGA
481 276	482 276	BWS	481 340	482 340	BGA
481 277	482 277	BWS	481 341	482 341	BGA
481 278	482 278	BWS	481 342	482 342	BGA
481 279	482 279	BWS	481 343	482 343	BGA
481 280	482 280	BWS	481 344	482 344	BGA
481 281	482 281	BWS	481 345	482 345	BGA
481 282	482 282	BWS	481 346	482 346	BGA
481 283	482 283	BWS	481 347	482 347	BGA
481 284	482 284	BWS	481 348	482 348	BGA
481 285	482 285	BWS	481 349	482 349	BGA
481 286	482 286	BWS	481 350	482 350	BGA
481 287	482 287	BWS	481 351	482 351	BGA
481 288	482 288	BWS	481 352	482 352	BGA
481 289	482 289	BWS	481 353	482 353	BGA
481 290	482 290	BWS	481 354	482 354	BGA
481 291	482 291	BWS	481 355	482 355	BGA
481 292	482 292	BWS	481 356	482 356	BGA
481 293	482 293	BWS	481 357	482 357	BGA
481 294	482 294	BWS	481 358	482 358	BGA
481 295	482 295	BWS	481 359	482 359	BGA
481 296	482 296	BWS	481 360	482 360	BGA
481 297	482 297	BWS	481 361	482 361	BGA
481 298	482 298	BWS	481 362	482 362	BGA
481 299	482 299	BWS	481 363	482 363	BGA
481 300	482 300	BWS	481 364	482 364	BGA
481 301	482 301	BWS	481 365	482 365	BGA
481 302	482 302	BWS	481 366	482 366	BGA
481 303	482 303	BWS	481 367	482 367	BGA
481 304	482 304	BWS	481 368	482 368	BGA
481 305	482 305	BWS	481 369	482 369	BGA
481 306	482 306	BWS	481 370	482 370	BGA
481 307	482 307	BWS	481 371	482 371	BGA
481 308	482 308	BWS	481 372	482 372	BGA
481 309	482 309	BWS	481 373	482 373	BGA
481 310	482 310	BWS	481 374	482 374	BGA
481 311	482 311	BWS	481 375	482 375	BGA
481 312	482 312	BWS	481 376	482 376	BGA
481 313	482 313	BWS	481 377	482 377	BGA
481 314	482 314	BWS	481 378	482 378	BGA
481 315	482 315	BWS	481 379	482 379	BGA
481 316	482 316	BWS	481 380	482 380	BGA
481 317	482 317	BWS	481 381	482 381	BGA
481 318	482 318	BWS	481 382	482 382	BGA
481 319	482 319	BWS	481 383	482 383	BGA
481 320	482 320	BWS	481 384	482 384	BGA
481 321	482 321	BWS	481 385	482 385	BGA
481 322	482 322	BWS	481 386	482 386	BGA
481 323	482 323	BWS	481 387	482 387	BGA
481 324	482 324	BWS	481 388	482 388	BGA
481 325	482 325	BWS	481 389	482 389	BGA
481 326	482 326	BWS	481 390	482 390	BGA
481 327	482 327	BWS	481 391	482 391	BGA
481 328	482 328	BWS	481 392	482 392	BGA
481 329	482 329	BWS	481 393	482 393	BGA
481 330	482 330	BWS	481 394	482 394	BGA
481 331	482 331	BWS	481 395	482 395	BGA
481 332	482 332	BWS	481 396	482 396	BGA
481 333	482 333	BGA	481 397	482 397	BGA
481 334	482 334	BGA	481 398	482 398	BGA
481 335	482 335	BGA	481 399	482 399	BGA
481 336	482 336	BGA	481 400	482 400	BGA

481 401	482 401	BGA	481 448	482 448	BGA
481 402	482 402	BGA	481 449	482 449	BGA
481 403	482 403	BGA	481 450	482 450	BGA
481 404	482 404	BGA	481 451	482 451	BGA
481 405	482 405	BGA	481 452	482 452	BGA
481 406	482 406	BGA	481 453	482 453	BGA
481 407	482 407	BGA	481 454	482 454	BGA
481 408	482 408	BGA	481 455	482 455	BGA
481 409	482 409	BGA	481 456	482 456	BGA
481 410	482 410	BGA	481 457	482 457	BGA
481 411	482 411	BGA	481 458	482 458	BGA
481 412	482 412	BGA	481 459	482 459	BGA
481 413	482 413	BGA	481 460	482 460	BGA
481 414	482 414	BGA	481 461	482 461	BGA
481 415	482 415	BGA	481 462	482 462	BGA
481 416	482 416	BGA	481 463	482 463	BGA
481 417	482 417	BGA	481 464	482 464	BGA
481 418	482 418	BGA	481 465	482 465	BGA
481 419	482 419	BGA	481 466	482 466	BGA
481 420	482 420	BGA	481 467	482 467	BGA
481 421	482 421	BGA	481 468	482 468	BGA
481 422	482 422	BGA	481 469	482 469	BGA
481 423	482 423	BGA	481 470	482 470	BGA
481 424	482 424	BGA	481 471	482 471	BGA
481 425	482 425	BGA	481 472	482 472	BGA
481 426	482 426	BGA	481 473	482 473	BGA
481 427	482 427	BGA	481 474	482 474	BGA
481 428	482 428	BGA	481 475	482 475	BGA
481 429	482 429	BGA	481 476	482 476	BGA
481 430	482 430	BGA	481 477	482 477	BGA
481 431	482 431	BGA	481 478	482 478	BGA
481 432	482 432	BGA	481 479	482 479	BGA
481 433	482 433	BGA	481 480	482 480	BGA
481 434	482 434	BGA	481 481	482 481	BGA
481 435	482 435	BGA	481 482	482 482	BGA
481 436	482 436	BGA	481 483	482 483	BGA
481 437	482 437	BGA	481 484	482 484	BGA
481 438	482 438	BGA	481 485	482 485	BGA
481 439	482 439	BGA	481 486	482 486	BGA
481 440	482 440	BGA	481 487	482 487	BGA
481 441	482 441	BGA	481 488	482 488	BGA
481 442	482 442	BGA	481 489	482 489	BGA
481 443	482 443	BGA	481 490	482 490	BGA
481 444	482 444	BGA	481 491	482 491	BGA
481 445	482 445	BGA	481 492	482 492	BGA
481 446	482 446	BGA	481 493	482 493	BGA
481 447	482 447	BGA	481 494	482 494	BGA

CLASS 481.5   4-CAR BERLIN S-BAHN UNITS

An innovation in 2003 was the delivery of three complete Halbzüge. These differ from previous practice in being gangwayed within the set. Details are as given for other class 481/482 vehicles.

481 501	482 501	482 601	481 601	BWS
481 502	482 502	482 602	481 602	BWS
481 503	482 503	482 603	481 603	BWS

CLASS 485   2-CAR UNITS

Units built to DR design. Many sets have been withdrawn and scrapped after Class 481 was introduced but the problems of recent years saw some sets taken back from scrapyards or from storage lines and reinstated after a thorough overhaul.

B + B (DMSO–TSO) Non-gangwayed.

Built: 1987–92.
Builder: LEW.
Wheel Arrangement: Bo-Bo + 2-2.
Traction Motors: 4 x 150 kW.
Accommodation: –/44 +–/56.
Weight: 34 + 26 tonnes.

Former DR Class: 285.
Length over Couplers: 18.00 + 18.00 m.
Maximum Speed: 90 km/h.

485 014	885 014	BGA		485 092	885 092	BGA
485 015	885 015	BGA		485 093	885 093	BGA
485 016	885 016	BGA		485 094	885 094	BGA
485 019	885 019	BGA		485 095	885 095	BGA
485 022	885 022	BGA		485 096	885 096	BGA
485 026	885 026	BGA		485 097	885 097	BGA
485 027	885 027	BGA		485 099	885 099	BGA (Z)
485 028	885 028	BGA		485 102	885 102	BGA
485 029	885 029	BGA		485 104	885 104	BGA
485 030	885 030	BGA		485 108	885 108	BGA
485 031	885 031	BGA		485 109	885 109	BGA
485 033	885 033	BGA		485 110	885 110	BGA
485 034	885 034	BGA		485 111	885 111	BGA
485 038	885 038	BGA		485 112	885 112	BGA
485 040	885 040	BGA		485 114	885 114	BGA
485 041	885 041	BGA		485 115	885 115	BGA
485 042	885 042	BGA		485 117	885 117	BGA
485 043	885 043	BGA		485 118	885 118	BGA
485 044	885 044	BGA		485 119	885 119	BGA
485 048	885 048	BGA		485 120	885 120	BGA
485 050	885 050	BGA		485 121	885 121	BGA
485 054	885 054	BGA		485 122	885 122	BGA
485 055	885 055	BGA		485 123	885 123	BGA
485 059	885 059	BGA		485 126	885 126	BGA
485 061	885 061	BGA		485 127	885 127	BGA
485 062	885 062	BGA		485 128	885 128	BGA
485 066	885 066	BGA		485 129	885 129	BGA
485 068	885 068	BGA		485 137	885 137	BGA
485 069	885 069	BGA		485 138	885 138	BGA (Z)
485 070	885 070	BGA		485 140	885 140	BGA
485 072	885 072	BGA		485 141	885 141	BGA
485 074	885 074	BGA		485 142	885 142	BGA
485 076	885 076	BGA		485 143	885 143	BGA (Z)
485 078	885 078	BGA		485 147	885 147	BGA
485 079	885 079	BGA		485 149	885 149	BGA
485 080	885 080	BGA		485 152	885 152	BGA
485 082	885 082	BGA		485 156	885 156	BGA
485 083	885 083	BGA		485 158	885 158	BGA
485 085	885 085	BGA		485 160	885 160	BGA
485 088	885 088	BGA		485 161	885 161	BGA
485 089	885 089	BGA		485 162	885 162	BGA
485 090	885 090	BGA		485 164	885 164	BGA
485 091	885 091	BGA		485 168	885 168	BGA

CLASS 488   PANORAMA TRAIN

The Berlin S-Bahn knowing that its lines across and around the city offer good sightseeing itineraries decided after unification to convert three carriages into a sightseeing train. Naturally much use has been made of glass on the sides and in the roof allowing wide views. Because of the amount of glass air-conditioning is provided and the middle car has a small bar. It is thus thought that there are gangways within the set.

488 001   (477 105)   888 001   (877 130)   488 501   (477 130)

BERLIN S-BAHN DEPARTMENTAL UNITS

SHUNTING LOCOMOTIVE   Bo

This electric locomotive is used for shunting at the main Berlin S-Bahn workshops at Berlin-Schöneweide and has never been numbered in the main stock list.

Built: 1932.   **Maximum Tractive Effort:** 44 kN.
Builder: AEG.   **Weight:** 29.1 tonnes.
Power: 220 kW.   **Maximum Speed:** 50 km/h.

E176 11

The Berlin S-Bahn has several departmental units which are grouped into the 478 series whether they are EMUs or locomotives.

BREAKDOWN TRAIN VEHICLES

Converted in 1994. One vehicle is the breakdown vehicle containing jacks, packing etc whilst the other vehicle is the staff messroom etc.

478 521   (475 137) 478 523   (478 021)   BWS
478 522   (475 148) 478 524   (478 022)   BFF

VACUUM CLEANER TRAIN

This is an experimental vacuum cleaner train (Stausaugerzug) run by contractor Wiebe and converted in 1998. The 478 numbers are unknown. Each time your author visits Berlin the unit is usually found standing outside Hundekehle depot so may now be withdrawn. It is understood these units were allocated departmental numbers 706 001/2. Cornfirmation welcomed!

478 xxx   (475 089) 478 xxx   (476 375)

STORES UNITS

Just as the former Southern Region of British Railways had stores units for ferrying materials between depots so does the Berlin S-Bahn.

478 821   (477 605) 878 821   (877 605)   BWS (Z)
478 822   (477 608) 878 822   (877 608)   BWS (Z)

6. DIESEL MULTIPLE UNITS

CLASS 605   ICE-TD   4-CAR UNITS

This DMU is a diesel version of an ICE3 unit intended to bring ICE comfort and standards to non-electrified lines. It was intended to be used on services between Nürnberg and Dresden and also München and Lindau/Zürich but in traffic they were deemed unsuitable. The tilt system is an electro-mechanical version by Siemens. At one point all the units were in store but problems with the electric ICE fleet saw some 605s standing in for them. Then the Danes came to the rescue! Danish railways had ordered a new batch of IC DMUs from Italy but deliveries have been seriously delayed. DSB hired in some DB 605s to cover for their existing IC DMUs on services from København to Hamburg. So a batch of units have been fitted with Danish safety systems and in fact carry DSB logos. 605s also work the København to Berlin service which now runs via Hamburg. Once allocated to Hof and later München their new duties meant a transfer to Hamburg was in order. 605 009 and 605 109 were withdrawn on 31/12/2002 after derailment damage in late 2002. Three units remain in store at Berlin, Hamm and Hagen. As the units no longer work in their original area the names given then have been replaced.

B + B + B + A (DMSO–MSO–MSORMB–DMFO).

Built: 1998–99.
Builders: Siemens-Duewag, SGP.
Wheel Arrangement: 2-Bo + Bo-2 + 2-Bo + Bo-2.
Engine: Four Cummins QSK 19R750 engines of 560 kW at 1800 rpm.
Transmission: Electric. 4 x 425 kW three-phase asynchronous traction motors.
Accommodation: –/63 + –/51 with children's compartment 1W 1T 1TD + –/40 with bistro & conductor's office 1T 1 staff T + 41/–.
Weight: 54 + 54 + 55 + 56 tonnes.   **Length over Couplers:** 27.45 + 25.90 + 25.90 + 27.45 m.
Wheel Diameter: 860 mm.   **Maximum Speed:** 200 km/h.

DK   Fitted with Danish safety equipment.

▲ Class 605 diesel ICE units were for a time hired by Danish Railways (DSB) to work services between København and Hamburg. 605 016 is seen en route to Hamburg with ICE35, passing through Roskilde (Denmark) in 2009.   **Robin Ralston**

605 001	605 101	605 201	605 501		AH1 (Z)	
605 002	605 102	605 202	605 502		AH1 (Z)	
605 003	605 103	605 203	605 503	DK	AH1	
605 004	605 104	605 204	605 504	DK	AH1	
605 005	605 105	605 205	605 505	DK	AH1	Ostseebad Heringsdorf
605 006	605 106	605 206	605 506	DK	AH1	
605 007	605 107	605 207	605 507	DK	AH1	Århus
605 008	605 108	605 208	605 508		AH1	
605 010	605 110	605 210	605 510	DK	AH1	Wehrheim (Taunus)
605 011	605 111	605 211	605 511	DK	AH1	
605 012	605 112	605 212	605 512		AH1 (Z)	
605 013	605 113	605 213	605 513		AH1 (Z)	
605 014	605 114	605 214	605 514	DK	AH1	
605 015	605 115	605 215	605 515		AH1	
605 016	605 116	605 216	605 516	DK	AH1	
605 017	605 117	605 217	605 517	DK	AH1	København
605 018	605 118	605 218	605 518	DK	AH1	Jever
605 019	605 119	605 219	605 519	DK	AH1	
605 020	605 120	605 220	605 520	DK	AH1	Rendsburg
Spare		605 209	605 509		AH1	

CLASS 610   2-CAR UNITS

These tilting units were inspired by the Italian "Pendolino" trains. DB wanted some new DMUs for its route from Nürnberg to Hof and Bayreuth where there are many curves. The units have operated quite successfully since introduction but in 2000 the bogies started to show signs of strain. The units were all withdrawn from service. A solution was found and the sets were back at work by late 2001. Recently the whole class was transferred from Nürnberg to Hof to give the latter depot a balanced workload after the loss of local DMU work to a private operator. The sets are now employed on Hof–Regensburg trains.

BD + AB (DMBSO–DMCO).

Built: 1991–92 for DB.
Builders: Duewag (610.0), MAN (610.5).
Wheel Arrangement: 2-A1 + 1A-A1.
Engine: 1 MTU 12V183TD12 of 485 kW.
Transmission: Electric. Three-phase asynchronous motors.
Accommodation: –/68 (4) + 16/46 (2).   **Length over Buffers:** 25.40 + 25.40 m.
Weight: 47.45 + 47.90 tonnes.   **Maximum Speed:** 160 km/h.

610 001	610 501	NHO	610 011	610 511	NHO	
610 002	610 502	NHO	610 012	610 512	NHO	
610 003	610 503	NHO	610 013	610 513	NHO	
610 004	610 504	NHO	610 014	610 514	NHO	
610 005	610 505	NHO	610 015	610 515	NHO	
610 006	610 506	NHO (Z)	610 016	610 516	NHO	
610 007	610 507	NHO (Z)	610 017	610 517	NHO (Z)	
610 008	610 508	NHO	610 018	610 518	NHO (Z)	
610 009	610 509	NHO	610 019	610 519	NHO	
610 010	610 510	NHO (Z)	610 020	610 520	NHO	

Names:

610 002	PEGNITZ		610 008	LANDKREIS CHAM
610 004	STADT HOF		610 010	STADT HERSBRUCK
610 005	HERZOG STADT SULZBACH-ROSENBERG		610 011	1194–1995 BAYREUTH 800 JAHRE
			610 014	STADT AMBERG
610 006	MARKT-NEUHAUS A.D. PEGNITZ		610 017	STADT SCHWANDORF
610 007	MARKTREDWITZ		610 018	STADT WEIDEN

CLASS 611 2-CAR UNITS

These tilting DMUs can be considered a German version of the Italian inspired but German built Class 610s. However the tilting system used on the 611s is based on the military system used in the Leopard tanks! Five years after delivery the trains were still giving problems often associated with the tilt which means slower running speeds have to apply and consequently trains are late. Rhineland-Pfalz refused to pay subsidies to DB Regio and had all the units allocated to Kaiserslautern transferred away being replaced by Class 612 units. The Germans, instead of calling the units Pendolinos often refer to them as "Pannelinos" (Panne = a breakdown!). They are currently in use on the following routes: Basel–Lindau, Ulm–Aulendorf–Tübingen–Stuttgart and Ulm–Friedrichshafen.

B + AB (DMSO–DMCO).

Built: 1996–97.
Builders: AEG/Adtranz, Hennigsdorf.
Wheel Arrangement: 2-B + B-2.
Engine: Two 12 cylinder MTU 183TD13 engines of 540 kW.
Transmission: Hydraulic – Voith.
Accommodation: –/77 + 24/37 1T.
Weight: 116 tonnes.
Length over Couplers: 25.87 + 25.87 m.
Maximum Speed: 160 km/h.

611 001	611 501	TU		611 009	611 509	TU
611 002	611 502	TU		611 010	611 510	TU
611 003	611 503	TU		611 011	611 511	TU
611 004	611 504	TU		611 012	611 512	TU
611 005	611 505	TU		611 013	611 513	TU
611 006	611 506	TU		611 014	611 514	TU
611 007	611 507	TU		611 015	611 515	TU
611 008	611 508	TU		611 016	611 516	TU

▲ 612 073 and 612 081 approach Buchloe with regional service 57588, the 1251 München Hauptbahnhof- Kempten (Allgäu) on 12 September 2012. **Quintus Vosman**

611 017	611 517	TU		611 034	611 534	TU
611 018	611 518	TU		611 035	611 535	TU
611 019	611 519	TU		611 036	611 536	TU
611 020	611 520	TU		611 037	611 537	TU
611 021	611 521	TU		611 038	611 538	TU
611 022	611 522	TU		611 039	611 539	TU
611 023	611 523	TU		611 040	611 540	TU
611 024	611 524	TU		611 041	611 541	TU
611 025	611 525	TU		611 042	611 542	TU
611 026	611 526	TU		611 043	611 543	TU
611 027	611 527	TU		611 044	611 544	TU
611 028	611 528	TU		611 045	611 545	TU
611 029	611 529	TU		611 046	611 546	TU
611 030	611 530	TU		611 047	611 547	TU
611 031	611 531	TU		611 048	611 548	TU
611 032	611 532	TU		611 049	611 549	TU
611 033	611 533	TU		611 050	611 550	TU

CLASS 612 — 2-CAR REGIO SWINGER

This class was designed as a follow on order to the 611s and again tilt is featured. An extra set has been provided as a mobile laboratory with car 612 902 fitted with a pantograph and camera. When there were problems with the 605s on the Nürnberg–Hof route they were replaced by 612s which were painted in IC livery and renumbered by adding 300 to the number. These are back in Regio use now and back in red. However the numbers never reverted back to the original ones. Over the years there have been various problems with the tilt with the apparatus being isolated and then reinstated many times. Currently it is understood that the apparatus is back in use.

Set 612 016 was involved in a fire and withdrawn with 612 516 becoming 612 508[II]. Set 612 063 was withdrawn following a crash at a level crossing.

AB + B (DMCO–DMSO).

Built: 1998–2003.
Builder: Adtranz Hennigsdorf.
Wheel Arrangement: 2-B + B-2.
Engine: One 12 cylinder Cummins QSK 19 of 559 kW.
Transmission: Hydraulic.
Accommodation: 24/37 (10) + –/71 (4) 1TD.
Weight: 119 tonnes.
Length over Couplers: 30.875 + 30.875 m.
Maximum Speed: 160 km/h.

612 001	612 501	MKP		612 023	612 523	UE
612 002	612 502	MKP		612 024	612 524	UE
612 003	612 503	MKP		612 025	612 525	UE
612 004	612 504	MKP		612 026	612 526	UE
612 005	612 505	SKL		612 027	612 527	UE
612 006	612 506	SKL		612 028	612 528	UE
612 007	612 507	SKL		612 029	612 529	UE
612 008	612 508[II]	SKL		612 030	612 530	UE
612 009	612 509	LH2		612 031	612 531	UE
612 010	612 510	LL1		612 032	612 532	UE
612 011	612 511	LL1		612 033	612 533	UE
612 012	612 512	LH2		612 034	612 534	UE
612 013	612 513	LH2		612 035	612 535	UE
612 014	612 514	LH2		612 036	612 536	UE
612 015	612 515	LH2		612 037	612 537	LL1
612 017	612 517	LL1		612 038	612 538	LL1
612 018	612 518	LL1		612 039	612 539	FK
612 019	612 519	DA		612 040	612 540	FK
612 020	612 520	DA		612 041	612 541	FK
612 021	612 521	UE		612 042	612 542	FK
612 022	612 522	UE		612 043	612 543	FK

612 044	612 544	FK	612 110	612 610	DA
612 045	612 545	FK	612 111	612 611	DA
612 046	612 546	FK	612 112	612 612	DA
612 047	612 547	FK	612 113	612 613	DA
612 048	612 548	FK	612 114	612 614	NHO
612 049	612 549	FK	612 115	612 615	NHO
612 050	612 550	FK	612 116	612 616	UE
612 051	612 551	SKL	612 117	612 617	UE
612 052	612 552	SKL	612 118	612 618	SKL
612 053	612 553	SKL	612 119	612 619	SKL
612 054	612 554	SKL	612 120	612 620	SKL
612 055	612 555	NHO	612 121	612 621	SKL
612 056	612 556	NHO	612 122	612 622	SKL
612 057	612 557	NHO	612 123	612 623	SKL
612 058	612 558	NHO	612 124	612 624	SKL
612 059	612 559	NHO	612 125	612 625	SKL
612 060	612 560	NHO	612 126	612 626	UE
612 061	612 561	NHO	612 127	612 627	DA
612 062	612 562	NHO	612 128	612 628	DA
612 064	612 564	NHO	612 129	612 629	DA
612 065	612 565	NHO	612 130	612 630	LL1
612 066	612 566	NHO	612 131	612 631	LL1 (Z)
612 067	612 567	LL1	612 132	612 632	NHO
612 068	612 568	LL1	612 133	612 633	UE
612 069	612 569	LL1	612 134	612 634	UE
612 071	612 571	DA	612 135	612 635	UE
612 072	612 572	DA	612 136	612 636	SKL
612 073	612 573	MKP	612 137	612 637	SKL
612 074	612 574	MKP	612 138	612 638	SKL
612 075	612 575	MKP	612 139	612 639	SKL
612 076	612 576	MKP	612 140	612 640	SKL
612 077	612 577	MKP	612 141	612 641	SKL
612 078	612 578	MKP	612 142	612 642	SKL
612 079	612 579	MKP	612 143	612 643	SKL
612 080	612 580	MKP	612 144	612 644	UE
612 081	612 581	MKP	612 145	612 645	UE
612 082	612 582	NHO	612 146	612 646	UE
612 083	612 583	MKP	612 147	612 647	UE
612 084	612 584	MKP	612 148	612 648	UE
612 085	612 585	MKP	612 149	612 649	MKP
612 086	612 586	MKP	612 150	612 650	MKP
612 087	612 587	MKP	612 151	612 651	NHO
612 088	612 588	MKP	612 152	612 652	NHO
612 089	612 589	MKP	612 153	612 653	NHO
612 090	612 590	MKP	612 154	612 654	NHO
612 091	612 591	MKP	612 155	612 655	NHO
612 092	612 592	NHO	612 156	612 656	NHO
612 093	612 593	NHO	612 157	612 657	NHO
612 094	612 594	NHO	612 158	612 658	NHO
612 095	612 595	NHO	612 159	612 659	LH2
612 096	612 596	NHO	612 160	612 660	LH2
612 097	612 597	NHO	612 161	612 661	LH2
612 098	612 598	NHO	612 162	612 662	LH2
612 099	612 599	UE	612 463	612 963	NHO
612 100	612 600	UE	612 464	612 964	NHO
612 101	612 601	UE	612 165	612 665	NHO
612 102	612 602	UE	612 166	612 666	NHO
612 103	612 603	DA	612 167	612 667	NHO
612 104	612 604	DA	612 168	612 668	NHO
612 105	612 605	DA	612 169	612 669	NHO
612 106	612 606	LL1	612 170	612 670	NHO
612 107	612 607	LL1	612 471	612 971	NHO
612 108	612 608	LL1	612 472	612 972	NHO
612 109	612 609	LL1	612 173	612 673	UE

612 174	612 674	UE		612 184	612 684	UE
612 175	612 675	UE		612 485	612 985	NHO
612 176	612 676	UE		612 486	612 986	NHO
612 477	612 977	NHO		612 487	612 987	NHO
612 178	612 678	UE		612 488	612 988	NHO
612 479	612 979	NHO		612 489	612 989	NHO
612 480	612 980	NHO		612 490	612 990	NHO
612 481	612 981	NHO		612 491	612 991	NHO
612 482	612 982	NHO		612 492	612 992	NHO
612 183	612 683	UE		612 901	612 902	STMI

Names:

612 058	STADT HOF		612 115	LANDKREIS KRONACH
612 065	STADT SCHWEINFURT		612 157	LANDKREIS HOF
612 074	IMMENSTADT im ALLGÄU		612 158	STADT HOF
612 090	LINDAU		612 170	LANDKREIS HOF
612 096	MARKT NEUHAUS A.D. PEGNITZ			

▲ 628 203 crosses the bridge over the river Ahr, near Kreuzberg, with a service from Ahrbrück to Remagen on 15 October 2011. **Matthias Müller**

CLASS 614 — 3-CAR UNITS

All these units are now out of service with most being in store at Hamm awaiting a purchaser. Some sets have been sold to eastern European countries with a view to being used by intending private operators.

ABD + B + ABD (DMBCso–TSO–DMBCso).

Built: 1971–76 for DB.
Builders: Orenstein & Koppel/Uerdingen.
Wheel Arrangement: B–2 + 2–2 + 2–B.
Engine: One MAN (Cummins QSK18*) of 335 kW (450 hp).
Transmission: Hydraulic.
Accommodation: 12/58 1T + –/88 2T + 12/58 1T. **Length over Buffers:** 26.65 + 26.16 + 26.65 m.
Weight: 45.5 + 32 + 45.5 tonnes. **Maximum Speed:** 140 km/h.

614 007		614 008		NN1 (Z)			614 052		BCS (Z)
614 011	914 006	614 012		NN1 (Z)	614 053		614 054	*	HBS (Z)
614 013	914 007	614 014		BCS (Z)	614 055		614 056		HBS (Z)
614 021	914 011	614 022		BCS (Z)	614 057	914 029	614 058		HBS (Z)
	914 013			BCS (Z)	614 059		614 060	*	HBS (Z)
614 027	914 014	614 028		NN1 (Z)		914 033			HBS (Z)
614 029	914 015	614 030		BCS (Z)	614 067	914 034	614 068	*	BCS (Z)
	914 004	614 036		BCS (Z)		914 035		*	BCS (Z)
614 037	914 019	614 038	*	NN1 (Z)		914 036			HBS (Z)
614 039	914 020	614 040		NN1 (Z)	614 073		614 074		HBS (Z)
614 041	914 021	614 042		BCS (Z)		914 040			HBS (Z)
614 043	914 022	614 044		BCS (Z)		914 041	614 082		HBS (Z)
614 047	914 024	614 048		BCS (Z)	614 083		614 084		BCS (Z)

CLASSES 620 & 621 — LINT 81H — 3-CAR UNITS

These new units from Alstom are part of the Coradia family of DMUs but differ from previous versions as no articulation is involved so the sets are longer. In fact these would appear to be the first Alstom three car units. 38 sets have been ordered for the Köln area. Surprisingly these three car sets will have four engines! The extra engine, unlike the principal engines, is for traction only not providing any power to auxiliaries and is capable of being switched off whilst in transit to save fuel. The MTU engines meet EU Stage IIIB emissions. The units additionally are fitted with Selective Catalytic Reduction equipment that cleans exhaust gases. The units are expected to enter service in December 2013.

ABD + B + AB (DMBSso–MSO–DMBCso).

Built: 2012–13.
Builder: Alstom Salzgitter.
Wheel Arrangement: .B–2 + B–2 + B–B.
Engine: MTU 6H 1800 R85L of 390kW (620.0 1 engine, 621 1 engine 620.5 2 engines).
Transmission: Hydraulic, Voith T 320 rz.
Accommodation: 12/58 1T + –/88 2T + 12/58 1T. **Length over Couplers:** 26.65 + 26.16 + 26.65 m.
Weight: 45.5 + 32 + 45.5 tonnes. **Maximum Speed:** 140 km/h.

620 001	621 001	620 501		620 015	621 015	620 515
620 002	621 002	620 502		620 016	621 016	620 516
620 003	621 003	620 503		620 017	621 017	620 517
620 004	621 004	620 504		620 018	621 018	620 518
620 005	621 005	620 505		620 019	621 019	620 519
620 006	621 006	620 506		620 020	621 020	620 520
620 007	621 007	620 507		620 021	621 021	620 521
620 008	621 008	620 508		620 022	621 022	620 522
620 009	621 009	620 509		620 023	621 023	620 523
620 010	621 010	620 510		620 024	621 024	620 524
620 011	621 011	620 511		620 025	621 025	620 525
620 012	621 012	620 512		620 026	621 026	620 526
620 013	621 013	620 513		620 027	621 027	620 527
620 014	621 014	620 514		620 028	621 028	620 528

620 029	621 029	620 529		620 034	621 034	620 534
620 030	621 030	620 530		620 035	621 035	620 535
620 031	621 031	620 531		620 036	621 036	620 536
620 032	621 032	620 532		620 037	621 037	620 537
620 033	621 033	620 533		620 038	621 038	620 538

CLASS 622   LINT 54H   2-CAR UNITS

This is another new version of the Alstom Coradia family but does not feature articulation so a two car set is longer. 18 sets have been ordered for the Köln area (2013 into service) and 24 for the Dieselnetz Südwest (2015 into service). The units have 3 engines one of which may be shut down in transit to save fuel. The MTU engines meet EU Stage IIIB emissions. The units additionally are fitted with Selective Catalytic Reduction equipment that cleans exhaust gases.

B + AB (DMSO–DMCO).

Built: 2012–13.
Builder: Alstom Salzgitter.
Wheel Arrangement: B-2 + B-B.
Engine: MTU 6H 1800 R85L of 390kW (622.0 1 engine, 622.5 2 engines).
Transmission: Hydraulic, Voith T 320 rz.
Accommodation: –/64 (8) 1T + 8/48 (13).   **Length over Couplers:** 22.70 + 22.70 m.
Weight: **Maximum Speed:** 140 km/h.

622 001	622 501		622 022	622 522
622 002	622 502		622 023	622 523
622 003	622 503		622 024	622 524
622 004	622 504		622 025	622 525
622 005	622 505		622 026	622 526
622 006	622 506		622 027	622 527
622 007	622 507		622 028	622 528
622 008	622 508		622 029	622 529
622 009	622 509		622 030	622 530
622 010	622 510		622 031	622 531
622 011	622 511		622 032	622 532
622 012	622 512		622 033	622 533
622 013	622 513		622 034	622 534
622 014	622 514		622 035	622 535
622 015	622 515		622 036	622 536
622 016	622 516		622 037	622 537
622 017	622 517		622 038	622 538
622 018	622 518		622 039	622 539
622 019	622 519		622 040	622 540
622 020	622 520		622 041	622 541
622 021	622 521		622 042	622 542

CLASS 628.2   2-CAR UNITS

The production series of lightweight DMUs for branch line use based on the 628.0 and 628.1 prototypes. Most units are fitted out for driver only operation whereby the driver can issue tickets as passengers join but with the installation of ticket machines at stations this is rarely the case these days. Some power cars have been rebuilt as Class 629 and paired with another 628 power car. The displaced trailers are spare or scrapped. The early units are now being replaced by more modern units from Alstom resulting in about 30 units being stored at Hamm awaiting sale or scrapping.

B + AB (DMSO–DTCO).

Built: 1987 onwards for DB.
Builders: Duewag, Uerdingen, LHB Salzgitter, MBB Donauwörth, AEG Hennigsdorf.
Wheel Arrangement: 2–B + 2–2.
Engine: 12 cylinder Daimler Benz OM 444A of 410 kW.
Transmission: Hydraulic, Voith T 320 rz.
Accommodation: –/64 (8) 1T + 10/48 (13).   **Length over Couplers:** 22.70 + 22.70 m.
Weight: 40 + 28 tonnes.   **Maximum Speed:** 120 km/h.

628 201	928 201	FL	628 223	928 223	FK
628 202	928 202	RL (Z)	628 224	928 224	NAH
628 203	928 203	RL (Z)	628 225	928 225	FK
628 204	928 204	RL (Z)	628 226	928 226	FK
628 205	928 205	RL (Z)	628 227	928 227	FK
628 206	928 206	RL	628 228	928 228	FK
628 207	928 207	RL	628 229	928 229	NAH
628 208	928 208	RL	628 230	928 230	NAH
628 209	928 209	RL	628 231	928 231	NAH
628 210	928 210	RL	628 232	928 232	NAH
628 211	928 211	RL	628 234	928 234	NAH
628 212	928 212	RL	628 235	928 235	FK
628 213	928 213	RL	628 236	928 236	RHL
628 214	928 214	RL	628 237	928 237	NAH
628 215	928 215	RL	628 238	928 238	AK
628 216	928 216	RL	628 239	928 239	MKP
628 217	928 217	RL	628 240	928 240	MKP
628 218	928 218	RL	628 241	928 241	MKP
628 219	928 219	RL	628 242	928 242	MKP
628 220	928 220	AK	628 243	928 243	WR
628 221	928 221	AK (Z)	628 244	928 244	FK
628 222	928 349	AK	628 245	928 245	WR

▲ 642 095 arrives at Memmingen with an RE service from Augsburg on 7 October 2009.
Robin Ralston

628 247	928 247	NAH	628 300	928 300	RL (Z)
628 248	928 248	NAH	628 302	928 302	RL
628 249	928 249	NHO (Z)	628 303		STR
628 250	928 250	FK	628 304	928 304	RL
628 251	928 251	NAH	628 305		STR
628 252	928 252	FK	628 307	928 307	RL
628 253	928 253	NAH (Z)	628 308	928 308	RL (Z)
628 254	928 254	MMF	628 309	928 309	RL (Z)
628 255	928 255	FK	628 310	928 310	RL
628 256	928 256	NAH	628 311	928 311	WR
	928 259	RL	628 312	928 312	RL (Z)
628 260	928 260	RL (Z)	628 314	928 314	WR
	928 261	RL	628 315	928 315	RL
628 262	928 262	NHO (Z)	628 316	928 316	FL
628 264	928 264	RL	628 317	928 317	FL
628 265	928 265	NAH	628 318	928 318	RHL
628 266	928 266	NAH	628 319	928 319	RL (Z)
628 267	928 267	NAH	628 320	928 320	RL (Z)
628 268	928 268	NAH	628 321	928 321	RL
628 269	928 269	NAH	628 322	928 322	RL (Z)
628 270	928 270	NAH	628 323	928 323	RL (Z)
628 271	928 271	RL (Z)		928 324	RL (Z)
628 272	928 272	RL (Z)	628 325	928 325	NAH
628 273	928 273	RL (Z)	628 326	928 326	FL (Z)
628 274	928 274	AK	628 327	928 327	NAH
628 275		RK (Z)	628 328	928 328	FL
628 277	928 277	NAH	628 329	928 329	FL (Z)
628 278	928 278	RHL	628 330	928 330	FL (Z)
628 280	928 280	RL (Z)	628 331	928 331	FL (Z)
628 281	928 281	AK	628 332	928 332	NAH
628 282	928 282	RL (Z)		928 333	TU
628 283	928 283	RL	628 334	928 334	TU
628 284	928 284	RL (Z)	628 335		TU
628 286	928 286	RL (Z)	628 336	928 336	TU (Z)
628 287	928 287	RL (Z)	628 337	928 337	TU (Z)
628 288	928 288	RL		928 338	TU (Z)
628 289	928 289	RHL	628 339	928 339	TU
628 290	928 290	MMF	628 340		TU
628 291	928 291	RL (Z)	628 342	928 342	TU
628 292	928 292	RL (Z)	628 343	928 343	TU
628 293	928 293	RL (Z)	628 344		TU
628 294	928 294	RL (Z)	628 345	928 345	TU
628 295	928 295	RL (Z)	628 346	928 346	TU
628 296	928 296	RL (Z)	628 347	928 347	TU
628 297	928 297	RL (Z)	628 348	928 348	TU
628 298	928 298	NAH		928 349	RL
628 299	928 299	RL (Z)	628 350	928 350	TU

Names:

628 201	Schleswig Holstein		628 255	Stadt Bad Laasphe
628 206	Niedersachsen		628 328	Landkreis Limburg-Weilburg
628 228	Region Siegen-Wittgenstein		628 345	Landkreis Altenkirchen
628 250	Region Burgwald-Ederbergland			

CLASS 628.4 2-CAR UNITS

The Class 628/4 features a more powerful engine, wider middle-entry doors and a different, more comfortable seat design. Sets 405–408 were not taken into DB stock being diverted to the EVB (Eisenbahnen und Verkehrsbetriebe Elbe-Weser GmbH). Sets 505 and 506 are actually owned by CFL but operated and maintained by DB at Trier.

B + AB (DMSO–DTCO).

Built: 1993–95.
Builders: Duewag, Uerdingen, LHB Salzgitter, MBB Donauwörth, AEG Hennigsdorf.
Wheel Arrangement: B–2 + 2–2.
Engine: 12 cyl MTU of 485 kW.
Transmission: Hydraulic, Voith T 320 rz.
Accommodation: –/62 (8) 1T + 12/48 (14). **Length over Couplers:** 23.20 + 23.20 m.
Weight: 40 + 29 tonnes. **Maximum Speed:** 120 km/h.

628 401	928 401	RL		628 453	928 453	SKL
628 402	928 402	MKP		628 454	928 454	SKL
628 403	928 403	RL		628 455	928 455	STR
628 404	928 404	RL		628 456	928 456	STR (Z)
628 409	928 409	EDO		628 457	928 457	SKL
628 410	928 410	RL		628 458	928 458	SKL
628 411	928 411	RL		628 459	928 459	SKL
628 412	928 412	RL		628 460	928 460	STR
628 413	928 413	RL		628 461	928 461	SKL
628 414	928 414	RL		628 462	928 462	STR
628 415	928 415	MKP		628 463	928 463	STR
628 416	928 416	MKP		628 464	928 464	RL
628 417	928 417	RL		628 465	928 465	SKL
628 418	928 418	RL		628 466	928 466	SKL
628 419	928 419	NHO		628 467	928 467	SKL
628 420	928 420	MKP		628 468	928 468	RL
628 421	928 421	RL		628 469	928 469	RL
628 422	928 422	MMF		628 470	928 470	SKL
628 423	928 423	MMF		628 471	928 471	SKL
628 424	928 424	MMF		628 472	928 472	SKL
628 425	928 425	MMF		628 473	928 473	SKL
628 426	928 426	MMF		628 474	928 474	SKL
628 427	928 427	NHO		628 475	928 475	SKL
628 428	928 428	MKP		628 476	928 476	SKL
628 429	928 429	NHO		628 477	928 477	SKL
628 430	928 430	RL		628 478	928 478	SKL
628 431	928 431	MKP		628 479	928 479	SKL
628 432	928 432	MMF		628 480	928 480	SKL
628 433	928 433	MMF		628 481	928 481	SKL
628 434	928 434	MMF		628 482	928 482	SKL
628 435	928 435	WR		628 483	928 483	SKL
628 436	928 436	FL		628 484	928 484	RL
628 437	928 437	RL		628 485	928 485	SKL
628 438	928 438	FL		628 486	928 486	SKL
628 439	928 439	RL		628 487	928 487	SKL
628 440	928 440	FL		628 488	928 488	STR
628 441	928 441	RL		628 489	928 489	STR
628 442	928 442	FL		628 490	928 490	STR
628 443	928 443	RL		628 491	928 491	STR
628 444	928 444	RL		628 492	928 492	SKL
628 445	928 445	RL		628 493	928 493	SKL
628 446	928 446	MKP		628 494	928 494	SKL
628 447	928 447	RL		628 495	928 495	KD
628 448	928 448	RL		628 496	928 496	KD
628 449	928 449	FL		628 497	928 497	KD
628 450	928 450	RL		628 498	928 498	STR
628 451	928 451	SKL		628 499	928 499	KD
628 452	928 452	SKL		628 500	928 500	KD

628 501	928 501	KD		628 567	928 567	MMF
628 502	928 502	KD		628 568	928 568	MMF
628 503	928 503	KD		628 569	928 569	MMF
628 504	928 504	KD		628 570	928 570	MMF
628 505	928 505	STR		628 571	928 571	MMF
628 506	928 506	STR		628 572	928 572	MMF
628 507	928 507	KD		628 573	928 573	TU
628 508	928 508	KD		628 574	928 574	MMF
628 509	928 509	KD		628 575	928 575	MMF
628 510	928 510	KD		628 576	928 576	MMF
628 511	928 511	KD		628 577	928 577	MMF
628 512	928 512	KD		628 578	928 578	MMF
628 513	928 513	KD		628 579	928 579	RL
628 514	928 514	EDO		628 580	928 580	MMF
628 515	928 515	EDO		628 581	928 581	MMF
628 516	928 516	EDO		628 582	928 582	SKL
628 517	928 517	EDO		628 583	928 583	SKL
628 518	928 518	EDO		628 584	928 584	MMF
628 519	928 519	STR		628 585	928 585	MMF
628 520	928 520	EDO		628 586	928 586	MMF
628 521	928 521	EDO		628 587	928 587	NAH
628 522	(628 696)	SKL		628 588	928 588	NAH
628 523	928 523	SKL		628 589	928 589	MMF
628 525	928 525	EDO		628 591	928 591	MMF
628 526	928 526	STR		628 592	928 592	STR
628 527	928 527	KD		628 593	928 593	MMF
628 528	928 528	EDO		628 594	928 594	SKL
628 529	928 529	EDO		628 595	928 595	SKL
628 530	928 530	EDO		628 596	928 596	HBS
628 531	928 531	KD		628 597	928 597	HBS
628 532	928 532	KD		628 598	928 598	HBS
628 533	928 533	KD		628 599	928 599	HBS
628 534	928 534	KD		628 600	928 600	HBS
628 535	928 535	KD		628 601	928 601	HBS
628 536	928 536	EDO (Z)		628 602	928 602	SKL
628 537	928 537	EDO		628 603	928 603	HBS
628 538	928 538	KD		628 604	928 604	RL
628 539	928 539	KD		628 605	928 605	HBS
628 540	928 540	KD		628 606	928 606	HBS
628 541	928 541	SKL		628 607	928 607	FL
628 542	928 542	TU		628 608	928 608	HBS
628 543	928 543	TU		628 609	928 609	HBS
628 544	928 544	TU		628 610	928 610	HBS
628 546	928 546	TU		628 611	928 611	RL
628 547	928 547	TU		628 612	928 612	MMF
628 548	928 548	TU		628 613	928 613	HBS
628 549	928 549	TU		628 614	928 614	HBS
628 550	928 550	TU		628 615	928 615	HBS
628 551	928 551	HBS		628 616	928 616	HBS
628 552	928 552	TU		628 617	928 617	HBS
628 553	928 553	HBS		628 618	928 618	HBS
628 554	928 554	TU		628 619	928 619	HBS
628 555	928 555	TU		628 620	928 620	HBS
628 556	928 556	MMF		628 622	928 622	HBS
628 557	928 557	MMF		628 623	928 623	HBS
628 558	928 558	MMF		628 624	928 624	HBS
628 559	928 559	MMF		628 625	928 625	HBS
628 560	928 560	MMF		628 626	928 626	SKL
628 561	928 561	RL		628 627	928 627	MMF
628 562	928 562	TU		628 628	928 628	MMF
628 563	928 563	AK		628 629	928 629	MMF
628 564	928 564	AK		628 630	928 630	MMF
628 565	928 565	MMF		628 631	928 631	WR
628 566	928 566	MMF		628 632	928 632	HBS (Z)

628 633	928 633	WR		628 668	928 668	KD
628 634	928 634	RL		628 669	928 669	KD
628 635	928 635	WR		628 670	928 670	KD
628 636	928 636	RL		628 671	928 671	STR
628 637	928 637	STR		628 672	928 672	STR
628 638	928 638	MKP (Z)		628 673	928 673	STR
628 639	928 639	MMF		628 674	928 674	STR
628 640	928 640	HBS		628 675	928 675	STR
628 641	928 641	WR		628 676	928 676	EDO
628 642	928 642	WR		628 678	928 678	MMF
628 643	928 643	HBS		628 681	928 681	STR
628 644	928 644	FL		628 682	928 682	WR
628 645	928 645	HBS		628 683	928 683	WR
628 646	928 646	MMF		628 684	928 684	WR
628 647	928 647	WR		628 685	928 685	AK
628 648	928 648	STR		628 686	928 686	STR
628 649	928 649	MMF		628 687	928 687	FL
628 650	928 650	WR		628 688	928 688	FL
628 651	928 651	WR		628 689	928 689	WR (Z)
628 652	928 652	WR		628 690	928 690	WR
628 653	928 653	MMF		628 691	928 691	WR (Z)
628 654	928 654	WR		628 692	928 692	WR
628 655	928 655	RL		628 693	928 693	RL
628 656	928 656	WR		628 694	928 694	RL
628 657	928 657	WR		628 695	928 695	RL
628 658	928 658	WR		628 696		SKL
628 659	928 659	WR		628 697	928 697	RL
628 660	928 660	EDO		628 698	928 698	FL
628 661	928 661	KD		628 699	928 699	RL
628 662	928 662	KD		628 700	928 700	RL
628 663	928 663	EDO		628 701	928 701	RHL
628 664	928 664	EDO		628 702	928 702	RHL
628 665	928 665	EDO		628 703	928 703	RHL
628 666	928 666	EDO		628 704	928 704	KD
628 667	928 667	KD		628 705	928 705	SKL

Names:

628 401	STADT HOF		628 560	LANDKREIS ALTÖTTLING
628 402	STADT MUNCHBERG		628 561	LANDKREIS DACHAU
628 403	1194–1994 BAYREUTH 800 JAHRE		628 562	LANDKREIS DACHAU
628 404	STADT REHAU		628 570	STADT MÜHLDORF AM INN
628 411	LANDKREIS KULMBACH		628 572	STADT WALDKRAIBURG
628 413	SELB		628 577	LANDKREIS STRAUBING BOGEN
628 414	BAYERISCHES STADTSBAD BAD STEBEN		628 578	GEMEINDE ZUBEN
			628 593	WALD KREIBURG
628 415	BINDLACH		628 612	STADT TRAUNREUT
628 417	SPEICHERSDORF		628 626	STADT BURGHAUSEN
628 423	STADT CHAM		628 627	MARKT TÜSSLING
628 432	STADT RIED IM INNKREIS			

CLASS 628.9/629   2-CAR UNITS

When first introduced these units were two Class 628.4 back to back. These units replaced the last of the original order for 628.4 as it was found a power car + trailer were under-powered when working on the Mainz–Alzey line. Thus the order was changed for extra power cars. Later, as 628.2 units became spare, pairs of these power cars were put together with the trailers being made spare or scrapped.

B + AB (DMSO–DMCO).

Built: 1995 (1999*).
Builders: Duewag, Uerdingen, LHB Salzgitter, MBB Donauwörth, AEG Hennigsdorf.
Wheel Arrangement: B–2 + 2–B.
Engine: 12 cylinder MTU of 485 kW.
Transmission: Hydraulic, Voith T 320 rz.
Accommodation: –/64 1T (8) + 10/48 (13).   **Length over Couplers:** 23.20 + 23.20 m.
Weight: 40 + 40 tonnes.   **Maximum Speed:** 120 km/h.

628 906 ex 628 522, 629 006 ex 928 607.

628 901	629 001		SKL	628 904	629 004		SKL
628 902	629 002		SKL	628 905	629 005		SKL
628 903	629 003		SKL	628 906	629 006	*	SKL
629 283	(628 261)			629 335	(628 345)		TU
629 288	(628 259)		RL	629 340	(628 341)		TU
629 301	(628 257)		STR	629 344	(628 349)		TU
629 303	(628 233)		STR	629 347	(628 333)		TU
629 305	(628 263)		STR	629 350	(628 338)		TU
629 313	(628 276)		STR				

CLASS 640   LINT 27   SINGLE CAR

30 of these single car LINT 27 were ordered on 21/06/96 (LINT = *Leichter Innovativer Nahverkehrs Triebwagen*; 27 = length in metres and now given the brand name Coradia). They were ordered along with many others to re-equip local services and give a good start to the 21st Century not to mention the State giving the soon to be privatised railways lots of modern stock to be inherited by the private buyers! They have welded stainless steel bodies, low floors, magnetic brakes, Scharfenberg couplers, and vacuum-toilets. Two sets of access doors. The cabs also have modern safety fittings etc including Sifa STG 545, Indusi I60R, Zugbahnfunk ZFM 90. The units can be found working around Finnentrop and Siegen as well as from their base at Dortmund.

AB (DMCO).

Built: 2000–01.
Builders: Alstom/LHB.
Wheel Arrangement: B-2.
Engine: Two six cylinder MTU 6R 183 TD 13H giving 315 kW at 1900 rpm.
Transmission: Hydrodynamic, Voith T211rzze.
Accommodation: 8/52 (13).   **Floor Height:** 580 mm.
Weight: 37 + 40.5 tonnes.   **Length over Couplers:** 27.21 m.
Wheel Diameter: 770 mm.   **Maximum Speed:** 120 km/h.

640 001	EDO	640 011	EDO	640 021	EDO
640 002	EDO	640 012	EDO	640 022	EDO
640 003	EDO	640 013	EDO	640 023	EDO
640 004	EDO	640 014	EDO	640 024	EDO
640 005	EDO	640 015	EDO	640 025	EDO
640 006	EDO	640 016	EDO	640 026	EDO
640 007	EDO	640 017	EDO	640 027	EDO
640 008	EDO	640 018	EDO	640 028	EDO
640 009	EDO	640 019	EDO	640 029	EDO
640 010	EDO	640 020	EDO	640 030	EDO

CLASS 641 SINGLE CAR

40 of these units were ordered on 21/06/96 and the Limburg area was expected to get the first units. In fact it got none and instead the units took over stopping services from Basel to Waldshut and similar work in Thüringen. The units are in fact basically the same as the SNCF TER sets of Class X 73500. Features include magnetic brakes, Scharfenberg couplers, and a welded aluminium body bolted to steel frames. Cabs are glass reinforced plastic. Magnetic brakes. Several of the Erfurt units are now stored at Hagen as the Erfurter Bahn has taken over many former DB services in the Erfurt area. 641 024/30 have been withdrawn following accident damage.

AB (DMCO).

Built: 2000–02.
Builders: Alstom/LHB, De Dietrich.
Wheel Arrangement: 1A-A1.
Engine: Two MAN D2866 LH21 of 257 kW.
Transmission: Hydrodynamic.
Accommodation: 8/55 (17).
Weight: 47 tonnes.
Wheel Diameter: 840 mm.

Floor height:
Length over couplers: 28.90 m.
Maximum Speed: 140 km/h.

641 001	RHL	641 010	RHL	641 019	UE
641 002	RHL	641 011	RHL	641 020	UE
641 003	RHL	641 012	RHL	641 021	UE
641 004	RHL	641 013	RHL	641 022	UE
641 005	RHL	641 014	RHL	641 023	UE
641 006	RHL	641 015	RHL	641 025	UE (Z)
641 007	RHL	641 016	RHL	641 026	UE
641 008	RHL	641 017	RHL	641 027	UE
641 009	RHL	641 018	RHL	641 028	RHL

▲ 643 216 working local service RB10619, the 1254 from Düsseldorf to Köln Messe-Deutz, arrives at Köln Hauptbahnhof on 29 August 2009. **Robin Ralston**

641 029	RHL	641 034	UE	641 038	UE (Z)
641 031	UE (Z)	641 035	UE	641 039	UE (Z)
641 032	UE	641 036	UE	641 040	RHL
641 033	UE (Z)	641 037	UE (Z)		

Name:

641 011 Haltingen

CLASS 642   2-SECTION ARTICULATED DMUS

150 of these articulated two-car units were ordered on 21/06/96 and were known at that time as the Duewag RVT2.2 but after the Siemens takeover of Duewag the marketing name of "Desiro" was applied. Welded aluminium features for the body whilst the cabs are glass reinforced plastic. There is rubber primary and air secondary suspension; Scharfenberg couplers. SIBAS microprocessor control system allows four sets to work in multiple. The arrival of these units has seen off many locos of Classes 202, 211, 212, 215, 219. At Innotrans 2012, DB presented set 642 129 as a hybrid unit – an electro-diesel. This unit now has 2 MTU hybrid power packs of 315 kW from MTU 6H1800R75 engines. There is an alternator and electric motor which is connected to the hydrodynamic gearbox. Additionally there is a lithium phosphate battery charged from the diesel engines but also by kinetic energy from braking. The unit is being tested in various areas with a view to converting more units if the scheme is judged successful.

B + AB (DMSO–DMCO).

Built: 1999–2003.
Builder: Siemens-Duewag.
Wheel Arrangement: B-2-B.
Engine: Two MTU engines of 275 kW.
Transmission: Hydrodynamic.
Accommodation: –/45 (13) +12/53.
Weight: 64 + 86 tonnes.
Wheel Diameter: 770 mm.

Floor height:
Length over couplers: 20.35 + 20.35 m.
Maximum Speed: 120 km/h.

*   Fitted with PKP safety systems for working Dresden to Wrocław.

642 001	642 501		RL	642 032	642 532		DA
642 002	642 502		FGM	642 033	642 533	*	DA
642 003	642 503		FGM	642 034	642 534	*	DA
642 004	642 504		FGM	642 035	642 535		DA
642 005	642 505		UE (Z)	642 036	642 536		SKL
642 006	642 506		NAH	642 037	642 537		DA
642 007	642 507		RL	642 038	642 538		DA
642 008	642 508		UE (Z)	642 039	642 539	*	DA
642 009	642 509		FGM	642 040	642 540		DA
642 010	642 510		UE (Z)	642 041	642 541		DA
642 011	642 511		UE (Z)	642 042	642 542		DA
642 012	642 512		FGM	642 043	642 543	*	DA
642 013	642 513		LL1	642 044	642 544		LL1
642 014	642 514		NN1	642 045	642 545		LL1
642 015	642 515		LL1	642 046	642 546		LL1
642 017	642 517		FGM	642 047	642 547		LL1
642 018	642 518		UE	642 048	642 548		WR
642 019	642 519		RL	642 049	642 549		WR
642 020	642 520		UE	642 050	642 550		WR
642 021	642 521		FGM	642 051	642 551		WR
642 022	642 522		UE	642 052	642 552		WR
642 023	642 523		UE	642 053	642 553		WR
642 024	642 524		SKL	642 054	642 554		WR
642 025	642 525		UE	642 055	642 555		DC
642 026	642 526		FGM	642 056	642 556		DC
642 027	642 527		FGM	642 057	642 557		DC
642 028	642 528		SKL	642 058	642 558		DC
642 029	642 529		SKL	642 059	642 559		DC
642 030	642 530		UE	642 060	642 560		NAH
642 031	642 531		UE	642 061	642 561		NAH

642 062	642 562	NAH
642 063	642 563	FGM
642 064	642 564	FGM
642 065	642 565	FGM
642 066	642 566	FGM
642 067	642 567	FGM
642 068	642 568	FGM
642 069	642 569	FGM
642 070	642 570	FGM
642 071	642 571	FGM
642 072	642 572	UE
642 073	642 573	RL
642 074	642 574	NN1
642 075	642 575	NN1
642 076	642 576	NN1
642 077	642 577	MKP
642 078	642 578	WR
642 079	642 579	WR
642 080	642 580	NN1
642 081	642 581	NN1
642 082	642 582	MKP
642 083	642 583	MKP
642 084	642 584	MKP
642 085	642 585	MKP
642 086	642 586	MKP
642 087	642 587	MKP
642 088	642 588	MKP
642 089	642 589	MKP
642 090	642 590	MKP
642 091	642 591	MKP
642 092	642 592	RL

642 093	642 593	MKP
642 094	642 594	MKP
642 095	642 595	RL
642 096	642 596	NN1
642 097	642 597	MKP
642 098	642 598	MKP
642 099	642 599	MKP
642 100	642 600	MKP
642 101	642 601	MKP
642 102	642 602	SKL
642 103	642 603	SKL
642 104	642 604	SKL
642 105	642 605	SKL
642 106	642 606	SKL
642 107	642 607	SKL
642 108	642 608	SKL
642 109	642 609	SKL
642 110	642 610	SKL
642 111	642 611	SKL
642 112	642 612	SKL
642 113	642 613	NN1
642 114	642 614	NN1
642 115	642 615	NN1
642 116	642 616	NN1
642 117	642 617	NN1
642 118	642 618	NN1
642 119	642 619	NN1
642 120	642 620	MKP
642 121	642 621	MKP
642 122	642 622	MKP
642 123	642 623	MKP

▲ One of the most attractive stations on the line from Bonn to Bad Münstereifel can be found at Kottenforst. 644 563 arrives at the station with a stopping service on 6 June 2010. **Matthias Müller**

642 124	642 624	NAH		642 185	642 685	WR
642 125	642 625	NAH		642 186	642 686	FGM
642 126	642 626	NAH		642 187	642 687	LMB
642 127	642 627	NAH		642 188	642 688	LMB
642 128	642 628	NAH		642 189	642 689	LMB
642 129	642 629	NAH		642 190	642 690	LMB
642 130	642 630	LL1		642 191	642 691	LMB
642 131	642 631	DA		642 192	642 692	LMB
642 132	642 632	LL1		642 193	642 693	LMB
642 133	642 633	DA		642 194	642 694	LMB
642 134	642 634	DA		642 195	642 695	LMB
642 135	642 635	DA		642 196	642 696	DC
642 136	642 636	LL1		642 197	642 697	DC
642 137	642 637	DA		642 198	642 698	LMB
642 138	642 638	DA		642 199	642 699	LMB
642 139	642 639	DA		642 200	642 700	DC
642 140	642 640	LL1		642 201	642 701	DC
642 141	642 641	LL1		642 202	642 702	LMB
642 142	642 642	SKL		642 203	642 703	LMB
642 143	642 643	DA		642 204	642 704	NAH
642 144	642 644	DA		642 205	642 705	NAH
642 145	642 645	DA		642 206	642 706	NAH
642 146	642 646	DA		642 207	642 707	NAH
642 147	642 647	DC		642 208	642 708	MKP
642 148	642 648	DC		642 209	642 709	MKP
642 149	642 649	DA		642 210	642 710	MKP
642 156	642 656	DA		642 211	642 711	MKP
642 157	642 657	DA		642 212	642 712	MKP
642 158	642 658	DA		642 213	642 713	MKP
642 159	642 659	DA		642 214	642 714	MKP
642 160	642 660	SKL		642 215	642 715	MKP
642 161	642 661	DA		642 216	642 716	MKP
642 162	642 662	LMB		642 217	642 717	MKP
642 163	642 663	LMB		642 218	642 718	MKP
642 164	642 664	LMB		642 219	642 719	LMB
642 165	642 665	LMB		642 220	642 720	LMB
642 166	642 666	LMB		642 221	642 721	LMB
642 167	642 667	LMB		642 222	642 722	LMB
642 168	642 668	LMB		642 223	642 723	LMB
642 169	642 669	LMB		642 224	642 724	LMB
642 170	642 670	LMB		642 225	642 725	LMB
642 171	642 671	LMB		642 226	642 726	LMB
642 172	642 672	LMB		642 227	642 727	LMB
642 173	642 673	LMB		642 228	642 728	DC
642 174	642 674	LMB		642 229	642 729	LMB
642 175	642 675	SKL		642 230	642 730	LMB
642 176	642 676	LMB		642 231	642 731	DC
642 177	642 677	RL		642 232	642 732	DC
642 178	642 678	LL1		642 233	642 733	LMB
642 179	642 679	LL1		642 234	642 734	DC
642 180	642 680	RL		642 235	642 735	DC
642 181	642 681	RL		642 236	642 736	DC
642 182	642 682	LL1		642 237	642 737	DC
642 183	642 683	WR		642 238	642 738	DC
642 184	642 684	WR				

Names:

642 029	Hinterweidenthal		642 059	Schwarzenberg –
642 036	Albersweiler			Perle des Erzgebirge
642 055	Stadt Augustusburg		642 082	Wittelsbacher Land
642 056	Gemeinde Pockau		642 085	Landsberg am Lech
642 057	Stadt Wilkau-Haßlau		642 089	Bad Wörishofen im Allgau
642 058	Berg und Adam Ries Stadt		642 102	Steinalben
	Annaberg-Buchholz		642 103	Bierbach

642 104	Dellfeld
642 105	Hassel
642 106	Rieschweiler – Mühlbach
642 107	Zweibrücken
642 108	Winnweiler
642 109	Langenlonsheim
642 110	Hochspeyer
642 111	Stadt Gräfenberg
642 112	Münchweiler/Alsenz
642 114	Neustadt (Aisch)
642 115	Stadt Amorbach
642 116	Markt Heroldsberg
642 117	Bad Kissingen
642 118	Stadt Roth
642 124	Liebliches Taubertal
642 127	Bad Mergentheim
642 142	Rinnthal
642 160	Hauenstein (Pfalz)
642 162	Hansestadt Gardelgen
642 172	Anhaltisches Theater Dessau
642 173	Bioshärenreservat Karstlandschaft Südharz
642 175	Wilgartswiesen
642 188	Joseph von Fraunhofer
642 192	Gartenräume Sachsen Anhalt
642 196	Olbernhau Spielzugland im Erzgebirge
642 197	Thermalbad Wiesenbad
642 198	Zoo Magdeburg
642 199	Kaiser und Hansestadt Tangermünde
642 200	Bergstadt Langenfeld
642 201	Gemeinde Burghardtsdorf
642 202	Johann Sebastian Bach
642 205	Stadt Miltenberg
642 206	Aschaffenburg
642 207	Amorbach
642 214	Stadt Krumbach
642 219	Sachsen Anhalt
642 220	Hansestadt Stendal
642 225	Scloss Hundisburg
642 226	Solepark Schönebeck/Bad Salzelmen
642 228	Stadt Zwönitz/Erzgebirge
642 229	Naturpark Drömling
642 230	Katharina die Grosse
642 231	Kreisstadt Aue
642 232	Johanngeorgenstadt
642 233	Local Heros
642 237	Thalheim/Erzgebirge
642 238	Stadt Zwickau

▲ Stadler designed 646 007 arrives at Berlin-Schönefeld Flughafen with a local service on 7 April 2011.   **Keith Fender**

CLASS 643.0   TALENT   3-SECTION ARTICULATED DMUS

Knowing that orders for new local trains were in the pipeline Talbot got a head start by producing a prototype set which it called the TALENT (= Talbots Leichtbau Niederflur Triebwagen). The unit was sent on promotional tours and Talbot was subsequently rewarded with many orders for the units. DB Regio ordered 75 diesel mechanical and 45 diesel-electric units on 21/06/96. Steel bodies have aluminium roofs and glass reinforced cabs. There is only one set of doors per vehicle.

B + B + AB (DMSO–TSO–DMCO).

Built: 1999–2001.
Builder: Bombardier Talbot.
Wheel Arrangement: B-2-2-B.
Engine: Two 6-cylinder MAN D2866 LH21 of 257 kW each.
Transmission: Hydrodynamic, Voith T311r.
Accommodation: –/24 1TD + –/40 (8) + 16/32.   **Floor Height:** 590 mm.
Weight: 89.3 tonnes.   **Length over Couplers:** 48.86 m.
Wheel Diameter: **Maximum Speed:** 120 km/h.

643 001	943 001	643 501	SKL		643 039	943 039	643 539	KK2
643 002	943 002	643 502	RK		643 040	943 040	643 540	EMST
643 003	943 003	643 503	RK		643 041	943 041	643 541	KK2
643 004	943 004	643 504	RK		643 042	943 042	643 542	EMST
643 005	943 005	643 505	SKL		643 043	943 043	643 543	KK2
643 006	943 006	643 506	SKL		643 044	943 044	643 544	EMST
643 007	943 007	643 507	RK		643 045	943 045	643 545	EMST
643 008	943 008	643 508	SKL		643 046	943 046	643 546	KK2
643 009	943 009	643 509	RK		643 047	943 047	643 547	KK2
643 010	943 010	643 510	SKL		643 048	943 048	643 548	EMST
643 011	943 011	643 511	RK		643 049	943 049	643 549	EMST
643 012	943 012	643 512	RK		643 050	943 050	643 550	KK2
643 013	943 013	643 513	RK		643 051	943 051	643 551	EMST
643 014	943 014	643 514	RK		643 052	943 052	643 552	EMST
643 015	943 015	643 515	SKL		643 053	943 053	643 553	KK2
643 016	943 016	643 516	SKL		643 054	943 054	643 554	EMST
643 017	943 017	643 517	RK		643 055	943 055	643 555	EMST
643 018	943 018	643 518	RK		643 056	943 056	643 556	EMST
643 019	943 019	643 519	SKL		643 057	943 057	643 557	EMST
643 020	943 020	643 520	SKL		643 058	943 058	643 558	EMST
643 021	943 021	643 521	SKL		643 059	943 059	643 559	EMST
643 022	943 022	643 522	SKL		643 060	943 060	643 560	EMST
643 023	943 023	643 523	SKL		643 061	943 061	643 561	EMST
643 024	943 024	643 524	SKL		643 062	943 062	643 562	EMST
643 025	943 025	643 525	SKL		643 063	943 063	643 563	EMST
643 026	943 026	643 526	SKL		643 064	943 064	643 564	EMST
643 027	943 027	643 527	SKL		643 065	943 065	643 565	EMST
643 028	943 028	643 528	SKL		643 066	943 066	643 566	EMST
643 029	943 029	643 529	SKL		643 067	943 067	643 567	EMST
643 030	943 030	643 530	SKL		643 068	943 068	643 568	EMST
643 031	943 031	643 531	SKL		643 069	943 069	643 569	EMST
643 032	943 032	643 532	SKL		643 070	943 070	643 570	EMST
643 033	943 033	643 533	KK2		643 071	943 071	643 571	EMST
643 034	943 034	643 534	EMST		643 072	943 072	643 572	EMST
643 035	943 035	643 535	EMST		643 073	943 073	643 573	EMST
643 036	943 036	643 536	EMST		643 074	943 074	643 574	EMST
643 037	943 037	643 537	KK2		643 075	943 075	643 575	EMST
643 038	943 038	643 538	EMST					

Names:

643 003	Knöringen		643 016	Fritz Walter
643 004	Kapsweyer		643 023	Matzenbaul
643 005	Alsenz		643 025	Niedermohr
643 011	Steinweiler		643 064	GEMEENTE ENSCHEDE
643 015	Ottmar Walter		643 065	STADT GRONAU

CLASS 643.2   TALENT   2-SECTION ARTICULATED DMUS

This batch of units is for the EUROBAHN service around Aachen. Several freight-only lines have been reactivated for passenger use and in fact an Aachen S-Bahn system has been created which includes the service to Heerlen on the NS. The units are fitted with cab systems including I160R, PZB90, ZBF and GSM-R. Four units can operate in multiple.

B + AB (DMSO–DMCO).

Built: 2002–03.
Builder: Bombardier Talbot.
Wheel Arrangement: B-2-B.
Engine: Two 6-cylinder MAN D2866 LH21 of 315 kW each.
Transmission: Hydrodynamic, Voith T311r.
Accommodation: –/32 (15) + 22/24.
Weight: 57 tonnes.
Wheel Diameter:

Floor Height: 800 mm.
Length over Couplers: 13.465 + 13.465 m.
Maximum Speed: 120 km/h.

643 201	643 701	KA		643 214	643 714	KA
643 202	643 702	KA		643 215	643 715	KA
643 203	643 703	KA		643 216	643 716	KA
643 204	643 704	KA		643 217	643 717	KA
643 205	643 705	KA		643 218	643 718	KA
643 206	643 706	KA		643 219	643 719	KA
643 207	643 707	KA		643 220	643 720	KA
643 208	643 708	KA		643 221	643 721	KA
643 209	643 709	KA		643 222	643 722	KA
643 210	643 710	KA		643 223	643 723	KA
643 211	643 711	KA		643 224	643 724	KA (Z)
643 212	643 712	KA		643 225	643 725	KA (Z)
643 213	643 713	KA		643 226	643 726	KA

▲ 648 349 is in charge of RB15985, the 1834 Bad St. Peter-Ording to Husum. It is seen here between Bad St. Peter Süd and Tating in the early evening of 1 August 2012.   **Matthias Müller**

CLASS 644 TALENT 3-SECTION ARTICULATED DMUS

An initial order for 45 sets was placed on 21/06/96 by DB Regio and was later increased to 63. These 3-car articulated Talbot Talents were the first of the new generation DMUs to appear and the design has been taken up by several other railway companies in Germany as well as in other countries. The units have Scharfenberg couplers, dynamic brakes (mounted on roof), welded bodies and GRP cabs. Vacuum toilets are fitted suitable for wheelchair access. The 644 is longer than the 643 and has more doors. Much larger set so thus a bigger engine. Not only that they are used amongst the Köln area S-Bahn services so a strong acceleration was needed so allow them to stay up there with the electric trains.

AB + B + B (DMCO–TSO–DMSO).

Built: 1998–2000.
Builder: Bombardier Talbot.
Wheel Arrangement: Bo-2-2-Bo.
Engine: Two 12 cylinder MTU 12V183TD13 of 505 kW at 1800 rpm.
Transmission: Electric, Elin Asynchronous 300 kW traction motors.
Accommodation: 16/32 + –/48 + –/24 (16) 1W 1TD.   **Floor Height:** 800 mm.
Weight: 33 + 19 + 33 tonnes.   **Length over Couplers:** 18.705 + 14.75 + 18.705 m.
Wheel Diameter: 760/630 mm.   **Maximum Speed:** 140 km/h.

644 001	944 001	644 501	KK2	644 012	944 012	644 512	KK2
644 002	944 002	644 502	KK2	644 013	944 013	644 513	KK2
644 003	944 003	644 503	KK2	644 014	944 014	644 514	KK2
644 004	944 004	644 504	KK2	644 016	944 016	644 516	KK2
644 005	944 005	644 505	KK2	644 017	944 017	644 517	KK2
644 006	944 006	644 506	KK2	644 018	944 018	644 518	KK2
644 007	944 007	644 507	KK2	644 019	944 019	644 519	KK2
644 008	944 008	644 508	KK2	644 021	944 021	644 521	KK2
644 009	944 009	644 509	KK2	644 022	944 022	644 522	KK2
644 010	944 010	644 510	KK2	644 023	944 023	644 523	KK2
644 011	944 011	644 511	KK2	644 024	944 024	644 524	KK2

▲ Regio Shuttle 650 309 is seen passing through the Main valley near Himmelstadt, making an empty stock movement from Kassel to Tübingen on 16 March 2012. **Matthias Müller**

644 025	944 025	644 525	KK2	644 046	944 046	644 546	KK2
644 027	944 027	644 527	KK2	644 047	944 047	644 547	KK2
644 028	944 028	644 528	KK2	644 048	944 048	644 548	KK2
644 029	944 029	644 529	KK2	644 049	944 049	644 549	KK2
644 030	944 030	644 530	KK2	644 050	944 050	644 550	KK2
644 031	944 031	644 531	KK2	644 051	944 051	644 551	KK2
644 032	944 032	644 532	KK2	644 052	944 052	644 552	KK2
644 033	944 033	644 533	KK2	644 053	944 053	644 553	KK2
644 034	944 034	644 534	KK2	644 054	944 054	644 554	KK2
644 035	944 035	644 535	KK2	644 055	944 055	644 555	KK2
644 036	944 036	644 536	KK2	644 056	944 056	644 556	KK2
644 037	944 037	644 537	KK2	644 057	944 057	644 557	KK2
644 038	944 038	644 538	KK2	644 058	944 058	644 558	KK2
644 039	944 039	644 539	KK2	644 059	944 059	644 559	KK2
644 040	944 040	644 540	KK2	644 060	944 060	644 560	KK2
644 041	944 041	644 541	KK2	644 061	944 061	644 561	KK2
644 042	944 042	644 542	KK2	644 062	944 062	644 562	KK2
644 043	944 043	644 543	KK2	644 063	944 063	644 563	KK2
644 044	944 044	644 544	KK2	644 064	944 064	644 564	KK2
644 045	944 045	644 545	KK2				

Name:

644 047   EIFEL

CLASS 646.0   GTW2/6   3-SECTION ARTICULATED DMUS

This strange design of articulation stems from the Swiss firm of Stadler. A centre "power pack" is flanked by two passenger coaches. The Swiss classification GTW 2/6 seems to have stuck with the design which is finding favour with many railway companies not only in Switzerland! (GTW = *Gelenktriebwagen* = articulated railcar). DB Regio ordered 44 sets (Classes 646.0 and 646.1) which was too much for the then small Swiss firm so a deal was struck with Adtranz and Bombardier. It is thought that Bombardier/DWA built the carriage bodies and fitting out was done by Adtranz at its Berlin Reinickendorf plant where the power car is built. Indeed a further deal has seen Stadler investing in this plant as Adtranz had too much capacity in Berlin. Class 646.0 is used on local services in Berlin and Brandenburg.

AB + B (DTCO–M–DTSO).

Built: 1999–2002.
Builders: Stadler, Adtranz, Bombardier/DWA.
Wheel Arrangement: 2-Bo-2.
Engine: 12 cylinder MTU 12V183 TDE2 of 550 kW at 2100 rpm.
Transmission: Electric, two three phase asynchronous traction motors type Adtranz 6R1A 4548.
Accommodation: 15/39 (5) + 0 + –/39 (10) 1T. **Floor Height:** 760 mm.
Weight: 55.6 tonnes.   **Length over Couplers:** 17.065 + 4.50 + 17.065 m.
Wheel Diameter: DT 680 mm, M 860 mm.   **Maximum Speed:** 120 km/h.

*   Fitted with PKP safety systems for working into Poland.

946 001	646 001	946 501		WNR	946 017	646 017	946 517	* WNR
946 002	646 002	946 502		WNR	946 018	646 018	946 518	WNR
946 003	646 003	946 503		WNR	946 019	646 019	946 519	WNR
946 004	646 004	946 504		WNR	946 020	646 020	946 520	WNR
946 005	646 005	946 505		WNR	946 021	646 021	946 521	WNR
946 007	646 007	946 507		WNR	946 022	646 022	946 522	WNR
946 008	646 008	946 508		WNR	946 023	646 023	946 523	WNR
946 009	646 009	946 509		WNR	946 024	646 024	946 524	WNR
946 010	646 010	946 510		WNR	946 025	646 025	946 525	WNR
946 011	646 011	946 511	*	WNR	946 026	646 026	946 526	WNR
946 012	646 012	946 512	*	WNR	946 027[II]	646 027	946 527	WNR
946 013	646 013	946 513		WNR	946 028	646 028	946 528	* WNR
946 014	646 014	946 514		WNR	946 029	646 029	946 529	* WNR
946 015	646 015	946 515		WNR	946 030	646 030	946 530	* WNR
946 016	646 016	946 516		WNR				

CLASS 646.1   GTW2/6   3-SECTION ARTICULATED DMUS

This class is similar to Class 646.0 but was specifically ordered for services on the Island of Usedom which have since been set up as a DB Regio subsidiary Usedomer Bäder Bahn. There are subtle differences such as lower floor height, heavier weight, no first class and high density seating (3+2) to cope with holiday crowds. They work all services on the island and the connection to the mainland at Zussow. The units are not in the standard livery, instead they are in a blue and white livery with the blue being formed into "waves" to denote the seaside area the line serves. Services have been extended to Stralsund and even to Barth for which eight additional units were obtained.

Details as Class 646/0 except:

B + B (DTSO–M–DTSO).

Accommodation: –/65 + 0 + –/46 (10) 1T.
Weight: 56.1 tonnes.   **Floor height:** 585 mm.

946 101	646 101	946 601	WHF
946 102	646 102	946 602	WHF
946 103	646 103	946 603	WHF
946 104	646 104	946 604	WHF
946 105	646 105	946 605	WHF
946 106	646 106	946 606	WHF
946 107	646 107	946 607	WHF
946 108	646 108	946 608	WHF
946 109	646 109	946 609	WHF
946 110	646 110	946 610	WHF
946 111	646 111	946 611	WHF
946 112	646 112	946 612	WHF
946 113	646 113	946 613	WHF
946 114	646 114	946 614	WHF
946 121	646 121	946 621	WHF
946 122	646 122	946 622	WHF
946 123	646 123	946 623	WHF
946 124	646 124	946 624	WHF
946 125	646 125	946 625	WHF
946 126	646 126	946 626	WHF
946 127	646 127	946 627	WHF

▲ Class 672 units were built for the Burgenlandbahn, at one time a joint venture between Karsdorfer Eisenbahn and DB. The units are now wholly owned by DB. 672 908 is pictured at Weissenfels on 15 August 2012.
Keith Fender

CLASS 646.2 GTW2/6 3-SECTION ARTICULATED DMUS

In 2003 deliveries began of a further batch of units for local services in Hessen around Darmstadt and for the Kurhessenbahn from Kassel.

946 201	646 201	946 701	FGM		946 208	646 208	946 708	FK
946 202	646 202	946 702	FGM		946 209	646 209	946 709	FK
946 203	646 203	946 703	FGM		946 210	646 210	946 710	FK
946 204	646 204	946 704	FGM		946 211	646 211	946 711	FK
946 205	646 205	946 705	FK		946 212	646 212	946 712	FK
946 206	646 206	946 706	FK		946 213	646 213	946 713	FK
946 207	646 207	946 707	FK					

CLASS 648 LINT 41 2-SECTION ARTICULATED DMUS

This railcar set is related to Class 640 (LINT 27). The LINT 41 is the same unit but extended to 41 m in length with two body sections instead of one. These units are similar to some delivered in 2000 to the private operator Nordostbahn that is working services in Schleswig Holstein. DB ordered some similar units to work alongside the private operator so that there is at least a common standard. The sets are known as "Coradia" by Alstom.

AB + B (DMCO–DMSO).

Built: 2000–01.
Builders: Alstom/LHB.
Wheel Arrangement: B-2-B.
Engine: One 6 cylinder MTU 6R 183TD 13H engine giving 315 kW at 1900 rpm.
Transmission: Hydrodynamic.
Accommodation: 16/46 (5) + –/52 1TD.
Weight: 63.5/92.0 tonnes.
Wheel Diameter: 770 mm.
Floor Height: 780 mm.
Length over Couplers: 20.905 + 20.905 m.
Maximum Speed: 120 km/h.

Class 648.0

648 001	648 501	AK		648 004	648 504	AK
648 002	648 502	AK		648 005	648 505	AK
648 003	648 503	AK		648 006	648 506	AK

Class 648.1

In February 2003 DB ordered 21 units for Sauerland services such as Dortmund–Iserlohn, Dortmund–Lüdenscheid, Dortmund–Winterberg and Unna–Menden–Fröndenberg–Neuenrade. These units have a floor height of 780 mm.

648 101	648 601	EDO		648 112	648 612	EDO
648 102	648 602	EDO		648 113	648 613	EDO
648 103	648 603	EDO		648 114	648 614	EDO
648 104	648 604	EDO		648 115	648 615	EDO
648 105	648 605	EDO		648 116	648 616	EDO
648 106	648 606	EDO		648 117	648 617	EDO
648 107	648 607	EDO		648 118	648 618	EDO
648 108	648 608	EDO		648 119	648 619	EDO
648 109	648 609	EDO		648 120	648 620	EDO
648 110	648 610	EDO		648 121	648 621	EDO
648 111	648 611	EDO				

Class 648.2

At the same time as the 648.1 order DB ordered seven Class 648.2. These units have a floor height of 598 mm and were intended for Siegen–Bad Berleburg/Dillenburg/Au and Finnentrop–Olpe services. Later DB announced another order; this time for 27 units for the Harz–Weser services. These units work over the following lines Bad Harzburg–Goslar–Kreiensen; Braunschweig–Salzgitter Ringelheim–Kreiensen; Göttingen–Northeim–Nordhausen; Braunschweig–Seesen–Herzberg; Kreiensen–Holzminden; Ottbergen–Northeim/Göttingen.

648 201	648 701	EDO		648 261	648 761	HBS
648 202	648 702	EDO		648 262	648 762	HBS
648 203	648 703	EDO		648 263	648 763	HBS
648 204	648 704	EDO		648 264	648 764	HBS
648 205	648 705	EDO		648 265	648 765	HBS
648 206	648 706	EDO		648 266	648 766	HBS
648 207	648 707	EDO		648 267	648 767	HBS
648 251	648 751	HBS		648 268	648 768	HBS
648 252	648 752	HBS		648 269	648 769	HBS
648 253	648 753	HBS		648 270	648 770	HBS
648 254	648 754	HBS		648 271	648 771	HBS
648 255	648 755	HBS		648 272	648 772	HBS
648 256	648 756	HBS		648 273	648 773	HBS
648 257	648 757	HBS		648 274	648 774	HBS
648 258	648 758	HBS		648 275	648 775	HBS
648 259	648 759	HBS		648 276	648 776	HBS
648 260	648 760	HBS		648 277	648 777	HBS

Name:

648 259   Stadt Goslar

Classes 648.3 & 648.4

DB Regio in continuing to improve local services ordered 30 sets for the Nürnberg area services followed by further orders for Schleswig Holstein Ost based in Kiel.

648 301	648 801	NN1		648 315	648 815	NN1
648 302	648 802	NN1		648 316	648 816	NN1
648 303	648 803	NN1		648 317	648 817	NN1
648 304	648 804	NN1		648 318	648 818	NN1
648 305	648 805	NN1		648 319	648 819	NN1
648 306	648 806	NN1		648 320	648 820	NN1
648 307	648 807	NN1		648 321	648 821	NN1
648 308	648 808	NN1		648 322	648 822	NN1
648 309	648 809	NN1		648 323	648 823	NN1
648 310	648 810	NN1		648 324	648 824	NN1
648 311	648 811	NN1		648 325	648 825	NN1
648 312	648 812	NN1		648 326	648 826	NN1
648 313	648 813	NN1		648 327	648 827	NN1
648 314	648 814	NN1				

Names:

648 302	Gräfenberg		648 306	Markt Erlbach
648 303	Schnaitatchtal		648 308	Bad Windsheim
648 304	Cadolzburg		648 310	Landkreis Fürth

648 331	648 831	AK		648 344	648 844	AK
648 332	648 832	AK		648 345	648 845	AK
648 333	648 833	AK		648 346	648 846	AK
648 334	648 834	AK		648 347	648 847	AK
648 335	648 835	AK		648 348	648 848	AK
648 336	648 836	AK		648 349	648 849	AK
648 337	648 837	AK		648 350	648 850	AK
648 338	648 838	AK		648 351	648 851	AK
648 339	648 839	AK		648 352	648 852	AK
648 340	648 840	AK		648 353	648 853	AK
648 341	648 841	AK		648 354	648 854	AK
648 342	648 842	AK		648 355	648 855	AK
648 343	648 843	AK				

648 450	648 950	AK	648 458	648 958	AK
648 451	648 951	AK	648 459	648 959	AK
648 452	648 952	AK	648 460	648 960	AK
648 453	648 953	AK	648 461	648 961	AK
648 454	648 954	AK	648 462	648 962	AK
648 455	648 955	AK	648 463	648 963	AK
648 456	648 956	AK	648 464	648 964	AK
648 457	648 957	AK	648 465	648 965	AK

CLASS 650   REGIO SHUTTLE   SINGLE CAR

The German private railways were ahead of the field in ordering new equipment and this Adtranz product having caught on well with the private lines DB Regio just had to have some. The design is a mix of bus, lorry and rail technologies. Waggon Union in Berlin thought out the design as a follow on to their successful NE81 design for the private lines. Waggon Union became part of Adtranz who continued the production with Stadler taking over the plant later. This single car DMU features a welded all steel frame but the roof, body, and cabs are glued glass fibre reinforced plastic. Bus engines and transmission are provided. MICAS computer controls allow up to 5 units to run in multiple. The units are air conditioned and have 2 sets of doorways.

B (DMSO).

Built: 1999–2002.
Builder: Adtranz Berlin Pankow (former Waggon Union) later becoming Stadler.
Wheel Arrangement: B-B.
Engine: Two 6 cylinder MAN D2866 LH21 of 257 kW.
Transmission: Hydrodynamic, Voith - DIWA.
Accommodation: –/75 (3) 1T.   **Floor Height:**
Weight: 40/56 tonnes.   **Length over Buffers:** 25.50 m.
Wheel Diameter: 770 mm.   **Maximum Speed:** 120 km/h.

Class 650/0. Units ordered by DB Zug-Bus, Regionalverkehr Alb-Bodensee.

650 001	TT	650 010	TT	650 019	TT
650 002	TT	650 011	TT	650 020	TT
650 003	TT	650 012	TT	650 021	TT
650 004	TT	650 013	TT	650 022	TT
650 005	TT	650 014	TT	650 023	TT
650 006	TT	650 015	TT	650 024	TT
650 007	TT	650 016	TT	650 025	TT
650 008	TT	650 017	TT	650 026	TT
650 009	TT	650 018	TT	650 027	TT

Class 650/1. Units ordered by Baden-Württemberg. In the Tübingen area sets can be seen working alongside similar ones belonging to the HzL – Hohenzollerische Landesbahn.

650 100	TU	650 108	TU	650 116	TU
650 101	TU	650 109	TU	650 117	TU
650 102	TU	650 110	TU	650 118	TU
650 103	TU	650 111	TU	650 119	TU
650 104	TU	650 112	TU	650 120	TU
650 105	TU	650 113	TU	650 121	TU
650 106	TU	650 114	TU	650 122	TU
650 107	TU	650 115	TU		

Class 650/2. Units with no toilets but instead having a space for bicycles.

650 201	TU	650 202	TU	650 203	TU

Name:

650 203   Seehänsele

Class 650/3. More units for Baden Württemberg and Bayern. These units were of an updated design using LED headlights, fire alarm systems for engines, disabled toilet, armrests, lift for wheelchair and an information display with speech. Two units can work in multiple but this version is understood not to work in multiple with earlier versions.

650 301	TT	650 311	TT	650 320	TU
650 302	TT	650 312	TU	650 321	TU
650 303	TT	650 313	TU	650 322	TU
650 304	TT	650 314	TU	650 323	TU
650 305	TT	650 315	TU	650 324	TU
650 306	TT	650 316	TU	650 325	TU
650 307	TT	650 317	TU	650 326	TU
650 308	TT	650 318	TU	650 327	TU
650 309	TT	650 319	TU	650 997	MMF
650 310	TT				

Names:

650 301	Landkreis Calw	650 305	Stadt Horb
650 302	Stadt Wildberg	650 306	Stadt Nagold
650 303	Stadt Calw	650 307	Bad Teinach-Zavelstein
650 304	Bad Liebenzell	650 308	Stadt Pforzheim

CLASS 672   SINGLE CAR

These units were built for the Burgenlandbahn which at one time was semi-private being owned by Karsdorfer Eisenbahn and DB. When the Karsdorfer Eisenbahn went bankrupt all the units passed to DB. Class originally VT3.01–20.

Built: 1998–99.
Builder: DWA Bautzen.
Wheel Arrangement: 1-A.
Engine: 265k/W.
Transmission: Hydraulic.
Accommodation: –/64 1T.
Weight: 40/56 tonnes.   **Length over Couplings:** 16.54 m.
Wheel Diameter: **Maximum Speed:** 120 km/h.
Non-Standard Livery: N Silver and yellow.

672 901	N	LL1	Querfurt Thaldorfer Pfingstbursche
672 902	N	LL1	Rotkäppchen-Sekt
672 903	N	LL1	Stadt Nebra
672 904	N	LL1	Happy Corax
672 905	N	LL1	Stadt Naumburg (Saale)
672 906	N	LL1	Auf den Spuren Otto's des Grossen
672 907	N	LL1	Stadt Braunsbedra
672 908	N	LL1	Kohlebau Deuben
672 909	N	LL1	Weissenfelser Schusterjunge
672 910	N	LL1	Stadt Weissenfels
672 911	N	LL1	Stadt Rossleben
672 913	N	LL1	Der Querfurter
672 914	N	LL1	Mitteldeutscher Verkehrsverbund
672 915	N	LL1	Mücheln im Geisetal
672 916	N	LL1	Bergenlandkreis gut in Fahrt
672 917	N	LL1	Johann Ernst Luther – Zeitz – die Stadt der Luther nach kommen
672 918	N	LL1	Finnebahn
672 919	N	LL1	
672 920	N	LL1	

CLASS 772   SINGLE CAR

These units amazingly are still in DB stock. They are based in Erfurt and used on tourist services by subsidiary company Oberweissbacher Berg – und Schwarztalbahn.

Built: 1965–69 for DR.
Former DR Class: 172.
Builder: VEB Waggonbau Görlitz
Engine: MAN 2866UH of 132 kW (175 hp).
Transmission: Mechanical.   **Length over Couplers:** 13.55 m.
Weight: 19.3 tonnes.   **Maximum Speed:** 90 km/h.

Class 772.1 B (DMSO). –/54 1T.

772 140	UE	772 141	UE

CLASS 798   SINGLE CAR

These two units are still in DB stock having been reinstated on 01/12/2005 for use on tourist services. Some trailer cars have also been saved to work with the power cars.

Built: 19xx for DB.
Builder: Uerdingen.
Engine: 2 x 112 kW.
Transmission: Mechanical.   **Length over Buffers:** 13.95 m.
Weight: 27 tonnes.   **Maximum Speed:** 90 km/h.

Class 798 B (DMSO). –/56 1T.

798 652	TU	798 653	TU

Class 996.0, 998.0. B (TSO). –/63 1T. 10.7 tonnes

998 069	TU	996 227	TU	996 300	TU
996 225	TU				

Class 998.8 BD (DTBSO). –/40 1T. 16.7 tonnes

998 896	TU

7. SELF-PROPELLED DEPARTMENTAL VEHICLES

Numbers may be painted on vehicles in this section but small white data panels are increasingly being used and are unreadable unless one is close to the vehicle! The introduction of European Vehicle Numbers has meant completely different numbers being applied in some cases; full details are not known. However, in most cases the old numbers are still shown on the vehicles.

CLASSES 701 & 702

Class 701.0 is the standard type of overhead line maintenance vehicle used by the old DB based on the Class 798 railbus. Class 702.0 was originally single-engined but most were subsequently re-equipped with two engines. However 702.0 and 702.1 types are in fact fitted with magnetic and dynamic brakes for working over steep lines.

The units are allocated to various depots for maintenance purposes but their operating base can be elsewhere at overhead line depots etc. In 1998/99 units marked * were converted to Diagnosetriebwagen (DVT). On these units the overhead work platform has been removed and a second pantograph mounted. These modified units have video and laser fittings for measuring the performance of the pantograph/catenary interface. In the lists below the first code is the depot for maintenance whilst the usual operating base if different is shown alongside.

Most other units have now been withdrawn but many still exist as maintenance contractors quickly bought them up; some have been sold to other countries. For its part DB has more modern vehicles now or uses road/rail vehicles.

Built: 1955–74.
Builder: WMD, Rathgeber, Uerdingen, MBB.
Wheel Arrangement: A-A.
Engine: Two 6 cylinder Bussing U10 of 110 kW at 1800 rpm. Water cooled.
Transmission: Mechanical.　　　**Weight:** 29 tonnes.
Accommodation: Two cabs, workshop area, overhead platform, pantograph.
Wheel Diameter: 900 mm.　　　**Length over Couplers:** 13.95 m.
Floor Height:　　　**Maximum Speed:** 90 km/h.
Non-Standard Livery: N Old red livery.
EVN: 99 80 1701 xxx, (99 80 9263 xxx for the Diagnose units)

Class 701

701 017	Y	*	HM	701 165	Y	*	STMI
701 069	Y		TU (Z)	701 167	Y	*	STMI
701 079	Y		HBH (Z)				

Class 702

702 055	Y		RF (Z)	702 133			TK (Z)
702 115	Y		MH1 (Z)	MFL	702 148	Y	*	HM
702 132	Y		TK (Z)	702 163	N	*	HM

CLASS 703.0 IFO

These units are clearly identified as IFO units-Instandhaltungsfahrzeuge Oberleitungsanlagen-maintenance units for overhead equipment. Their arrival has allowed some Class 701s to be withdrawn. Class 703 has a large cab at one end but with two driving positions. There is a pantograph on the cab roof and an observation window at roof level. The remaining area is taken up by a hydraulic platform. Many 703.0 have been withdrawn; it is understood weak frames were a problem.

Built: 1995–96.
Builder: Windhoff.
Wheel Arrangement: A-A.
Engine: One 5 cylinder MAN D2865 LF24 Euro 2 of 213 kW at 2000 rpm (for traction) and one 4 cylinder MAN D 0824 4FL04 of 81 kW at 2400 rpm for auxiliaries.
Transmission: Hydrodynamic, mechanical.
Wheel Diameter: 840 mm.   **Length over Couplers:** 13.94 m.
Weight: 32 tonnes.   **Maximum Speed:** 90 km/h.
EVN: 99 80 xxxx xxx

703 004"	**Y**	KD		703 009	**Y**	EHG	
703 005"	**Y**	RF (Z)					

CLASS 703.1 IFO

These new OHLE units are based on the GAF 200 engineer's trolley/draisine. The vehicles have one complete frame upon which are mounted a cab with crew room behind which is a hydraulic lifting platform. The main engine is for traction; there is an auxiliary engine to power the lifting platform. (This is a MAN four cylinder D 8024 LFL 06 of 89 kW.)

Built: 2000–01.
Builder: Gleisbaumechanik Brandenburg.
Wheel Arrangement: A-A.
Engine: MAN 6-cylinder D.2876 LOH 01 of 338 kW.
Transmission: Hydraulic. Voith T211 rc3.
Wheel Diameter: 840 mm.   **Length over Couplers:** 14.95 m.
Weight: 40 tonnes.   **Maximum Speed:** 100 km/h.
EVN: 99 80 xxxx xxx

703 101	**Y**	RK		703 106	**Y**	FFU
703 102	**Y**	BSE		703 107	**Y**	TC
703 103	**Y**	RSI		703 108	**Y**	NN2
703 104	**Y**	FD		703 109	**Y**	FFU
703 105	**Y**	FH (Z)		703 110	**Y**	HO

CLASS 704

This overhead line unit is based on the Class 627 single car DMU. One end has a pantograph fitted whilst at the other end there is a hydraulic platform which can be turned to allow work to take place on an adjoining line. The units have a higher speed than others and thus tend to find employment on NBS lines. Class 704 has now been replaced by Class 711 resulting in most 704s being stored out of service at Cottbus works.

Built: 1977–78.
Builder: MBB.
Wheel Arrangement: B-B.
Engine: Two 12 cylinder KHD F12L413 engines of 204 kW.
Transmission: Hydraulic, Voith T320r.
Accommodation: Mess room (8 people), kitchen, WC, workshop.
Wheel Diameter: 760 mm.   **Length over Couplers:** 23.40 m.
Weight: 53 tonnes.   **Maximum Speed:** 140 km/h.
EVN: 99 80 xxxx xxx

704 001	**Y**	SSR (Z)		704 004	**Y**	NWH (Z)
704 002	**Y**	RK (Z)		704 005	**Y**	FFU (Z)
704 003	**Y**	FMZ (Z)				

CLASS 705   TIF

TIF = Tunnelinstandhaltungsfahrzeuge-tunnel maintenance unit. This new unit was ordered to cope with all the extra tunnels the DB acquired when the NBS lines were built. The unit is based on the Austrian X 552 departmental unit also built by Plasser. At No. 1 end there is a small hydraulic platform to carry two persons whilst No. 2 end has a much larger hydraulic crane arm. Steps are provided to give access to the roof which is also used as a work or inspection area.

Built: 1992.
Builder: Deutsche Plasser 2454/1992.
Wheel Arrangement: B-2.
Engine: One 12 cylinder KHD BF12L513C engine of 367 kW at 2300 rpm for principal traction and one 4 cylinder KHD BF4L1011T of 44 kW at 2500 rpm for the auxiliaries.
Transmission: Hydrodynamic, mechanical.
Accommodation: 2 cabs, mess room with kitchen and washroom, 2 beds, office.
Wheel Diameter: 840 mm.   **Length over Couplers:** 15.92 m.
Weight: 52 tonnes.   **Maximum Speed:** 120 km/h (140 km/h hauled).
EVN: 99 80 xxxx xxx

705 001   **Y**   RK

▲ Windhoff overhead line maintenance vehicle 711 102 is seen at Neuwied on 2 March 2009.
                                                                    Keith Fender

CLASS 708.3   OBERLEITUNGSREVISIONTRIEBWAGEN (ORT)

The oil crisis of the 1980s gave a spurt to DR electrification; consequently there was a need for a new batch of ORTs. Apart from the expected workshop area a mess room and toilet are also provided. Some units have recently been withdrawn; some have been taken over by private maintenance contractors whilst about a dozen are stored at Mukran awaiting sale or scrap.

Built: 1987–91 for DR.
Builder: VEB Waggonbau Görlitz.
Engine: Rosslau 6VD18/15 AL–2 of 330 kW (* MAN D2876 LUE 604 of 371 kW).
Transmission: Electric.
Accommodation: 2 cabs, mess room, workshop and toilet.
Length over Buffers: 22.40 m.   **Former DR Class:** 188.3.
Weight: 58 tonnes.   **Maximum Speed:** 100 km/h.
EVN: 99 80 xxxx xxx

708 303	Y		MH4
708 305	0		AK (Z)
708 306	Y	*	KD
708 310	0		LLW (Z)
708 311	Y		BSE
708 314	Y		WR (Z)
708 315	Y	*	SSR (Z)
708 319	Y	*	MA (Z)
708 320	0	*	BSE
708 322	0		EHM (Z)
708 323	Y		HB
708 324	0	*	WR
708 325	0	*	EDO
708 326	Y		BSE
708 327	0	*	NWH
708 329	0		TU
708 330	0	*	AM
708 331	0		KD
708 332	0		NN2
708 333	Y		TH
708 334	Y	*	LL1
708 336	Y		LLW
708 337	Y		KK2

CLASS 709

This class is similar to ÖBB X 552 and in fact was ordered by the DR in 1992. Two hydraulic arms are provided with the larger one supporting the working platform. The smaller arm can support a small platform or be fitted with a crane. A video camera is providing for recording the state of the OHLE.

Built: 1993.
Builder: Plasser & Theurer.
Wheel Arrangement: B-B.
Engine: One 12 cylinder KHD BF L513C of 367 kW for principal traction and one 4 cylinder KHD BF4L1011T for auxiliaries.
Transmission: Hydrodynamic, mechanical.
Accommodation: 2 cabs, workshop, office, pantograph.
Wheel Diameter: 840 mm.   **Length over Couplers:** 15.84 m.
Weight: 59 tonnes.   **Maximum Speed:** 120 km/h (140 km/h hauled).
EVN: 99 80 xxxx xxx

709 002	Y	LL1		709 003	Y	BSE (Z)

CLASSES 711.0 & 711.1 HIOB

HIOB = *Hubarbeitsbuhnen Instandhaltungsfahrzeug Oberleitungsanlagen.*

Windhoff not only built the two-axle Class 703 but also these bogie vehicles as a bigger version of the same machine. The units have a pantograph, hydraulic platform and an observation post at roof level. Video recording gear is also provided. Some units have been withdrawn having had similar problems as Class 703.

Built: 1995–96.
Builder: Windhoff.
Wheel Arrangement: 2-B.
Engine: One 6 cylinder MAN D 2876 of 338 kW at 1800 rpm for principal traction and one 4 cylinder MAN D 0824 of 118 kW at 2400 rpm for auxiliaries.
Transmission: Hydrodynamic, mechanical.
Accommodation: 2 cabs, office, mess room, workshop.
Wheel Diameter: 840 mm.   **Length over Couplers:** 17.24 m.
Weight: 66 tonnes.   **Maximum Speed:** 120 km/h.
EVN: 99 80 xxxx xxx

Class 711.0

711 003	**Y**	RK		711 006	**Y**	FMB (Z)
711 004	**Y**	DF (Z)		711 008	**Y**	HS (Z)
711 005	**Y**	EOB				

Class 711.1

711 101"	**Y**	NWH		711 112	**Y**	RF
711 102	**Y**	LMR		711 113	**Y**	HG
711 103	**Y**	LH1		711 114	**Y**	NN2
711 104	**Y**	EMST		711 115	**Y**	DF
711 105	**Y**	NRH		711 116	**Y**	WP
711 106	**Y**	RM		711 117	**Y**	DC
711 107	**Y**	KK		711 118	**Y**	EWAN
711 108	**Y**	WW		711 119	**Y**	MP
711 109	**Y**	HS		711 120	**Y**	AHAR
711 110	**Y**	BCS		711 121	**Y**	TS
711 111	**Y**	HB		711 122	**Y**	BRG

▲ The Würzburg emergency train awaits the call to service on 27 August 2012, headed by 714 007 (714 010 at the rear). Note how the train is connected to "shore" supplies. **Brian Garvin**

CLASS 711.2 IFO

Built: 2009–11.
Builder: Robel, type 57.44.
Wheel Arrangement: B-B.
Engine. Two Deutz TCD 2015V08 of 480 kW.
Transmission: Hydraulic.
Accommodation: 2 cabs, office, personnel room for 5, workshop, pantograph, work platform.
Wheel Diameter: 840 mm. **Length over Couplers:** 17.24 m.
Weight: **Maximum Speed:** 140 km/h.
EVN: 99 80 9136 001–008

711 201	Y	KK2		711 205	Y	KKO
711 202	Y	UE		711 206	Y	FMB
711 203	Y	FF		711 207	Y	LL1
711 204	Y	FK		711 208	Y	EOB

CLASS 714 RETTUNGSDIENSTFAHRZEUG (RTZ)

These are Class 212 locomotives converted for use with the RTZ trains. Originally numbered as Class 214 and retaining the original Class 212 running number they have subsequently been renumbered into the departmental series and given completely new numbers. For working with the RTZ trains the locomotives have been given many extra fittings such as two Halogen headlights, heat-sensitive cameras fitted at the front as well as video cameras. Yellow flashing lights denote that the train may be approaching remotely controlled from within the train. Two powerful main headlights are also provided.

The RTZ trains were built for use in emergencies on the NBS lines that have many tunnels and are often going through remote areas. The RTZ trains comprise several vehicles usually formed as follows:

1. **Locomotive.**
2. **Transportwagen:** Special containers on a flat wagon. The containers are fitted with a driving position from which the driver can remotely control the locomotive and use TV monitors that are linked to cameras on the front of the locomotives. 60-80 people can be accommodated including 24 on beds and 24 on seats. Loudspeakers provided on the outside.
3. **Gerätewagen:** This is a rebuilt former postal coach for fire brigade use, pumps hoses, etc.
4. **Löschmittelwagen:** This wagon contains 20,000 litres of water.
5. **Sanitätswagen:** This is a hospital coach with an operating theatre.
6. **Transportwagen:** Similar to (2) above.
7. **Locomotive.**

Going into a tunnel where a train has crashed people can be rescued and walk through the train into the rear transport wagon. People can be given instructions and advice over the loudspeakers fixed to the exterior of the vehicles. Having walked through the train to the rear transport wagon the train can be divided and the rear half go out of the tunnel to a point where people can be detrained into waiting ambulances etc. There is an automatic coupling between the two halves of the train.

All Class 714s are based at the DB Netz depot at Fulda but the locos are normally permanently coupled to their trains ready to go at a moment's notice. The emergency trains are normally stationed at Stuttgart (Kornwestheim), Mannheim, Würzburg, Fulda, Kassel and Hildesheim. Taking Kassel as an example the NBS north to Göttingen has 20 km of tunnels (in 50 km) and to the south the NBS to Fulda has 47 km of tunnels in 70 km. Thus if there is an incident on the NBS line it is highly likely that a tunnel would be involved. The EBA has considered Class 714 locomotives to be still Class 212 locomotives and consequently the EVN gives the old 212 number!

In late 2012 it was learnt that some new rescue trains are to be ordered to replace the existing trains. The new trains are likely to be formed of multi-purpose vehicles. But subsequently it was learnt two more Class 212s are at Bremen works for conversion to 714s so the situation is somewhat unclear.

Built: 1963–1965, rebuilt 1989–1997.
Builder: MaK, Deutz, Henschel.
Engine: MTU 12V652TZ.
Transmission: Hydraulic.
Wheel Diameter: 950 mm.
Weight: 63 tonnes.

Power: 990 kW.
Maximum Tractive Effort: 183 kN.
Length over Buffers: 12.30 m.
Maximum Speed: 100 km/h.

714 001	(212 033)	FFU		714 009	(212 257)	FFU
714 002	(212 046)	FFU		714 010	(212 260)	FFU
714 003	(212 235)	FFU		714 011	(212 271)	FFU
714 004	(212 236)	FFU		714 012	(212 277)	FFU
714 005	(212 244)	FFU		714 013	(212 252)	FFU
714 006	(212 245)	FFU		714 014	(212 269)	FFU
714 007	(212 246)	FFU		714 015	(212 160)	FFU
714 008	(212 251)	FFU			(212 076)	

CLASS 716 B-B

Class 716 is the designation given to two rotary snowploughs specially built for service on the new NBS lines especially Hannover–Würzburg but they can also see general use. There are three engines; one for traction and the other two for powering the two rotary ploughs. The machine carries its own turntable and can thus turn for ploughing in the reverse direction.

Built: 1994.
Builder: Beilhack/DB Meiningen.
Engine: Three 12 cylinder Daimler Benz OM 4441a of 605 kW at 600 rpm.
Transmission: Hydraulic, Voith T 311.
Maximum Tractive Effort:
Wheel Diameter: 850 mm.
Weight: 80 tonnes.
EVN: 99 80 xxxx xxx

Length over Buffers: 16.50 m.
Maximum Speed: 120 km/h.

716 001 **Y** MP | 716 002 **Y** FFU

CLASS 719.0; 720.0; 719.5 ULTRASONIC TEST TRAIN 1

This three car set is an ultrasonic test train which is in effect a modified Class 614 DMU. The two power cars contain offices, mess rooms, kitchen and overnight accommodation. The trailer car is the actual test car and has two extra sets of wheels in the centre to support the testing equipment; these can all be raised and locked out of use when the train is in transit and not testing.

Built: 1974.
Builder: MAN, MBB.
Wheel Arrangement: B-2 + 2-2 + 2-B.
Engine: MAN 12 cylinder D 3560 HM 12 of 360 kW.
Transmission: Hydraulic.
Weight: 48.5 tonnes (719); 51.3 tonnes (720).
Length over Buffers: 26.65 m + 26.16 m + 26.65 m.
Maximum Speed: 140 km/h.
EVN: 99 80 9429 001, 99 80 9529 001, 99 80 9429 002

719 001 720 001 719 501 **Y** HM

CLASS 719.045/46   LIMEZ III

This two car DMU is formed of the power cars 614 045/046 suitably modified and is a replacement for the former LIMEZ II train of Class 712/713. LIMEZ = *Lichtraumprofil Messtriebwage,* a profile measuring train full details of which remain unclear.

EVN: 99 80 9160 001 + 002

Technical details as for Class 614.

719 045   719 046   **Y**   HM

CLASS 719.1   ULTRASONIC TEST TRAIN 1

This is a new state of the art purpose built ultrasonic test train, built in 1995 and exhibited at the Hannover Fair in 1996. Cab fittings include Sifa, Indusi I60R, ZBF, ZFG90.

Built: 1995.
Builder: Plasser, Linz, Austria.
Wheel Arrangement: B-2 + 2-2 + 2-B.
Engine: One 12 cylinder MTU 12V183TD13 of 540 kW.
Transmission: Hydraulic.
Accommodation: Mess room, working area, WC, washroom.
Length over Couplers: 23.70 m (719); 23.70 m (720).
Wheel Diameter: 920 mm.
Weight: 62.6 tonnes (719); 67.5 tonnes (720).
Maximum Speed: 160 km/h.
EVN: 99 80 xxxx xxx

719 101   720 101   710 102   **Y**   HM

▲ LIMEZ III profile measuring train 719 046 passes through Köln Hauptbahnhof on 30 June 2010.
Keith Fender

CLASS 725   TRACK RECORDING TRAIN

These track recording trains have two vehicles. The 725 is the power car and was converted from older units but the 726 vehicles were built new based on a Class 701 unit. The 725 car has a dormitory. The sets are normally used to test on secondary routes or even private lines where DB has running rights.

Built: 1959–61 (725); 1974 (726).
Builder: MAN, Uerdingen, WMD (725s); MBB (726).
Engine: Two 6 cylinder Bussing U10 of 110 kW.
Transmission: Mechanical.
Length over Couplers: 13.95 m. (725); 13.40 m. (726).
Wheel Diameter: 900 mm (725); 800 mm (726).
Weight: 23 tonnes (725); 18 tonnes (726).
Maximum Speed: 90km/h (80 km/h if testing).
EVN: 99 80 xxxx xxx

725 002	726 002	Y	HM	725 004	726 004	Y	HM
725 003	726 003	Y	HM	725 005	726 005	Y	HM

CLASS 740   SIGNALDIENST

These units were converted from Class 798 railbuses when it was realised that more test units would be required in the light of the expanding high speed network. The units cover the testing of NBS signalling and radio. Some have been withdrawn.

Built: 1955–1960, Rebuilt 1990–1992.
Builder: MAN, Uerdingen, WMD.
Wheel Arrangement: A-A.
Engine: Two 6 cylinder Bussing U10 engines of 110 kW.
Transmission: Mechanical.
Wheel Diameter: 900 mm.   **Length over Buffers:** 3.95 m.
Weight: 22.4 tonnes.   **Maximum Speed:** 90 km/h.
EVN: 99 80 xxxx xxx

740 002	(798 705)	Y	FK (Z)	740 004	(798 735)	Y	FK

8. INTERNAL USER LOCOMOTIVES

AKKUMULATOR SCHLEPP FAHRZEUGE (ASF)

ASFs are small battery shunters that the DR used at all its depots and workshops for shunting locomotives into place inside the depot/workshop and thus not fill these places with fumes. With the closure of many former DR depots spare ASFs have moved west where they have been welcomed. Additionally some former industrial ASFs have also been acquired. Regretfully many have lost their workplates and so the identities of the new additions to the list are unclear. Another complication is that some depots have numbered their locomotives in to their own series adding yet another complication. To help matters the date of observation has been shown; those not seen in the last few years are probably now scrapped or moved on and obtained a new number. Some allocations are shown as bracketed - this was the last known location of a particular locomotive. (WL = Werklok; 17767 = LEW works number). Some of these diminutive shunters still move around with No. 15 having appeared at NN2 when last known to be at the closed depot in Vacha. It is possible that others are still locked away in closed depots! Those ASFs not reported/sighted in the current century have been deleted.

Note: although referred to as a locomotive the Germans refer to these and departmental locomotives as a "Gerate" - basically a tool or piece of equipment. Thus they are not counted as capital stock and presumably not considered for an EVN.

Built: 1966–89.
Builder: LEW.
Weight: 12 tonnes.

Power Rating: 17kW.
Maximum Speed: 6 km/h.

No.	Location	Date	No.	Location	Date	No.	Location	Date
3	BWS	4/10	55	WNT	08/12	107	WR	03/12
5	LH1	05/11	56	WRS	08/02	108	US	02/07
7	FK	03/10	58	LH2	04/00	109	HO	07/03
9	DF	04/08	61	EHG	02/00	110	US	02/07
12	BCSX	09/09	62	AK	03/12	111	DZW	03/02
13	BCSX	12/08	64	BRG	11/11	112	BSN	03/02
14	LH2	06/09	66	BRG	08/02	114	LL2	10/09
15	NN2	08/12	68	DF	04/08	116	RHL	03/09
16	BSE	09/12	69	RF	05/09	117	NN1	03/07
17	NN1	02/09	70	NN2	12/11	118	LH1	08/04
19	DF	04/08	73	UE	09/08	119	LS	08/04
20	FL	12/09	74	TU	03/07	120	BSE	09/12
21	HBS	12/09	75	WNTX	08/12	121	TS	03/10
25	BSN	04/08	77	LMR	03/12	123	UN	09/02
26	BHF	08/02	80	LS	08/04	124	WM	07/04
27	DG	03/00	81	HBS	12/09	125	LS	08/04
28	WNTX	08/12	82	TS	03/10	126	WRS	03/01
29	BCSX	11/11	83	TK	03/07	127	WM	03/04
31	HBS	03/00	84	LH2	06/09	128	WA	03/01
33	UN	09/02	85	LH1	12/09	130	DF	04/08
34	UE	03/02	86	BSE	09/12	131	BLO	04/10
35	LH2	12/09	87	BFG	04/08	132	LE	03/02
36	LMR	03/12	88	DZW	03/02	133	UE	09/08
37	HS	6/05	89	DF	04/08	134	BLO	03/01
38	FB	11/00	90	WA	03/04	135	BRG	08/02
39	AK	03/12	92	NN2	02/12	136	BSE	09/12
40	BSE	08/11	96	AH1	07/03	137	BFG	05/01
42	BCS	02/08	97	LS	08/04	138	BSN	03/02
43	UE	04/01	99	LMR	03/12	140	NN2	08/12
44	US	03/02	100	MH1	05/02	141	DZW	03/02
47	HB1	06/09	102	BFG	05/01	142	AH1	07/00
48	(LF)	03/08	103	WR	03/12	143	UE	04/01
49	LE	10/09	104	BSE	09/12	145	NN1	02/09
50	LH2	06/09	105	WNR	03/12	148	AK	08/02
52	WR	03/12	106	WR	03/12	149	BCS	02/08

150	WRS WL3	03/12		156	US	02/07		162	LL2	10/09
151	UG	09/12		157	WHF	06/10		163	LMR	03/12
152	HB1	06/09		158	LL2	05/02		164	FK	03/10
153	BSE	09/12		159	LL1	08/04		165	MH1	03/07
155	AH1	08/02		161	LDX	10/01		166	LH2	09/09

Duplicates

1	WRS	03/12		7	WRS	03/12		1005	LE	10/09
001	NN2	02/07		9	WRS	03/12		1006	BFG	04/08
1	AM	03/12		20	DH	04/08		404 001	MH1	
01	HS	03/12		20	FLX	05/09		?	NN1	11/01
01	M. NORD	02/09		192	FLX	05/09		?	AK	10/02
02	HS	03/12		200	UE	09/08		?	TK	02/03
2	WRS	02/08		222	UG	03/02		14868	TK	12/11
03	HS	03/12		303	AM	03/12		17767	TK	12/11
04	HS	03/12		333	US	03/02		?	FG	10/02
4	WRS	03/12		1001	FF1	02/02		?	FG	10/02
5	WRS	03/12		1002	FF1	02/02		17230	KD	06/05
5	WM	07/10		1003	FF1	02/02		383 001	KK2	07/12
6	WRS	03/12		1004	LL2	05/02				

▲ ASF 102 takes a break from pilot duties at Engelsdorf, near Leipzig   **Brian Denton**

9. PRESERVED LOCOMOTIVES AND RAILCARS

DB Museum seems to be out on a limb. Having been under Fernverkehr for a while and until recently using its locomotives and stock for excursion and relief trains this has now ceased. Amazingly the Class 103 electric locomotives it was using have been taken back into active stock! The main museum remains in Nürnberg with the nearby shed at Lichtenfels being used to store locomotives. It was thought that once the new Regio depot opened in Nürnberg the museum would take over the old depot but this has not happened. DB Museum has in the meantime taken over the old wagon shop at Koblenz Lützel as an annexe but this building is too small and many locomotives are stored in the open. It appears DB does not wish to bite the bullet and get something properly organised for its vast collection. Just as in Britain some locomotives are loaned to museum groups to be looked after particularly at Halle and Leipzig. More recently the museums at Bahnpark Augsburg and Horb have received stock on loan. The situation needs careful attention as some interesting relics could fall by the wayside.

9.1. STANDARD GAUGE STEAM LOCOMOTIVES

The following are technical details of former DB and DR classes which are often seen on mainline use, either on excursions run with DBM locomotives or by preservation societies etc.

CLASSES 01/01.5   4-6-2 (2'C1'h2)

After the First World War, the various German state railways were nationalised and the first of the new standard locomotives to appear was the Class 01 pacific. A few were built each year, there being altogether 232 locos plus 9 more rebuilt from Class 02. At the end of the Second World War most of the class ended up on the DB. Both DB and DR modernised some of their locos in the 1950s and 1960s fitting new boilers, but only on the DR were the locos reclassified to 01.5.

Built: 1925–38. Rebuilt 1962–65.
Builder: Henschel.
Driving Wheel Diameter: 2000 mm.
Length over Buffers: 23.94 m.
Maximum Speed: 130 km/h.

Boiler Pressure: 16 bar.
Weight: 170.6 tonnes.
Cylinders: (2) 600 x 660 mm.

Some locos oil fired.

CLASS 01.10   4-6-2 (2'C1'h3)

Introduced in 1939, a three-cylinder heavy duty express locomotive built for a Germany that was expanding its borders. After the Second World War all of the class ended up on the DB. Originally streamlined this was removed soon after the Second World War and in the 1950s most locos received new boilers and many became oil fired. 01 1102 has been re-streamlined.

Built: 1940. Rebuilt 1953–58.
Builder: BMAG.
Driving Wheel Diameter: 2000 mm.
Length over Buffers: 24.13 m.
Maximum Speed: 140 km/h.

Boiler Pressure: 16 bar.
Weight: 180 tonnes.
Cylinders: (3) 500 x 600 mm.

Oil fired.

CLASS 03 4-6-2 (2'C1'h2)

This class is a lightweight version of Class 01. After the Second World War, the class was more or less evenly split between the DB and the DR. 03 001 has been retained in original condition, but other DR locos were rebuilt in the 1960s with modern boilers from withdrawn Class 22s.

Built: 1930–37.
Builder: Borsig.
Driving Wheel Diameter: 2000 mm.
Length over Buffers: 23.90 m.
Maximum Speed: 130 km/h.

Boiler Pressure: 16 bar.
Weight: 160 tonnes.
Cylinders: (2) 570 x 660 mm.

CLASS 03.10 4-6-2 (2'C'1'h3)

As with Class 01.10 the 03.10 is a three cylinder version of Class 03 and the class was also streamlined. All streamlining was removed after the Second World War and both DB and DR rebuilt their locomotives with new boilers. On the DB the locos took on a completely different appearance having the same boiler as on Class 41, but all these locos lost out to diesels and electrics in the 1960s. The DR locos had new boilers, and the survivor owes its longevity to being fitted with counter pressure brakes and being kept by Halle Test Plant long after others had been scrapped.

Built: 1940. Rebuilt RAW Meiningen 1959.
Builder: Borsig.
Driving Wheel Diameter: 2000 mm.
Length over Buffers: 23.90 m.
Maximum Speed: 140 km/h.

Boiler Pressure: 16 bar.
Weight: 163 tonnes.
Cylinders: (3) 470 x 660 mm.

CLASS 18.2 4-6-2 (2'C1'h3)

This one is a real cross-breed. In the aftermath of the Second World War, the DR found itself with a damaged 4–6–4T (61 002) for which there was no use. The driving wheels from this loco together with parts from a 2–10–2 (45 024) and a new boiler were put together by RAW Meiningen to make a new pacific tender locomotive. Fitted with counter pressure brakes the loco became part of the Halle Test Plant fleet and was the only steam loco passed for 160 km/h. It is now the fastest steam loco in the world as it is still passed for 160 km/h! It now has a supplementary tender.

Built: 1961.
Builder: RAW Meiningen.
Driving Wheel Diameter: 2300 mm.
Length over Buffers: 25.14 m.
Maximum Speed: 160 km/h.

Boiler Pressure: 16 bar.
Weight:
Cylinders: (3) 520 x 660 mm.

Oil fired.

CLASS 23 2-6-2 (1'C1'h2)

After the Second World War, the DB wanted to modernise its fleet of locomotives and to replace the ageing KPEV P8 4–6–0s, the Class 23 2–6–2 was introduced.

Built: 1959 for DB.
Builder: Jung.
Driving Wheel Diameter: 1750 mm.
Length over Buffers: 22.94 m.
Maximum Speed: 110 km/h.

Boiler Pressure: 16 bar.
Weight: 136.6 tonnes.
Cylinders: (2) 550 x 650 mm.

CLASS 23.10   2-6-2 (1'C1'h2)

This locomotive was the DR answer to the same problem that faced DB with the KPEV P8s. Between 1955 and 1959 the DR produced 113 of these and like the DB preserved the last example built. The class was renumbered as Class 35 in the DR computer numbering scheme.

Built: 1959 for DR.
Builder: LKM.
Driving Wheel Diameter: 1750 mm.
Length over Buffers: 22.66 m.
Maximum Speed: 110 km/h.

Boiler Pressure: 16 bar.
Weight:
Cylinders: (2) 550 x 660 mm.

CLASS 38.10   4-6-0 (2'Ch2)

The famous Prussian P8. Some 3950 locomotives of this type were built between 1906 and 1925, and it is interesting to note that this "pre-nationalisation" design lasted right to the last days of steam operation, in some cases outliving locos built to replace it! The P8 was known as the "maid of all work" and was a good all round loco. Some examples have been repatriated from Romania.

Built: 1910–23.
Builder: BMAG.
Driving Wheel Diameter: 1750 mm.
Length over Buffers: 18.59 m.
Maximum Speed: 100 km/h.

Boiler Pressure: 12 bar.
Weight: 120.2 tonnes.
Cylinders: (2) 575 x 630 mm.

CLASS 41   2-8-2 (1'D1'h2)

366 examples of this basically mixed traffic locomotive were built between 1936 and 1941. The surviving locos differ in appearance because both DB and DR rebuilt their locos in the 1950s. DB provided its locos with wide boilers, together with a large diameter chimney. 40 locos became oil burners and it is these that DB has preserved. On the DR the new boilers did not change the appearance dramatically.

Built: 1938–41. Rebuilt AW Braunschweig 1958.
Builder: MBA, Borsig, Jung.
Driving Wheel Diameter: 1600 mm.
Length over Buffers: 23.90 m.
Maximum Speed: 90 km/h.

Boiler Pressure: 26 bar.
Weight: 162.7 tonnes.
Cylinders: (2) 520 x 720 mm.

Some Oil fired.

CLASS 44   2-10-0 (1'Eh3)

The standard heavy freight locomotive built 1926–1944. These three cylinder locos were called "Jumbos" as all the real heavy loads were entrusted to them. DB had by far the largest part of the class after the Second World War. Both DB and DR had oil fired locos and the DR Traditionslok was converted back to coal burning.

Built: 1926–44.
Builder: Floridsdorf.
Driving Wheel Diameter: 1400 mm.
Length over Buffers: 22.62 m.
Maximum Speed: 80 km/h.

Boiler Pressure: 16 bar.
Weight: 170.8 tonnes.
Cylinders: (3) 550 x 660 mm.

CLASS 50 2-10-0 (1'Eh2)

Built 1939–1948, this class was intended as the standard locomotive to replace ageing KPEV G10 and G12 locos. However, with the outbreak of the Second World War large numbers of this new class were built for the war effort until the class totalled over 3000. Its 15 tonnes axle load gave it a wide ranging route availability, making the class popular for main and branch line use.

Built: 1939–43.
Builder: Henschel, Krauss Maffei.
Driving Wheel Diameter: 1400 mm.
Length over Buffers: 22.94 m.
Maximum Speed: 80 km/h

Boiler Pressure: 16 bar.
Weight: 135.1 tonnes.
Cylinders: (2) 600 x 660 mm.

CLASS 50.35 2-10-0 (1'Eh2)

Between 1958 and 1963, the DR re-boilered many locomotivess with new welded steel boilers and the Class 50 locos so treated were renumbered from 50 3501 upwards.

Rebuilt: 1958–63.
Builder: Henschel, Krauss Maffei.
Driving Wheel Diameter: 1400 mm.
Length over Buffers: 22.94 m.
Maximum Speed: 80 km/h.

Boiler Pressure: 16 bar.
Weight:
Cylinders: (2) 600 x 660 mm.

CLASS 52.8 2-10-0 (1'Eh2)

Basically a Class 50 stripped of all non-essential parts to become a wartime "Austerity" locomotive. Over 6000 were built, and the class ended up all over Europe with the Soviet Union having over 2000 of them. Again the light axle weight meant the loco had a good route availability. 200 locos were rebuilt by the DR with feed-water heaters, welded boilers etc.

Built: 1943. Rebuilt RAW Stendal 1965–67.
Builder: Skoda.
Driving Wheel Diameter: 1400 mm.
Length over Buffers: 23.05 m.
Maximum Speed: 80 km/h.

Boiler Pressure: 16 bar.
Weight: 129.8 tonnes.
Cylinders: (2) 600 x 660 mm.

CLASS 64 2-6-2T (1'C1'h2t)

A lightweight tank engine for branch line use, the class is a tank version of the Class 24 2-6-0 tender engine. 520 were built.

Built: 1928.
Builder: Borsig.
Driving Wheel Diameter: 1500 mm.
Length over Buffers: 12.40 m.
Maximum Speed: 90 km/h.

Boiler Pressure: 14 bar.
Weight: 71 tonnes.
Cylinders: (2) 500 x 660 mm.

CLASS 65.10 2-8-4T (1'D2'h2t)

The DR built a very modern tank engine after the Second World War, intended for use on suburban services and branch lines. Many worked in the Leipzig and Magdeburg areas. In the 1960s all were fitted with Giesl ejectors, but the preserved example has been restored to original condition.

Built: 1956 for DR.
Builder: LEW.
Driving Wheel Diameter: 1600 mm.
Length over Buffers: 17.50 m.
Maximum Speed: 90 km/h.

Boiler Pressure: 16 bar.
Weight: 120 tonnes.
Cylinders: (2) 600 x 660 mm.

CLASS 86   2-8-2T (1'D1'h2t)

A standard locomotive which despite being classed as a freight locomotive, saw most use on mixed duties in mountainous areas. On the DR many were used in Saxony, and Aue was a well known centre for the class.

Built: 1928, 1942.
Builder: Karlsruhe, DWM.   **Boiler Pressure:**
Driving Wheel Diameter: 1400 mm.   **Weight:** 83 tonnes.
Length over Buffers: 13.82 m.   **Cylinders:** (2) 570 x 660 mm.
Maximum Speed: 80 km/h.

9.2. LIST OF PRESERVED LOCOMOTIVES

The current status of motive power is indicated at follows:

M   Museum, on display (not active)
MA   Museum, active
MR   Museum, under repair
MS   Museum, stored
P   Plinthed
S   Stored

▲ Preserved former DR 44 2546 from Bayerischen Eisenbahnmuseum Nördlingen is seen here with a steam special from Köln to Trier near Linz in the Rhine valley. The date was 24 April 2010.

Matthias Müller

9.2.1. STEAM LOCOMOTIVES

Old No.	Computer No.	Co.	Wheel	Type	Built	Status	Location
01 005	-	DR	4-6-2	2C1h2	1925	M	VMD, Stassfurt.
01 008	001 008	DB	4-6-2	2C1h2	1925	M	Stiftung Eisenbahnmuseum. Bochum Dahlhausen
01 066	01 2066	DR	4-6-2	2C1h2	1928	MA	BEM. Nördlingen.
01 111	001 111	DB	4-6-2	2C1h2	1934	M	DDM. Neuenmarkt Wirsberg.
01 118	01 2118	DR	4-6-2	2C1h2	1934	MA	HE. Frankfurt/Main.
01 137	01 2137	DR	4-6-2	2C1h2	1935	M	DBM. Dresden Altstadt.
01 150	001 150	DB	4-6-2	2C1h2	1935	MA	DBM. SEH Heilbronn.
01 164	001 164	DB	4-6-2	2C1h2	1935	MS	Lichtenfels.
01 173	001 173	DB	4-6-2	2C1h2	1936	M	DTM. Berlin.
01 180	001 180	DB	4-6-2	2C1h2	1936	MR	SEH, Heilbronn.
01 202	001 202	DB	4-6-2	2C1h2	1936	MA	Lyss, Switzerland.
01 204	01 2204	DR	4-6-2	2C1h2	1936	M	Hermeskeil.
01 220	001 220	DB	4-6-2	2C1h2	1937	P	Treuchtlingen.
01 509	01 0509	DR	4-6-2	2C1h2	1963	MA	UEF. Heilbronn.
01 514	01 1514	DR	4-6-2	2C1h2	1964	M	TM. Speyer.
01 519	01 1519	DR	4-6-2	2C1h2	1964	MR	EFZ. Rottweil.
01 531	01 1531	DR	4-6-2	2C1h2	1964	M	DBM. Arnstadt.
01 533	01 1533	DR	4-6-2	2C1h2	1964	MA	ÖGEG. Ampflwang, Austria.
01 1056	011 056	DB	4-6-2	2C1h3	1940	M	DME. Darmstadt Kranichstein.
01 1061	012 061	DB	4-6-2	2C1h3	1940	M	DDM. Neuenmarkt Wirsberg.
01 1063	012 063	DB	4-6-2	2C1h3	1940	P	Braunschweig Hbf.
01 1066	012 066	DB	4-6-2	2C1h3	1940	MA	UEF. Heilbronn.
01 1075	012 075	DB	4-6-2	2C1h3	1940	MA	SSN. Rotterdam Noord, Netherlands.
01 1081	012 081	DB	4-6-2	2C1h3	1940	M	UEF. Bahnpark Augsburg.
01 1082	012 082	DB	4-6-2	2C1h3	1940	M	DTM. Berlin.
01 1100	012 100	DB	4-6-2	2C1h3	1940	MA	DBM Oberhausen Osterfeld.
01 1102	012 102	DB	4-6-2	2C1h3	1940	M	UEF/SEH Heilbronn.
01 1104	012 104	DB	4-6-2	2C1h3	1940	MS	DBK Crailsheim.
03 001	03 2001	DR	4-6-2	2C1h2	1930	M	DBM. Dresden Altstadt.
03 002	03 2002	DR	4-6-2	2C1h2	1930	M	TM. Prora.
03 098	03 2098	DR	4-6-2	2C1h2	1933	M	TM. Speyer.
03 131	003 131	DB	4-6-2	2C1h2	1933	M	DDM. Neuenmarkt Wirsberg.
03 155	03 2155	DR	4-6-2	2C1h2	1934	MA	WFL, Nossen.
03 188	003 188	DB	4-6-2	2C1h2	1935	P	DBM. Kirchheim (Teck).
03 204	03 2204	DR	4-6-2	2C1h2	1936	MR	LDC. Cottbus.
03 295	03 2295	DR	4-6-2	2C1h2	1937	M	BEM. Bahnpark Augsburg.
03 1010	03 1010	DR	4-6-2	2C1h3	1940	MA	DBM. Halle P.
03 1090	03 0090	DR	4-6-2	2C1h3	1940	M	DBM. Schwerin.
05 001	-	DB	4-6-4	2C2h3	1935	M	DBM. Nürnberg.
10 001	010 001	DB	4-6-2	2C1h3	1957	M	DDM. Neuenmarkt Wirsberg.
15 001	-	DRG	4-4-4	2B2h4v	1906	M	DBM. Nürnberg.
17 008	-	DRG	4-6-0	2Ch4	1911	M	DTM. Berlin.
17 1055	-	DR	4-6-0	2Ch4v	1913	M	VMD. Dresden Altstadt.
18 201	02 0201	DR	4-6-2	2C1h3	1961	MA	Dampf Plus, Lutherstadt Wittenberg.
18 314	02 0314	DR	4-6-2	2C1h4v	1919	M	TM. Sinsheim.
18 316	018 316	DB	4-6-2	2C1h4v	1919	M	LTA/HEM. Mannheim.
18 323	018 323	DB	4-6-2	2C1h4v	1920	P	DBM. Offenburg.
18 451	-	DB	4-6-2	2C1h4v	1912	M	Deutsches Museum, München.
18 478	-	DB	4-6-2	2C1h4v	1918	M	BEM. Nördlingen.
18 505	018 505	DB	4-6-2	2C1h4v	1924	M	DGEG Neustadt (Weinstrasse).
18 508	-	DB	4-6-2	2C1h4v	1924	M	Locorama, Romanshorn, Switzerland.
18 528	-	DB	4-6-2	2C1h4v	1928	M	Siemens, München Allach.
18 612	-	DB	4-6-2	2C1h4v	1926	M	DDM. Neuenmarkt Wirsberg.
19 017	-	DR	2-8-2	1D1h4v	1922	M	VMD. Dresden Altstadt.
22 029	39 1029	DR	2-8-2	1D1h3	1959	MS	BEM. Nördlingen.

22 047	39 1047	DR	2-8-2	1D1h3	1960	M	Falkenberg/Elster.
22 064	39 1064	DR	2-8-2	1D1h3	1960	MS	BEM Nördlingen.
22 066	39 1066	DR	2-8-2	1D1h3	1960	M	Hermeskeil.
22 073	39 1073	DR	2-8-2	1D1h3	1961	M	Falkenberg/Elster.
23 019	023 019	DB	2-6-2	1C1h2	1952	M	DDM. Neuenmarkt Wirsberg.
23 023	023 023	DB	2-6-2	1C1h2	1952	MA	SSN. Rotterdam Noord, Netherlands.
23 029	023 029	DB	2-6-2	1C1h2	1954	P	Aalen.
23 042	023 042	DB	2-6-2	1C1h2	1954	MA	DME. Darmstadt Kranichstein.
23 058	023 058	DB	2-6-2	1C1h2	1955	MA	Eurovapor, Sissach, Switzerland.
23 071	023 071	DB	2-6-2	1C1h2	1956	MA	VSM. Beekbergen, Netherlands.
23 076	023 076	DB	2-6-2	1C1h2	1956	MA	VSM. Beekbergen, Netherlands.
23 105	023 105	DB	2-6-2	1C1h2	1959	MS	DBM. SEH, Heilbronn.
23 1019	35 1019	DR	2-6-2	1C1h2	1958	MA	LDC. Cottbus.
23 1021	35 1021	DR	2-6-2	1C1h2	1958	M	TM. Prora.
23 1074	35 1074	DR	2-6-2	1C1h2	1959	MS	Eisenbahnwelt, Gera.
23 1097	35 1097	DR	2-6-2	1C1h2	1959	MA	IG. Glauchau.
23 1113	35 1113	DR	2-6-2	1C1h2	1959	MS	DBM. Nossen.
24 004	37-1004	DR	2-6-0	1Ch2	1928	M	VMD. Dresden Altstadt.
24 009	37 1009	DR	2-6-0	1Ch2	1928	MS	Gelsenkirchen Bismarck.
24 083	(Oi2-22)	PKP	2-6-0	1Ch2	1938	MA	Loburg.
38 205	38 5205	DR	4-6-0	2Ch2	1910	M	DBM, SEM Chemnitz Hilbersdorf.
38 1182	38 1182	DR	4-6-0	2Ch2	1910	M	DBM. Arnstadt.
38 1444	-	DB	4-6-0	2Ch2	1913	M	LHB. Salzgitter.
38 1772	038 772	DB	4-6-0	2Ch2	1915	M	Siegen.
38 2267	38 2267	DR	4-6-0	2Ch2	1918	MA	Stiftung Eisenbahnmuseum Bochum Dahlhausen.
38 2383	038 382	DB	4-6-0	2Ch2	1918	M	DDM. Neuenmarkt Wirsberg.
38 2425	(Ok1-296)	PKP	4-6-0	2Ch2	1919	M	DTM. Berlin.
38 2460	(230 094)	CFR	4-6-0	2Ch2	1919	MA	Eisenbahnwelt Gera. Restored as Posen 2455.
38 2884	038 884	DB	4-6-0	2Ch2	1921	M	DBM. Nürnberg.
38 3650	038 650	DB	4-6-0	2Ch2	1922	P	Böblingen.
38 3711	038 711	DB	4-6-0	2Ch2	1922	P	Berebostel.
38 3180	(230 105)	CFR	4-6-0	2Ch2	1921	MA	BEM Nördlingen.
38 3199	(230 106)	CFR	4-6-0	2Ch2	1921	MA	SEH Heilbronn.
38 3999	(230 111)	CFR	4-6-0	2Ch2	1923	MA	DME Darmstadt.
39 184	-	DB	2-8-2	1D1h3	1924	M	LHB. Salzgitter.
39 230	-	DB	2-8-2	1D1h3	1925	M	DBM. DDM Neuenmarkt Wirsberg.
41 018	042 018	DB	2-8-2	1D1h2	1938	MA	IG 41 018. Bahnpark Augsburg.
41 024	042 024	DB	2-8-2	1D1h2	1938	M	DME. Darmstadt Kranichstein.
41 025	41 1025	DR	2-8-2	1D1h2	1938	M	Hermeskeil.
41 052	042 052	DB	2-8-2	1D1h2	1938	MR	Osnabrück.
41 073	042 073	DB	2-8-2	1D1h2	1939	MR	Club 41 073, SEH Heilbronn.
41 096	042 096	DB	2-8-2	1D1h2	1938	MA	IG 41 096. Salzgitter.
41 105	042 105	DB	2-8-2	1D1h2	1938	MR	SSN. Rotterdam Noord, Netherlands.
41 113	042 113	DB	2-8-2	1D1h2	1938	M	TM. Sinsheim.
41 122	41 1122	DR	2-8-2	1D1h2	1938	MS	Meiningen Works.
41 125	41 1125	DR	2-8-2	1D1h2	1938	MS	Falkenberg/Elster.
41 137	41 1137	DR	2-8-2	1D1h2	1938	M	Hermeskeil.
41 144	41 1144	DR	2-8-2	1D1h2	1938	MA	IG Werrabahn, Eisenach.
41 150	41 1150	DR	2-8-2	1D1h2	1938	MA	BEM. Nördlingen.
41 185	41 1185	DR	2-8-2	1D1h2	1938	M	DBM Halle P.
41 186	042 186	DB	2-8-2	1D1h2	1938	M	Dieringhausen.
41 225	41 1225	DR	2-8-2	1D1h2	1938	M	SEM. Chemnitz Hilbersdorf.
41 226	042 226	DB	2-8-2	1D1h2	1938	M	Tuttlingen.
41 231	41 1231	DR	2-8-2	1D1h2	1939	MA	Stassfurt.
41 241	042 241	DB	2-8-2	1D1h2	1939	MA	DBM Oberhausen Osterfeld Süd.
41 271	042 271	DB	2-8-2	1D1h2	1939	S	EF Rendsburg. Neumünster.
41 289	41 1289	DR	2-8-2	1D1h2	1939	M	Falkenberg/Elster.
41 303	41 1303	DR	2-8-2	1D1h2	1939	S	Röbel (Exists?).
41 360	042 360	DB	2-8-2	1D1h2	1939	MA	DBM Oberhausen Osterfeld Süd.

41 364	042 364	DB	2-8-2	1D1h2	1941	M	DDM. Neuenmarkt Wirsberg.
42 1504	(Ty43-127)	PKP	2-10-0	1Eh2	1944	M	TM. Speyer.
42 2754	(16.15)	BDZ	2-10-0	1Eh2	1949	M	Hermeskeil.
42 2768	(16.18)	BDZ	2-10-0	1Eh2	1949	M	BEM Nördlingen.
43 001	-	DR	2-10-0	1Eh2	1926	M	VMD. Chemnitz Hilbersdorf.
44 100	043 100	DB	2-10-0	1Eh3	1937	M	TM. Sinsheim.
44 105	44 2105	DR	2-10-0	1Eh3	1938	M	Falkenberg/Elster.
44 140	44 2140	DR	2-10-0	1Eh3	1938	M	Falkenberg/Elster.
44 154	44 2154	DR	2-10-0	1Eh3	1938	M	Falkenberg/Elster.
44 167	44 2167	DR	2-10-0	1Eh3	1939	M	Hermeskeil.
44 177	44 2177	DR	2-10-0	1Eh3	1939	M	Hermeskeil.
44 196	44 2196	DR	2-10-0	1Eh3	1939	M	Hermeskeil.
44 225	44 2225	DR	2-10-0	1Eh3	1939	S	Meiningen (For Denmark?).
44 264	44 2264	DR	2-10-0	1Eh3	1939	M	Hermeskeil.
44 276	044 276	DB	2-10-0	1Eh3	1940	M	DDM. Neuenmarkt Wirsberg.
44 351	44 0351	DR	2-10-0	1Eh3	1941	S	VSE. Wülknitz.
44 381	043 381	DB	2-10-0	1Eh3	1941	M	BEM. Nördlingen.
44 389	044 389	DB	2-10-0	1Eh3	1941	P	Altenbeken.
44 394	44 2394	DR	2-10-0	1Eh3	1941	M	Falkenberg/Elster.
44 397	44 2397	DR	2-10-0	1Eh3	1941	M	TM. Prora.
44 404	044 404	DB	2-10-0	1Eh3	1941	M	DME. Darmstadt Kranichstein.
44 434	044 434	DB	2-10-0	1Eh3	1941	M	Hermeskeil.
44 481	044 481	DB	2-10-0	1Eh3	1941	M	Technikmuseum, Kassel.
44 500	44 2500	DR	2-10-0	1Eh3	1941	M	Hermeskeil.
44 508	044 508	DB	2-10-0	1Eh3	1941	MS	Westerburg.
44 546	44 2546	DR	2-10-0	1Eh3	1941	M	BEM. Nördlingen.
44 594	044 594	DB	2-10-0	1Eh3	1941	M	Wittenberge.
44 606	043 606	DB	2-10-0	1Eh3	1941	M	Bahnpark, Augsburg.
44 635	44 2635	DR	2-10-0	1Eh3	1941	M	Hermeskeil.
44 661	44 2661	DR	2-10-0	1Eh3	1941	MA	ÖGEG. Ampflwang Austria.
44 663	44 2663	DR	2-10-0	1Eh3	1941	M	Stassfurt.
44 687	44 2687	DR	2-10-0	1Eh3	1941	M	Altenbeken.
44 903	043 903	DB	2-10-0	1Eh3	1943	P	Emden Hbf.
44 1040	44 1040	DR	2-10-0	1Eh3	1942	M	Hermeskeil.
44 1056	44 1056	DR	2-10-0	1Eh3	1942	M	Hermeskeil.
44 1085	043 085	DB	2-10-0	1Eh3	1942	MT	VSM Beekbergen, Netherlands.
44 1093	44 1093	DR	2-10-0	1Eh3	1942	M	DBM Arnstadt.
44 1106	44 1106	DR	2-10-0	1Eh3	1942	M	Hermeskeil.
44 1121	043 121	DB	2-10-0	1Eh3	1942	M	Tuttlingen.
44 1182	44 1182	DR	2-10-0	1Eh3	1942	MA	Stassfurt.
44 1203	043 196	DB	2-10-0	1Eh3	1942	P	Salzbergen Bhf.
44 1251	44 1251	DR	2-10-0	1Eh3	1942	M	Hermeskeil.
44 1315	043 315	DB	2-10-0	1Eh3	1943	M	SEH Heilbronn.
44 1338	44 1338	DR	2-10-0	1Eh3	1943	M	SEM Chemnitz Hilbersdorf.
44 1377	044 377	DB	2-10-0	1Eh3	1943	M	Stiftung Eisenbahnmuseum Bochum Dahlhausen.
44 1378	44 1378	DR	2-10-0	1Eh3	1943	M	Crailsheim.
44 1412	44 1412	DR	2-10-0	1Eh3	1943	M	Hermeskeil.
44 1424	044 424	DB	2-10-0	1Eh3	1943	MR	Heilbronn, for Ingolstadt.
44 1486	44 1486	DR	2-10-0	1Eh3	1943	MA	Stassfurt.
44 1489	44 1489	DR	2-10-0	1Eh3	1943	MR	SEH Heilbronn.
44 1537	44 1537	DR	2-10-0	1Eh3	1943	M	Hermeskeil.
44 1558	044-556	DB	2-10-0	1Eh3	1943	M	Gelsenkirchen Bismarck
44 1593	44 1593	DR	2-10-0	1Eh3	1943	MA	VSM. Beekbergen, Netherlands.
44 1595	44 1595	DR	2-10-0	1Eh3	1943	S	ÖGEG. Ampflwang. Austria.
44 1614	44 1614	DR	2-10-0	1Eh3	1943	S	ÖGEG. Ampflwang. Austria.
44 1616	44 1616	DR	2-10-0	1Eh3	1943	S	SEH Heilbronn.
44 1681	043 681	DB	2-10-0	1Eh3	1942	M	Eisenbahn Erlebniswelt, Horb.
45 010	045 010	DB	2-10-2	1E1h3	1941	S	DBM. Lichtenfels.
50 001	050 001	DB	2-10-0	1Eh2	1939	M	DTM. Berlin.
50 413	050 413	DB	2-10-0	1Eh2	1940	M	TM. Sinsheim.
50 607	050 607	DB	2-10-0	1Eh2	1940	M	Hermeskeil.
50 622	050 622	DB	2-10-0	1Eh2	1940	MR	Meiningen.
50 682	050 682	DB	2-10-0	1Eh2	1940	P	Grafenwöhr.

50 685	(50.685)	GKB	2-10-0	1Eh2	1940	M	TM. Speyer.
50 778	050 778	DB	2-10-0	1Eh2	1941	M	BEM. Nördlingen.
50 794	050 794	DB	2-10-0	1Eh2	1941	P	Tolk, Kreis Schleswig.
50 849	50 1849	DR	2-10-0	1Eh2	1941	MA	DBM Glauchau.
50 904	050 904	DB	2-10-0	1Eh2	1940	M	DDM. Neuenmarkt Wirsberg.
50 955	50 1955	DR	2-10-0	1Eh2	1941	S	BEM. Nördlingen.
50 975	050 975	DB	2-10-0	1Eh2	1941	M	DDM. Neuenmarkt Wirsberg.
50 1002	50 1002	DR	2-10-0	1Eh2	1941	MS	ÖGEG. Ampflwang, Austria.
50 1255	051 255	DB	2-10-0	1Eh2	1941	MR	SSN. Rotterdam Noord, Netherlands.
50 1446	051 446	DB	2-10-0	1Eh2	1941	M	Hermeskeil.
50 1650	051 650	DB	2-10-0	1Eh2	1942	MS	Moers, Rheinkamp.
50 1724	051 724	DB	2-10-0	1Eh2	1941	MS	Siegen.
50 1832	051 832	DB	2-10-0	1Eh2	1941	M	Hermeskeil.
50 2146	50 2146	DR	2-10-0	1Eh2	1943	P	Weiden.
50 2404	052 404	DB	2-10-0	1Eh2	1942	MS	Gelsenkirchen Bismarck.
50 2429	052 429	DB	2-10-0	1Eh2	1942	MS	Oberhausen.
50 2613	052 613	DB	2-10-0	1Eh2	1942	P	Seifertshofen.
50 2652	50 2652	DR	2-10-0	1Eh2	1943	P	Kaiserslautern.
50 2740	50 2740	DR	2-10-0	1Eh2	1942	MR	UEF Menzingen.
50 2838	052 838	DB	2-10-0	1Eh2	1943	M	Tuttlingen.
50 2908	052 908	DB	2-10-0	1Eh2	1942	P	Lauda (Bhf).
50 2988	052 988	DB	2-10-0	1Eh2	1942	MA	WTB. Fützen.
50 3014	50 3014	DR	2-10-0	1Eh2	1942	M	Hermeskeil.
50 3031	053 031	DB	2-10-0	1Eh2	1942	M	SEH. Heilbronn.
50 3075	053 075	DB	2-10-0	1Eh2	1943	M	Stiftung Eisenbahnmuseum Bochum Dahlhausen.
50 3502	50 0072	DR	2-10-0	1Eh2	1957	MA	BEM. Nördlingen.
50 3506	50 3506	DR	2-10-0	1Eh2	1957	MS	ÖGEG. Ampflwang, Austria.
50 3517	50 3517	DR	2-10-0	1Eh2	1958	M	Falkenberg/Elster,
50 3518	50 3518	DR	2-10-0	1Eh2	1958	M	Falkenberg/Elster,
50 3519	50 3519	DR	2-10-0	1Eh2	1958	MS	ÖGEG. Ampflwang. Austria,
50 3520	50 3520	DR	2-10-0	1Eh2	1958	M	VSM. Beekbergen, Netherlands.
50 3521	50 3521	DR	2-10-0	1Eh2	1958	P	Meyenberg.
50 3522	50 3522	DR	2-10-0	1Eh2	1958	MS	Röbel.
50 3523	50 3523	DR	2-10-0	1Eh2	1958	M	Selb.
50 3527	50 3527	DR	2-10-0	1Eh2	1958	M	Pasewalk.
50 3539	50 3539	DR	2-10-0	1Eh2	1958	MA	SEH. Heilbronn.
50 3540	50 3540	DR	2-10-0	1Eh2	1958	M	Tuttlingen.
50 3545	50 3545	DR	2-10-0	1Eh2	1958	MA	Crailsheim.
50 3552	50 3552	DR	2-10-0	1Eh2	1958	MA	Hanau.
50 3553	50 3553	DR	2-10-0	1Eh2	1958	M	Hermeskeil.
50 3554	50 3554	DR	2-10-0	1Eh2	1959	MS	Tuttlingen.
50 3555	50 3555	DR	2-10-0	1Eh2	1959	M	Hermeskeil.
50 3556	50 3556	DR	2-10-0	1Eh2	1958	M	Stassfurt.
50 3557	50 3557	DR	2-10-0	1Eh2	1959	M	Falkenberg/Elster.
50 3559	50 3559	DR	2-10-0	1Eh2	1959	P	Liblar/Erfstadt.
50 3562	50 3562	DR	2-10-0	1Eh2	1959	P	Kirchweyhe.
50 3564	50 3564	DR	2-10-0	1Eh2	1959	MA	VSM. Beekbergen, Netherlands. (Restored as 50 307).
50 3568	50 3568	DR	2-10-0	1Eh2	1959	M	Falkenberg/Elster.
50 3570	50 3570	DR	2-10-0	1Eh2	1959	M	Wittenberge.
50 3576	50 3576	DR	2-10-0	1Eh2	1959	MA	NTB. Wiesbaden.
50 3580	50 3580	DR	2-10-0	1Eh2	1960	P	Triberg Bhf (Restored as 50 245).
50 3600	50 3600	DR	2-10-0	1Eh2	1960	MA	BEM. Nördlingen.
50 3603	50 3603	DR	2-10-0	1Eh2	1960	M	Tuttlingen.
50 3604	50 3604	DR	2-10-0	1Eh2	1960	M	Tuttlingen.
50 3606	50 3606	DR	2-10-0	1Eh2	1960	MA	Stassfurt.
50 3610	50 3610	DR	2-10-0	1Eh2	1960	MA	Nossen.
50 3616	50 3616	DR	2-10-0	1Eh2	1960	MA	VSE. Schwarzenberg.
50 3618	50 3618	DR	2-10-0	1Eh2	1960	M	VSM Apeldoorn (Netherlands) for spares.
50 3624	50 3624	DR	2-10-0	1Eh2	1960	M	Wittenberge.
50 3626	50 3626	DR	2-10-0	1Eh2	1960	M	Weimar.

50 3628	50 3628	DR	2-10-0	1Eh2	1960	M	SEM Chemnitz Hilbersdorf.
50 3631	50 3631	DR	2-10-0	1Eh2	1960	M	Falkenberg/Elster.
50 3635	50 3635	DR	2-10-0	1Eh2	1960	M	Falkenberg/Elster.
50 3636	50 3636	DR	2-10-0	1Eh2	1960	MA	GES. Kornwestheim.
50 3638	50 3638	DR	2-10-0	1Eh2	1960	MS	Röbel.
50 3642	50 3642	DR	2-10-0	1Eh2	1960	M	Falkenberg/Elster.
50 3645	50 3645	DR	2-10-0	1Eh2	1961	MS	STAR, Stadskanaal, Netherlands.
50 3648	50 3648	DR	2-10-0	1Eh2	1961	MA	SEM Chemnitz Hilbersdorf.
50 3649	50 3649	DR	2-10-0	1Eh2	1961	M	Hermeskeil.
50 3652	50 3652	DR	2-10-0	1Eh2	1961	M	Falkenberg/Elster.
50 3654	50 3654	DR	2-10-0	1Eh2	1961	MA	VSM. Beekbergen, Netherlands.
50 3655	50 3655	DR	2-10-0	1Eh2	1961	MA	ET. Lengerich.
50 3657	50 3657	DR	2-10-0	1Eh2	1961	M	Tuttlingen.
50 3658	50 3659	DR	2-10-0	1Eh2	1961	P	Biblis-Wattenheim Golfpark.
50 3661	50 3661	DR	2-10-0	1Eh2	1961	MS	CFT Pontarlier – Vallorbe, France.
50 3662	50 3662	DR	2-10-0	1Eh2	1961	M	Hermeskeil.
50 3666	50 3666	DR	2-10-0	1Eh2	1961	MA	VSM Apeldoorn, Netherlands.
50 3670	50 3670	DR	2-10-0	1Eh2	1961	MS	Fischamend, Austria.
50 3673	50 3673	DR	2-10-0	1Eh2	1961	MA	Luino, Italy.
50 3680	50 3680	DR	2-10-0	1Eh2	1961	P	Linde bei Lindlar.
50 3681	50 3681	DR	2-10-0	1Eh2	1961	MA	VSM. Beekbergen, Netherlands.
50 3682	50 3682	DR	2-10-0	1Eh2	1961	M	Wittenberge.
50 3684	50 3684	DR	2-10-0	1Eh2	1961	MS	Oebisfelde.
50 3685	50 3685	DR	2-10-0	1Eh2	1961	M	Wittenberge.
50 3688	50 3688	DR	2-10-0	1Eh2	1961	M	DBM. Arnstadt.
50 3689	50 3689	DR	2-10-0	1Eh2	1961	M	ÖGEG Ampflwang, Austria.
50 3690	50 3690	DR	2-10-0	1Eh2	1961	MR	Nossen.
50 3691	50 3691	DR	2-10-0	1Eh2	1961	M	Falkenberg/Elster.
50 3693	50 3693	DR	2-10-0	1Eh2	1961	M	Falkenberg/Elster.
50 3694	50 3694	DR	2-10-0	1Eh2	1961	M	Schwerin.
50 3695	50 3695	DR	2-10-0	1Eh2	1961	MA	Stassfurt.
50 3696	50 3696	DR	2-10-0	1Eh2	1961	MA	CFV3V. Mariemburg, Belgium.
50 3700	50 3700	DR	2-10-0	1Eh2	1961	M	Stassfurt.
50 3703	50 3703	DR	2-10-0	1Eh2	1961	M	Prora.
50 3705	50 3705	DR	2-10-0	1Eh2	1962	M	Treysa.
50 3707	50 3707	DR	2-10-0	1Eh2	1962	P	Berlin Naturpark Süd.
50 3708	50 3708	DR	2-10-0	1Eh2	1962	MA	Blankenburg.
50 4073	50 4073	DR	2-10-0	1Eh2	1959	MR	BEM. Nördlingen.
52 360	52 1360	DR	2-10-0	1Eh2	1942	MA	Vienenburg.
52 662	52 1662	DR	2-10-0	1Eh2	1944	M	Hermeskeil.
52 1423	52 1423	DR	2-10-0	1Eh2	1943	M	Hermeskeil.
52 2093	52 2093	DR	2-10-0	1Eh2	1943	M	Hermeskeil.
52 2195	52 2195	DR	2-10-0	1Eh2	1943	M	BEM. Nördlingen.
52 2751	52 2751	DR	2-10-0	1Eh2	1943	M	Marl.
52 3109	(152.3109)	GKB	2-10-0	1Eh2	1943	M	TM. Sinsheim.
52 3548	52 3548	DR	2-10-0	1Eh2	1943	M	BEM. Nördlingen.
52 3915	(TE-3915)	SZD	2-10-0	1Eh2	1944	M	Speyer (ex TE-3915).
52 4544	(Ty2-4544)	PMP	2-10-0	1Eh2	1943	MR	Naumburg.
52 4867	(152.4867)	GKB	2-10-0	1Eh2	1943	MA	HEF.Frankfurt/M.
52 4900	52 9900	DR	2-10-0	1Eh2	1943	MS	Halle P.
52 4924	52 4924	DR	2-10-0	1Eh2	1943	M	SEM Chemnitz Hilbersdorf.
52 4966	52 4966	DR	2-10-0	1Eh2	1943	M	DTM. Berlin.
52 5448	52 5448	DR	2-10-0	1Eh2	1943	MS	Leipzig.
52 5679	52 5679	DR	2-10-0	1Eh2	1943	P	Falkenberg/Elster.
52 5804	(52.5804)	ÖBB	2-10-0	1Eh2	1943	M	DDM. Neuenmarkt Wirsberg.
52 5933	(TE-5933)	SZD	2-10-0	1Eh2	1943	MA	Stadskanaal, Netherlands (STAR).
52 6666	52 6666	DR	2-10-0	1Eh2	1943	MS	DBM Berlin Schöneweide.
52 6721	52 6721	DR	2-10-0	1Eh2	1943	M	Hermeskeil.
52 7409	(52.7409)	ÖBB	2-10-0	1Eh2	1943	MA	Würzburg.
52 7596	(52.7596)	ÖBB	2-10-0	1Eh2	1944	MR	EFZ. Rottweil.
52 8001	52 8001	DR	2-10-0	1Eh2	1960	M	Gera.
52 8003	52 8003	DR	2-10-0	1Eh2	1960	MS	ÖGEG Ampflwang, Austria.
52 8006	52 8006	DR	2-10-0	1Eh2	1960	M	Hermeskeil.
52 8008	52 8008	DR	2-10-0	1Eh2	1960	M	Falkenberg/Elster.

52 8009	52 8009	DR	2-10-0	1Eh2	1961	M	Falkenberg/Elster.
52 8010	52 8010	DR	2-10-0	1Eh2	1961	MR	VSM. Beekbergen, Netherlands.
52 8012	52 8012	DR	2-10-0	1Eh2	1961	P	Zollhaus Blumberg.
52 8013	52 8013	DR	2-10-0	1Eh2	1961	M	Falkenberg/Elster.
52 8015	52 8015	DR	2-10-0	1Eh2	1961	P	Lehrte.
52 8017	52 8017	DR	2-10-0	1Eh2	1961	P	Kirchmoser.
52 8019	52 8019	DR	2-10-0	1Eh2	1961	M	Tuttlingen.
52 8020	52 8020	DR	2-10-0	1Eh2	1961	M	Tuttlingen.
52 8021	52 8021	DR	2-10-0	1Eh2	1961	M	Falkenberg/Elster.
52 8023	52 8023	DR	2-10-0	1Eh2	1961	M	Falkenberg/Elster.
52 8028	52 8028	DR	2-10-0	1Eh2	1961	MS	Belzig.
52 8029	52 8029	DR	2-10-0	1Eh2	1961	MA	Hei na Ganzlin, Berlin?
52 8034	52 8034	DR	2-10-0	1Eh2	1961	P	Simbach (Inn).
52 8035	52 8035	DR	2-10-0	1Eh2	1961	M	Falkenberg/Elster.
52 8036	52 8036	DR	2-10-0	1Eh2	1961	M	Falkenberg/Elster.
52 8037	52 8037	DR	2-10-0	1Eh2	1961	M	Falkenberg/Elster.
52 8038	52 8038	DR	2-10-0	1Eh2	1961	MA	DEW Rinteln.
52 8039	52 8039	DR	2-10-0	1Eh2	1962	MS	AKO, Scharzerden.
52 8041	52 8041	DR	2-10-0	1Eh2	1962	MS	Lutherstadt Wittenberg.
52 8042	52 8042	DR	2-10-0	1Eh2	1962	M	Falkenberg/Elster.
52 8043	52 8043	DR	2-10-0	1Eh2	1962	M	Tuttlingen.
52 8044	52 8044	DR	2-10-0	1Eh2	1962	M	Falkenberg/Elster.
52 8047	52 8047	DR	2-10-0	1Eh2	1962	MS	Nossen.
52 8051	52 8051	DR	2-10-0	1Eh2	1962	M	Tuttlingen.
52 8053	52 8053	DR	2-10-0	1Eh2	1962	MA	VSM. Beekbergen, Netherlands.
52 8055	52 8055	DR	2-10-0	1Eh2	1962	MA	DLM. Schaffhausen, Switzerland.
52 8056	52 8056	DR	2-10-0	1Eh2	1962	P	Bautzen Bhf.
52 8057	52 8057	DR	2-10-0	1Eh2	1962	M	Tuttlingen.
52 8058	52 8058	DR	2-10-0	1Eh2	1962	M	Falkenberg/Elster.
52 8060	52 8060	DR	2-10-0	1Eh2	1962	MS	Stadskanaal, Netherlands. (STAR).
52 8062	52 8062	DR	2-10-0	1Eh2	1962	P	Treuenbritzen.
52 8064	52 8064	DR	2-10-0	1Eh2	1962	MR	Krefeld.
52 8068	52 8068	DR	2-10-0	1Eh2	1962	M	SEM. Chemnitz Hilbersdorf.
52 8070	52 8070	DR	2-10-0	1Eh2	1962	MS	Peitz.
52 8072	52 8072	DR	2-10-0	1Eh2	1963	M	Falkenberg/Elster.
52 8075	52 8075	DR	2-10-0	1Eh2	1963	MA	IG Werrabahn. Eisenach.
52 8077	52 8077	DR	2-10-0	1Eh2	1963	MS	DBK. Crailsheim.
52 8079	52 8079	DR	2-10-0	1Eh2	1963	MA	Dampf Plus, Nossen.
52 8080	52 8080	DR	2-10-0	1Eh2	1963	MA	Löbau.
52 8082	52 8082	DR	2-10-0	1Eh2	1963	MR	STAR, Stadskanaal, Netherlands.
52 8083	52 8083	DR	2-10-0	1Eh2	1963	MS	Falkenberg/Elster.
52 8085	52 8085	DR	2-10-0	1Eh2	1963	M	Falkenberg/Elster.
52 8086	52 8086	DR	2-10-0	1Eh2	1963	M	Dalhausen (Wupper).
52 8087	52 8087	DR	2-10-0	1Eh2	1963	MS	Neuoffingen.
52 8089	52 8089	DR	2-10-0	1Eh2	1963	M	Falkenberg/Elster.
52 8090	52 8090	DR	2-10-0	1Eh2	1963	M	Hermeskeil.
52 8091	52 8091	DR	2-10-0	1Eh2	1963	M	VSM Beekbergen, Netherlands.
52 8092	52 8092	DR	2-10-0	1Eh2	1963	M	Falkenberg/Elster.
52 8095	52 8095	DR	2-10-0	1Eh2	1963	MA	VEB, Gerolstein, (Restored as 52 6106).
52 8096	52 8096	DR	2-10-0	1Eh2	1963	M	ÖGEG Ampflwang, Austria.
52 8098	52 8098	DR	2-10-0	1Eh2	1963	M	Leipzig Plagwitz.
52 8100	52 8100	DR	2-10-0	1Eh2	1963	M	Falkenberg/Elster.
52 8102	52 8102	DR	2-10-0	1Eh2	1964	M	Falkenberg/Elster.
52 8104	52 8104	DR	2-10-0	1Eh2	1964	M	Falkenberg/Elster.
52 8106	52 8106	DR	2-10-0	1Eh2	1964	MR	Treysa.
52 8109	52 8109	DR	2-10-0	1Eh2	1964	M	Weimar.
52 8111	52 8111	DR	2-10-0	1Eh2	1964	M	Tuttlingen.
52 8113	52 8113	DR	2-10-0	1Eh2	1964	M	Hermeskeil.
52 8115	52 8115	DR	2-10-0	1Eh2	1964	M	Knappenrode.
52 8116	52 8116	DR	2-10-0	1Eh2	1964	MS	Osnabruck-Piesberg.
52 8117	52 8117	DR	2-10-0	1Eh2	1964	M	Falkenberg/Elster.
52 8120	52 8120	DR	2-10-0	1Eh2	1964	M	Hermeskeil.

52 8122	52 8122	DR	2-10-0	1Eh2	1964	M	Falkenberg/Elster.
52 8123	52 8123	DR	2-10-0	1Eh2	1965	M	Hermeskeil.
52 8124	52 8124	DR	2-10-0	1Eh2	1965	M	ÖGEG Ampflwang, Austria.
52 8125	52 8125	DR	2-10-0	1Eh2	1965	M	Tuttlingen.
52 8126	52 8126	DR	2-10-0	1Eh2	1965	M	Falkenberg/Elster.
52 8130	52 8130	DR	2-10-0	1Eh2	1965	M	Tuttlingen.
52 8131	52 8131	DR	2-10-0	1Eh2	1965	MR	Nossen.
52 8132	52 8132	DR	2-10-0	1Eh2	1965	M	Falkenberg/Elster.
52 8133	52 8133	DR	2-10-0	1Eh2	1965	M	Falkenberg/Elster.
52 8134	52 8134	DR	2-10-0	1Eh2	1965	MA	Siegen.
52 8135	52 8135	DR	2-10-0	1Eh2	1965	P	Wildau.
52 8137	52 8137	DR	2-10-0	1Eh2	1965	M	Stassfurt.
52 8138	52 8138	DR	2-10-0	1Eh2	1965	M	Tuttlingen.
52 8139	52 8139	DR	2-10-0	1Eh2	1965	MA	VSM Beekbergen, Netherlands.
52 8141	52 8141	DR	2-10-0	1Eh2	1965	MS	Löbau.
52 8145	52 8145	DR	2-10-0	1Eh2	1965	S	Frankfurt/O.
52 8147	52 8147	DR	2-10-0	1Eh2	1965	MR	Schwarzerden.
52 8148	52 8148	DR	2-10-0	1Eh2	1965	MR	Mönchengladbach.
52 8149	52 8149	DR	2-10-0	1Eh2	1965	M	SEM Chemnitz Hilbersdorf.
52 8150	52 8150	DR	2-10-0	1Eh2	1965	MS	VSM Beekbergen Netherlands, (Spares).
52 8154	52 8154	DR	2-10-0	1Eh2	1965	MA	Leipzig.
52 8156	52 8156	DR	2-10-0	1Eh2	1966	MS	Belzig.
52 8157	52 8157	DR	2-10-0	1Eh2	1966	S	Falkenberg/Elster.
52 8160	52 8160	DR	2-10-0	1Eh2	1966	MA	VSM Beekbergen, Netherlands.
52 8161	52 8161	DR	2-10-0	1Eh2	1966	M	Stassfurt.
52 8163	52 8163	DR	2-10-0	1Eh2	1966	MS	Pontarlier, France.
52 8168	52 8168	DR	2-10-0	1Eh2	1966	M	BEM. Nördlingen.
52 8169	52 8169	DR	2-10-0	1Eh2	1966	M	Tuttlingen.
52 8170	52 8170	DR	2-10-0	1Eh2	1966	M	Falkenberg/Elster.
52 8171	52 8171	DR	2-10-0	1Eh2	1966	M	Tammbach Dietharz.
52 8173	52 8173	DR	2-10-0	1Eh2	1966	MS	Berlin Schöneweide.
52 8174	52 8174	DR	2-10-0	1Eh2	1966	M	Flakenberg/Elster.
52 8175	52 8175	DR	2-10-0	1Eh2	1966	M	Falkenberg/Elster.
52 8176	52 8176	DR	2-10-0	1Eh2	1966	M	Tuttlingen.
52 8177	52 8177	DR	2-10-0	1Eh2	1966	MA	Berlin Schöneweide.
52 8183	52 8183	DR	2-10-0	1Eh2	1967	M	VSE Schwarzenberg.
52 8184	52 8184	DR	2-10-0	1Eh2	1967	MA	Stassfurt.
52 8186	52 8186	DR	2-10-0	1Eh2	1967	M	ÖGEG Ampflwang, Austria.
52 8187	52 8187	DR	2-10-0	1Eh2	1967	M	Falkenberg/Elster.
52 8189	52 8189	DR	2-10-0	1Eh2	1967	M	Stassfurt.
52 8190	52 8190	DR	2-10-0	1Eh2	1967	M	Prora.
52 8191	52 8191	DR	2-10-0	1Eh2	1967	M	Tuttlingen.
52 8194	52 8194	DR	2-10-0	1Eh2	1967	M	Falkenberg/Elster.
52 8195	52 8195	DR	2-10-0	1Eh2	1967	MA	FME. Nürnberg.
52 8196	52 8196	DR	2-10-0	1Eh2	1967	M	ÖGEG Ampflwang, Austria.
52 8197	52 8197	DR	2-10-0	1Eh2	1967	M	Hermeskeil.
52 8198	52 8198	DR	2-10-0	1Eh2	1967	M	Tuttlingen.
52 8199	52 8199	DR	2-10-0	1Eh2	1967	M	Oelsnitz.
52 8200	52 8200	DR	2-10-0	1Eh2	1967	MA	CFV3V. Mariembourg, Belgium. (Restored as 52 467).
53 7002	-	DRG	0-6-0	Cn2	1884	M	DBM. Nürnberg.
55 669	-	DR	0-8-0	Dn2	1905	M	VMD. Dresden Altstadt.
55 3345	055 345	DB	0-10-0	DH2	1915	M	DGEG. Bochum Dahlhausen.
55 3528	055 528	DB	0-10-0	DH2	1915	M	TM. Speyer.
56 3007	-	DB	0-10-0	1DH2	1928	M	DME. Darmstadt Kranichstein.
57 1841		CFR	0-10-0	Eh2	1919	MR	Dieringhausen (Was sold to CFR and became 50 259).
57 3088	057 088	DB	0-10-0	Eh2	1922	M	DBM/EFB Siegen.
57 3297		DR	0-10-0	Eh2	1923	M	VMD. Dresden Altstadt.
"57 3525"	(50.277)	CFR	0-10-0	Eh2	1926	M	BEM Nördlingen.
"57 3597"	(50.397)	CFR	0-10-0	Eh2	1930	M	SEH. Heilbronn.
58 261	58 1261	DR	2-10-0	1Eh3	1921	M	VMD. Chemnitz Hilbersdorf.
58 311	58 1111	DR	2-10-0	1Eh3	1921	MR	UEF. Menzingen.

58 1616	58 1616	DR	2-10-0	1Eh3	1920	M	Hermeskeil.
58 3047	58 3047	DR	2-10-0	1Eh3	1963	MS	DBM Glauchau.
58 3049	52 3049	DR	2-10-0	1Eh3	1963	MR	VSE Schwarzenberg.
62 015	62 1015	DR	4-6-4T	2C2h2t	1928	M	DBM Dresden Altstadt.
64 006	064 006	DB	2-6-2T	1C1h2t	1926	M	DGEG. Neustadt/Weinstr.
64 007	64 1007	DR	2-6-2T	1C1h2t	1928	M	DBM Schwerin.
64 019	064 019	DB	2-6-2T	1C1h2t	1927	M	Selb.
64 094	064 094	DB	2-6-2T	1C1h2t	1928	MS	GES. Kornwestheim.
64 250	064 250	DB	2-6-2T	1C1h2t	1932	MA	CFV3V. Mariembourg, Belgium.
64 289	064 289	DB	2-6-2T	1C1h2t	1933	M	EFZ. SEH Heilbronn.
64 295	064 295	DB	2-6-2T	1C1h2t	1933	M	DDM. Neuenmarkt Wirsberg.
64 305	064 305	DB	2-6-2T	1C1h2t	1934	MR	NVR Peterborough, UK.
64 317	64 1317	DR	2-6-2T	1C1h2t	1934	P	Frankfurt/Oder Hbf.
64 344	064 344	DB	2-6-2T	1C1h2t	1934	M	DBM. Passau.
64 355	064 355	DB	2-6-2T	1C1h2t	1934	P	Hillstedt.
64 393	064 393	DB	2-6-2T	1C1h2t	1935	P	Konz.
64 415	064 415	DB	2-6-2T	1C1h2t	1935	MA	VSM Beekbergen, Netherlands.
64 419	064 419	DB	2-6-2T	1C1h2t	1935	MA	DBK. Crailsheim.
64 446	064 446	DB	2-6-2T	1C1h2t	1938	M	DBM. Bahnpark, Augsburg.
64 491	064 491	DB	2-6-2T	1C1h2t	1940	MA	DFS Ebermannstadt.
64 518	064 518	DB	2-6-2T	1C1h2t	1940	MA	Eurovapor, Huttwil, Switzerland.
64 520	064 520	DB	2-6-2T	1C1h2t	1940	MR	BEM Nördlingen.
65 018	065 018	DB	2-8-4T	1D2h2t	1955	MA	SSN. Rotterdam Noord, Netherlands.
65 1008	65 1008	DR	2-8-4T	1D2h2t	1955	M	Pasewalk.
65 1049	65 1049	DR	2-8-4T	1D2h2t	1956	MA	DBM Arnstadt.
65 1057	65 1057	DR	2-8-4T	1D2h2t	1956	M	Basdorf.
66 002	066 002	DB	2-6-4T	1C2h2t	1955	M	Stiftung Eisenbahnmuseum Bochum Dahlhausen.
70 083	-	DB	2-4-0T	1Bn2t	1913	MA	BLV, Landshut.
74 231	-	DR	2-6-0T	1Ch2t	1908	MA	MEM, Minden.
74 1192	-	DR	2-6-0T	1Ch2t	1915	M	Stiftung Eisenbahnmuseum Bochum Dahlhausen.
74 1230	74 1230	DR	2-6-0T	1Ch2t	1916	MS	DBM Berlin Schöneweide.
75 501	-	DR	2-6-2T	1C1h2t	1916	M	DDM. Neuenmarkt Wirsberg loaned to VSE Schwarzenberg.
75 515	-	DR	2-6-2T	1C1h2t	1911	M	VMD. SEM. Chemnitz Hilbersdorf.
75 634	-	DB	2-6-2T	1C1h2t	1929	M	VVM. Aumühle.
75 1118	-	DR	2-6-2T	1C1h2t	1921	MA	UEF. Gerstetten.
78 009		DR	4-6-4T	2C2h2t	1912	M	VMD. Dresden Altstadt.
78 192	078 192	DB	4-6-4T	2C2h2t	1920	M	Tuttlingen.
78 246	078 246	DB	4-6-4T	2C2h2t	1922	M	DDM. Neuenmarkt Wirsberg.
78 468	078 468	DB	4-6-4T	2C2h2t	1923	MA	Lengerich.
78 510	078 510	DB	4-6-4T	2C2h2t	1924	M	DBM. Nürnberg.
80 009	-	DR	0-6-0T	Ch2t	1928	P	Berlin Bohnsdorf.
80 013	-	DB	0-6-0T	Ch2t	1928	M	DDM. Neuenmarkt Wirsberg.
80 014	-	DB	0-6-0T	Ch2t	1928	M	SEH. Heilbronn.
80 023	-	DR	0-6-0T	Ch2t	1928	M	VMD. Chemnitz Hilbersdorf.
80 030	-	DB	0-6-0T	Ch2t	1929	M	Stiftung Eisenbahnmuseum Bochum Dahlhausen.
80 036	-	DB	0-6-0T	Ch2t	1929	M	VSM. Beekbergen, Netherlands.
80 039	-	DB	0-6-0T	Ch2t	1929	MA	Hamm.
81 004	-	DB	0-8-0T	DH2t	1928	MS	Naumburg.
82 008	082-008	DB	0-10-0T	Eh2t	1950	M	DBM. Siegen.
85 007		DB	2-10-2T	1E1h3t	1932	P	DBM. Freiburg/Brsg.
86 001	86 1001	DR	2-8-2T	1D1h2t	1928	M	DBM, SEM Chemnitz Hilbersdorf.
86 049	86 1049	DR	2-8-2T	1D1h2t	1932	M	VSE Schwarzenberg.
86 056	86 1056	DR	2-8-2T	1D1h2t	1932	M	ÖGEG Ampflwang, Austria.
86 283	086 283	DB	2-8-2T	1D1h2t	1937	M	DDM. Neuenmarkt Wirsberg.
86 333	86 1333	DR	2-8-2T	1D1h2t	1939	MA	WTB. Fützen.
86 346	086 346	DB	2-8-2T	1D1h2t	1939	MS	UEF. Menzingen.
86 348	086 348	DB	2-8-2T	1D1h2t	1939	MS	Kornwestheim.
86 457	086 457	DB	2-8-2T	1D1h2t	1942	M	DBM Heilbronn.

86 501	86 1501	DR	2-8-2T	1D1h2t	1942	MA	ÖGEG Ampflwang, Austria.
86 607	86 1607	DR	2-8-2T	1D1h2t	1942	M	Adorf.
86 744	86 1744	DR	2-8-2T	1D1h2t	1942	MR	MEM. Prussisch Oldendorf.
88 7306		DB	0-4-0T	Bn2t	1892	M	DGEG. Neustadt/Weinstr.
88 "7405"		DB	0-4-0T	Bn2t	1899	M	DTM, Berlin.
89 008		DR	0-6-0T	Ch2t	1938	M	VMD. Schwerin.
89 312		DB	0-6-0T	Cn2t	1896	M	LTA. Mannheim.
89 339		DB	0-6-0T	Cn2t	1901	M	DME. Darmstadt Kranichstein.
89 357		DB	0-6-0T	Cn2t	1903	P	Kornwestheim.
89 363		DB	0-6-0T	Cn2t	1905	MA	GES, Neuffen.
89 407		DB	0-6-0T	Cn2t	1912	M	SEH. Heilbronn.
89 801		DB	0-6-0T	Cn2t	1921	M	DBM. Koblenz Lützel.
89 837	(789.837)	ÖBB	0-6-0T	Cn2t	1921	M	BEM Nördlingen.
89 1004	89 1004	DR	0-6-0T	Ch2t	1906	M	DBM Halle P.
89 6009	89 6009	DR	0-6-0T	Ch2t	1902	MA	DBM Dresden Altstadt.
89 6024		DR	0-6-0T	Ch2t	1914	MA	DDM. Neuenmarkt Wirsberg.
89 6237		DR	0-6-0T	Ch2t	1924	MR	MEM. Prussisch Oldendorf.
"89 6311"	-	DR	0-6-0T	Ch2t		M	DBM Arnstadt.
89 7005			0-6-0T	Ch2t	1882	M	Hochdahl.
89 7077		DB	0-6-0T	Ch2t	1899	MS	Lübeck (Private).
89 7159			0-6-0T	Ch2t	1910	MA	DGEG. Neustadt/Weinstr.
89 7220			0-6-0T	Ch2t	1896	M	MBS. Haaksbergen, Netherlands.
89 7296		DB	0-6-0T	Ch2t	1899	M	Gramzow.
89 7462		DB	0-6-0T	Ch2t	1904	M	DBM. Koblenz.
89 7513		DB	0-6-0T	Ch2t	1911	M	Loburg.
89 7531		DB	0-6-0T	Ch2t	1898	M	SEH. Heilbronn.
89 7538		DB	0-6-0T	Ch2t	1914	M	Location unknown (Italy?).
90 009			0-6-2T	C1n2t	1893	M	Stiftung Eisenbahnmuseum Bochum Dahlhausen.
90 042			0-6-2T	C1n2t	1895	M	SHE, Heilbronn.
91 134		DR	2-6-0T	1Cn2t	1898	M	DBM. Schwerin.
91 319			2-6-0T	1Cn2t	1902	P	Münster-Gremmendorf (Westf).
91 896^{II}		DR	2-6-0T	1Cn2t	1912	M	SEM, Chemnitz Hilbersdorf.
91 936	(TKi3-112)	PKP	2-6-0T	1Cn2t	1903	M	DTM. Berlin.
91 6580	-	DR	2-6-0T	1Ch2t	1939	M	DBM Arnstadt.
92 011	-	DRG	0-8-0T	DH2t	1917	P	Rust/Lahr.
92 442	-	DRG	0-8-0T	DH2t	1928	MR	GES, Kornwestheim.
92 503	-	DR	0-8-0T	DH2t	1910	M	VMD. Dresden Altstadt.
92 638	-	DR	0-8-0T	DH2t	1912	M	MEM. Minden.
92 739	-	DB	0-8-0T	DH2t	1914	M	DBM/DGEG. Neustadt/Weinstr.
93 230	-	DR	2-8-2T	1D1h2t	1917	M	VMD. Dieringhausen.
93 526	093 526	DB	2-8-2T	1D1h2t	1918	M	DDM. Neuenmarkt Wirsberg.
94 002	-	DRG	0-10-0T	Eh2t	1907	M	DGEG. Neustadt/Weinstr.
94 249	-	DR	0-10-0T	Eh2t	1908	M	Heiligenstadt Ost.
94 1184	094 184	DB	0-10-0T	Eh2t	1921	MR	Crailsheim.
94 1292	94 1292	DR	0-10-0T	Eh2t	1922	MA	DBM. Ilmenau.
94 1538	094 538	DB	0-10-0T	Eh2t	1922	MR	Ilmenau.
94 1640	094 640	DB	0-10-0T	Eh2t	1923	P	Gennep, Netherlands.
94 1692	094 692	DB	0-10-0T	Eh2t	1924	M	DBM. Ilmenau.
94 1697	094 697	DB	0-10-0T	Eh2t	1924	M	BEM Nördlingen.
94 1730	094 730	DB	0-10-0T	Eh2t	1924	M	DDM. Neuenmarkt Wirsberg.
94 2105	-	DR	0-10-0T	Eh2t	1923	M	VMD. Schwarzenberg.
95 009	95 0009	DR	2-10-2T	1E1h2t	1922	M	Dieringhausen.
95 016	95 1016	DR	2-10-2T	1E1h2t	1922	M	Neuenmarkt Wirsberg.
95 020	95 0020	DR	2-10-2T	1E1h2t	1923	M	TM. Speyer (As "95 007").
95 027	95 1027	DR	2-10-2T	1E1h2t	1923	MA	DBM Blankenberg.
95 028	95 0028	DR	2-10-2T	1E1h2t	1923	M	Stiftung Eisenbahnmuseum Bochum Dahlhausen.
95 6676	95 6676	DR	2-10-2T	1E1h2t	1919	MS	Rubeland.
97 501	-	DB	0-10-0RT	Ezzh2t	1923	MA	ZHL, Reutlingen.
97 502	-	DB	0-10-0RT	Ezzh2t	1923	M	Stiftung Eisenbahnmuseum Bochum Dahlhausen.
97 504	-	DB	0-10-0RT	Ezzh2t	1925	M	DTM. Berlin

98 001	-	DR	0-4-4-0T	BBn4vt	1910	M	VMD. Industrie Museum, Chemnitz.
98 307	-	DB	0-4-0T	Bh2t	1909	M	DBM. Neuenmarkt Wirsberg.
98 507	-	DB	0-6-2T	C1h2t	1903	P	DBM. Ingolstadt, Bhf.
98 727	-	DRG	0-4-4-0T	BBn4vt	1903	M	DME. Darmstadt Kranichstein.
98 812	098 812	DB	0-8-0T	DH2t	1914	MA	UEF. Gerstetten.
98 886	098 886	DB	0-8-0T	DH2t	1924	MA	Fladungen.
98 7056	-	DR	0-4-0T	Bn2t	1886	M	VMD. Dresden Altstadt.
98 7508	-	DRG	0-4-0T	Bn2t	1883	M	DGEG. Neustadt/Weinstr.
98 7658	-	DRG	0-6-0T	Cn2t	1892	M	Bayerische Eisenstein.
99 162	-	DR	0-4-4-0T	BBn4vt	1902	M	Oberhainsdorf.
99 193	-	DB	0-10-0T	Eh2t	1927	MA	Blonay Chamby, Switzerland.
99 211	-	DB	0-6-0T	Ch2t	1929	P	Wangerooge.
99 253	-	DB	0-6-2T	C1n2t	1908	P	Regensburg.
99 516	99 1516	DR	0-4-4-0T	BBn4vt	1892	MA	Schöneheide Mitte.
99 534	99 1534	DR	0-4-4-0T	BBn4vt	1898	P	Geyer.
99 535	99 1535	DR	0-4-4-0T	BBn4vt	1898	M	VMD. Dresden.
99 539	99 1539	DR	0-4-4-0T	BBn4vt	1899	MA	Radeburg.
99 542	99 1542	DR	0-4-4-0T	BBn4vt	1899	MA	Jöhstadt.
99 555	99 1555	DR	0-4-4-0T	BBn4vt	1908	MS	Bertsdorf.
99 562	99 1562	DR	0-4-4-0T	BBn4vt	1909	M	DDM. Neuenmarkt Wirsberg.
99 564	99 1564	DR	0-4-4-0T	BBn4vt	1909	MR	Radebeul Ost.
99 566	99 1566	DR	0-4-4-0T	BBn4vt	1909	M	SEM. Chemnitz Hilbersdorf.
99 568	99 1568	DR	0-4-4-0T	BBn4vt	1910	MA	Jöhstadt.
99 579	99 1579	DR	0-4-4-0T	BBn4vt	1912	P	Oberrittersgrün.
99 582	99 1582	DR	0-4-4-0T	BBn4vt	1912	MA	Schöneheide Mitte.
99 585	99 1585	DR	0-4-4-0T	BBn4vt	1913	MS	Schöneheide Mitte.
99 586	99 1586	DR	0-4-4-0T	BBn4vt	1913	MA	Radebeul Ost.
99 590	99 1590	DR	0-4-4-0T	BBn4vt	1913	MA	Jöhstadt.
99 594	99 1594	DR	0-4-4-0T	BBn4vt	1913	MS	Putbus.
99 604	99 1604	DR	0-4-4-0T	BBn4vt	1914	MA	VSSB, Radebeul.
99 606	99 1606	DR	0-4-4-0T	BBn4vt	1916	MR	VSSB Carlsfeld.
99 633	-	DB	0-4-4-0T	BBn4vt	1899	MA	Ochsenhausen.
99 637	-	DB	0-4-4-0T	BBn4vt	1904	P	Bad Buchau.
99 651	-	DB	0-10-0T	Eh2t	1919	P	Steinheim.
99 713	99 1713	DR	0-10-0T	Eh2t	1927	MA	Radebeul.
99 715	99 1715	DR	0-10-0T	Eh2t	1927	MR	Jöhstadt.
99 716	-	DB	0-10-0T	Eh2t	1927	MA	Ochsenhausen.
99 750	99 1750	DR	2-10-2T	1E1h2t	1929	P	Trixipark, Gross Schönau.
99 759	99 1759	DR	2-10-2T	1E1h2t	1933	M	Oberrittersgrün.
99 788	99 1788	DR	2-10-2T	1E1h2t	1955	MA	Ochsenhausen.
99 790	99 1790	DR	2-10-2T	1E1h3	1957	P	Freital Hainsberg.
99 3301	99 3301	DR	0-6-0T	Cn2t	1895	MA	Cottbus Park.
99 3310	99 3310	DR	0-8-0T	Dn2t	1917	MA	Ohs Bruk Jvg. Sweden.
99 3311	99 3311	DR	0-8-0T	Dn2t	1917	MR	Schinznach, Switzerland.
99 3312	99 3312	DR	0-8-0T	Dn2t	1912	MA	Weisswasser.
99 3313	99 3313	DR	0-8-0T	Dn2t	1914	MA	DRM. Frankfurt/M.
99 3314	99 3314	DR	0-8-0T	Dn2t	1917	M	MPSF. Schwichtenberg.
99 3315	99 3315	DR	0-8-0T	Dn2t	1917	MA	DKM. Muhlenstroth.
99 3316	99 3316	DR	0-8-0T	Dn2t	1919	M	TM. Speyer.
99 3317	99 3317	DR	0-8-0T	Dn2t	1918	MS	Weisswasser.
99 3318	99 3318	DR	0-8-0T	Dn2t	1918	MR	DKM. Muhlenstroth.
99 3351	99 3351	DR	0-6-2T	C1n2t	1906	MR	DRM. Frankfurt/M.
99 3352	99 3352	DR	0-6-2TT	C1n2t	1907	P	Friedland.
99 3353	99 3353	DR	0-6-2T	C1n2t	1908	MA	Brecon, UK.
99 3361	99 3361	DR	0-8-0	Dn2t	1938	MA	Hesston, Indiana, USA.
99 3461	99 3461	DR	0-8-0	Dn2t	1934	MA	Froissy, France.
99 3462	99 3462	DR	0-8-0	Dn2t	1934	MA	DKM. Muhlenstroth.
99 4301		DR	0-6-0T	Cn2t	1920	P	Gommern.
99 4503		DR	0-6-0T	Cn2t	1920	P	Gramzow.
99 4511		DR	0-6-2T	C1n2t	1899	MA	Jöhstadt.
99 4532	99 4532	DR	0-8-0T	Dn2t	1924	M	Bertsdorf.
99 4631	99 4631	DR	0-8-0T	Dh2t	1913	MS	Kanzach.
99 4644	99 4644	DR	0-8-0T	Dh2t	1923	MR	Lindenberg.

99 4652		DR	0-6-0TT	Cn2t	1941	MS	Putbus.
99 4701		DR	0-6-0T	Cn2t	1914	P	Wollstein.
99 5001		DR	0-4-0T	Bn2t	1922	MS	Portes la Valence, France.
99 5605	99 5605	DR	0-4-0T	Bn2t	1925	MA	DEV. Bruchhausen Vilsen.
99 5606	99 5606	DR	0-4-0T	Bn2t	1894	MS	Schwäbisch Gmünd.
99 5611		DR	0-6-0T	Cn2t	1925	MS	Tence, France.
99 5633		DR	2-6-0T	1Cn2t	1917	MA	DEV. Bruchhausen Vilsen.
99 5703		DR	0-6-0T	Cn2t	1897	M	Lubbenau.
99 7201		DB	0-6-0T	Cn2t	1904	MR	Tambach-Dietharz.
99 7202		DB	0-6-0T	Cn2t	1904	P	Mudau.
99 7203		DB	0-6-0T	Cn2t	1904	MA	UEF. Amstetten.
99 7204		DB	0-6-0T	Cn2t	1904	M	MME. Hersheid-Hünigshausen.

9.2.2. ELECTRIC LOCOMOTIVES

Old No.	Computer No.	Co.	Wheel	Built	Status	Location
E03 001	103 001	DB	Co-Co	1965	MS	DBM Nürnberg.
E03 002	103 002	DB	Co-Co	1965	P	Herrnried.
E03 004	103 004	DB	Co-Co	1966	MS	DBM. Lichtenfels.
	103 101	DB	Co-Co	1971	M	DME. Darmstadt.
	103 132	DB	Co-Co	1971	MS	LDX (Spares for 103 235/245).
	103 167	DB	Co-Co	1971	M	Lokwelt Freilassing, Freilassing.
	103 197	DB	Co-Co	1972	P	Herrnried.
	103 220	DB	Co-Co	1973	M	DGEG. Neustadt (Weinstrasse).
	103 226	DB	Co-Co	1973	MS	Wildenrath.
	103 233	DB	Co-Co	1973	MS	Koblenz Lützel.
E04 01	204 001	DR	1Co1	1932	MS	Leipzig.
E04 07	204 007	DR	1Co1	1933	M	Stassfurt.

▲ For a while in 2011, Bayernbahn hired a preserved Class 194 from Bayerischen Eisenbahnmuseum Nördlingen to operate its Henkelzug freight train from Langenfeld to Wassertrüdigen. E94 192 heads the train through Bonn-Beuel on 10 August 2011. **Matthias Müller**

E04 11	204 011	DR	1Co1	1934	M	Weimar.
E04 20	104 020	DB	1Co1	1934	P	DB HQ Frankfurt/Main.
E10 002	110 002	DB	Bo-Bo	1952	MS	Lichtenfels.
E10 005	110 005	DB	Bo-Bo	1952	M	BEM Nördlingen.
E10 121	110 121	DB	Bo-Bo	1957	M	DBM Koblenz Lützel.
E10 152	110 152	DB	Bo-Bo	1956	MS	Köln Nippes.
E10 210	110 210	DB	Bo-Bo	1957	M	DBM Koblenz Lützel.
E10 223	110 223	DB	Bo-Bo	1961	M	DBM Koblenz Lützel.
E10 228	110 228	DB	Bo-Bo	1961	MA	DBM Stuttgart (TS).
E10 281	110 281	DB	Bo-Bo	1963	M	Eisenbahn Erlebniswelt, Horb.
E10 292	110 292	DB	Bo-Bo	1964	M	DBM Koblenz Lützel.
E10 300	110 300	DB	Bo-Bo	1963	MS	Köln Nippes.
E10 348	110 348	DB	Bo-Bo	1964	MA	DBM Koblenz Lützel.
E10 468	110 468	DB	Bo-Bo	1966	MS	Rottweil.
E10 488	110 488	DB	Bo-Bo	1968	MS	Rottweil.
E10 1239	110 239	DB	Bo-Bo	1961	M	Köln.
E10 1311	113 311	DB	Bo-Bo	1963	M	DBM Koblenz Lützel.
E11 001	211 001	DR	Bo-Bo	1961	MS	Halle P.
E11 049	109 049	DR	Bo-Bo	1970	M	Weimar.
	111 003	DB	Bo-Bo	1975	MR	Euskirchen.
E16 03	116 003	DB	1Do1	1926	M	DBM. Koblenz Lützel.
E16 07	116 007	DB	1Do1	1926	M	Lokwelt Freilassing.
E16 08	116 008	DB	1Do1	1926	M	DME, Darmstadt Kranichstein.
E16 09	116 009	DB	1Do1	1926	M	Bahnpark Augsburg.
E17 103	117 103	DB	1Do1	1929	MS	Lichtenfels.
E17 113	117 113	DB	1Do1	1928	M	DGEG. Neustadt (Weinstr).
E18 03	118 003	DB	1Do1	1935	MS	DBM. Koblenz Lützel.
E18 08	118 008	DB	1Do1	1936	M	Bahnpark Augsburg.
E18 19	218 019	DB	1Do1	1936	MS	Glauchau.
E18 24	118 024	DR	1Do1	1936	M	Weimar.
E18 31	218 031	DR	1Do1	1937	MA	Halle P.
E18 047	118 047	DB	1Do1	1939	MA	DBM, Halle P.
E19 01	119 001	DB	1Do1	1938	M	DTM. Berlin.
E19 12	119 012	DB	1Do1	1939	MS	DBM. Lichtenfels.
-	120 003	DB	Bo-Bo	1979	M	Bahnpark Augsburg.
-	120 005	DB	Bo-Bo	1979	M	ThEV, Weimar.
-	128 001		Bo-Bo	1994	M	Bombardier, Hennigsdorf.
E32 27	132 027	DB	1C1	1925	M	Stiftung Eisenbahnmuseum Bochum Dahlhausen.
E41 001	141 001	DB	Bo-Bo	1956	M	DBM. Koblenz Lützel.
E41 006	141 006	DB	Bo-Bo	1956	M	Dieringhausen.
E41 011	141 011	DB	Bo-Bo	1956	MR	Private. NN1.
E41 055	141 055	DB	Bo-Bo	1958	MS	Koblenz Lützel.
E41 068	141 068	DB	Bo-Bo	1958	MS	Private. FF1.
E41 228	141 228	DB	Bo-Bo	1962	M	DBM/DME. Darmstadt.
E41 248	141 248	DB	Bo-Bo	1963	M	DBM/EFB. Siegen.
E41 366	141 366	DB	Bo-Bo	1965	M	DBM, Koblenz Lützel.
E41 401	141 401	DB	Bo-Bo	1965	P	Bombardier, Kassel.
E42 001	142 001	DR	Bo-Bo	1963	MA	Glauchau.
E42 002	142 002	DR	Bo-Bo	1963	M	SEM. Chemnitz Hilbersdorf.
E42 151	142 151	DR	Bo-Bo	1968	M	Weimar.
E42 255	142 255	DR	Bo-Bo	1976	M	Halle P.
-	143 007	DR	Bo-Bo	1984	M	Weimar.
-	143 117	DR	Bo-Bo	1986	M	ThEV Weimar. Painted as 243 001.
-	143 806	DR	Bo-Bo	1988	MS	Falkenberg/Elster (Belongs to group In Zinnowitz).
E44 001	144 001	DB	Bo-Bo	1930	MS	DBM, Lichtenfels.
E44 002	144 002	DB	Bo-Bo	1933	MS	DBM. Koblenz.
E44 044	244 044	DR	Bo-Bo	1936	MA	Dessau Works.
E44 045	244 045	DR	Bo-Bo	1936	M	SEM. Chemnitz Hilbersdorf.
E44 046	244 046	DR	Bo-Bo	1936	MS	Leipzig Hbf.
E44 049	244 049	DR	Bo-Bo	1936	M	Falkenberg/Elster.
E44 051	244 051	DR	Bo-Bo	1936	M	Lokwelt Freilassing.
E44 059	144 059	DB	Bo-Bo	1937	MS	DBM/Pflazbahn, Worms.

E44 084	144 084	DB	Bo-Bo	1938	M	DBM/ Eisenbahn Erlebniswelt, Horb.
E44 103	244 103	DR	Bo-Bo	1940	M	Weimar.
E44 105	244 105	DR	Bo-Bo	1940	M	Weimar.
E44 108	244 108	DR	Bo-Bo	1939	M	DBM. Halle P.
E44 119	144 119	DB	Bo-Bo	1941	MS	DBM. Lichtenfels.
E44 131	244 131	DR	Bo-Bo	1942	M	DTM. Berlin.
E44 137	244 137	DR	Bo-Bo	1942	MS	Fortezza (I)?
E44 139	244 139	DR	Bo-Bo	1942	M	ETM. Prora.
E44 143	244 143	DR	Bo-Bo	1942	M	Weimar.
E44 148	244 148	DR	Bo-Bo	1942	M	Hermeskeil.
E44 150	144 150	DB	Bo-Bo	1942	M	DGEG. Neustadt (Weinstr).
E44 502	144 502	DB	Bo-Bo	1933	P	Freilassing.
E44 507	144 507	DB	Bo-Bo	1934	M	Weimar.
E44 508	144 508	DB	Bo-Bo	1934	M	Lokwelt, Freilassing.
E44 1170	145 170	DB	Bo-Bo	1944	M	DBM, Seebrugg.
E44 1180	145 180	DB	Bo-Bo	1947	MS	DBM/Pfalzbahn, Worms.
E50 091	150 091	DB	Co-Co	1963	M	DBM. Koblenz Lützel.
150 186	150 186	DB	Co-Co	1972	M	DBM/SEH. Heilbronn.
151 121	151 121	DB	Co-Co	1976	M	DBM, Koblenz Lützel.
E52 34	152 034	DB	2B-B2	1924	MS	DBM. Lichtenfels.
E60 09	160 009	DB	1-C	1932	M	DME, Darmstadt Kranichstein.
E60 10	160 010	DB	1-C	1932	M	DBM. Koblenz.
E60 12	160 012	DB	1-C	1932	M	TM. Sinsheim.
E63 01	163 001	DB	C	1935	P	Stuttgart, Bw Rosenstein (TS).
E63 02	163 002	DB	C	1935	M	BEM, Nördlingen.
E63 05	163 005	DB	C	1936	M	Bahnpark Augsburg.
E63 08	163 008	DB	C	1938	M	DBM, SEH Heilbronn.
E69 01	-	DB	Bo	1905	M	Lokwelt Freilassing.
E69 02	169 002	DB	Bo	1909	M	Bahnpark, Augsburg.
E69 03	169 003	DB	Bo	1922	M	DBM, Koblenz Lützel.
E69 04	169 004	DB	Bo	1922	P	Murnau.
E69 05	169 005	DB	Bo	1922	M	BLM. Landshut.
E71 19	-	DB	B-B	1921	M	DBM. Koblenz Lützel.
E71 28	-	DB	B-B	1922	M	DTM. Berlin.
E71 30	-	DR	B-B	1922	M	VMD. Dresden.
E75 09	175 009	DB	1B-B1	1928	MS	Bauhof Nürnberg Rbf.
E77 10	-	DR	1B-B1	1925	MS	VMD. Dresden Friedrichstadt.
	180 014	DR	Bo-Bo	1991	M	ThEV, Weimar.
E91 99	191 099	DB	C-C	1929	M	Bahnpark Augsburg.
E93 07	193 007	DB	Co-Co	1936	MS	DBM, Koblenz Lützel.
E93 08	193 008	DB	Co-Co	1936	P	AKW Neckarwestheim.
E93 12	193 012	DB	Co-Co	1936	M	DGEG. Neustadt (Weinstr).
E94 040	254 040	DR	Co-Co	1942	M	Hermeskeil.
E94 052	254 052	DR	Co-Co	1941	MA	Dieringhausen (Now in traffic).
E94 056	254 056	DR	Co-Co	1942	MS	Leipzig Hbf.
E94 058	254 058	DR	Co-Co	1941	M	Falkenberg/Elster.
E94 059	254 059	DR	Co-Co	1942	M	SEM. Chemnitz Hilbersdorf.
E94 066	254 066	DR	Co-Co	1942	M	Hermeskeil.
E94 080	194 080	DB	Co-Co	1942	M	Stiftung Eisenbahnmuseum Bochum Dahlhausen.
E94 106	254 106	DR	Co-Co	1943	M	ThEV, Weimar.
E94 110	254 110	DR	Co-Co	1943	M	Hermeskeil.
E94 135	1020 017	ÖBB	Co-Co	1945	MS	BEM. Nördlingen.
E94 158	194 158	DB	Co-Co	1944	A	Krefeld.
E94 192	194 192	DB	Co-Co	1956	MA	BEM Nördlingen.
E94 279	194 579	DB	Co-Co	1955	MA	DBM. Kornwestheim.
E94 281	194 581	DB	Co-Co	1955	MS	Kornwestheim (Spares for E94 278).
E94 580	194 580	DB	Co-Co	1955	A	Back in traffic as "194 178".
E95 02	-	DR	1Co-Co1	1910	MS	Halle P.
E244 31	-	DB	Bo-Bo	1936	MS	HEM. Mannheim.
250 001	155 001	DR	Co-Co	1974	M	Halle P.
250 250	155 250	DR	Co-Co	1984	M	ThEV, Weimar.
E251 001	171 001	DR	Co-Co	1964	MS	DBM, Blankenberg.
E251 002	171 002	DR	Co-Co	1964	MS	DBM, Blankenberg.

E251 012	171 012	DR	Co-Co	1965	M	Weimar.
E310 001	181 001	DB	Bo-Bo	1967	M	DBM. Koblenz Lützel.
181 206-4		DB	Bo-Bo	1974	M	DBM. Koblenz Lützel.
E320 01	182 001	DB	Bo-Bo	1959	M	DBM. Koblenz Lützel.
E410 003	184 003	DB	Bo-Bo	1968	M	DBM. Koblenz Lützel.
E410 012	184 112	DB	Bo-Bo	1967	M	DTM. Berlin.

9.2.3. DIESEL LOCOMOTIVES

Old No.	Computer No.	Co.	Wheel	Built	Status	Location
V15 002	-	DB	B DM	1935	M	Göteborg, Sweden.
V15 005	-	DB	B DH	1943	M	Göteborg, Sweden.
V16 100	-	DB	B DM	1936	M	MEM Minden.
V20 022	-	DB	B DM	1942	M	Almstedt.
V20 035	270 035	DB	B DH	1943	M	BLME, Braunschweig.
V20 036	270 036	DB	B DH	1943	P	DBM. Glückstadt.
V20 039	270 039	DB	B DH	1943	M	VVM. Schonberger Strand.
V20 051	270 051	DB	B DH	1943	M	EKF. Bhf Sinsheim.
V20 058	-	DB	B DH	1943	M	BLME, Braunschweig.
V29 952	-	DB	B-B DH	1952	MA	Bruchhausen Vilsen.
V36 027	103 027	DR	C DH	1939	M	DBM, Schwerin.
V36 102	236 102	DB	C DH	1945	M	DME Darmstadt.
V36 107	236 107	DB	C DH	1940	P	AW Bremen.
V36 108	236 108	DB	C DH	1940	MS	DBM. Lichtenfels.
V36 114	236 114	DB	C DH	1945	M	Oberhausen.
V36 116	236 116	DB	C DH	1941	M	DGEG. Neustadt (Weinstr).
V36 123	236 123	DB	C DH	1940	MA	Ebermannstadt.
V36 211	236 211	DB	C DH	1942	MA	BEM. Nördlingen.
V36 225	236 225	DB	C DH	1944	MA	BLME, Braunschweig.
V36 231	236 231	DB	C DH	1939	MA	Stiftung Eisenbahnmuseum Bochum Dahlhausen.
V36 237	236 237	DB	C DH	1947	M	Bruchhausen Vilsen?
V36 262	236 262	DB	C DH	1948	M	Bodenwerder.
V36 311	-	DB	C DM	1940	M	BLME. Braunschweig.
V36 314	-	DB	C DM	1941	M	MEM Minden.
V36 316	-	DB	C DM	1942	M	Dieringhausen.
V36 401	236 401	DB	C DH	1950	MA	DME. Darmstadt Kranichstein.
V36 405	236 405	DB	C DH	1950	MA	HE Frankfurt/M.
V36 406	236 406	DB	C DH	1950	M	HE Frankfurt/M.
V36 411	236 411	DB	C DH	1950	M	DME. Darmstadt Kranichstein.
V36 412	236 412	DB	C DH	1950	MR	ET. Lengerich.
V45 009	245 009	DB	B DH	1956	M	DDM. Neuenmarkt Wirsberg.
105 072	345 072	DR	D DH	1977	M	Wittenberge (On loan from MEG).
V60 1001	-	DR	D DH	1959	M	SEM. Chemnitz Hilbersdorf.
V60 1067	346 067	DR	D DH	1962	M	Belzig.
V60 1068	346 068	DR	D DH	1962	M	Aschersleben.
V60 1078	346 078	DR	D DH	1963	M	Falkenberg/Elster.
V60 1095	346 095	DR	D DH	1963	M	Heilgenstadt Ost.
V60 1100	346 100	DR	D DH	1963	M	Arnstadt.
V60 1120	346 120	DR	D DH	1963	M	SEM Chemnitz.
106 182-9	346 182	DR	D DH	1981	M	Falkenberg/Elster.
106 521-8	346 521	DR	D DH	1968	M	Oelsnitz.
106 660-4	346 660	DR	D DH	1970	M	Falkenberg/Elster.
260 114-4	360 114	DB	C DH	1956	MA	DFS, Ebermannstadt.
260 303-3	360 303	DB	C DH	1957	M	DBM. Koblenz Lützel.
260 583-0	360 583	DB	C DH	1960	M	DGEG, Bochum Dahlhausen.
260 615-0	360 615	DB	C DH	1961	M	HEF, Hamm.
260-786-9	364 786	DB	C DH	1960	M	Battenberg/Eder.
261 815-9	363 815	DB	C DH	1960	M	PEF, Passau.
260 860-2	360 860	DB	C DH	1960	M	BEM, Nördlingen.
261 234-9	361 234	DB	C DH	1960	M	Vienenburg.

261 715-7	365 715	DB	C DH	1960	M	LTA, Mannheim.
	360 366	DB	C DH	1957	M	SEH, Heilbronn.
V65 001	265 001	DB	D DH	1956	MA	Osnabrück.
V65 011	265 011	DB	D DH	1956	M	DBM, Koblenz Lützel.
V80 001	280 001	DB	B-B DH	1952	MR	Private, Frankfurt/M.
V80 005	280 005	DB	B-B DH	1952	MR	DBM, Meiningen Works.
V80 007	280 007	DB	B-B DH	1952	MR	Altenbeken.
V90 001	290 001	DB	B-B DH	1964	M	DBM, Koblenz Lützel.
V100 003	201 003	DR	B-B DH	1968	MA	Lutherstadt Wittenberg.
V100 019	201 019	DR	B-B DH	1967	MR	Brieske.
V100 025	201 025	DR	B-B DH	1967	M	SEM Chemnitz.
V100 068	201 068	DR	B-B DH	1968	P	Plau am See.
V100 093	201 093	DR	B-B DH	1968	MA	VSM Beekbergen, Netherlands.
V100 101	201 101	DR	B-B DH	1968	MA	Nossen.
V100 143	201 143	DR	B-B DH	1969	M	Schwerin.
110 228-4	201 228	DR	B-B DH	1970	M	Belzig.
110 380-3	201 380	DR	B-B DH	1971	MS	Zinnowitz.
DE 2500	202 002	DB	Co-Co DE	1971	P	Bombardier Transportation, Kassel.
-	202 003	DB	Bo-Bo DE	1973	M	DTM Berlin.
-	202 004	DB	Co-Co DE	1983	M	LTA. Mannheim.
110 331-6	202 331	DR	B-B DH	1971	M	Löbau.
110 457-9	202 457	DR	B-B DH	1972	M	Halle P.
110 516-2	202 516	DR	B-B DH	1973	M	VSE Schwarzenberg.
110 565-7	202 565	DR	B-B DH	1973	MA	PRESS, Espenhain.
110 792-9	201 792	DR	B-B DH	1975	MS	Zinnowitz.
110 885-1	202 885	DR	B-B DH	1978	M	SEM, Chemnitz Hilbersdorf.
114 774	204 774	DR	B-B DH	1975	M	Wittenberge (On loan from MEG).
V100 1042	211 042	DB	B-B DH	1962	P	Eschenau.
V100 1200	211 200	DB	B-B DH	1962	MA	DGEG Würzburg.
V100 1357	211 357	DB	B-B DH	1962	MA	GES Kornwestheim.
V100 2001	212 001	DB	B-B DH	1959	MS	DBM. Gelsenkirchen Bismarck.
V100 2007	212 007	DB	B-B DH	1962	M	DGEG. Bochum Dahlhausen.
V100 2062	212 062	DB	B-B DH	1963	MS	Wiesbaden.
V100 2077	212 077	DB	B-B DH	1964	MS	DBM, Osnabrück Piesberg.
V100 2084	212 084	DB	B-B DH	1964	M	DBM/DBK, Crailsheim.
V100 2372	212 372	DB	B-B DH	19665	M	DBM/EFB, Siegen.
V140 001	-	DB	1-C-1 DH	1935	M	Deutsches Museum, München.
	215 049	DB	B-B DH	1970	M	DBM Oberhausen.
	215 122	DB	B-B DH	1970	M	DBM Oberhausen.
V160 003	216 003	DB	B-B DH	1960	MA	DBM Lübeck.
V160 067	216 067	DB	B-B DH	1966	M	DBM, Koblenz Lützel.
V160 221	216 221	DB	B-B DH	1968	M	DBM Lübeck
V162 001	217 001	DB	B-B DH	1965	M	Eisenbahn Erlebniswelt, Horb.
	217 014	DB	B-B DH	1968	M	DBM, Koblenz Lützel.
	218 128	DB	B-B DH	1971	MS	Siegen.
	218 137	DB	B-B DH	1971	M	DBM, Koblenz Lützel.
	218 217	DB	B-B DH	1973	M	DBM, Koblenz Lützel.
	218 225	DB	B-B DH	1972	M	HE, Mannheim.
119 003-2	219 003	DR	B-B DH	1978	M	DBM/SEM. Chemnitz Hilbersdorf.
119 084-2	219 084	DR	B-B DH	1981	M	DBM/ThEV, Weimar.
119 158-4	219-158	DR	B-B DH	1983	MS	DBM/RSB. Ilmenau.
	229 184	DB	B-B DH	1992	M	Gera (On loan from MEG)
	229 188	DB	B-B DH	1992	M	ThEV, Weimar.
	229 199	DB	B-B DH	1993	M	ThEV, Weimar.
V180 005	228 505	DR	B-B DH	1963	M	Arnstadt.
V180 048	228 548	DR	B-B DH	1964	MR	Prora.
V180 075	118 075	DR	B-B DH	1965	M	DTM. Berlin.
V180 078	228 578	DR	B-B DH	1965	M	ThEV, Weimar.
V180 086	228 586	DR	B-B DH	1965	M	Stassfurt.
V180 118	228 118	DR	B-B DH	1965	M	Schwerin.
V180 141	228 141	DR	B-B DH	1965	M	SEM Chemnitz.
V240 001	228 202	DR	C-C DH	1971	M	Dresden Altstadt.
V180 078	228 578	DR	B-B DH	1965	M	ThEV Weimar.
V180 217	228 617	DR	C-C DH	1967	M	Tuttlingen.

V180 283	228 683	DR	C-C DH	1968	M	Löbau.
V180 292	228 692	DR	C-C DH	1968	M	Wittenberge.
V180 314	228 714	DR	C-C DH	1968	M	Rennsteigbahn, Ilmenau.
V180 349	228 749	DR	C-C DH	1968	MA	Arnstadt.
V180 376	228 776	DR	C-C DH	1969	M	VSE Schwarzenberg.
V180 382	228 782	DR	C-C DH	1969	M	SEM Chemnitz.
V180 388	228 788	DR	C-C DH	1969	M	ThEV, Weimar.
V180 402	228 802	DR	C-C DH	1970	M	Halle P.
130 002-9	230 002	DR	Co-Co DE	1971	M	Dresden.
130 101-9	754 101	DR	Co-Co DE	1973	M	DBM. Halle P.
131 001-0	231 001	DR	Co-Co DE	1973	M	DBM. Halle P.
131 060-6	231 060	DR	Co-Co DE	1973	M	SEM Chemnitz.
131 070-5	231 070	DR	Co-Co DE	1973	M	Falkenberg/Elster.
131 072-0	231 072	DR	Co-Co DE	1973	M	Arnstadt.
132 010-0	232 010	DR	Co-Co DE	1973	M	ThEV, Weimar (On loan from MEG).
132 372-4	232 372	DR	Co-Co DE	1976	M	Schwerin.
232 304-6	234 304	DR	Co-Co DE	1976	M	Nossen.
132 500	232 500	DR	Co-Co DE	1977	M	Wittenberge (On loan from MEG).
V200 001	220 001	DB	B-B DH	1953	MR	FME. Nürnberg.
V200 007	220 007	DB	B-B DH	1956	MA	HE, Lübeck.
V200 009	220 009	DB	B-B DH	1956	M	TM. ETM Prora.
V200 017	220 017	DB	B-B DH	1957	S	Düsseldorf (Classic Train Tours).
V200 018	220 018	DB	B-B DH	1957	M	DTM. Berlin.
V200 033	220 033	DB	B-B DH	1956	MA	HEF. Hamm.
V200 058	220 058	DB	B-B DH	1959	M	TM. Speyer.
V200 071	220 071	DB	B-B DH	1959	M	TM. Speyer.
V200 077	220 077	DB	B-B DH	1959	S	Düsseldorf (Classic Train Tours).
V200 001	220 001	DR	Co-Co DE	1966	M	Schwerin.

▲ Now under the custodianship of Historische Eisenbahn, Lübeck, V200 007 stands at Dagebuell-Mole on 5 August 2012. **Matthias Müller**

120 198-7	220 198	DR	Co-Co DE	1969	M	ThEV, Weimar.
V200 269	220 269	DR	Co-Co DE	1969	M	SEM Chemnitz.
120 274-6	220 274	DR	Co-Co DE	1969	M	Arnstadt.
	120 338	DR	Co-Co DE	1973	M	VMD. Dresden Altstadt.
120 366-0	220 366	DR	Co-Co DE	1975	M	Stassfurt.
V200 101	221 101	DB	B-B DH	1962	M	SEH. Heilbronn.
V200 104	221 104	DB	B-B DH	1963	MS	EOB (Spares).
V200 116	221 116	DB	B-B DH	1963	MS	DBM. Lübeck.
V200 120	221 120	DB	B-B DH	1963	M	SEH. Heilbronn.
Kö 0049	-	DR	B DM	1933	M	VSE Schwarzenberg.
Kö 0073	-	DB	B DM	1933	M	Dresden Altstadt.
Kö 0082	-	DB	B DM	1934	MS	Heiligenstadt.
Kö 0099	-	DB	B DM	1934	M	ETM Prora.
Kö 0107	-	DB	B DM	1935	M	DBB Mittenwalde Ost.
Kö 0110	-	DB	B DM	1935	MS	EF Kraichgau, Sinsheim.
Kö 0116	-	DB	B DM	1935	MA	BEM Nördlingen.
Kö 0128	-	DB	B DM	1934	MA	MKB Berlin Lichterfelde.
Kö 0181	-	DB	B DM	1935	M	Selb.
Kö 0186	311 186	DB	B DM	1936	M	Stadt Museum, Schörndorf.
Kö 0188	311 188	DB	B DM	1936	M	Siegen.
Kö 0203	-	DB	B DM	1936	M	RIM Köln.
Kö 0204	311 204	DB	B DM	1936	MS	RSWE, Regensburg.
Kö 0206		DB	B DM	1936	M	Herborn.
Kö 0210	100 010	DR	B DM	1936	MA	LDC Cottbus.
Kö 0211	311 211	DB	B DM	1936	MR	HE Mannheim.
Kö 0221	311 221	DB	B DM	1936	MA	Gerolstein (98 80 3311 221).
Kö 0225	311 225	DB	B DM	1936	MA	DBM. Bielefelder EF, Bielefeld.
Kö 0227	311 227	DB	B DM	1936	MS	Altenbeken.
Kö 0229	311 229	DB	B DM	1936	MA	DBM Koblenz Lützel.
Kö 0232	311 232	DB	B DM	1936	MR	HE Mannheim.
Kö 0237	-	DR	B DN	1936	M	OSE Löbau.
Kö 0242	100 042	DR	B DM	1936	MA	DLF, Berlin Schöneweide.
Kö 0245	100 045	DR	B DM	1936	MS	SEM Chemnitz Hilbersdorf.
Kö 0247	311 247	DB	B DM	1936	P	Modellbahnausstellung, Mölschow (Usedom).
Kö 0255	311 255	DB	B DM	1936	M	Vienenburg.
Kö 0258	311 258	DB	B DM	1936	MS	IG Nebenbahn Nordhessen, Kassel-Rothenditmold.
Kö 0260	311 260	DB	B DM	1936	MA	BEF Basdorf (98 80 3311 260).
Kö 0262	311 262	DB	B DM	1936	P	Warthausen.
Kö 0265	311 265	DB	B DM	1936	M	Eisenbahn Museum Oderland, Wriezen.
Kö 0274	311 274	DB	B DM	1936	MS	Almstedt-Segeste VL 4.
Kö 0278	311 278	DB	B DM	1936	P	Neustadt/Aisch.
Kö 0281	311 281	DB	B DM	1936	MA	Hespertalbahn V 2, Essen-Kupferdreh.
Kö 0289	100 089	DR	B DM	1936	M	Falkenberg/Elster.
Kö 1002	-	DRG	B DM	1940	MA	DME Darmstadt.
Kö 4002	310 102	DR	B DM	1961	M	Tuttlingen.
Kö 4006	310 106	DR	B DN	1961	P	Bad Langensalza-Merxleben.
Kö 4009	310 109	DR	B DM	1940	M	Wismar.
Ks 4013	-	DB	Bo BE	1930	M	Stiftung Eisenbahnmuseum Bochum Dahlhausen.
Ks 4015	381 101	DB	Bo BE	1930	M	BEM Nördlingen.
Kö 4024	310 124	DR	B DM	1961	MS	Blumberg.
Kb 4026	310 126	DR	B DM	1962	MA	Glauchau.
Kö 4028	399 110	DR	B DM	1962	M	Georgenthal, (Thüringen).
Kb 4031	310 131	DR	B DM	1962	M	Hermeskeil.
Kb 4066	310 769	DR	B DM	1932	M	ETB Stassfurt.
Ks 4071	381 201	DB	Bo BE	1932	P	DBM Bhf. Limburg.
Kbe 4090	310 190	DR	Bo DE	1934	P	Tottleben.
Kbe 4096	310 196	DR	Bo DE	1934	M	Magdeburg.
Kb 4103	323 906	DB	B DH	1933	P	Oberthingau.
Kb 4117	310 217	DR	B DM	1933	M	Falkenberg/Elster.
Kb 4118	310 218	DR	B DM	1933	M	Falkenberg/Elster.
Kb 4140	323 004	DB	B DH	1934	M	MEM. Prussisch Oldendorf.

Kb 4146	322 128	DB	B DH	1934	MA	Hanau.
Kö 4150	322 174	DB	B DM	1934	P	Reichelshofen.
Kö 4175	310 275	DR	B DM	1933	MA	Worms.
Kö 4178	310 278	DR	B DM	1933	MA	Marnheim.
Kö 4180	310 280	DR	B DM	1933	P	Wetzlar-Garbenheim.
Kö 4181	310 281	DR	B DM	1933	P	Rostock Seehafen.
Kö 4201	310 201	DR	B DM	1933	P	Stadtwerke Mainz.
Kö 4202	322 656	DB	B DH	1933	MA	HEF, Hamm 98 80 3322 656-0 D-MEH.
Kö 4210	310 212	DR	B DM	1933	P	Weisswasser.
Kö 4211	310 211	DR	B DM	1934	M	SEM Chemnitz Hilbersdorf.
Kö 4228	310 228	DR	B DM	1934	M	Private, Stendal.
Kö 4270	323 903	DB	B DH	1933	M	OEF. Giessen.
Kö 4274	322 141	DB	B DM	1934	M	DBG. Loburg. (V21 04).
Kö 4280	323 605	DB	B DH	1934	MA	BEF. Basdorf (9880 3322 605-7 D-BEF).
Kö 4285	322 137	DB	B DH	1934	M	Hermeskeil.
Kö 4287	322 613	DB	B DH	1934	M	Fladungen.
Kö 4290	322 143	DB	B DH	1934	MA	DME Darmstadt.
Kö 4293	322 607	DB	B DH	1934	MA	NTB. Wiesbaden (9880 3322 607-3 D-PBE).
Kö 4294	322 635	DB	B DH	1934	MS	ZHL Reutlingen (3).
Kö 4309	310 309	DR	B DM	1934	M	Hermeskeil.
Kb 4323	322 636	DB	B DH	1934	M	DDM Neuenmarkt Wirsberg.
Kb 4324	310 324	DR	B DM	1934	P	Bad Segeberg - Fredesdorf.
Kb 4326	310 326	DR	B DM	1934	P	Bad Segeberg - Fredesdorf.
Kö 4350	322 628	DB	B DH	1934	M	Petite Roselle, France.
Kö 4352	310 532	DR	B DM	1934	M	Rheinsberg.
Kö 4353	310 353	DR	B DM	1934	M	DBB Mittenwalde Ost.
Kö 4371	310 371	DR	B DM	1934	M	Falkenberg/Elster.
Kö 4375	322 106	DB	B DH	1934	M	Braunschweig.
Kö 4407	310 407	DR	B DM	1934	P	Annaberg Buchholz.
Kö 4412	310 412	DR	B DM	1934	P	Potsdam Rehbrücke.
Kö 4418	310 418	DR	B DM	1934	P	Berlin Tempelhof (Bosepark).
Kö 4430	310 430	DR	B DM	1934	M	ETM Prora.
Kö 4439	310 439	DR	B DM	1934	P	Mainz-Mombach.
Kö 4445	310 445	DR	B DM	1935	M	Eschwege.
Kö 4471	310 471	DR	B DM	1934	P	Lichtenau-Ottendorf.
Kö 4492	100 492	DR	B DM	1934	M	Meuselwitz.
Kö 4498	310 498	DR	B DM	1934	MA	Nossen.
Kö 4500	310 500	DR	B DM	1934	MA	Dresden - Glittersee.
Kö 4501	310 501	DR	B DM	1934	P	Parkeisenbahn, Cottbus.
Kö 4528	310 528	DR	B DM	1934	M	Falkenberg/Elster.
Kö 4537	310 537	DR	B DM	1935	MA	VSE Schwarzenberg.
Kö 4543	310 543	DR	B DM	1935	M	EF Grossheringen.
Kö 4547	310 547	DR	B DM	1935	M	Wittenberge.
Kö 4572	322 618	DB	B DH	1934	MS	Gerolstein.
Kö 4573	310 573	DR	B DM	1934	P	Hotel Alterbahnhof, Prerow.
Kö 4579	310 579	DR	B DM	1934	M	Walburg.
Kö 4594	310 594	DR	B DM	1934	P	Neumarkt (Sachs).
Kö 4604	310 604	DR	B DM	1934	MS	Eisenbahn Club, Aschersleben.
Kö 4607	322 660	DB	B DH	1934	MA	Blumberg.
Kö 4610	322 109	DB	B DH	1934	M	Krefeld.
Kö 4617	310 617	DR	B DM	1934	M	Stassfurt.
Kb 4630	310 630	DR	B DM	1934	MA	Löbau.
Kö 4632	100 632	DR	B DM	1934	P	Zughotel, Wolkenstein.
Kb 4634	100 634	DR	B DM	1934	MA	Buckow (9880 3310 634).
Kö 4638	X110.02	ÖBB	B DM	1934	MA	ÖGEG Ampflwang (A).
Kö 4642	X112.02	ÖBB	B DM	1935	M	TM Berlin.
Kö 4646	100 646	DR	B DM	1935	MA	Finsterwalde (Klein Bahren).
Kö 4667	323 016	DB	B DH	1935	MA	FME. Nürnberg.
Kö 4669	323 508	DB	B DH	1935	M	Mittenwalde Ost.
Kö 4696	323 510	DB	B DH	1934	M	Private, Remagen.
Kö 4701	310 701	DR	B DM	1934	P	Rostock Stadthafen.
Kö 4706	323 922	DB	B DH	1934	P	Hofheim.
Kö 4714	322 602	DB	B DH	1934	MA	SEH Heilbronn.
Kö 4731	-	DRG	B DM	1934	M	Alter Bahnhof, Coesfeld Lette.

Kbf 4736	100 736	DR	B DM	1935	P	Sachsendorf.
Kö 4737	323 482	DB	B DH	1935	M	Stiftung Eisenbahnmuseum Bochum Dahlhausen (9880 3323 482).
Köe 4744	310 744	DR	B DM	1934	MA	Belzig.
Köe 4751	310 751	DR	B DM	1935	P	Bitterfeld.
Köe 4755	310 755	DR	B DM	1935	M	Stassfurt.
Kb 4757	310 757	DR	B DM	1935	M	Falkenberg/Elster.
Kö 4772	322 121	DB	B DH	1935	MA	Private, Frankfurt/M.
Kö 4796	310 796	DR	B DM	1935	MS	Eisenach.
Kö 4798	310 798	DR	B DM	1935	M	Tuttlingen.
Kö 4800	310 700	DR	B DM	1935	M	Neuf Brisach, France.
Kö 4809	322 646	DB	B DM	1935	MS	Ingolstadt.
Kö 4842	323 017	DB	B DH	1936	M	Hanau.
Kö 4853	310 773	DR	B DH	1937	M	Meuselwitz.
Kbf 4858	310 758	DR	B DM	1935	MA	Rostock Seehafen.
Kö 4872	310 774	DR	B DM	1936	MS	IG Altensteigerle e V. Nagold.
Kö 4879	323 484	DB	B DH	1936	P	Hallstadt.
Kö 4880	322 157	DB	B DH	1936	MA	BEM Nördlingen.
Kö 4900	310 703	DR	B DM	1936	M	Bad Segeberg- Fredesdorf.
Kö 4902	310 704	DR	B DM	1936	P	Berlin Bohnsdorf.
Ks 4909	381 011	DB	Bo BE	1937	MS	BEM Nördlingen.
Ks 4910	381 012	DB	Bo BE	1937	P	Dorfen.
Kö 4911	310 711	DR	B DM	1937	M	Mittenwalde Ost.
Kö 4915	323 448	DB	B DM	1938	M	EHEH, Hochdahl.
Kö 4923	322 009	DB	B DH	1938	P	School, Mönchengladbach-Hardt.
Kö 4934	310 735	DR	B DM	1938	MA	Belzig.
Kö 4936	310 738	DR	B DM	1937	MA	Oelsnitz.
Köf 4959	310 759	DR	B DM	1937	P	Erfurt Mittelhausen.
Köf 4962	310 765	DR	B DM	1938	MS	Adorf.
Kö 4963	310 763	DR	B DM	1938	MA	Hafenbahn Neustrelitz.
Ks 4969	310 709	DR	B DM	1938	MS	Belzig.
Ks 4972	310 782	DR	B DM	1938	M	Adorf.
Köf 4978	310 778	DR	B DM	1939	P	Lontzen, Belgium.
Ks 4986	381 013	DB	Bo DE	1938	MS	Rottau.
Köf 4999	310 789	DR	B DM	1942	M	Tuttlingen.
Köf 5009	310 809	DR	B DH	1941	M	Belzig.
Kö 5044	323 442	DB	B DH	1943	P	Merzen.
Köf 5046	310 846	DR	B DH	1937	MS	Cottbus.
Kö 5048	322 150	DB	B DH	1938	MS	Reutlingen.
Kö 5049	310 849	DR	B DH	1939	M	Gramzow.
Kbf 5057	323 036	DB	B DH	1943	M	Stadskanaal, Netherlands.
Kbf 5064	310 864	DR	B DH	1943	MA	Cloppenburg.
Kbf 5067	310 867	DR	B DH	1943	M	ETM Prora.
Kbf 5072	100 872	DR	B DH	1943	MS	Kalbe (Milde).
Kbf 5116	323 044	DB	B DH	1943	M	DTM Berlin.
Kb 5142	310 842	DR	B DH	1944	M	DBM Halle P.
Kb 5159	X111.04	ÖBB	B DH	1944	M	Strasshof, Austria.
Köf 5182	310 882	DR	B DH	1941	P	Cottbus Works.
Kö 5186	324 043	DB	B DH	1938	M	Treysa.
Köf 5193	310 892	DR	B DH	1942	MA	BEM Nördlingen.
Köf 5226	100 826	DR	B DH	1944	M	Aschersleben.
Kbf 5231	323 049	DB	B DH	1944	M	Verden.
Kbf 5250	-	DB	B DH	1944	M	Private, Braunschweig.
Kbf 5261	310 881	DR	B DH	1944	M	Hermeskeil.
Kbf 5262	310 822	DR	B DH	1944	P	Erfurt.
Kbf 5266	100 886	DR	B DH	1944	MA	Weimar.
Kbf 5271	323 463	DB	B DH	1944	MS	Hamburg Wilhelmsburg.
Köf 5274	323 470	DB	B DH	1944	M	Siegen.
Köf 5712	310 912	DR	B DH	1942	MA	Frankfurt/M (9880 3310 0912).
Köf 5714	310 914	DR	B DH	1942	MA	Adorf.
Kö 5722	-	DR	B DH	1935	P	Wittenberge Works.
Köf 5727	310 927	DR	B DH	1936	S	Lübbenau.
Kö 5729	310 929	DR	B DH	1939	S	Lübbenau.
Kö 5730	310 930	DR	B DH	1934	MS	Helbra.

Kö 5731	100 931	DR	B DH	1934	MA	Putlitz.
Köf 5736	100 936	DR	B DH	1939	M	ETM Prora.
Kö 5742	310 942	DR	B DH	1941	P	Espenhain.
Kö 5743	-	DR	B DH	1935	MA	Magdeburg.
Kö 5746	310 946	DR	B DH	1943	P	Landgasthof St. Moritz, Möllenbeck-Quadenschonfeld.
Kö 5752	310 952	DR	B DH	1938	M	Schwerin.
Köf 5753	310 953	DR	B DH	1943	P	Beierfeld.
Kö 5755	310 955	DR	B DH	1952	M	Weimar.
Köf 6007	322 609	DB	B DH	1937	MA	Bad Salzdetfurth.
Kö 6020	-	DB	B DH	1937	M	Dieringhausen.
Köe 6042	-	DB	Bo DE	1938	M	ETM, Prora.
Köf 6046	322 173	DB	B DH	1941	M	Treysa.
Köf 6119	324 044	DB	B DH	1951	MA	Oberhausen.
Köf 6124	322 036	DB	B DH	1951	M	IGN Kassel.
Köf 6136	322 039	DB	B DH	1952	M	Werra Fulda Bahn e.V, Schenklengsfeld.
Köf 6139	322 172	DB	B DH	1952	M	Hermeskeil.
Köf 6152	322 041	DB	B DH	1953	MA	Norden.
Köf 6157	323 440	DB	B DH	1953	MS	DB (current situation not known).
Köf 6158	322 147	DB	B DH	1953	P	Nürnberg Langwasser.
Köf 6159	323 942	DB	B DH	1953	MA	Marnheim (98 80 3323 942-3 D-PBE).
Köf 6168	323 525	DB	B DH	1954	MA	Oberhausen Osterfeld Süd.
Köf 6169	323 526	DB	B DH	1954	MA	GES. Kornwestheim.
Köf 6170	322 510	DB	B DH	1954	M	DGEG Neustadt/Weinstr.
Köf 6182	322 640	DB	B DH	1954	MR	HEF, Mannheim.
Köf 6183	323 958	DB	B DH	1954	MA	FME. Nürnberg (98 80 3323 958-9 D-FME).
Köf 6190	322 614	DB	B DH	1954	M	FME. Nürnberg.
Köf 6203	322 043	DB	B DH	1954	M	Darmstadt.
Köf 6204	322 044	DB	B DH	1954	MA	DFS 5, Ebermannstadt.
Köf 6211	322 047	DB	B DH	1955	M	København, Denmark.
Köf 6265	323 582	DB	B DH	1956	M	Treysa.
Köf 6276	323 593	DB	B DH	1957	M	Haltingen.
Köf 6277	323 597	DB	B DH	1956	P	Duingen.
Köf 6280	323 597	DB	B DH	1957	M	Struer, Denmark.
Köf 6286	323 602	DB	B DH	1957	M	NTB. Wiesbaden.
Köf 6306	323 617	DB	B DH	1957	M	H.E. Gelsenkirchen e.V, Gelsenkirchen.
Köf 6311	323 626	DB	B DH	1958	MA	Bahnpark, Augsburg (98 80 3323 626-2 D – DGM).
Köf 6322	323 634	DB	B DH	1958	M	Private, Frankfurt/Main.
Köf 6325	323 637	DB	B DH	1958	M	BSW Oberhausen Osterfeld Süd.
Köf 6330	323-642	DB	B DH	1958	S	Drachten, Netherlands.
Köf 6334	323 646	DB	B DH	1958	M	RSWE, Regensburg.
Köf 6338	323 650	DB	B DH	1958	M	MEH, Hanau.
Köf 6349	323 655	DB	B DH	1958	M	Struer, Denmark.
Köf 6359	322 058	DB	B DH	1959	MA	Neustadt/Weinstr.
Köf 6372	323 102	DB	B DH	1959	M	VVM, Schönberg Strand.
Köf 6383	322 521	DB	B DH	1959	P	Osnabrück, Hafen Strasse.
Köf 6406	323 119	DB	B DH	1959	M	DGEG, Neustadt (Weinstrasse).
Köf 6424	323 137	DB	B DH	1959	MS	IGN, Kassel Rothenditmold.
Köf 6436	323 149	DB	B DH	1959	MA	Linz/Rhein.
Köf 6449	323 156	DB	B DH	1960	M	Hermeskeil.
Köf 6454	323 210	DB	B DH	1960	M	Battenberg/Eder.
Köf 6470	323 225	DB	B DH	1969	MS	Oebisfelde.
Köf 6472	323 227	DB	B DH	1960	MA	Kassel.
Köf 6482	323 237	DB	B DH	1960	MA	Rahden.
Köf 6498	323 680	DB	B DH	1959	MA	BEM München (98 80 3323 680-9 D-BYB).
Köf 6499	323 681	DB	B DH	1959	M	Walburg.
Köf 6501	323 683	DB	B DH	1959	MA	BEM Nördlingen.
Köf 6510	323 710	DB	B DH	1960	M	Vienenburg.
Köf 6524	323 724	DB	B DH	1960	M	GES Kornwestheim.
Köf 6525	323 725	DB	B DH	1960	MS	Crailsheim.
Köf 6526	323 726	DB	B DH	1960	M	MEC Losheim.
Köf 6528	323 728	DB	B DH	1960	M	Azpeitia, Spain.
Köf 6533	323 733	DB	B DH	1960	MA	FME. Nürnberg.

Köf 6541	323 741	DB	B DH	1960	M	Gedser, Denmark.
Köf 6546	323 746	DB	B DH	1960	P	St. Engimar.
Köf 6547	323 747	DB	B DH	1960	M	Petite Roselle, France.
Köf 6551	323 751	DB	B DH	1960	M	DEW Rinteln.
Köf 6557	323 757	DB	B DH	1960	MS	DBM. Lichtenfels.
Köf 6571	323 771	DB	B DH	1960	MR	Schwaben Dampf, Neuoffingen.
Köf 6579	323 871	DB	B DH	1961	M	DDM, Neuenmarkt Wirsberg.
Köf 6580	323 872	DB	B DH	1961	M	Bahnpark, Augsburg.
Köf 6606	323 174	DB	B DH	1959	MA	Hamm.
Köf 6617	323 185	DB	B DH	1959	M	MEC, Losheim.
Köf 6642	323 268	DB	B DH	1960	M	ET Lengerich.
Köf 6648	323 274	DB	B DH	1960	MA	Oberhausen.
Köf 6705	323 703	DB	B DH	1959	MA	BEM. München.
Köf 6712	323 782	DB	B DH	1959	M	St. Sulpice, Switzerland.
Köf 6731	323 801	DB	B DH	1960	M	DGEG, Würzburg.
Köf 6732	323 802	DB	B DH	1960	MA	BEM. München Neuaubing.
Köf 6741	323 811	DB	B DH	1960	M	EF Untermain, Aschaffenburg.
Köf 6772	323 842	DB	B DH	1960	MA	Westerwälder EF, Westerburg.
Köf 6782	323 852	DB	B DH	1960	M	DBM. Koblenz.
Köf 6791	323 861	DB	B DH	1960	M	Hermeskeil.
Köf 6796	323 866	DB	B DH	1960	P	Gerwisch, Magdeburg.
Köf 6797	323 867	DB	B DH	1960	P	Dronsfeld.
Köf 6803	323 323	DB	B DH	1965	MA	DEW Rinteln.
Köf 6808	323 328	DB	B DH	1965	M	Crailsheim.
Köf 6815	323 335	DB	B DH	1965	MA	Bösingfeld.
Köf 6816	323 336	DB	B DH	1965	M	Herborn.
Köf 6817	323 337	DB	B DH	1965	P	Bischofsmais.
Köf 6833	323 353	DB	B DH	1965	M	Braunschweig.
Köf 11 066	332 066	DB	B DH	1964	M	Frankisch Thüringische Museumsbahn e.V. Fladungen.
Köf 11 098	332 098	DB	B DH	1964	MA	Schwarzenden (98 80 3332 098-3 D-AKO).
Köf 11 114	332 114	DB	B DH	1964	MA	DGEG, Neustadt (Weinstrasse).
Köf 11 139	332 139	DB	B DH	1964	MA	ZLSM, Simpelveld, Netherlands. (332-06).
Köf 11 156	332 156	DB	B DH	1964	MA	Westerstede Ocholt.
Köf 11 187	332 187	DB	B DH	1964	MS	ZLSM, Simpelveld, Netherlands (332-3).
Köf 11 204	332 204	DB	B DH	1964	P	Adlerwerke, Frankfurt/Main.
Köf 11 227	332 227	DB	B DH	1966	M	Treysa.
Köf 11 238	332 238	DB	B DH	1966	M	HE, Frankfurt/M.
Köf 11 262	332 262	DB	B DH	1965	M	DBM, Lichtelfels.
Köf 11 271	332 271	DB	B DH	1966	M	FME, Nürnberg.
-	335 039	DB	B DH	1968	M	Schwarzenden.
-	335 059	DB	B DH	1969	M	Schwarzenden.
-	333 068	DB	B DH	1969	M	DBM. Koblenz.
-	335 200	DB	B DH	1976	P	DB Systems, Frankfurt/M.
V15 1001	-	DR	B DH	1959	MA	Dresden Altstadt.
V15 1002	-	DR	B DH	1959	M	Magdeburg.
V15 1018	-	DR	B DH	1960	M	Speyer.
V15 2020	311 020-2	DR	B DH	1961	M	Löbau.
V15 2035	311 705-8	DR	B DH	1961	M	Falkenberg/Elster.
V15 2065	311 681	DR	B DH	1961	M	SEM, Chemnitz Hilbersdorf.
V15 2082	311 559-9	DR	B DH	1962	M	BEF. Basdorf (98 80 3311 559-9 D-BEF).
V15 2232	311 544-1	DR	B DH	1962	M	Wittenberge.
V15 2299	311 535-9	DR	B DH	1963	MA	Wittenberge.
V23 001	312 001-1	DR	B DH	1967	M	DBM. Halle P.
V23 004	312 004	DR	B DH	1968	M	Lutherstadt Wittenberg.
V23 009	312 009-4	DR	B DH	1968	M	Falkenberg/Elster.
V23 072	312 072-2	DR	B DH	1968	M	Falkenberg/Elster.
102 125-8	312 125	DR	B DH	1970	M	Weimar.
102 131	312 131	DR	B DH	1970	M	VSE, Schwarzenberg.
102 140-1	312 140	DR	B DH	1970	M	SEM. Chemnitz Hilbersdorf.
102 172-0	312 172	DR	B DH	1970	MA	Stassfurt.
102 182-3	312 182	DR	B DH	1970	M	Glauchau.
102 187-2	312 187	DR	B DH	1970	M	SEM. Chemnitz Hilbersdorf.

102 188	312 188	DR	B DH	1970	MA	Dresden Altstadt.
						(98 80 3312 188-6 D-IGDA).
329 501-1	399 101	DB	C DH	1952	MS	Stiftung Deutsche Kleinbahnen,
						Schwichtenberg.
329 502-9	399 102	DB	C DH	1957	MS	Stiftung Deutsche Kleinbahnen,
						Schwichtenberg.
329 503-7	399 103	DB	C DH	1957	MS	Stiftung Deutsche Kleinbahnen,
						Schwichtenberg.
329 504-5	399 104	DB	B DH	1957	MS	Stiftung Deutsche Kleinbahnen,
						Schwichtenberg.
199 007-6	399 701	DR	C DH	1972	MA	Jöhstadt.
199 101-7	399 601	DR	C DM	1980	MA	Berlin Park Railway.
199 102-5	399 602	DR	C DM	1980	MA	Berlin Park Railway.
199 103-3	399 603	DR	C DM	1980	MA	Berlin Park Railway.
Kdl 91-0001		DB	B DM	1953	M	Gerolstein.
Kdl 91-0005		DB	B DM	1958	P	Hemmor.
Kdl 91-0006		DB	B DM	1958	M	DBM. Walburg.
Kdl 91-0012		DB	B DM	1958	M	Fredesdorf.
ASF 01		DR	Bo BE	1964	MA	SEM. Chemnitz Hilbersdorf.
ASF 2		DR	Bo BE	1983	MA	Weimar.
ASF 4		DR	Bo BE	1966	MA	Halle.
ASF 8		DR	Bo BE	1966	MA	SEM. Chemnitz Hilbersdorf.
ASF 24		DR	Bo BE	1969	M	Weimar.
ASF 32		DR	Bo BE	1969	M	Weimar.
ASF 45		DR	Bo BE	1971	M	Pasewalk.
ASF 59		DR	Bo BE	1973	M	Glauchau.
ASF 60		DR	Bo BE	1973	M	Bitterfeld.
ASF 75		DR	Bo BE	1974	MA	Arnstadt.
ASF 76		DR	Bo BE	1974	M	Weimar.
ASF 94[II]		DR	Bo BE	1979	M	Nossen.
ASF 114		DR	Bo BE	1981	M	SEM. Chemnitz Hilbersdorf.
ASF 115		DR	Bo BE	1981	M	Glauchau.
ASF 122[I]		DR	Bo BE	1977	M	Schwerin.
ASF 122[II]		DR	Bo BE	1983	M	SEM. Chemnitz Hilbersdorf.
ASF 139		DR	Bo BE	1987	M	Weimar.
ASF 144		DR	Bo BE	1987	M	Lutherstadt Wittenberg.
ASF 146		DR	Bo BE	1987	M	Aschersleben.
ASF 14271			Bo BE	1974	M	Arnstadt.
ASF 17762	ASF 1		Bo BE	1982	M	Arnstadt.

9.2.4. ELECTRIC MULTIPLE UNITS

Old No.	Computer No.	Co.	Type	Built	Status	Location
1624ab		DB	2-car	1927	M	VVM. Aumuhle.
ET 11 01		DB	2-car	1935	M	DGEG. Neustadt (Weinstr).
-	410 001	DB	Bo-Bo	1985	P	ST Minden.
745 002-6	410 002	DB	Bo-Bo	1985	M	Deutsches Verkehrsmuseum,
						München.
-	420 001	DB	3-car	1969	MA	S-Bahn München.
	420 300	DB	3-car	1978	M	Eisenbahn Erlebniswelt, Horb.
ET25 015	425 115	DB	2/3/4-car	1935	MR	Haltingen.
ET25 020	425 120	DB	2/3/4-car	1935	MA	Stuttgart.
ET26 002	426 002	DB	2-car	1941	M	Peenemünde.
ET27 005	427 105	DB	3-car	1965	MR	Stuttgart.
ET30 414	430 114	DB	1 of 3-car	1956	MS	DBM. Eisenbahn Erlebniswelt, Horb.
ET 32 201 a	432 201	DB	1 of 3-car	1936	M	Eisenbahn Erlebniswelt, Horb.
ET 65 005	465 005	DB	Bo-Bo	1933	MS	Stuttgart.
ET 65 006	465 006	DB	Bo-Bo	1933	MS	Eisenbahn Erlebniswelt, Horb.
ET85 07	485 007	DB	Bo-Bo	1927	M	Eisenbahn Erlebniswelt, Horb.
ET183 05	-	DB	1Ao-Ao1	1899	M	DTM. Berlin.
ET188 511	-	DR	Bo	1930	MS	Dresden Altstadt.
ET188 521	-	DR	Bo	1930	MS	Dresden Altstadt.

-	470 136	DB	3-car	1969	M	Kulturbahnhof Schmilau.
ET171 039	471 139	DB	3-car	1943	MS	Schönberger Strand or SFW Delitzsch.
ET171 044	471 144	DB	3-car	1942	M	LHB Salzgitter.
ET171 082	471 182	DB	2-car	1958	MR	S-Bahn Hamburg.
270 001-1	-	DR	2-car	1985	MS	HSB Berlin.
275 003-2	475 001	BVG	2-car	1929	P	B-Kleistpark (Bar).
275 031-3	475 003	BVG	2-car	1928	M	Stiftung Eisenbahnmuseum Bochum Dahlhausen.
275 045-3	475 005	BVG	2-car	1928	MA	HSB Berlin.
275 061-0	475 008	BVG	2-car	1928	P	Dresdener Tor on A4 road.
275 081-8	475 009	BVG	2-car	1928	P	Beelitz Süd.
275 085-9	475 011	BVG	2-car	1928	P	Herzhausen (34516).
275 109-7	475 013	BVG	2-car	1928	P	Gaststätte, Breitenbrunn.
275 169-1	475 017	BVG	2-car	1928	MS	Walburg (?).
275 247-5	475 024	BVG	2-car	1929	MS	Beelitz.
275 343-2	475 037	BVG	2-car	1929	P	Luckenwalde (Gottower Strasse).
275 319-2	475 601	BVG	2-car	1929	MS	Walburg (?).
275 407-5	475 049	BVG	2-car	1928	MS	Walburg (?).
275 411-7	475 050	BVG	2-car	1928	P	B-Falkensee, Bar.
275 417-4	475 053	BVG	2-car	1928	P	B-Falkensee, Bar.
275 429-9	475 057	BVG	2-car	1928	M	ETM. Prora.
275 517-1	475 075	BVG	2-car	1929	P	Gaststätte, Dabendorf.
275 519-7	475 076	BVG	2-car	1928	P	Hohenschonhausen Bhf.
275 625-2	475 161	BVG	2-car	1927	M	Deutsches Museum Verkehrszentrum, München.
275 641-9	475 605	BVG	2-car	1928	MA	S-Bahn Berlin.
275 659-1	488 165	DR	2-car	1928	MA	HSB Berlin.
275 683-1	475 608	BVG	2-car	1928	MS	Berlin Schöneweide.
275 693-0	488 166	DR	2-car	1928	MA	S-Bahn Berlin.
275 701-1	475 612	BVG	2-car	1928	P	Lübars.

▲ As part of the celebrations to mark 175 years of railways in Germany, a large festival was held in Rheinland Pfalz, involving many preserved locomotives and multiple units. Preserved EMU 425 120 is seen leaving Oberbillig in the afternoon of 5 April 2010 with a special service Trier–Wellen–Trier.

Matthias Müller

275 737-5	475 162	DR	2-car	1928	M	DBM. Nürnberg.
275 747-4	488 167	BVG	2-car	1928	M	DTM Berlin.
275 783-0	488 168	DR	2-car	1928	MA	S-Bahn Berlin.
275 815-9	488 169	DR	2-car	1929	MA	S-Bahn Berlin.
275 959-5	475 126	DR	2-car	1932	MA	S-Bahn Berlin (As 488 167[II] ?).
276 031-2	476 601	DR	2-car	1935	M	HSB Berlin.
276 035-3	-	DR	2-car	1949	MS	DTM Berlin.
276 069-2	-	DR	2-car	1938	M	HSB Berlin.
276 243-3	476 033	DR	2-car	1928	M	DME. Darmstadt.
276 301-9	476 352	DR	2-car	1930	MS	Private, Berlin-Modersohnbrücke.
276 347-2	476 372	DR	2-car	1930	P	Stadthalle, Kirchberg (55481).
276 415-7	476 396	DR	2-car	1928	P	Tiroler Stadl, Senftenberg.
276 513-9	476 002	DR	2-car	1928	P	HSB Berlin.
276 519-6	476 005	DR	2-car	1928	P	Bornholmerstrasse, Berlin.
276 535-2	476 013	DR	2-car	1928	P	School, Berlin Spandau.
277 003-0	477 197	DR	2-car	1938	M	HSB Berlin.
277 087-3	477 206	DR	2-car	1939	M	HSB Berlin.
277 129-3	477 053	DR	2-car	1939	P	Töpchin.
277 195-4	477 085	DR	2-car	1940	M	Ziesar-Bucknitzer Eisenbahn.
277 263-0	477 117	DR	2-car	1943	P	Töpchin.
277 267-1	477 119	DR	2-car	1943	P	Berlin-Schönefeld (Bar).
	477 601	DR	2-car	1939	M	Horb.
277 405-7	477 602	DR	2-car	1940	M	HSB Berlin.
277 407-3	477 603	DR	2-car	1936	M	Ziesar-Bucknitzer Eisenbahn.
277 415-6[II]	477 606	DR	2-car	1936	P	Berlin school.
278 005-4	478 004	DR	2-car	1925	M	S-Bahn Berlin.
278 007-0	478 005	DR	2-car	1925	M	S-Bahn Berlin (Now in Technologie Park Köln ??).
278 107-8	-	DR	2-car	1928	MS	HSB Berlin.
279 001-2	479 601	DR	Bo	1930	MS	Buckow.
279 003-8	479 602	DR	Bo	1930	MS	Buckow.
279 005-3	479 603	DR	Bo	1930	MS	Buckow.
ET91 01	491 001	DB		1936	M	Bahnpark Augsburg.
ETA150 011	515 011	DB	Bo BE	1955	M	BEM Nördlingen.
ETA150 556	515 556	DB	Bo BE	1960	M	Stiftung Eisenbahnmuseum Bochum Dahlhausen.
ETA176 001	517 001	DB	Bo-Bo BE	1956	MS	DBM. Lichtenfels.
AT 589/590	-	DR	2A-A2 DE	1927	MR	VMD. Gotha

9.2.5. DIESEL MULTIPLE UNITS

Old No.	Computer No.	Co.	Type	Built	Status	Location
VT 4.12.01	173 001	DR	1A-A1dm	1964	MR	Hoyerswerda.
VT 4.12.02	173 002	DR	1A-A1dm	1964	MR	Dessau.
VT 06 104ab		DB	2-car	1938	M	LHB Salzgitter.
VT 06 106a		DB	1/3 3-car	1938	P	Lübeck Travemünde Hafen.
VT 06 106bc		DB	2/3 3-car	1938	P	Konstanz.
VT 137 856a	182 009	DR	2-car	1938	MS	Leipzig.
VT 137 856b	182 010	DR	2-car	1938	MS	Leipzig.
VT 08 503	613 603	DB	B-2 DH	1952	MS	DBM/VBV Braunschweig.
VT 08 520	613 620	DB	B-2 DH	1954	MS	DBM/VBV Braunschweig.
VT 11 5003	602 003	DB	B-2 GTH	1957	M	Eisenbahn Erlebniswelt, Horb.
VT 11 5006	601 006	DB	B-2 DH	1957	M	Bahnpark Augsburg (Restaurant train).
VT 11 5008	601 008	DB	B-2 DH	1957	M	Eisenbahn Erlebniswelt, Horb.
VT 11 5012	602 012	DB	B-2 GTH	1957	M	DBM. Nürnberg.
VT 11 5013	601 013	DB	B-2 DH	1957	M	Bahnpark Augsburg.
VT 11 5014	601 014	DB	B-2 DH	1957	M	Bahnpark Augsburg (Restaurant train).
VT 11 5014	601 014	DB	B-2 DH	1957	M	Eisenbahn Erlebniswelt, Horb.
VT 11 5016	601 016	DB	B-2 DH	1957	S	Private, Solignano Nuovo, Italy.
VT 11 5018	601 018	DB	B-2 DH	1957	M	Eisenbahn Erlebniswelt, Horb.
VT 11 5019	601 019	DB	B-2 DH	1957	M	Bahnpark Augsburg.
VT 12 506	612 506	DB	B-2 DH	1957	MA	DBM Stuttgart.

VT 12 507	612 507	DB	B-2 DH	1957	MA	DBM Stuttgart.
614 005		DB	B-2 DH	1973	MS	DBM Nürnberg.
614 006		DB	B-2 DH	1973	MS	DBM Nürnberg.
VT 18.16.03a	175 005	DR	B-2 DH	1966	M	SEM, Chemnitz.
VT 18.16.03b	175 006	DR	B-2 DH	1966	M	SEM, Chemnitz.
VT 18.16.07b	175 014	DR	B-2 DH	1968	MS	Berlin Rummelsburg.
VT 18.16.08a	175 015	DR	B-2 DH	1968	MS	Berlin Lichtenberg.
VT 18.16.08b	175 016	DR	B-2 DH	1968	MS	Berlin Lichtenberg.
VT 18.1610a	175 019	DR	B-2 DH	1968	MS	Berlin Rummelsburg.
VT 60 531	723 003	DB	1A-2 DH	1940	MR	Osnabrück Piesberg.
VT 66 904	-	DB	1A-A1 DM	1927	MA	Harsefeld.
VT 66 906	-	DB	B-B DM	1928	MR	UEF. Gerstetten (WEG T401).
VT 70 919	-	DB	A-1 DM	1937	MA	Ebermannstadt.
VT 70 921	-	DB	A-1 DM	1937	MR	DME. Darmstadt.
VT 78 901	-	DB	A-1 DM	1932	M	Ebermannstadt.
VT 79 902	-	DB	A-1 DM	1932	M	DME, Darmstadt.
VT 88 902	-	DB	A-1 DM	1934	M	CFV3V, Mariemborg, Belgium.
VT 92 501	692 501	DB	B-2 DH	1932	MR	EVB, Hesedorf.
701 065		DB	A-A DM	1962	MS	Deutsches Museum, Freilassing.
701 067	DB	A-A DM		1962	MS	DBM, Halle.
701 095	DB	A-A DM		1964	MS	Deutsches Museum, Freilassing.
VT 95 9122	795 122	DB	A-1 DM	1953	MR	Münster.
VT 95 9164	795 164	DB	A-1 DM	1953	P	Wuppertal Cronenberg.
VT 95 9240	795 240	DB	A-1 DM	1952	M	DBM, Koblenz Lützel.
VT 95 9256	795 256	DB	A-1 DM	1952	MA	VEB, Gerolstein.
VT 95 9286	795 286	DB	A-1 DM	1955	A	HWB 3.
VT 95 9326	795 326	DB	A-1 DM	1957	P	Rehlingen. Tennis court clubhouse.
VT 95 9396	795 396	DB	A-1 DM	1954	MA	BEF, Basdorf.
VT 95 9414	795 414	DB	A-1 DM	1954	M	Dieringhausen.
VT 95 9445	795 445	DB	A-1 DM	1954	M	Wesseling.
VT 95 9465	795 465	DB	A-1 DM	1954	M	DTM. Berlin.
VT 95 9626	795 626	DB	A-1 DM	1955	M	VEB, Gerolstein.
VT 95 9627	795 627	DB	A-1 DM	1955	M	KBE VT 12, Wesseling.
VT 95 9662	795 662	DB	A-1 DM	1955	MA	CFV3V, Mariembourg, Belgium (As 551.662).
VT 95 9669	795 669	DB	A-1 DM	1955	MA	AMTF, Train 1900 Petange, Luxembourg.
VT 98 9597	796 597	DB	A-A DM	1956	MA	Giessen.
VT 98 9625	796 625	DB	A-A DM	1956	MR	EFZ. Rottweil.
VT 98 9680	796 680	DB	A-A DM	1960	MA	Goes, Netherlands.
VT 98 9690	796 690	DB	A-A DM	1960	M	DBM, Nürnberg.
VT 98 9702	796 702	DB	A-A DM	1960	MA	Hagen.
VT 98 9739	796 739	DB	A-A DM	1960	MA	Volkach.
VT 98 9740	796 740	DB	A-A DM	1960	MA	DDM. Neuenmarkt Wirsberg.
VT 98 9744	796 744	DB	A-A DM	1960	P	Dransfeld.
VT 98 9760	796 760	DB	A-A DM	1960	MS	Schenklengsfeld.
VT 98 9761	796 761	DB	A-A DM	1960	MA	EVG, Linz/Rh.
VT 98 9784	796 784	DB	A-A DM	1960	MR	Kassel.
VT 98 9790	796 790	DB	A-A DM	1961	MA	Gerolstein.
VT 98 9796	796 796	DB	A-A DM	1961	S	Reutlingen.
					MA	Stiftung Eisenbahnmuseum Bochum Dahlhausen.
VT 98 9802	796 802	DB	A-A DM	1961	MA	Hagen.
VT 97 902	797 502	DB	A-A DM	1962	MR	Reutlingen.
VT 97 903	797 503	DB	A-A DM	1962	MR	Reutlingen.
VT 97 904	797 504	DB	A-A DM	1962	MS	Wuppertal.
VT 97 905	797 505	DB	A-A DM	1962	MR	Reutlingen.
VT 98 9514	798 514	DB	A-A DM	1955	MR	Werlte.
VT 98 9522	798 522	DB	A-A DM	1955	MA	BEM. Nördlingen.
VT 98 9554	798 554	DB	A-A DM	1955	MS	Krefeld.
VT 98 9585	798 585	DB	A-A DM	1956	MR	Wesseling.
VT 98 9589	798 589	DB	A-A DM	1956	MA	Giessen.
VT 98 9598	798 598	DB	A-A DM	1956	MA	EVG. Linz/Rh.
VT 98 9622	798 622	DB	A-A DM	1956	MA	Worms.

VT 98 9623	798 623	DB	A-A DM	1956	M	Horb.
VT 98 9629	798 629	DB	A-A DM	1956	MA	Frankfurt/M (Leased out).
VT 98 9632	798 632	DB	A-A DM	1956	MS	BEM. Nördlingen.
VT 98 9643	798 643	DB	A-A DM	1956	MA	Goes, Netherlands (Via StLB VT 23).
VT 98 9647	798 647	DB	A-A DM	1956	MA	Simpelveld, Netherlands.
VT 98 9652	798 652	DB	A-A DM	1959	MA	Ulm.
VT 98 9653	798 653	DB	A-A DM	1959	MA	Ulm.
VT 98 9659	798 659	DB	A-A DM	1959	MS	Ocholt.
VT 98 9668	798 668	DB	A-A DM	1959	MR	ZLSM. Simpelveld, Netherlands.
VT 98 9670	798 670	DB	A-A DM	1959	MR	Gerolstein.
VT 98 9675	798 675	DB	A-A DM	1959	MA	BEM. Nördlingen.
VT 98 9677	798 677	DB	A-A DM	1959	MS	Dorsten.
VT 98 9706	798 706	DB	A-A DM	1960	MA	Passau.
VT 98 9726	798 726	DB	A-A DM	1960	P	Schiltach.
VT 98 9729	798 729	DB	A-A DM	1960	MS	Waldbahn Almetalbahn, Büren.
VT 98 9731	798 731	DB	A-A DM	1960	P	Nordhalben.
VT 98 9751	798 751	DB	A-A DM	1960	MR	Gerolstein.
VT 98 9752	798 752	DB	A-A DM	1960	MA	Gerolstein.
VT 98 9766	798 766	DB	A-A DM	1960	S	Altenbeken.
VT 98 9776	798 776	DB	A-A DM	1960	MR	Passau.
VT 98 9778	798 778	DB	A-A DM	1960	MR	Wilburgstetten.
VT 98 7979	798 794	DB	A-A DM	1961	MS	Seelze.
VT 98 9818	798 818	DB	A-A DM	1962	MS	Pfalzbahn, Worms.
VT 98 9823	798 823	DB	A-A DM	1962	M	Minden.
VT 98 9828	798 828	DB	A-A DM	1962	MS	Eisenbahn Tours, Hermeskeil ?
VT 98 9829	798 829	DB	A-A DM	1962	MR	Giessen.
VT 133 522	187 001	DR	A-1 DM	1933	MA	Wernigerode HSB.
VT 135 054	186 257	DR	A-1 DM	1935	M	Stassfurt.
VT 135 057		DB	A-1 DM	1935	M	MEM. Minden.
VT 135 060		DB	A-1 DM	1935	M	MEM. Pr. Oldendorf.
VT 137 063	723 101	DR	2-Bo DE	1934	MR	Berlin-Schöneweide.
VT 137 099	185 254	DR	2-Bo DE	1935	MS	DBM. Schwerin.
VT 137 110	786 258	DR	A-1 DM	1935	MS	DBM. Halle P.
VT137 225ab	183 252	DR	2-car	1935	P	Leipzig Hbf.
VT 137 234	183 251	DR	2-car	1935	MR	SFW Delitzsch.
VT 137 322	-	DR	B-2 DM	1938	MS	Bertsdorf.
VT 137 527	185 256	DR	1A-A1 DM	1939	M	Gramzow.
VT 137 532	187 101	DR	1A-A1 DM	1939	MA	DEV. Bruchhausen Vilsen.
VT 137 566	187 025	DR	1A-A1 DM	1940	MA	HSB Wernigerode.
188 001-2	708 001	DR	A-1 DM	1956	M	Magdeburg.
188 005-3	708 005	DR	A-1 DM	1959	M	Finsterwalde.
188 006-1	708 006	DR	A-1 DM	1959	MA	DB Leipzig.
188 201-8	708 201	DR	2-Bo DE	1968	MR	Weimar.
188 202-6	708 202	DR	2-Bo DE	1968	M	Dresden.
188 203-4	708 203	DR	2-Bo DE	1968	M	SEM. Chemnitz Hilbersdorf.
699 001-4	699 101	DB	B-2 DM	1933	MA	DEV. Bruchhausen Vilsen.
Köl 6204	701 018	DB	A-A DM	1955	MA	Wesseling.
VT38 002	712 001	DB	Bo-2 DE	1936	MA	Stiftung Eisenbahnmuseum Bochum Dahlhausen.
VT2.09 003	771 003	DR	A-1 DM	1962	MA	Gramzow.
VT2.09 101	772 001	DR	A-1 DM	1964	MA	Neustrelitz.
VT2.09.103	772 003	DR	A-1 DM	1965	MA	Lugauer EF, Oelsnitz.
VT2.09 201	772 101	DR	A-1 DM	1965	P	Peckfitz.
VT2.09 203	772 103	DR	A-1 DM	1965	MA	Oelsnitz.
VT2.09 231	772 131	DR	A-1 DM	1968	MA	Belzig.
VT2.09 250	772 150	DR	A-1 DM	1968	M	Adorf.
VT2.09 255	772 155	DR	A-1 DM	1968	M	Adorf.
VT2.09 271	772 171	DR	A-1 DM	1968	MA	Oelsnitz.
771 012	772 312	DR	A-1 DM	1968	M	Adorf.
771 042	772 342	DR	A-1 DM	1968	MA	LDC, Cottbus.
771 067	772 367	DR	A-1 DM	1968	M	Adorf.
772 013	772 413	DR	A-1 DM	1968	MA	Oelsnitz.
772 014	772 414	DR	A-1 DM	1968	M	Adorf.
SVT 877		DB	Part only	1932	M	DBM. Nürnberg.

APPENDIX I. BUILDERS

The following list of builder codes is not an exhaustive list of all builders of rolling stock shown in this book, but details only those builders for which an abbreviation is used.

ABB Henschel	ASEA/Brown Boveri Henschel, Kassel (to Adtranz)
Adtranz	ABB Daimler Benz Transportation, 2001 to Bombardier
Alstom/LHB	Alstom/Linke Hofmann Busch, Salzgitter
AEG	Allgemeine Elektricitäts Gesellschaft Berlin-Hennigsdorf
Bautzen	Waggon und Maschinenfabrik AG, (vorm Busch), Bautzen
Beilhack	Martin Beilhack GmbH, Rosenheim
Bergmann	Bergmann Elektricitäts Werke AG, Berlin
BMAG	Berliner Maschinenfabrik AG, vormals Schwartzkopff, Berlin
Bombardier	Bombardier Transportation. Various works but principally Kassel (locomotives), Hennigsdorf (dmu/emu).
Borsig	Borsig, Berlin Tegal
Brown Boveri	Brown, Boveri & Cie (BBC), Mannheim. 1999 to Adtranz, 2001 to Bombardier
Deutz	Motoren Fabrik Deutz AG Köln, later Klockner Humboldt Deutz AG
Düewag	Düsseldorfer Waggonfabrik AG, Düsseldorf
DWA	Deutsche Waggonbau AG works at Bautzen, Berlin, Görlitz, Halle Ammendorf, Nieksy, Vetschau. 2001 most to Bombardier
DWM	Deutsche Waffen und Munitionsfabriken AG, Werk Posen, Poland
Esslingen	Maschinenfabrik Esslingen, Esslingen am Neckar
Floridsdorf	Wiener Lokomotivfabrik AG, Wien Floridsdorf, Austria
Gmeinder	Gmeinder & Co GmbH, Mosbach, Baden.
Hanomag	Hannoversche Maschinenbau AG, Hannover-Linden
Hartmann	Sächsiche Maschinenfabrik Rich. Hartmann AG, Chemnitz
Henschel	Henschel & Sohn, Kassel
Humboldt	Humboldt Lokomotivbau, Köln Kalk
Jung	Arn.Jung Lokomotivfabrik Gmbh Jungenthal bei Kirchberg an der Sieg
Krauss Maffei	Krauss Maffei AG München Allach, 1999 to Siemens-Krauss Maffei Lokomotiven GmbH now just Siemens.
Krupp	Friedrich Krupp AG Essen
Karlsruhe	Maschinenbau Gesellschaft, Karlsruhe
LEW	VEB Lokomotivbau Elektrotechnische Werke Hans Beimler, Hennigsdorf. (To Bombardier).
LHB	Linke Hofmann Busch, Salzgitter, 1994 to Alstom/LHB
Linke Hofmann	Linke Hofmann Werke Breslau
LKM	VEB Lokomotivbau Karl Marx, Babelberg (= O&K)
Maybach	Maybach Motorenbau Gmbh, Friedrichshafen
MaK	Maschinenbau Kiel Gmbh, Kiel
MAN	Maschinenfabrik Augsburg Nürnberg AG. 1999 to Adtranz
MBA	Maschinenbau und Bahnbedarf AG, Berlin (= O&K)
MBB	Messerschmidt Bölkow Blohm GmbH, München and Donauwörth
O&K	Orenstein & Koppel, Berlin Drewitz, Lübeck or Dortmund
Plasser & Theurer	Plasser & Theurer, Linz Austria or Freilassing Germany
Rathgeber	Waggonfabrik Josef Rathgeber AG, München
SACM	Société Alsacienne de Constructions Mechaniques, France
Schöma	Christoph Schöttler Maschinenfabrik GmbH, Diepholz
SFT Krupp	Siemens Schienfahrzeugtechnik Krupp, Essen
SGP	Simmering Graz Pauker, Granz and Wien, Austria
Siemens	Siemens AG Berlin, Erlangen, Krefeld and München
Skoda	Skoda Werke, Plzen, Czechoslovakia
SSW	Siemens Schuckertwerke, Berlin und Erlangen
Stadler	Stadler Fahrzeug AG, Bussnang (CH) and Berlin Pankow later Stadler Pankow GmbH
Talbot	Waggonfabrik Talbot, Aachen (to Bombardier)
U23A	Uzinele 23 August, Bucuresti, Romania
Uerdingen	Waggonfabrik Uerdingen AG, Krefeld, Uerdingen and Düsseldorf (now Siemens)
Vulcan	Vulcan Werke, Stettin
Wegmann	Wegmann & Co., Kassel-Rothenditmold
Wismar	Triebwagen und Waggonfabrick AG, Wismar

Westwaggon	Vereingte Westdeutsche Waggonfabriken AG Köln Deutz
Wumag	Waggon und Maschinenbau AG Görlitz
Waggon Union	Waggon Unionh, Berlin. 1996 to Adtranz, 2001 to Bombardier and later Stadler
Windhoff	Rheiner Maschinenfabrik, Rheine, Windhoff AG Rheine.
WMD	Waggon und Maschinenbau GmbH, Donauwörth, to MBB

APPENDIX II. VEHICLE TYPE CODES FOR RAILCARS & MULTIPLE UNITS

These are given in the European system with the British codes in parentheses.

(1) EUROPEAN SYSTEM:

A   1st Class
B   2nd Class
D   Luggage, i.e., vehicle with luggage space and guard's compartment
R   Restaurant
K   Buffet Kitchen

Examples:

BD   Second Class with luggage/guard's compartment.
AB   Composite

(2) BRITISH SYSTEM:

Coaching Stock codes are as used in the Platform 5 BR Pocket Books and "British Railways Locomotives & Coaching Stock", e.g., F=first, S=second, C=composite, B=brake, O=open, K=side corridor with lavatory, so=semi-open.

Under 'accommodation' are shown the number of first and second class seats with tip-up seats in saloons in parentheses, followed by the number of toilets, e.g. 24/49(3) 1T indicates 24 first class seats, 49 second class seats, three additional tip-up seats and one toilet. TD indicates a toilet suitable for disabled people, W indicates a wheelchair space.

APPENDIX III. COMMON TERMS IN GERMAN AND ENGLISH

Lokomotive (Lok) – locomotive (loco).
Reisezugwagen – passenger coach.
Gleis – track.
die Fahrkarte – ticket.
Ausbesserungswerke (abbreviated to AW) – works.
Reichsbahnausbesserungswerke (abbreviated to RAW) – works (former DR).
Bahnbetriebswerke (abbreviated to Bw) – depot.
Bundesbahndirektion (abbreviated to BD) – division (DB).
Reichsbahndirektion (abbreviated to RBD) – division (former DR).
Baureihe – Class (as in "Class 110").
Speisewagen – restaurant car.
Klasse – Class (as in *Erste Klasse* – First Class).
Schlafwagen – sleeping car.
Bier – Beer.
Liegewagen – couchette.
Verspätung – lateness.
Dampflok – steam loco.
Lokführer – driver.
Ellok – electric loco.

Zugführer – guard.
Diesellok – diesel loco.
Bahnsteig – platform.
Schienenbus – railbus.
Bahnhof (abbreviated to Bhf) – station.
Hauptbahnhof (abbreviated to Hbf) – main station.
Hauptguterbahnhof (abbreviated to Hgbf) – main goods depot.
Rangierbahnhof (abbreviated to Rbf) – marshalling yard.

APPENDIX IV. DB DEPOT CODES

Code	Sector	Depot name			
AH1	F	Hamburg Eidelstedt including Hamburg Langenfelde	KA	R	Aachen Hbf.
			KD	R	Düsseldorf Abstellbahnhof
AM	S	Maschen	KG	S	Gremberg
AK	R	Kiel	KK2	R	Köln Deutzerfeld
ANB	A	Niebüll	LH1	S	Halle G
AOP	R	Hamburg Ohlsdorf	LH2	R	Halle P
BCS	R	Cottbus	LL1	R	Leipzig Hbf Süd
BFF	R	Berlin Friedrichsfelde.	LMB	R	Magdeburg Buckau
BGA	R	Berlin Grunau	LMR	S	Magdeburg Rothensee
BLO	R	Berlin Lichtenberg	MH1	F, R	München Hbf Süd (F),
BRG	F	Berlin Rummelsburg			München Hbf West (R),
BSE	S	Seddin			(depots side by side)
BSN	S	Senftenberg	MH2	R	München Pasing
BWS	S	Berlin Wannsee	MH6	R	München Steinhausen
DA	R	Dresden Altstadt	MAOB	N	Augsburg Oberhausen
DBN	N	DB Netz	MKP	R	Kempten
DC	R	Chemnitz Hbf	MMF	R	Mühldorf
DF	S	Dresden Friedrichstadt	NHO	R	Hof
DZW	S	Zwickau	NN1	R	Nürnberg West
EDEF	N	Duisburg Wedau Entenfang	NN2	S	Nürnberg Rbf
EDO	R	Dortmund	NWH	R	Würzburg
EE	R	Essen	RF	R	Freiburg
EHGV	S	Hagen Vorhalle	RHL	R	Haltingen
EHM	-	Hamm (Storage point)	RK	N	Karlsruhe
EMST	R	Münster (Westf)	RL	R	Ludwigshafen
EOB	S	Oberhausen Osterfeld Süd	RM	S	Mannheim
FB	S	Bebra	RO	S	Offenburg
FF	R	Frankfurt/M Hbf (Old postal depot)	SKL	R	Kaiserslautern
			SSR	S	Saarbrücken Rbf
FFU	N	Fulda	STMI		System Technik Minden
FGM	F & R	Frankfurt/M Griesheim (two depots at same site)	STMU		System Technik München
			STR	R	Trier
FK	R	Kassel	TK	S	Kornwestheim
FL	R	Limburg	TP	R	Plochingen
FMB	S	Mainz Bischofsheim	TS	R	Stuttgart
HB	S	Bremen (locos maintained at Bremen Works)	TT	R	Tübingen
			TU	R	Ulm
HBH	S	Bremerhaven	UE	R	Erfurt
HBS	R	Braunschweig	UMX		Meiningen Works
HE	S	Emden	US	S	Saalfeld
HHL	R	Hannover Leinhausen	WHF	R	Heringsdorf
HO	S	Osnabrück	WR	R	Rostock Hbf
HS	S	Seelze	WRS	S	Rostock Seehafen
HWG	F	Wangerooge			

DBN: DB Netz includes DB Netz and DB Fahrweg. Some locomotives are shown with a particular depot but all are controlled nationally and maintained at any suitable depot when maintenance is due.

Stored locos are denoted by (Z) after the depot code. Z= *Zurückgestellt* ("put back").

Allocation shown in parentheses are provisional.

SECTOR CODES

F	DB Fernverkehr
N	DB Netze
R	DB Regio.
S	DB Schenker

APPENDIX V. ABBREVIATIONS

AKW	Atom Kraftwerk
AMTF	Association des Musées et Tourisme Ferroviaires
AW	Ausbesserungswerk
BEF	Berliner Eisenbahn Freunde
BEM	Bayerische Eisenbahn Museum
BLME	Braunschweigische Landes Museums Eisenbahn
BLV	Bayerische Lokalbahn Verein
CFV3V	Chemin de Fer Vapeur Trois Vallées
DBB	Draisinenbahn Berlin Brandenburg
DBG	Dampfzug Betriebsgemeinschaft
DBK	Dampfbahn Kochertal
DBM	DB Museum
DDM	Deutsches Dampflok Museum
DEV	Deutsche Eisenbahn Verein
DEW	Dampf Eisenbahn Weserbergland
DFS	Dampfbahn Fränkische Schweiz
DGEG	Deutsche Gesellschaft für Eisenbahn Gesichte
DKM	Dampf Kleinbahn Mühlenstroth
DLF	Dampflokfreunde (Berlin)
DME	Deutsche Museums Eisenbahn
DRM	Dampfbahn Rhein Main = Frankfurter Feldbahnmuseum
DTM	Deutsches Technik Museum
EF	Eisenbahn Freunde
EFB	Eisenbahn Freunde Betzdorf
EFZ	Eisenbahn Freunde Zollernbahn
EHEH	Eisenbahn und Heimatmuseum Erkrath - Hochdahl
ET	Eisenbahn Tradition
ETB	Eisenbahnfreunde Traditionsbahnbetriebeswerk Stassfurt
ETM	Eisenbahn Technik Museum
EVG	Eifelbahn Verkehrs GmbH
FME	Fränkische Museums Eisenbahn
GES	Gesellschaft zur Erhaltung von Schienenfahrzeuge e.V.
HE	Historische Eisenbahn
HEM	Historische Eisenbahn Mannheim
HSB	Harzer Schmalspur Bahn
HSB	Historische S-Bahn, Berlin
HWB	Hochwaldbahn
IG	Interessengemeinschaft
IGN	IG Nebenbahn, Kassel
KBE	Köln Bonner Eisenbahn
LDC	Lausitzer Dampflok Club
LTA	Landesmuseum für Technik und Arbeit
MBS	Museum Buurt Spoorweg
MEC	Modell Eisenbahn Club
MEG	Mitteldeutsche Eisenbahn Gesellschaft
MEM	Museums Eisenbahn Minden
MME	Märkische Museums Eisenbahn
NTB	Nassauische Touristik Bahn
NVR	Nene Valley Railway
ÖGEG	Österreichische Gesellschaft für Eisenbahngesichte
OSE	Ostsächsische Eisenbahnfreunde
PRESS	Eisenbahn-Bau- und Betriebsgesellschaft Pressnitztalbahn mbH

RSB	Rennsteigbahn
SEH	Süddeutsche Eisenbahnmuseum Heilbronn
SEM	Sächsische Eisenbahn Museum
SFW	Schienen Fahrzeuge Werk
SSN	Stoom Stichting Nederlanse
ST	Systems Technik
STAR	Stadskanaal Rail
ThEV	Thüringer Eisenbahn Verein
TM	Technik Museum
VBV	Verein Braunschweiger Verkehrsfreunde
VEB	Vulkan Eifel Bahn
UEF	Ulmer Eisenbahn Freunde
VMD	Verkehrs Museum Dresden
VSE	Verein Sächsische Eisenbahnfreunde
VSM	Veluwse Stoomtrein Maaatschappij
VSSB	Verein zur Förderung Sächsische Schmalspurbahnen
VVM	Verein Verkehrsamateure und Museumsbahnen
WFL	Wedler Franz Logistik GmbH & Co KG
WTB	Wuchtachtalbahn
ZHL	Zahnradbahn Honau-Lichtenstein e. V
ZLSM	Zuid Limbugse Stoomtrein Maatschappij